STRANGE FIRE?

Assessing the Vineyard movement
and
the Toronto Blessing

Eric E. Wright

 **EVANGELICAL PRESS**

EVANGELICAL PRESS
12 Wooler Street, Darlington, Co. Durham, DL1 1RQ, England

© Evangelical Press 1996
First published 1996

British Library Cataloguing in Publication Data available

ISBN 0 85234 349 3

Printed and bound in Great Britain at the Bath Press, Avon.

Contents

Acknowledgements

I would like to acknowledge the help and encouragement I received from many to carry on this project.

Michael Haykin, Doug Adams, Sharon Cavers and Debbie Marling read crucial chapters and made helpful suggestions.

John Noble and Barry Foster read through the entire manuscript as it issued from my computer. They kept me motivated!

Russ Irwin, a friend whose consultation and help I used to receive on a regular basis while working on theological education by extension courses in Pakistan, returned home just in time to be of service again. His grammatical and practical suggestions were of immense help.

Most of all I want to express my debt to Mary Helen, a helpmate of thirty-four years, whose support during this time undergirded everything I have done. She became a 'computer widow' until 'after the book'. She saw household projects put off, weekends lost, walks in the woods postponed and lots of late nights. Despite it all, she happily read and reread the manuscript making the kind of frank suggestions that only a loving wife can make.

The strange fire from Toronto — an overview

'On January 20th, 1994 we were "zapped by the Spirit," claim the leaders at the Toronto Airport Christian Fellowship. They believe 'fire from the Spirit' fell on their congregation that night initiating a 'renewal' that is preparing the way for the final worldwide revival leading up to the return of Christ.

Since then strange things have been happening. Waves of uproarious laughter ripple through the congregation. People fall prone to the floor. Some shake uncontrollably. Others roar, bark like dogs, or cackle like chickens. People come forward to give 'words of prophecy' and others tell of healings. Exotic manifestations such as these have attracted thousands of visitors from all over the world to their nightly meetings. Early on the British press dubbed it 'the Toronto Blessing' and the name has stuck.

Each issue of the Toronto church's new magazine tells more stories of the spread of the 'renewal' to different parts of the world. India, Korea, Thailand, Indonesia, Zimbabwe, Switzerland and Germany are mentioned, along with many other venues where local expressions of the Toronto Blessing have broken out. Some estimate that as many as 7,500 churches in Great Britain have been engulfed in this spreading fire.

'Fire' is one of the most common metaphors used to describe the phenomenon. Guy Chevreau's best-selling book *Catch the Fire* chronicles events surrounding the 'renewal'. People from all over the world subscribe to the Toronto church's magazine, *Spread the Fire*. In July 1994 the Anaheim, California, Vineyard held a 'Let the Fire Fall' conference. In January 1995 and again in January 1996, thousands attended 'Catch the Fire Again!' conferences in Toronto to celebrate the first and second anniversaries of the 'laughing revival'. News reports in the Christian media proclaim, 'Fire still ablaze at Toronto church.' Their new radio and TV ministries go to air under this slogan. Their new School of Ministry is subtitled 'Fire to the Nations'.

Should we attribute the strange happenings in Toronto to 'fire from heaven', or are they the effect of 'strange fire' — akin to that offered up by Aaron's sons so many years ago? (Lev. 10:1-7). Is it holy fire, heavenly fire, Holy Spirit fire? Or is it the potent product of mankind's restless search for spirituality mixed with elements of Christianity? Could it be a volatile and dangerous new mixture fuelled by a post-modern hunger for experience?

The answers to questions such as these cannot be found without exploring the Vineyard movement's long-time expectation of a great season of extra-biblical revelation marked by signs, wonders and mystical experiences. The Toronto Blessing is the progeny of the Vineyard movement, which itself gave birth to the Third Wave of the charismatic movement.

If we would respond adequately to the 'fire from Toronto', we must understand Vineyard terminology — 'power evangelism', 'signs and wonders', 'words of prophecy' and many other in-house terms of a like nature. We need to become acquainted with Rodney Howard-Browne, the Kansas City Prophets and John Arnott, but particularly with the visionary of the movement — John Wimber.

I was first exposed to John Wimber's emphasis on power evangelism well over twenty years ago while I was a missionary in a Muslim land. His panacea — power evangelism through signs and wonders — seemed to many like the open sesame they had searched for to penetrate hard Muslim lands with the gospel. Unfortunately, like most other cure-alls, it has not proved itself in the heat of missionary ministry.

Down through the years I continued to collect material on Wimber and on the Vineyard movement. Then in 1994 the Toronto Airport Vineyard made front-page headlines with the news that 'The Holy Spirit has landed.' But instead of an unmixed blessing, the events have stirred up a storm of controversy that has left in its wake many troubled churches and confused Christians.

Nothing but a heaven-sent return to 'the faith once for all delivered to the saints' can save the confused evangelical church from splintering in several more directions. Speaking of the spiritual movements in America in the 1970s, with special reference to the

Third Wave, Tom Wolfe has written, 'There is no ecumenical spirit within this Third Great Awakening. If anything, there is a spirit of schism.'[1] I saw the signs of this around me in Toronto in 1994-95 — long before John Wimber asked the Toronto church to disengage itself from the Vineyard denomination.

I hesitated for some time about writing this book. For me there is something distasteful about becoming polemical. However, the way even pastors have joined the movement calls for a thorough response. To my mind the books that have come out thus far are either too euphoric in their praise, too muted in their criticism, too historical in their approach, or too vitriolic in their condemnation. Most focus on the physical phenomena. Further analysis is needed. The movement is challenging principles that have been cherished by evangelicals for generations. For this reason, I have sought to approach the subject on a broader level. This work deals with experiences, but emphasizes their biblical and doctrinal implications. It is not enough to discuss the Toronto Blessing. I do that, but I analyse as well the Vineyard movement which gave it birth. Even this is not enough. I have also sought to address broader issues as they relate to the role of preaching, doctrine, subjective experience and revival, to name a few.

Let me state at the outset that I do not question the integrity of those involved on a personal level. Many of those involved are very likeable people. I have seen nothing to make me doubt the sincerity of those who attend or lead the meetings. Many in our day have a deep hunger for God. Pastors seek a new vitality in their ministry. One cannot fault people for seeking more of the Lord. However, I do not believe that this movement will ever provide the dynamic necessary for genuinely revitalized lives. It bears no resemblance to the Great Awakening when Jonathan Edwards and George Whitefield hammered home the great truths of Scripture in awesome sermons that moved a generation. Instead Vineyard leaders routinely allow physical phenomena, such as hysterical laughter, to interrupt the ministry of the Word. How can this encourage revival when it is the Word, under the Holy Spirit, that lights revival fires?

Although I grant that the leaders of the Toronto Blessing seem to be sincere, sincerity is not enough. None of us is perfect and even a sincere man may be sincerely wrong. Real spiritual vitality is mediated by the Spirit of truth. Genuine renewal cannot be sustained in a climate of doctrinal error or practical confusion. The Toronto Blessing, however, is encouraging the disparaging of doctrine, the decentralization of preaching and the exaltation of personal impressions and experiences. Recent history should warn us about the inevitable result. Uncounted thousands of sincere people have been swallowed up by the cults — cults that had their beginnings in the evangelical church. We cannot sacrifice truth on the altar of sincerity or experience.

You may ask what right I have to write a critique of a movement of which I am not a member. Besides pointing to the fact that this movement is affecting Christians in churches in which I minister, I would answer that I have a solemn responsibility. 'Test everything. Hold on to the good' (1 Thess. 5:21). The process of sanctification is a process of stumbling and being lifted up, of making mistakes and having the Lord correct us. All of us, including those in the Vineyard, have to be open to correction as well as to encouragement. Without repeated mid-course corrections in our lives we shall not 'grow in grace and in the knowledge of our Lord and Saviour Jesus Christ'.

All of us have feet of clay. Luther was wrong in his views about the Jews. John Wesley treated George Whitefield shabbily. Missionaries from his own family found C. T. Studd impossible to get on with. Spurgeon could be criticized for smoking. Livingstone dragged his wife and children all over Africa. Every Christian has foibles.

Unfortunately, many of those who embrace an outstanding experience, such as the Toronto Blessing, tend to imagine themselves dwelling in a rarefied atmosphere of blessing far above criticism. This itself is a cause for concern because the outpourings of repentance and sorrow for sin that brought balance to the historical revivals are largely missing here. Instead participants 'laugh in the Spirit' while they keep on 'soaking in the Spirit'.

I do not write, however, because I believe I have obtained a more exalted personal walk with Christ. I don't doubt that many in the movement love Christ as much as I do and have a deeper prayer life than mine. I am sure some are more effective soul-winners and exhibit more zeal and commitment. I write with a profound consciousness of my own weaknesses and the distance I yet need to travel in the Christian faith. Yet whenever I dipped into the Word of God, or compared the writings of great Christians with Vineyard belief and practice, I felt a strong sense of unease. Something was wrong.

Months of study combined with attendance at Vineyard meetings in Toronto have confirmed my fears. In the Toronto Blessing, and its parent the Vineyard movement, we face a serious departure from apostolic practice. The evangelical church raised the standard against liberalism early in this century and fought against those who would attack innerrancy in the sixties, but now we face another challenge. While we were fending off attacks from without, Satan has run around our defences to raise up foes from within the evangelical camp. Let me explain. Modernists attacked our commitment to the Scriptures as an objective revelation of God's will for man. They lost. But suddenly we have a new generation of charismatics who, on the one hand, proclaim their absolute loyalty to the Scriptures, while on the other hand, they act as if the Scriptures were irrelevant. It is a matter of emphasis. By advocating a theology of subjective experience and fallible, but genuine, revelation they effectively shunt Holy Writ offstage.

This subtle attack on the sufficiency of the Scriptures is being waged by the current intoxication of so many Christians with their own subjective impressions, feelings and experiences. What good is it to proclaim to the heavens one's faith in the Bible as the Word of God if it is not used as the touchstone of experience? What good is this profession, if preaching and teaching are downgraded? What good is it to sing about Jesus and then fail to give him the pre-eminence he deserves? Unfortunately, those caught up in the Toronto Blessing lay more stress on the Spirit, prophecy and the physical phenomena than on Christ Jesus the Lord. We have serious problems here.

Of course, it is to be expected. This latest movement is a child of the 'me generation'. The excitement arises out of an unconscious adoption of values and practices that are part and parcel of our culture. The style and beat of the music, the use of story and testimonials, the emphasis on visual effect and dramatic experiences, the sense of mystery and spirituality, the emphasis on inner healing and victimology — all these reflect the culture around us.

Cheryl Thomson and her husband Steve left a Toronto-area Vineyard fellowship because they were disillusioned by their lack of concern for evangelism and discipleship. She found them as self-absorbed as others of this generation. She writes, 'Did the Vineyard emphasize evangelism? I thought they would. But I discovered, instead, an inward-looking self-absorption, a "bless me," "thrill me," "heal me," "minister to me" mindset. It was an unending cycle.'[2]

John Armstrong writes, 'I have recently read several books produced by these 1995 revival movements... In every case the pattern of the movement is the same. People are caught up in movements where feelings of ecstasy are enjoyed during days of revival... What we are seeing is more of the Me generation. It is producing a newer more virulent revivalism that is far more opposed to the historic faith than anything which came out of the Second Great Awakening. (The Second Great Awakening produced heresies galore and sects and cults that are still with us to this very day!)'[3]

The signs are ominous. Tom Wolfe writes, 'This third wave has built up from more diverse and exotic sources than the first two, from therapeutic movements as well as overtly religious movements, from hippies and students of the "psi phenomena" and Flying Saucerites as well as from charismatic Christians.'[4]

I am seriously disturbed by events in Toronto. I want to be scrupulously fair, however. For this reason, in the earlier chapters of this book I will describe what I have seen, what Vineyard leaders say is happening and how a range of Christians interpret these events. In the main part of the book, I will compare Vineyard beliefs and practices with the biblical pattern and the history of the church. Since it will take some time to gauge all the fruit of this movement it is possible that those in the movement will recognize the dangers and pull back from the brink. We cannot wait, however. We must let the Scriptures speak now.

Since I first wrote those unconsciously 'prophetic words', the Vineyard denomination has asked its Toronto stepchild to leave the nest. On 5 December 1995 John Wimber arrived in Toronto along with Todd Hunter, Bob Fulton and Gary Best, representatives from the Association of Vineyard Churches (AVC). They delivered to John Arnott and other senior members of the Toronto Vineyard leadership team the decision of the AVC board to ask the Toronto church to disassociate itself from the AVC.

The Toronto church was shocked and dismayed by the AVC action. John Arnott, founder and senior pastor of the Toronto Airport Vineyard, writes, 'We were suprised by the finality of the decision. We had hoped to have input into the process ... we were offered no opportunity for discussion. We were removed without due process.'[5]

Since much of this leaked out immediately through the Internet, Toronto leaders moved quickly to repair the breach. John Arnott writes that they have 'apologized to the AVC Board for misreading the intent and extent of their concerns... They have accepted our apology.'[6] John Arnott and John Wimber have exchanged cordial letters admitting there were some communication problems on both sides and expressing their fraternal respect for each other.

Toronto leaders then moved to put the best interpretation possible on events. In an open letter on 12 December John Arnott wrote, 'Rather than revamp the renewal meetings, they [the AVC] released us to continue on as we believe God is leading us. Wimber agrees that the Holy Spirit is moving in Toronto, it's just that he [Wimber] feels the AVC board is not called to shepherd something outside the ministry model God has given them.'[7] They explain that 'We are not saying goodbye. We simply recognize that the Sovereign Lord is moving this stream of the Holy Spirit along a new tributary.'[8] Toronto leaders explain that this move gives them a new freedom, with the blessing of the AVC but without their oversight, to promote renewal. The AVC, in turn, are freed to pursue their own church-planting goals without being burdened to continually answer questions about the Toronto Blessing.

This withdrawal of Vineyard endorsement became official on 20 January 1996, when the Toronto Airport Vineyard Christian Fellowship changed its name to the Toronto Airport Christian Fellowship. Since most of the events described in this book took place before that date, in many cases I will retain the older name.

Disengagement from the AVC will not erase the perception that the Toronto Blessing is a Vineyard phenomenon. In fact in an interview with Toronto Airport Christian Fellowship administrator Steve Long on 22 February 1996 he assured me that little has changed. John Wimber has blessed their ministry as an authentic move of the Spirit, but cut them loose to follow their own leading in whatever direction the Lord takes them. A Vineyard doctrinal statement remains in force. Vineyard beliefs and practices continue as before. Believers from Vineyard churches all over the world continue to attend the Toronto meetings. Many of the speakers they use continue to be from Vineyard churches.

Whatever shape or direction the Toronto Blessing takes in the future, it is clearly a mid-nineties mutation of Vineyardism. The move by John Wimber to withdraw Vineyard endorsement from the Toronto Vineyard is like shutting the gate after the horse has bolted.

The Toronto Blessing is a colt raised by John Wimber on a rich diet of Vineyard presuppositions that has bolted. It is running at full gallop. Nothing can stop it.

The Toronto church has already moved to establish a worldwide 'renewal' network of like-minded church leaders. In Toronto over 400 church leaders from many denominations continue to meet weekly in a renewal fellowhip ignited by the Toronto Airport Vineyard but now led from without. Toronto Airport 'renewal' teams continue to travel the world passing on the Toronto Blessing. Steve Long assured me that their travel docket is full for the foreseeable future.

Whatever happens in the years ahead, the Vineyard movement has altered the evangelical landscape. John Wimber's emphasis on 'signs and wonders' has opened Pandora's box. It is too late to close the lid. An approach to 'renewal' has been spawned that depends heaily upon bizarre manifestations for its authenticity. An attitude towards the Holy Spirit has been generated that is mystical and experiential without being necessarily biblical.

In this book I explore the events and beliefs that have triggered this movement in the firm belief that serious assessment is necessary if we are to recover a view of revival that is biblical and historical.

1.
Experiencing the Toronto Blessing

In September 1994, I lined up with scores of others outside a plain warehouse in an industrial park not far from the runway of Toronto's international airport. I had come to witness events being reported around the globe.

As I write this, well over a year after that initial visit, a thousand or more, from all over North America and from distant countries, still gather six nights a week to catch the Toronto Blessing in a much larger, air-conditioned building. In October 1995 five thousand attended a Catch The Fire Again conference held at a nearby hotel. The Toronto Airport Christian Fellowship has bought a second building to house offices and a School of Ministry. A moderate-sized church has grown until in 1996 it employs seventy-five staff members, fifty of whom are full-time. Its budget has ballooned to six million dollars and the church acts as a travel agent for visitors booking several hundred hotel rooms every night.[1]

Between 20 January 1994 and 20 January 1996 events at the Airport Vineyard Christian Fellowship in Toronto attracted approximately 700,000 people from many countries and denominations.[2] What would cause people to change their holiday plans, hop on a flight to Toronto and come night after night to a nondescript industrial complex not far from the runway of Toronto's international airport?

They come to witness what Vineyard leaders believe is an outpouring of the Holy Spirit. It is the latest and the most spectacular manifestation of the Vineyard movement's emphasis on 'power evangelism' through a revival of signs and wonders. Some come out of curiosity. Many arrive with a deep longing to know more of the Spirit. Many 'catch the Toronto Blessing' and take it home to plant in distant congregations. It has been estimated that up to 40% of evangelical churches in Britain have been affected by it.

I found a seat near the back with a friend who had attended before. A group of musicians in blue jeans and tee-shirts tuned up their instruments. The song leader invited people to stand and sing. We stood for forty-five minutes of rousing songs accompanied by the upbeat tempo of a drummer and a battery of skilful guitarists. The leader occasionally interjected a few comments or a prayer. The six or seven choruses sung during this time were repeated over and over again. All were simple and contemporary, although unknown to me. One concerned the Bridegroom coming. Several others began with: 'Glory and honour for ever...', 'Send revival fire again', and 'Do it again, Lord'. As the singing progressed the audience became increasingly animated. Many waved their hands high in the air. Some swayed back and forth. Some shook. Over to the far right I saw someone bouncing up and down. Just to the right, one man violently bounced forwards and backwards. Clapping and amens came fast and furious. Strange sounds rose above the singing — groans, shrieks of laughter, cries.

About halfway into the meeting a woman took over from the song leader. John Arnott, the senior pastor, was away. She asked people where they were from. While most of the Canadian provinces and many of the US states were represented, the largest contingent seemed to be from England, Ireland, Scotland and Wales. Others had come from Norway, Germany, Australia, Bermuda and Nicaragua.

'Testimony time' came next on the agenda. The leader interviewed a number of people, asking what they had experienced at the meetings. Several shared how they had taken the blessing back to their home churches where physical manifestations had also broken out. One or two admitted it had taken some time to be 'slain in the Spirit', a term they use for falling backwards onto the carpet. While these interviews were going on several were 'slain in the Spirit' until the space below the stage was strewn with prone figures, some of whom were shaking, some laughing uproariously, some making other strange noises. After one of the interviews, the leader asked for a 'foot anointer' to come forward — perhaps to anoint the person for service?

Midway through the evening the leader gave a thirty-minute talk. She explained that God was wooing us from our denominational preoccupations to go deeper into the Spirit. She compared this experience to wading into the river that Ezekiel saw flowing from the temple. She stated that we were ministering from dry wells and playing church. 'What's missing? The river! God is pulling us deeper.' She went on to explain that God brings on the phenomena to bring glory to his name. She said, 'I've seen more praise and worship in these seven months' (since it began). Another purpose was 'to build up the church. Prodigals are returning home. So many of us have had the elder brother attitude.' (This theme about the prodigal son and his elder brother seems to be repeated often in their circles.) She also mentioned that signs and wonders are intended to draw people to Jesus. She gave a couple of examples.

She went on to assert that the physical manifestations taking place were not new but could be found throughout the Scriptures. God, 'in the context of prophetic intercession is shaking our status quo... Everything not built on the rock will shake — crumble. This is progressive. He is cleansing the temple from the leadership down.' She continued by giving her view of the biblical support for 'doing carpet time' — their expression for falling backward, being 'slain in the Spirit'. She tried to convince us of its authenticity by drawing parallels from the lives of Old Testament priests as well as Ezekiel, Daniel, Abraham, Balaam and Saul.

She cautioned us not to rely upon experiences but to grow in Christ: 'They are not the measuring stick of spirituality. If we don't fall, that is not a sign we are resisting the Spirit.'

But she quickly went on to illustrate from the lives of different people who had done 'carpet time' how they had been either anointed for ministry, given a new dimension of ministry, made sensitive, heard the voice of God, received visionary revelations, or had begun to prophesy. Others were put into a 'state of anaesthesia for inner healing. Deep wounds were being healed.' She asserted that power from God was not on any one person but came as a sovereign act of God. She qualified this by asserting that 'Some walk in the anointing.'

She concluded her talk by asking the pastors present to stand. About forty stood up. (Toronto Vineyard leaders state that 15% of those who attend are pastors while another 30% are lay leaders. This would mean 30,000 pastors had visited up to May 1995.[3]) She warned them that 'the blessing', when taken back to one's home church, might rock the ship a bit. 'You might lose some of your strong workers,' she told them, but encouraged them not to worry about this. She then urged counsellors to go from pastor to pastor praying for the Spirit to lift 'the yoke of discouragement'. She had earlier asked for volunteer 'catchers' to stand behind those being prayed for to catch them when they were 'slain in the Spirit'.

This prayer session for pastors signalled the beginning of 'ministry time', during which specially trained people from the local congregation wearing badges went around praying for those desirous of 'the blessing'. The aisles soon filled with men and women lying prone on their backs 'doing carpet time'. At this point chairs were moved to the side to create more space. After three hours, I left with the friend who had come with me.

What I saw was typical of what others have reported. These evening meetings often stretch on into the early hours of the morning. In their March 1994 bulletin the Toronto Airport Vineyard reported, 'Laughter, joy, shaking and falling are very common. Others lie still and receive; others tremble and shake; others pogo and dance. Some become speechless; some can only belly-laugh; some become so drunk with the Spirit that they have to be helped from the meeting and driven home.'

In its second year, 1,300 attended the weekday services with 2,000 at weekends.[4] The Christian media has widely reported the Toronto Blessing. Secular newspapers, magazines and TV networks from all over the world have run features on it. Toronto columnist Lynda Hurst writes, 'The nightly renewal meetings begin at 7:30 with an hour of folk-rock spiritual music and everyone swaying to the beat. About 9:30 p.m. they sit down as small plastic pails are passed around for collection.'[5]

'Then, for the next six or seven hours, depending on your mindset, it can look and sound like bedlam, like primal scream therapy for fundamentalists or like *something* — but what? is genuinely happening here. It ends in the early hours of the morning with almost everyone flat on the floor, exhausted, yes, but invigorated — "slain", as they put it, "in the Spirit".' She writes of people being urged to dance. She describes a pregnant woman not wanting to get down on the floor who nevertheless after a five-minute prayer 'is felled and jerking compulsively on the floor before resting, seemingly asleep, for the next half hour'.[6]

Toronto Star columnist on religious affairs Tom Harpur writes, 'The sound system belted out loud folk-song-style music with a heavy beat until, at 7:30, several musicians took the stand for a solid hour of extremely repetitive hymn-singing. But the tunes were infectious and made it impossible not to join in the toe-tapping, hand-clapping, body-swaying mood. Many in the throng waved their hands high in the air, as charismatics are wont to do, and several bobbed and jumped in ecstatic dancing.' He goes on to describe how 400 or so lined up for prayer during the ministry time along 'tapes stuck on the floor in rows about two metres apart. Almost at once weird cries ... otherwise normal-looking people started to shake as if seized by an epileptic fit. Eventually they would slump to the floor writhing, trembling or in an apparent fainting spell. Soon there were hundreds lying on every side. The din was chaotic as some brayed like donkeys, others gave short grunts, screams, or giggles.'[7]

Toronto Life magazine, somewhat tongue-in-cheek, called it Toronto's best 1994 tourist attraction. As I write the interest continues to spread around the world.

Meanwhile in Scotland Nick Needham writes about what he saw at a 'Fire Conference' in St Andrew's and St George's Church, Edinburgh. His description of the meeting parallels what I saw in Toronto. Needham describes how Toronto Vineyard speaker Jim Paul 'explained to people that when they receive the Toronto Blessing and felt themselves beginning to fall over, this was "the sweet heaviness of Jesus" descending on them. Once they had fallen, he encouraged them to remain on the floor for a long time. "The floor is God's operating table where he does business with his men and women, boys and girls." People then formed long queues to be prayed for by members of the conference team who were marked out by badges.'[8]

He goes on to describe people collapsing, trembling, pogoing, dancing, yelling and running on the spot with unbelievable swiftness. 'Two people started barking loudly like dogs. The barks were interspersed with howling noises like wolves ... one person screeching like a cat ... wailing, laughing hysterically.'[9]

According to Airport Vineyard associate pastor Steve Long, quoted in August 1994, laughing is less common than it was in the early stages of the renewal: 'Weeks take different patterns. We've gone through prophetic times, physical healing times, and now people are sensing a call for evangelism and personal holiness.'[10]

In May 1995 Long wrote, 'We have seen a dramatic increase in the number of salvations, and my conclusion is that it has taken our people a year to fully evidence the changes in their lives that they are seen as changed people by their friends, family and colleagues.'[11]

When I visited the Toronto Airport Vineyard several times in July and October 1995 I noted some of the changes Steve Long mentioned. Roaring, crying out, laughing, shaking, pogoing and falling backwards were much less in evidence. The basic format of the evening was unchanged, but the meeting progressed to a more carefully choreographed script, ending with those seeking ministry lining up along lines marked on the carpet to wait for the ministry team to pray for them. Less spontaneity seemed to require more coaching and manipulation. The musical introduction to the meeting, however, injected the same note of wild, emotional abandon that prepared the way for the phenomena at other times. The place was rocking as people began dancing in their places or dancing up the aisles and across the front of the auditorium.

Let me fill out the picture with observations from my visit in July 1995. That evening, 'testimony time' concentrated on three 'healings' and one 'blessing'. Peter and Heather, who head up the Toronto church's School of Ministry, led this session in the greatly expanded new facilities.

Heather first gave 'a word of knowledge' to urge those in ministry who were given to being 'performers and strivers' to just let the 'mercy fall... He's going to cause the river to flow.'

After asking people where they were from, Peter went on to interview the four called forward for 'testimony time'. To much applause, Loraine told how after four years of being unable to talk due to fear, a miracle had occurred in Toronto opening up her mouth to speak. Esther hopped up and down as she praised God for healing a pinched nerve. Peter asked her, 'Would you like more? Fill her up, Lord. Let it flow.' Like Loraine earlier, she fell backwards to begin 'carpet time'. Tracy joined them on the floor after praising God for freedom from memories of abuse and fear of men that made her unable to sleep in the dark.

Keith, an ex-marine and son of a fundamentalist Baptist pastor, told of returning to God after drifting far away. He jerked back and forth, ostensibly under the influence of the Spirit, as he told of receiving the spirit of adoption. Peter, the leader, joked about 'how hard it was to play golf with this guy jerking in the Spirit'. (A man I sat beside in the meeting told me about a woman who was still jerking after having received the 'blessing' the previous autumn. She had, he said, to plan her days around her involuntary shaking. He explained that it evidently stopped when she drove her car.)

A young girl of about ten then came to the front and gave 'a word of knowledge' about 'gushers flowing all over the earth'.

Next a husband-and-wife team from Texas, Byran and Jan Mode, came forward to bring the message of the evening. First of all, Jan brought a devotional message about the fountains, wells and streams of the physical water cycle. She used them to illustrate a kind of spiritual water cycle in which we drink in the rain of heaven and then send it back to God in the form of praise.

Byran spoke for about forty minutes. He explained that the Spirit had led him to set aside his prepared message to talk about the spirit of adoption. The Spirit, he said, had redirected him by moving those who gave testimonies to focus on this theme. Then he gave another reason. He clarified his leading by pointing out that the crowd was too small that night to benefit fully from the crucial words of relief and deliverance he was planning to give. He asked how many felt disconnected from their churches. A number indicated by a show of hands their sense of alienation from their churches. He promised, 'God is going to reconnect you tomorrow night.' He then asked for people to raise their hands if they had pain anywhere in their joints. Many did. He said, 'I've been on a ten-day fast. Tomorrow night God will heal you.' 'Praise the Lord!' echoed from many lips. (How he could justify delaying important ministry until he had a larger crowd mystifies me. This pattern of setting aside prepared messages and engaging in extemporaneous speech seems to be common.)

Using the parable of the prodigal son, he emphasized our need to come to the Father, as the wandering son did, to receive a robe, a ring and sandals. He warned us about the elder brother, who failed to enjoy the spirit of adoption. Much of what he said most evangelicals could relate to. The audience, however, seemed singularly inattentive. People who shortly before had been wildly cheering and dancing seemed to wilt. Some talked to each other; some closed their eyes and rested. An epidemic of loud laughter off to the right captured the attention of many. People seemed too worn out by the two hours leading up to Byran's preaching.

The message led into 'ministry time', during which Byran gave a threefold invitation. He first asked those who were really prodigals, in that they had never received Christ, to come forward. Twenty or so did — the majority of them men. Without any explanation of the gospel and without any appeal for faith and repentance, he proceeded down the line anointing each one to receive the spirit of adoption. They were then sent back to receive five minutes of instruction on being a Christian before returning to the front for some 'soaking time' — evidently where these newly 'adopted' prodigals would also be 'slain in the Spirit'.

Next he called for supposedly saved prodigals to come forward. He especially appealed to 'elder-brother prodigals' as well as anyone who did not feel the spirit of adoption. He invited all these to gather at the back along the taped lines in the carpet. Well over half the audience responded. Ministry team members, identified by badges, and catchers went along these lines praying for the Spirit to come. Soon most were lying prone on their backs.

The final invitation was for those who understood the spirit of adoption but wanted more. This third group pressed to the front as he cried, 'We're really going to soak you good!'

The board chairman of a large Baptist church in the Toronto area, where I was ministering at the time, attended with me. Far from being narrowly Baptistic or insular, Barry and his wife, from a Russian Baptist background, demonstrate considerable openness. He wanted to see for himself what was happening at the Toronto Airport Vineyard. He was appalled: 'From the beginning to the end, I did not sense the Holy Spirit. One doesn't want to be too judgemental but I don't see how laughing during the message, or the jerking of someone giving a testimony can glorify God.'

Almost everyone has an opinion about the events at the Vineyard. Lynda Hurst writes, 'When the Archbishop of Canterbury flew into Toronto this June [1994], almost the first question he put to the two men who met him was, "Well, what do you think of this airport Vineyard thing?"'[12] The talk shows have even got into the act! In May1995 American talk-show host Phil Donahue interviewed seven representatives of various Christian renewal movements. Three from the Toronto Airport Vineyard joined one from England and one from Florida 'where unusual manifestations of the Holy Spirit's presence have accompanied church meetings'. Two others represented a movement on colleges throughout America. The producer of the show is a born-again Christian who saw an opportunity to present a 'hot news story'. Janice Chevreau, whose husband Guy Chevreau is author of the best-selling book on Vineyard apologetics, *Catch the Fire*, said, 'It was a great opportunity to share with a broad, secular audience what God is doing all over the world... Donahue explored the topic graciously, thoughtfully and with great sincerity.'[13]

Well, what has been happening here? Revival? Renewal? Delusion? Manipulation? Is it demonic? Is it mass hypnosis? Is it a mixture? Opinions vary widely. Before we can properly analyse these phenomena, we need to understand their context as part of the cresting of the 'Third Wave' of Pentecostalism.

2.
Surfing the Third Wave —
without going under

These events at Toronto can only be understood 'in the context of the 20th century phenomenon known as Pentecostalism', the fastest-growing segment of the church in the world today.[1] The Toronto Blessing is the most spectacular happening so far in what Peter Wagner has called 'the Third Wave'.[2] According to Wagner's terminology the First Wave embraces the rise of modern Pentecostalism at the turn of the century. The Second Wave crested with the upsurge of the charismatic movement in the 1960s. This Second Wave washed over many non-Pentecostal, mainline churches in the intervening years.

Victor Budgen traces the scattered appearance of charismatic phenomena during church history. He notes the prophetic fervour of the Montanists (declared heretical by the early church) and the disruptive effects the French Prophets had on emerging Methodism and the career of Edward Irving in the nineteenth century. Concerning Irving and his followers, who sought to revive primitive prophecy, healing and tongues he writes, 'Central to everything was the customary view that in great experiences such as tongues and prophecy God delights to bypass the understanding.'[3]

Charles H. Spurgeon dismissed Irving's movement. He said, 'Every now and then there comes up a heresy; some woman turns prophetess and raves; or some lunatic gets the idea that God has inspired him, and there are always fools ready to follow any impostor.'[4]

Out of this restless search for the spectacular, but without any direct link to Irving, Pentecostalism was born. Pentecostals look back to the events that took place in the Azusa Street Mission in Los

Angeles in 1906 as a modern Pentecost. In the congregation at that time there came a 'public weeping, shouting, dancing, leaping, lying in a heap on the rostrum before the congregation: falling backward across steps, constant speaking in tongues often simultaneously... At other gatherings many, including the preachers, were lying on the floor, purportedly "slain in the Lord". One preacher "had his feet tangled up in a chair".'[5]

Pentecostalism spread around the world, arriving even in India in 1909. Cecil Polhill, one of the Cambridge Seven, temporarily embraced the movement. Inside his house people were found 'rolling and kicking, bellowing, rattling, cackling, singing, shouting in tongues, with words and without words'.[6]

As Pentecostal churches matured, they mellowed and began to move theologically more towards the historic evangelical faith. Occasionally a new outbreak, such as the 'Latter Rain' movement in North Battleford, Saskatchewan, would call Pentecostals to return to their roots. Of this 'latter rain' it is said that in 1948, 'People came from near and far to experience healing, exorcism, speaking in tongues, and exhortation to holy living as all around them men and women swayed and shook, many falling to the ground.'[7]

The rise of the charismatic movement in the 1960s, however, took Pentecostal phenomena into the very churches that had earlier frowned on their Pentecostal cousins. Before long charismatic renewal movements sprang up in all the mainline Protestant denominations and also spread into the Roman Catholic fold.

In a Vineyard meeting I attended, a Roman Catholic man from Ottawa informed me that he had been a member of the charismatic renewal movement for twenty years. He had travelled to Toronto four times, so far, to embrace this latest 'move of the Spirit', which he asserted had made him a better Roman Catholic. A Vineyard team has been in his church passing on the Toronto Blessing! This is an interesting point. Both the Second and Third Waves have gained a following within the Roman Catholic community, without rescuing Catholics from their extra-biblical practices.

The charismatic movement set the stage for the Third Wave. This new emphasis began to gather momentum in the late 1970s. It gained ground among evangelical groups largely untouched by Pentecostalism and among those somewhat disenchanted by the charismatic movement. This new wave, instead of insisting on a 'second blessing' evidenced by tongues, emphasizes 'signs and wonders'.

John Wimber is the chief architect, although not the founder, of the Vineyard movement that is largely spearheading this Third Wave. In brief, he claims that the church has succumbed to a rationalistic and materialistic Western world-view that derails the biblical emphasis on the miraculous. He asserts that the types of power-encounters that occurred when Christ clashed with demonic forces need to be revived in order to make an impact on modern pagans. The word of the gospel, he believes, is not enough to break through the rationalistic shell of this generation. He claims that the word needs to be supplemented by 'power evangelism' as evidenced by signs and wonders. He urges Christians to revive their faith in the supernatural by emphasizing miraculous 'power healings', deliverance from demonic powers and prophetic 'words of wisdom'.[8]

Since the Toronto Blessing is rooted in the Vineyard movement and Vineyardism largely reflects the teachings and experience of John Wimber, let me give a brief chronology of his life and career.

1934	John Wimber was born in the American midwest. His father was an alcoholic and left the family while John was very young.
1955	John married Carol, a nominal Roman Catholic.
1962	John and Carol separated. The marriage was saved when John turned to God for help.
Early 1970s	Wimber served as co-pastor of an evangelical Quaker church in southern California.
1976	Carol received a dramatic experience of tongues.
1977	Carol worked with a growing home prayer group.
1978	John became the pastor of this group and began his 'healing ministry rooted in his memory of [his son] Sean's healing, his own gift in tongues when he was a young Christian and his wife's rather dramatic experience'.[9]
Late '70s-82	Wimber was associated with Chuck Smith's group of Calvary Chapels.
1981	The sudden appearance of radical phenomena among hundreds of young people in his church shook Wimber until their authenticity 'was confirmed' by the 6:00 a.m. phone call of his friend Tom Stipe from Colorado.

1982	He left his association with Calvary Chapels to lead 'a small group of churches known as the Vineyard, founded in 1974 by Kenn Gulliksen'.
Jan. 1982	Wimber began teaching a controversial, but explosively popular course on 'Signs and Wonders and Church Growth' at Fuller Theological Seminary in Pasadena, California.
1982	Vineyard Ministries International was founded to promote Wimber's teaching, healing and music ministry.
1984	The death by cancer of David Watson, an English leader in the renewal movement, whom Wimber had expected to be healed, proved traumatic.
1985	Fuller Seminary, in the midst of doctrinal skirmishes, put Wimber's course on hold — but reinstated it later. He continued as an adjunct faculty member until 1992.
1985	He published, with Kevin Springer, *Power Evangelism*, which became the seminal book of the movement.
1986	Wimber suffered a heart attack, but recovered. He published *Power Healing*, also with Kevin Springer.
1987	The publication of *Riding the Third Wave* presented the movement in quite euphoric terms.
1988	Wimber said God had told him the movement was actually in a desperate condition in 1987.
1987-88	Mike Bickle, of the Kansas City Prophets, offered encouragement and advice.
1988-91	Wimber embraced the prophetic movement out of Kansas City.
1990	Mike Bickle's Kansas City Fellowship became Metro Vineyard. Controversy erupted over prophets such as Paul Cain, Bob Jones, John Paul Jackson and, to a lesser extent, Mike Bickle.
1991	Wimber moved beyond the prophetic movement. 'The prophetic glory days, allegedly flowing out of the Spirit are over.'[10]
1994	Many Vineyard churches were impacted by phenomena spreading from Toronto.

1 Sept. 1994   John Wimber convened a meeting of the Associ-
               ation of Vineyard Churches (AVC) to discuss the
               phenomena associated with the Toronto Blessing.
               John Arnott, Randy Clark and Wes Campbell, key
               leaders in this 'renewal', also attended and sub-
               scribed to the conclusions of the Board.
14 Oct. 1994   The AVC board issued a memorandum urging re-
               straint in the promotion of the phenomena, but
               asserting that the Toronto 'renewal' was a move-
               ment of the Holy Spirit.
1995   Wimber retired from official positions while re-
               maining the de-facto leader and voice of the move-
               ment.

Allied with the chronology of Wimber's amazing career we need to
explore several other streams of influence that came together to
produce the Toronto Blessing.

'In the late '60s and early '70s John [Arnott] was significantly
               impacted by Kathryn Kuhlman's ministry, and later
               on, Benny Hinn's which began in Toronto.'[11]
1986   John and Carol Arnott went to a John Wimber
               Conference in Vancouver and another in Ohio.[12]
1987   The Arnotts officially joined the Vineyard. Teaming
               up with Jeremy and Connie Sinnot they began a
               house group in West Toronto.
1987   Rodney Howard-Browne came to America from
               South Africa with what he believed to be a special
               mission to renew the church with the power of the
               Holy Spirit. He is a leading 'practitioner' of 'holy
               laughter'.
1992   The Arnotts attended Benny Hinn's meetings in
               Toronto. They had been friends with him and ad-
               mired him for a number of years.[13]
June 1993   The Arnotts visited a Rodney Howard-Browne
               meeting in Texas where Carol was 'slain' but John
               was left standing.
1993   Randy Clark, founding pastor of the Vineyard
               Christian Fellowship in St Louis, Missouri, went to
               Tulsa, Oklahoma, to receive the laying on of

Howard-Browne's hands in a revival meeting. There he experienced many of the manifestations that have come to be associated with the Toronto Blessing. Howard-Browne comments, 'I remember him coming to me with his hands ablaze and said, "My hands are burning." I said, "Yeah, that's the anointing. You know what it's for?" I said, "Go back to your church and lay hands on everything that moves." And he went back to his church, laid hands on everything that moved; the next week he went to Toronto and the rest is history.'[14]

Autumn 1993 John Arnott, pastor of the Toronto Airport Vineyard, was impressed by Randy Clark's testimony and the discussion by others of renewal in the church through holy laughter.

Nov. 1993 The Arnotts went to Argentina with a ministry team and met Claudio Freidzon, head of the Argentinian Pentecostal Assemblies of God, who had been powerfully 'anointed' at a Benny Hinn meeting. Both John and Carol were 'slain in the Spirit'.[15]

20 Jan. 1994 John Arnott asked Randy Clark to preach at the Airport Vineyard and, as they say, 'The Holy Spirit landed.'

5 Dec. 1995 John Wimber, along with AVC board members Todd Hunter, Bob Fulton and Gary Best, informed John Arnott and the senior staff of the Toronto Airport Vineyard of their decision to withdraw endorsement from the Toronto church. Although the Toronto leadership were shocked and chagrined, they accepted the decision.

12 Dec. 1995 In an open letter John Arnott explained the disengagement from the AVC, asserted Wimber's acceptance of the Toronto 'renewal' as a genuine move of the Holy Spirit, announced the formation of an International Renwal Network and charted a new and freer course while asserting the continuing goodwill of the AVC.

20 Jan. 1996 The Toronto Airport Vineyard Christian Fellowship was formally disassociated from the AVC to become the Toronto Airport Christian Fellowship.

As we can see, the Vineyard is a movement in transition. One of the main difficulties we face in trying to analyse it is the difficulty encountered in pinning its practitioners down. Their pragmatism and openness to new and novel ideas and practice produce a state of flux. John Wimber has undergone a series of metamorphoses himself. He embraced the prophetic movement in 1988 only to distance himself from it in 1991. Both John Wimber and John Arnott, in common with the whole movement, used to interpret physical phenomena of the type now being experienced at Toronto as demonic.[16] And yet the same type of phenomena have occured, and been encouraged, in Vineyard meetings for well over a decade.

In late 1995 James Beverley, who calls himself the Vineyard's friendly critic, wrote that 'There remain further questions to ask about the famous manifestations. The greater Vineyard world itself is now divided about their place and importance. Even local leaders cannot seem to make up their minds about them.'[17] The events centring on 5 December 1995 have brought that division into the open.

From time to time, I shall quote from James Beverley's *Holy Laughter and The Toronto Blessing*. Beverley has had extensive interviews with Vineyard personalities and done considerable research on the subject. His grasp of the facts and people involved has been extremely helpful. I wish he had gone on to tackle the underlying doctrinal issues because I find his conclusions too lenient. But I do appreciate much about his approach to the subject. After discussing Wimber's relationship with the Kansas City Prophets (see chapter 18) Beverley concludes, 'On the one hand, it illustrates that Wimber can be vulnerable to excesses typical of charismatic Christianity. However, it also shows his ability to be self-critical and to redirect the movement once errors are detected.'[18] The errors which Wimber detected in the Toronto 'renewal' will become clear as this book progresses.

While this quality in Wimber may be endearing, it nevertheless indicates a movement adrift without clear moorings. Why did it take two years to discern serious errors? Herein lies considerable danger. In the chapters ahead, I shall fill in more detail about the nature and beliefs of those who surf the Third Wave.

3.
Confusing signals — diverse Vineyard interpretations of events in Toronto

The people most closely affected by events in Toronto interpret them as a mighty renewal of the Spirit. They write, 'On January 20, 1994, Randy Clark, a Vineyard pastor from St. Louis, Missouri in the US came with a team to share at our church. The intent was to have a family night on Thursday, kids' meeting on Friday, youth and young adults on Saturday, and a regular worship service on Sunday morning.'[1]

'At the conclusion of the Thursday service Randy invited three groups of people to respond: those who had never trusted Christ; those who had at one time made a commitment to Christ but were now prodigal sons or daughters; and those believers who needed a fresh touch of God in their lives. Respondents who came forward were prayed for by our prayer counselors. God began to impact people immediately.'[2]

According to John Arnott, senior pastor of the Airport Vineyard, 'An explosion, as the Spirit of God just sort of fell on people ... suddenly "kaboom" and 80 per cent of the congregation was all over the floor, laughing and rolling and totally overtaken by the Spirit of God.'[3]

John Arnott invited Randy Clark to stay for a prolonged period. Nightly meetings continued through most of January and February. Other conservative evangelicals joined the meetings. As the word spread, people began to come from all over. 'By the summer months of last year [1994], it was not uncommon for people from the US and the UK to begin lining up at 4:30 p.m. for the 7:30 service.'[4]

From Toronto the 'blessing' spread to other Vineyard churches in Canada, USA and the UK and before long many non-Vineyard churches had been affected. 'Mainstream denominations, charismatic Church of England parishes, in particular, are studying and adopting its style in hopes of a similar visitation. Indeed, there are now more "Vineyard Anglican churches — 1,500 — than there are pure Vineyards, with 550 worldwide.'[5]

How has the Toronto Blessing changed lives? Guy Chevreau, who left the Baptist ministry to join the Airport team writes, 'When interviewed, people declare time and again that there is a deeper love for Jesus, a greater sense of the power of the gospel, a personal sense of the Lord's love, and a profound experience of the Spirit's transformative work. With all of that, there is also a renewed hunger for the Bible and prayer, a profound sense of gratitude, and a humble submission to the Lord's sovereign care, as well as a sense of recommissioning for ministry, often with a new sense of power, authority, and boldness.'[6]

Numerous people testify to the impact of the events on their lives. In his book, *Catch the Fire*, Guy Chevreau assembles, 'from a thick file of written testimonies that nearly a hundred people submitted',[7] seventeen stories of people young and old affected by the 'renewal'.

Thirteen-year-old Sarah lay near death's door until her friend Rachel attended a Vineyard meeting, received prayer, saw a vision and went to her friend to pray for her healing.[8]

Dr Dora Bitterman from Switzerland 'was able to soak hour after hour in the Spirit, and drink again and again' in Toronto until she found release and a fulness of Jesus' love.[9]

Belma Vardy, dancer, teacher and choreographer from a Christian Reformed background, writes that at first she was shocked. However, after continuing to go to the meetings three times a week her attitudes changed. She learned to forgive and she became more aware of things for which she needed to repent. One night, 'It was as if the heavens opened up and a bucket of laughter was dumped.' In another meeting while she was doing 'carpet time' she saw a beautiful vision. She walked hand in hand with Jesus into a river. Later that night she realized a large growth on her leg had been healed.[10]

But the Vineyard hope is not in individual transformations alone. Steve Long, who left the Fellowship Baptists — my own denomination — to join the Airport Vineyard writes, 'Encouraging to us is the fact that 15% of attendees are pastors, another 30% lay leaders. If there is any group that is cautious about heresy or deception it is pastors... Every denomination and fellowship you can think of has

attended... We estimate that 5,000 people trusted Christ or recon-
nected with Christ during 1994.'[11] With this kind of input, Toronto
leaders hope that the renewal will eventually unite all believers in a
full-scale revival.

John Arnott adds, 'This is a heaven-sent renewal meant for the
local church, to build up the body of Christ so that eventually it will
overflow into the community and usher in revival.'[12] Many Vineyard
leaders consider their whole movement, and the Toronto Blessing
in particular, to be a precursor of the Second Coming of Christ. This
revival of signs and wonders heralds the outpouring of the Spirit
they believe necessary before the return of Christ.

While many Vineyard pastors from all over the world have been
unequivocal in their assurance that this is a mighty move of God,
others have expressed doubts. It was for this reason that John
Wimber called together the board of the AVC in September 1994.
John Arnott, Randy Clark and Wes Campbell, leaders in the Toronto
Blessing, were asked to participate.

In a letter attached to the Board Report Wimber sought to explain
his views about phenomena such as 'roaring under the anointing'
and 'people shaking, falling or having other kinds of exotic phenomena': 'I would say that there is no biblical or theological framework
for such phenomena. I don't see anywhere in the New Testament
where Jesus and/or the apostles encouraged such phenomena or
encountered such phenomena. Therefore, I think these kinds of
things have to be put in a category of "non-biblical" and "exotic"...
I know of no biblical mandate for encouraging anyone to "roar"...
We do not equate phenomena with God; we see these usually as
human responses to God... Having said that, I do not, personally
hold the opinion that this is "demonic" and/or necessarily "divine".
I put this in the category of "pondering/I don't know".'[13]

In the same memorandum the Board of the Association of
Vineyard Churches summarized their approach to the phenomena:
'We are willing to allow "experiences" to happen without endors-
ing, encouraging or stimulating them; nor should we seek to
"explain" them by inappropriate "proof-texting"... The absence of
a proof-text, however, does not necessarily disallow an experience... The board was not prepared to make a blanket statement
rejecting or "barring" any particular manifestation unless it is
prohibited by Scripture... The ultimate test of manifestations
should be long-term fruit in a person's life, and the edification of the
body of Christ.'[14]

Wimber went on to suggest that it was too early to evaluate the renewal movement since genuine fruit takes considerable time to grow. He admitted, 'We can't rule out the possibility of demonic activity either, or else why do we read in the epistles, "Test everything"?'[15]

He explained that in the 'excitement of the infilling and empowering, and moving of the Spirit, some people ... do things they think are in vogue, like "Fall, fall, fall ..." or "Roar, roar, roar... Frankly that zeal is excusable — for now — but ... needs correction.'[16]

For Wimber the ultimate test is: 'Do you love Jesus more?'[17] Clearly, John Wimber was either perplexed or straddling the fence when he wrote this. He obviously believed many of the phenomena were from the Spirit. He promoted a cautious acceptance and encouragement of those who claimed that their experiences had been positive. It is noteworthy that he urged Vineyard leaders to do exactly what many in the movement condemn others for doing — 'testing all things'. His test, of course, is extremely questionable, as I will note later.

According to John Wimber, Vineyard leaders spoke and corresponded on numerous occasions during the next fifteen months with John Arnott and the Toronto leadership team. They sought to lovingly urge them to change their 'renewal' practices in order to comply with Vineyard policy (i.e. the policy that had been agreed on in the AVC board in September 1994). They did not sense any appreciable response to their correction. It became clear that the Toronto Airport Vineyard (TAV) was charting its own course instead of accepting John Wimber's leadership. Finally, on 27-28 November, the AVC board met to discuss the situation.

According to Gary Best, the National Director for the Association of Vineyard Churches of Canada, the AVC Board concluded that the 'TAV had firmly set their direction and that their lack of compliance was simply an indication that our differences were not just methodological but much deeper... There was a strong consensus that the theological and philosophical foundation that the Blessing was being constructed upon was significantly divergent from what we [the AVC] have felt is our foundation... The best course of action would be to recognize those differences and release them to what obviously was in their hearts.' [18]

Consequently John Wimber and three other Vineyard representatives, including Gary Best, met with the leaders of the Toronto Airport Vineyard to inform them that the AVC was 'formally withdrawing our endorsement from those who have operated in visible leadership in the Toronto Airport Vineyard'.[19] They explained, 'In no way was the origin of the Blessing being called into question (we all believe it has been from the Spirit) nor was there any accusatory spirit.'[20]

John Arnott responded within two hours by accepting the Vineyard decision. On the surface, at least, he expressed chagrin: 'We were surprised at the finality of the decision. We had hoped to have some input into the process... We were removed without due process.'[21] He went on, however, to apologize to John Wimber for 'misreading the intent and extent of their concerns',[22] to assert his love for Wimber and appreciation for his leadership, and to request that the Toronto Airport Vineyard leave with Wimber's blessing.

Actually, the Toronto leadership must have known about the pending decision the day before Wimber arived. And they must have already decided it was a good thing. In E-mail on 4 December, Richard Riss notes that Toronto staff member Daina Doucet had requested that he prepare a paper showing the historical precedent for such a separation. Riss wrote to John Arnott, 'Daina mentioned that you see this as a good thing.'[23] In E-mail on 6 December Riss writes, 'John Arnott and his staff there feel this is a positive thing — a new beginning, no longer encumbered by various constraints. In connection with these events, my wife Kathryn had a vision of a ship being launched from its moorings, now able to move forward.'

On 12 December John Arnott's open letter struck a positive note: 'We do want to publicly thank John Wimber and the AVC Board. This current move of God's Spirit would not have achieved its worldwide reach and impact without them... We are not saying goodbye. We simply recognize that the Sovereign Lord is moving this stream of the Holy Spirit along a new tributary... It is onward and upward for us.'[24]

John Arnott and the Toronto team are relieved to be released to promote their brand of 'renewal', with all the accompanying phenomena. As mentioned in the introductory overview, their calendar is full of conferences, global travel, radio and TV programmes all designed to promote the Toronto Blessing.

Why was John Wimber so decisive in pursuing this separation? On 13 December he released a 'Notice of Withdrawal of Endorsement from the Toronto Airport Vineyard'. He wrote, 'We cannot at any time endorse, encourage, offer theological justification or biblical proof-texting for any exotic practices that are extra-biblical

— whether in Toronto or elsewhere. Neither can these practices be presented as criteria for true spirituality or as a mark of true renewal... There may be phenomena that we do not understand; it is our conviction that these manifestations should not be promoted, placed on stage, nor used as the basis for theologizing that leads to new teaching.' Wimber's position had hardened.

'We believe the leaders at the TAV have repeatedly violated the guidelines in this report, both in practice and in print, in spite of expressions of concern.' Wimber and the AVC believed that the Toronto Airport Vineyard had poorly pastored a genuine move of the Spirit.

In a letter to AVC pastors on the same date, he explained what had happened and why. He went into more detail about his concerns about the way the Toronto leadership were guiding the 'renewal'. He basically outlined four main areas of concern.

1. The TAV had an approach to pastoring and administering the work of the Spirit that was diverse from the AVC model.

a. Instead of refusing to encourage, spotlight, explain, defend, or pray for 'exotic, non-biblical manifestantions ... the leaders of TAV have continued to encourage, spotlight and defend these manifestations. They have attempted to establish scriptural precedents based on metaphorical language of scriptures, which we do not believe is a valid use of the scriptures. They have attempted to give these manifestations prophetic and eschatological meanings, which we also do not accept as valid.'[25]

b. The TAV leadership seem fearful of doing anything to administer or pastor the 'renewal for fear of quenching' the Spirit.

c. While the TAV acknowledges 'that any renewal contains a mixture of spirit and flesh...', they refuse to 'publicly and pastorally test the spirits or manifestations or to sort out the good fron the bad' — contrary to 1 Thessalonians 5:19-20; 1 John 4:1-3; 1 Corinthians 14:29.

d. The TAV has a naïve belief that 'their good intent and many good results relieve them of the responsibility to deal with abuses and excesses. We believe that we must deal with abuses and excesses if we want renewal to be healthy and to achieve its full purpose.'

2. The TAV emphasizes 'exotic and extra-biblical experience' as if it was a necessary part of ministry and renewal. This focus has led them to make equipping incidental.

3. The TAV fails to understand how crowds can be hyped and manipulated by suggestions and emotions. 'Examples of this are the featuring of manifestations in testimonies, use of tape on floor and assigning catchers to each person being prayed for, conveying the strong impression and suggestion that if ministry is successful the recipient will fall down or manifest in some way.'

4. 'Acceptance of prophecies which set up an élitist mentality among churches, that incite a division between "haves" and "have nots" and which treat expressions of concern or correction as quenching and opposing the work of the Holy Spirit.'[26]

Wimber raises some very serious issues. Many of us might agree with his assessment. But when we probe further into Vineyard history and explore their presuppositions, we may wonder why he was so surprised by the Toronto Blessing, especially when, as Steve Long explains, 'Outward manifestations are not new at the Vineyard ... however, the number of people experiencing them was unique.'[27] Could this be more of an evidence of church politics — the clash of internationally known leaders — than a concern for principles?

The Vineyard movement is now openly divided. No matter how gracious and polite Vineyard leaders are to each other and to the Toronto leadership, tensions course beneath the surface, Unwisely, Richard Riss brought this into the open in his E-mail transmission of 4 December. He compared John Wimber's treatment of John Arnott to King Saul persecuting David. He predicted that 'The vast majority of Vineyard churches will probably be split right down the middle... There will be a separation of the sheep from the goats [Is he labelling Toronto Blesing advocates as sheep and the rest as goats?], and I do see this as a good thing ... there will be greater liberty for the Spirit of God to move unhindered.'

The Toronto Airport Vineyard immediately jumped on Riss for this communication. On 7 December he published 'his sincere apologies' for caricaturing John Wimber. But the damage had already been done. Several churches have left the AVC to side with the Toronto church, who, it must be said, are striving to avoid creating divisions in the Vineyard movement.

But freed from the constraints of the AVC, the Toronto Airport Fellowship is now aiming for the 'renewal' statosphere. In the period ahead we can expect their booster rockets to be activated. With many evangelicals expressing a more euphoric interpretation of the Toronto Blessing than John Wimber, it has become increasingly urgent to examine this 'fire from Toronto'.

4.
A pot-pourri of evangelical responses

Evangelicals from a wide spectrum of churches have been attending the meetings at the Toronto Airport Christian Fellowship. Some come away euphoric. Multitudes return to their churches to plant the Toronto Blessing in their home soil. Many others are cautious, alarmed or even highly critical.

Favourable comments

That many have responded favourably is clear from Peter Fenwick's comment that 'Up to 40% of evangelical churches [in the UK] had embraced the experience, including virtually all charismatic and most Pentecostal churches.'[1]

Faith Today, Canada's leading Christian magazine, writes, 'Most observers are viewing the movement as a renewal of the church, the first wave of a revival that will eventually reach out to non-believers.'[2] Interest and restrained acceptance are widespread among evangelical churches.

I interviewed a Baptist pastor whom I know well. He explained: 'I went to find out, not that I felt a great need. During the ministry time I suddenly fell down. Just a feeling of awe at the Lord, like I've had before — but more intense — came over me. I couldn't get up for at least forty minutes. The sense of the Lord's presence was so strong. I went back again to observe. On that occasion, someone asked if anyone had prayed for me. I said, "No." After prayer I fell back and my head began to bang back and forth on the floor. Someone put a coat under my head to cushion it. It was like the Lord saying, "I can do whatever I want with you. Remember, I am the Lord."'

Dr Grant Mullen, a specialist in mood disorders says, 'I've seen powerful psychological changes take place spontaneously, that could never happen with years of counselling.' He believes that 'God is rehabilitating minds and rewiring them emotionally so that people stop thinking negative thoughts which separate them from God's love.'[3]

Author Clark H. Pinnock, professor of theology at McMaster Divinity College says, 'Personally, I have found myself made more radically open to God's presence and have come away with my faith enhanced... Unquestionably there are dangers here... The teaching ministry, which is sometimes flat ... the pattern does not have to be replicated in local churches... My belief is that God's Spirit is moving in a special way in the Toronto Blessing (and not only there) and my hope for us is that the fire which Jesus promised will spread into all our communities.'[4]

Stan Fowler, academic dean of Heritage Theological Seminary, a Fellowship Baptist school in Ontario writes, 'It's undeniable that God is doing a powerful work.' Stan mentioned to me several individuals he knew, including an alcoholic, who had been transformed by their experience at the Airport Vineyard: 'I know too many people who have borne witness to this; in fact, anyone who denies this isn't looking at real people.' Fowler went on to question whether God had worked 'because of the Vineyard context or despite it'.[5] His ambivalence is shared by many.

Cautious responses

Numerous Christian leaders urge us to be temperate in our comments about the phenomena lest we should quench the Spirit.

Dr David Reed, professor at Wycliffe College, University of Toronto, in an address entitled 'The Toronto Mixed Blessing', believes that it is giving the charismatic movement, which had reached a kind of plateau, a second wind. He notes both benefits and concerns. He theorizes that the Vineyard movement is a bridge to the future in the face of weaknesses in the established churches. He believes it is a prophetic movement standing against apathy and lethargy as a 'gift from God during an interim period'.[6]

Dr Justin Dennison, pastor of one of the Fellowship Baptist's largest churches in Canada comments, 'There are points about the Vineyard movement with which I would disagree theologically but I also appreciate their unique contribution to the body of Christ... We need to be careful about judging other groups without searching our own hearts.'[7]

Daniel Lundy, pastor of Toronto's historic Jarvis Street Baptist Church, points out that we all share some common ground with the Vineyard. He believes we need a sense of the presence and power of the Holy Spirit as well as a focus on the victory of Christ. We also need to go beyond the abstract doctrinal knowledge of the Scriptures that leads to barren orthodoxy to walk with God experientially on a moment-by-moment basis. He then goes on to express his concerns by requesting the Vineyard to reaffirm biblical truths, namely:

1. God's work is not normally done through extraordinary manifestations of his power in human affairs.
2. Suffering is central to discipleship prior to glory.
3. Walking with God is not a matter of gaining direct communications from God but of holiness.[8]

In an editorial in *The Canadian Baptist* Larry Matthews gives examples of unhelpful responses to the Toronto Blessing, including outright condemnation. Then he comments, 'No matter the official teaching, Vineyard meetings communicate that unless you are in on the "blessing", you are leading a sub-standard Christian life. The "train is leaving", or this is a "window of opportunity, like a space shot", or "This calls for a decision." The unspoken subtext of a Vineyard meeting is that this allegedly new and powerful movement of the Holy Spirit is not available any way but the Vineyard way. I don't accept that.'[9]

James Beverley, in his helpful volume *Holy Laughter and the Toronto Blessing*, expresses no doubt that the Toronto Blessing is an outpouring of the Holy Spirit but he does offer some critiques. He presents ten tests of a genuine movement and gives the Vineyard a passing grade on five: their allegiance to the God of the Scriptures, their high Christology, their morality and love and their connection with the church at large. He goes on to probe their weaknesses in the areas of biblical authority, commitment to rationality, prophecy, their emphasis on the Spirit and their openness to different opinions and views. He comments, 'Vineyard leaders clearly want the blessing of the Holy Spirit. However, there are some serious issues to be explored concerning the controversial and well-known manifestations ... the Airport Vineyard has duplicated some common errors about the Spirit-filled life that have been made by their Pentecostal and charismatic cousins.'[10]

Responses of alarm from many evangelicals

I have talked with a number of pastors who went along with an open mind and a real desire to meet God. Some were convinced. Many, however, have serious reservations. Indeed, in an in-depth study of the pros and cons made by *Faith Today,* 'Many people express private concerns ... but refused to go on record for fear of causing more division. One commented, "It's difficult to be critical when others are obviously benefiting — it's like throwing water in their faces."'[11]

Others said, 'I don't know what is happening there but it is certainly not produced by the Holy Spirit.' 'I was repelled.' 'I did not sense the presence of the Spirit.' 'I believe demonic activity is involved.'

Nick Needham went to a conference in Edinburgh where the Toronto Blessing was explained. He saw similar phenomena: 'I went to the conference in a spirit of prayer, with a calm, impartial mind, determined to judge what happened on its own merits. If God was going to be there, I was ready to meet him there.'[12]

As Needham left, he asked a minister friend 'who had been slightly less sceptical than I had been about the Toronto Blessing... "Now, tell me honestly. Do you feel any sense of God's presence in the building?" He replied that he did not.'[13]

Needham goes on to comment, 'By the time we left it was beginning to sound like a zoo! But by the same token, I had absolutely no sense that it was divine.'[14]

He mentions the speakers' apparent sincerity and then expresses some serious concerns: 'I did observe a distressing tendency towards jokiness and flippancy... Where does the Holy Spirit say in Scripture that it is a manifestation of his work for people to behave like animals? ... It seems to me to contradict Scripture teaching about spiritual renewal to claim that the Spirit's sanctifying presence can reduce human beings to the level of animal behaviour... I long for spiritual renewal in my own heart ... but sadly, I see no prospect of either in the Toronto Blessing.'[15]

Ken Fast writes, 'The comment by John Arnott, "It's about time the church had more faith in God's ability to bless us than Satan's ability to deceive us," reminds me of advice I received from Mormons. They told me to put down the Bible and just pray for the *burning in my bosom* (an ecstatic experience). Then I would know that Mormonism is true... The written Word is our only reliable guide. It is truly a lack of spiritual leadership that prefers emotionalism and opinion as the yardstick for measuring truth.'[16]

Norman McLeod, a longtime member of Spring Garden Baptist Church in Toronto, whose pastor has embraced the experience said, 'I was horrified at the horrendous antics. I think it's become excessive ... going out five nights a week — it's like a drug.'[17]

John Allison, pastor at St Andrew's Islington Presbyterian Church in Toronto, comments about the priorities evident in an Airport Vineyard service. He voices a common complaint that the manifestations became so loud and distracting that the speaker was forced to stop preaching. 'Is the focus on Jesus, or is it on experiences? They explained that we should just let the Holy Spirit do his work, but I'm less than comfortable with what they thought was important.'[18]

Harold Lutzer, director of the Canadian Revival Fellowship, states unequivocally that the events in Toronto lack 'the marks of true revival. Historically, revivals included an overwhelming sense of reverence and awe toward God... Revival is anything but euphoric — until afterwards... I don't see any sense of genuine repentance.'[19]

John MacArthur, in *Reckless Faith*, categorizes the 'laughing revival' as anti-intellectual emotionalism. He quotes Jonathan Edwards' explanation that the Great Awakening filled people with a kind of joy 'that did not corrupt and debase the mind'.[20] MacArthur comments, 'So it should be clear what Jonathan Edwards would think of twentieth-century emotionalism. "Holy laughter" epitomizes the fanaticism he blamed for the demise of the Great Awakening... When the laughing revival has run its course, what will be next? How can a movement stoked by the heat of raw passion rekindle the flames when people's emotions finally grow cold?'[21]

My visits to the Toronto Airport Fellowship have certainly upheld MacArthur's concern. He laments 'the tragedy that thousands swept up in the emotionalism of the movement have never been exposed to enough objective truth and sound doctrine to come to a saving knowledge of the Christ of Scripture. The Christ they worship is a figment of their imagination. So inevitably, their imagination is where they will turn when they want to hear Him speak.'[22]

Pentecostal responses critical of the movement

Back in February 1994, just after the initial manifestations at the Airport Vineyard, Ken Birch, a columnist with the *Pentecostal Testimony*, wrote a column on 'holy laughter'. His comments relate to what he saw in a television programme run by one of the Toronto Blessing's key progenitors. He does not mention the name, but the context makes it clear that he is speaking of either Benny Hinn or Rodney Howard-Browne. Birch states that this 'dean of Pentecostal televangelists … is supposedly being used by the Lord in releasing people from their bondages and cares by dispensing the "gift" of laughter'.[23]

Birch describes a meeting in which waves of people fall, supposedly 'slain in the Spirit'. He notes the 'ubiquitous presence of "catchers"' and goes on to comment: 'Holy Spirit-inspired laughter? Hardly. It was pure, suggestive manipulation.' He concludes, 'When will they (we!) grow up to the point where we will no longer be blown about by every wind of aberrant doctrine, or behavior? To me, it's no laughing matter… This too, will pass.'[24]

Pentecostal pastor Joseph R. Chambers writes, 'No segment of people within the body of Jesus Christ has suffered so many impostors as we Pentecostals… Satan approaches men by titillating their flesh. He scorns the use of one's mind to believe and receive on the basis of faith and truth and convinces men to act on the basis of feeling and excitement… [This] is utterly false and is another gospel… Holy laughter … is nothing less than the rotten fruit of a downward trend … raw witchcraft mixed with a religious experience… It is unbiblical to give your body to emotions that are not controlled by your reason and spirit. This is Satan's style, not God's… The Holy Spirit is a gentleman. He does not induce men to act like fools, but to honour the Lord Jesus Christ.'[25]

Responses that warn of demonic influence

According to Steve Long, associate pastor at the Airport Vineyard, 'Demonic stuff is happening. The bigger question is: is it stuff coming out [demons coming out?] or going in? If it is stuff going in, we are obviously very much against that; but to the best of my knowledge that doesn't happen. Many people, however, are becoming free from bondages they have been weighed down by.'[26]

As mentioned in a previous chapter, confusion on how to discern demonic activity has been part of Vineyard experience for years. In a statement of John Wimber to "All Vineyard Pastors" in October 1994 he writes, '... I recognize that there are certain manifestations of the Spirit that have gone on in our meetings for fifteen years that we supposed were demonic in origin.'[27]

Is this confusion now laid to rest? Steve Long explains about practice at the Toronto Airport Vineyard: 'Demonic activity is usually very easy to recognize. If a person begins to scream, shake violently or speak in a different voice, our team will quickly take them to a private area so they don't embarrass themselves, or they will pray the peace of God into their lives. Those from our congregation are encouraged to make appointments with our prayer team should we feel that the deliverance process may be a long one.'[28]

Obviously, practitioners at the Toronto Airport Fellowship accept that Christians can be possessed by demons. (I competely disagree with this view. Christians may be tempted and even oppressed by the devil, but not possessed.) A puzzling question immediately arises: how can they tell the difference between the demonic and the spiritual when the manifestations are so similar? Most of us find them identical. With deliverance from demonic oppression and possession being such a large part of the Vineyard agenda of power evangelism through signs and wonders we must ask ourselves why they are so confused.

Cheryl and Steve Thomson left a Toronto-area Vineyard Church in 1989. They became disillusioned by what they label the 'New Age overtones' in the movement as well as by Bible studies degenerating into group therapy sessions and by serious discernment problems on the part of the Vineyard leadership team in the US. They have followed the movement as insiders. Cheryl writes, 'My husband and I have heard story after story in the past year

[1994] of demonic attacks on people who have visited the Toronto Airport Vineyard.'[29]

Gordon Williams, a Pentecostal evangelist, reports that he has no problems with shaking or laughter. In describing the manifestations he saw in a Vineyard meeting, he writes that at first 'I didn't think too much about this because this physical movement was what the old-time Pentecostals called "one of the excesses" by which people tried to pump up the experience of the Holy Spirit.'[30]

Williams goes on, however, to express his alarm at the way in which roaring and other manifestations interrupted testimonies and preaching. He rejects the claim of various speakers that the presence of an 'anointing' is proved by the physical manifestations. 'Proof of the anointing is in the message not in any particular shaking... But when things ... become disruptive and the preaching of the Gospel is prevented, then laughter is not from God... Because of the demonic attacks that are occurring in the Vineyard ministry, it is obvious that there is no Gift of Discerning Spirits.'[31]

Critiques of the Toronto Blessing as mass hypnotism or hysteria

Professor Edward Shorter of the University of Toronto is a student of 'the history of religious hysteria'. A CBC television crew showed him a series of videos they had taken at the Airport Vineyard. He believes they exhibit the classic signs of an epidemic of religious hysteria. He explains that outbreaks such as this have occurred repeatedly in history, particularly since the seventeenth century. 'Two hundred years ago the same symptoms were described as evidence of demonic possession. These people are "primed," they have a script in their mind, not consciously but deep in their unconscious mind. They know what kind of manifestation they are to reproduce.'[32]

Professor Shorter went on to comment on the claims of physical healing. Pointing to the example of the thousands who claim healing at Lourdes, he explains that their healing is really the subjective relief that people feel. No physical cures have ever been substantiated.[33] Although one hesitates to agree with a non-Christian observer, I have no doubt that B. B. Warfield, who wrote *Counterfeit Miracles* to prove a similar point, would agree.[34]

Tom Harpur, a liberal Toronto columnist writes, 'My judgment is that some people are genuinely being helped or healed in some way by this movement but that much of it is induced hysteria that will ultimately fizzle out. I hope I'm wrong.'[35]

Claims that the Toronto Blessing is cultic

In declining to attend a consultation on the Toronto Blessing, sponsored by the Evangelical Alliance for UK evangelical leaders, Alan Morrison, 'a veteran of the New Age movement and Eastern mysticism', writes the following: 'After having counselled many hundreds of people who have been affected by this psycho-religious experience (which has often been extremely harrowing), I have come to regard it as displaying all the marks of a cult. Within the churches which propagate the "Toronto Experience" we find a great many traits which characterize the cults: (1) extra-biblical revelation; (2) a false basis of salvation; (3) arrogant personal claims of the leaders; (4) doctrinal double-talk; (5) defective Christology; (6) defective pneumatology; (7) unjustified scriptural proof-texting; (8) vicious and threatening denunciation of those who disagree; (9) syncretistic practices and associations.'[36] Some other critics agree with Morrison's assessment.

The Toronto Blessing has provoked a bewildering range of responses. Leaving aside the opinions of secular and liberal critics, we still face a range of opinions within the evangelical camp from 'This is a revival!' to 'This is demonic.' It will not be easy to sort through the issues raised. Nor will it be easy to pierce the armour of those enamoured by the phenomena. One can understand why they bristle at criticism.

5.

Shots across the bow — will criticism of the movement quench the Spirit?

Such a confusion of opinions calls for careful analysis. However, as soon as people begin to voice any doubts, they hear the rumble of shots across the bow. Warnings about quenching the Spirit fall thick and fast. Indeed, criticizing a movement when so many testify to the blessing they have received may appear petty and churlish. Some sources in the secular media assert that detractors are engaged in skirmishes motivated by jealousy at the attention the Toronto Blessing is receiving.

Vineyard warnings

The warnings delivered by some 'prophets' in the movement persuade some Christians to swallow their concerns and hop on the bandwagon. In the first issue of the Toronto Vineyard's magazine, *Spread the Fire*, Stacey Campbell 'delivers a thunderous warning on the need to "Choose! Choose! Choose!" about the Toronto Blessing while we are "in the days of power, and in the days of sight when many miraculous things are being done".' The prophecy announces wrath on those who cause division: 'It will be better for Sodom and Gomorrah than it will be for that one on that day.' Readers are then told they have a choice: accept the Toronto Blessing and 'call it "God" or follow after human wisdom and reasoning"'.[1]

Apologists of the movement commonly assert that detractors come from the same stock as the Pharisees who crucified Christ. This accusation surfaces not only in relationship to the Toronto

Blessing. Vineyard pastor James Ryle writes, 'A group of people who promote themselves as Biblical purists, the faithful remnant who alone preach the Word and who evidently possess the power to judge and criticize anyone who is not like them... It was, in fact, this very kind of people who crucified Jesus Christ. They are Scribes and Pharisees, religious and angry, attacking and persecuting anyone who dares to differ from their exclusive views... These watchdogs of moral purity... have turned their swords against the Vineyard and its leaders. Why? Since there is no truth to their accusations one must ask why then do they accuse? What motivates them to tear down another church? The answer is pride, jealousy, fear, hatred, or ignorance — take your pick. You can be sure one of these factors is at the heart of this present contention.'[2]

Irked by his critics, John Arnott warns that 'People come [to criticize] with no anointing, no power, just words. This is how to kill a revival. Satan has done this again and again.'[3]

Guy Chevreau, in *Catch the Fire,* calls up Jonathan Edwards to hammer the opposition. He quotes him as saying, 'Censoring others is the worst disease with which this affair has been attended. Critics pass judgment, and make their own experience the rule... Persons are very ready to be suspicious of what they have not felt them-selves...'[4] As we shall see later, quotes like this from Edwards fail to tell the whole story.

William DeArteaga, in his book *Quenching the Spirit,* labours to prove by historical precedent that phenomena inside the present 'renewal' cannot derail it, while criticism from without may quench it. He specifically targets Calvinistic theology by paradoxically appealing to Edwards. He comments, 'Calvin has no theology of discernment... Jonathan Edwards developed the Protestant theol-ogy of discernment as far as I can see... His theology is probably the best that there has ever come around. So, that's one incident where the Pharisees stopped revival.'[5]

DeArteaga's view, contained both in a taped message and in his book, claims that it was the pharisaism of Calvinists that stopped the Great Awakening. He writes, 'Calvinist theology could not interpret the spiritual experiences that were to accompany the Great Awak-ening. In spite of Edwards' own theories, it seems that the Great Awakening was not quenched because of extremists [within the movement]. It was quenched because of the condemnation of its op-ponents [Calvinists outside of the movement]. This condemnation demoralized the supporters and marred the faith of the public to the point where they no longer welcomed the presence of the Spirit.'[6]

What a charge! Think of all those whose minds have been stretched and whose spirits have been led to soar in worship through exposure to the great Calvinist writers of the past! Were they all Pharisees? Are we to believe that Augustine and Luther, Calvin and Whitefield, Spurgeon and Carey knew nothing of the fire of the Spirit? Preposterous! DeArteaga's analysis is totally contrary to historic fact. He blatantly, or ignorantly, discounts the fact that Jonathan Edwards was not only one of the greatest Calvinistic thinkers of all time but believed in the cessation of the charismatic gifts! It was his fiery Calvinistic preaching, along with that of George Whitefield, that stoked the fires of revival.

At least DeArteaga credits Edwards with a highly developed theology of discernment. True! But Edwards' discernment led to the opposite conclusion to that presented by DeArteaga. As the revival ran its course, Jonathan Edwards 'came to believe that there was one principal cause of the reversal, namely, the unwatchfulness of the friends of the Awakening who allowed genuine and pure religion to become so mixed with "wildfire" and carnal "enthusiasm", that the Spirit of God was grieved and the advantage given to Satan... Trouble first appeared in connection with the cases of sudden physical collapse, of outcries, and of swoonings which were witnessed in many congregations from the summer of 1741 onwards.'[7] These are the very kind of phenomena that the Vineyard seems to want to encourage.

In a footnote Murray notes that 'These phenomena do not appear to have been present at the beginning of the Great Awakening. Thomas Prince remembered nothing of the kind under the preaching of Whitefield or Tennent.'[8]

The earlier quotation from Edwards concerning censoriousness was tempered by his later reflections. He wrote extensively about the excesses that began to occur as the revival progressed. In his view these excesses, not the warnings and criticisms of others, hindered — indeed might very well have quenched — the work of the Spirit.

These warnings about 'quenching the Spirit' hang like the sword of Damocles in the air over the heads of those who would assess the present movement. Since we long for genuine revival in our midst, such warnings must be taken seriously. They might make us stop with our pens poised in mid-air. Is it true that we have 'no anointing, no power, just words'? Are we being censorious and judgemental, pharisaical even?

It is not only those from within the Vineyard movement at large who warn of the danger of criticism. Many evangelical leaders seem content either to embrace the movement wholeheartedly or to 'wait and see.' I cannot follow that route.

Failure to make assessments is irresponsible

Fortunately, into this maelstrom of confusion and spiritual blackmail, John MacArthur has cast his book *Reckless Faith.* It is a ringing call for the church to recover its discernment. He notes, 'It is fashionable today to characterize anyone who is concerned with biblical doctrine as Pharisaical. The biblical condemnation of the Pharisees' legalism has been misread as a denunciation of doctrinal precision... But love for truth is *not* the same as legalism.'[9]

MacArthur points out that 'Sometimes the Pharisees are accused of being overly concerned with orthodoxy. But that was not at all where they went astray. Their error was that they became so wrapped up in their own traditions that they *downplayed* the truth of Scripture and distorted sound doctrine.'[10]

MacArthur's approach is right on track. It is not pharisaical to evaluate a movement that professes to be leading the way in a worldwide renewal — it would be pharisaical not to do so!

I have given considerable space in this book to trying to be fair and objective. We need to hear all sides. Nevertheless, neither the testimonies of blessing nor the warnings about quenching the Spirit have allayed my concerns. And I am not alone. There is a chorus of alarm rising from many serious and godly Christians who do not have an axe to grind. People from within Pentecostal churches as well as evangelicals of every spectrum point to serious flaws in the movement. Even John Wimber has expressed his alarm at some practices associated with the Toronto Airport Fellowship.

These flaws pose a serious danger both to individuals and to the church at large. Far from leading us to revival, this movement could very well be hindering genuine revival and leading us down a twisted path towards the birth of a new cult or heresy.

Spiritual blackmail

What really disturbs me is the sense of 'spiritual blackmail' hanging over the heads of all critics of the movement. The 'blackmail' comes as an overt charge, or a subtle insinuation, that those not in the movement have no right to question what God is doing. That we might quench the Spirit's work is a very powerful concern indeed. Who among us wants to grieve the gracious Spirit who comforts and counsels and illumines the Word in order to conform us to the image of Christ?

Is the Spirit calling us to either get on board or remain silent? Many pastors and leaders have given us this impression. Such a warning, whether taken from Jonathan Edwards or John Arnott — surely on opposite sides of the issue — holds us hostage to unfounded spiritual fears. Are we to suspend our rational faculties? Is the Spirit of truth only a Spirit of enthusiasm and experience?

After warning us against making quick and simplistic 'black-and-white' judgements about the Toronto Blessing, Larry Matthews, in an editorial in *The Canadian Baptist,* comments, 'But there is no grounds for looking down on those who abstain [from the Airport Vineyard experiences] in good faith. It's sheer presumption to ask us automatically to set aside our critical faculties and our historic understanding of our faith.'[11]

We must assess the movement. If we do nothing we shall still feel the heat. Many churches are already being scorched! If the heat is from the Spirit — wonderful! If not, we need to cool the saints by laying a channel to the refreshing streams of living water found in the Word of God. And if the 'fire' is not of the Spirit — what is it? How will it burn in the years ahead?

The biblical meaning of quenching the Spirit

Consider the phrase 'quench the Spirit' that is being thrown around so vehemently. This phrase is found in the context of instructions about personal sanctification given by the apostle Paul to the Thessalonians. He urges them to hard work, respect, patience, joyfulness, prayerfulness and thanksgiving (1 Thess. 5:12-18). Then he says, 'Do not put out [AV, 'quench'] the Spirit's fire; do not treat prophecies with contempt. Test everything. Hold on to the good. Avoid every kind of evil. May God himself, the God of peace, sanctify you through and through' (1 Thess. 5: 19-23).

This passage, far from being a warning to avoid making assessments, urges us to 'test everything'. The context forces us to conclude that we can quench the Spirit either by ungodly behaviour or by failing to evaluate carefully the messages people bring.

We are also urged not to treat prophecies carelessly. Prophecy, as it is spoken of here, is not foretelling. It is forth-telling — preaching, prophecy in the classic biblical mould. In his First Epistle to the Corinthians, Paul defines prophecy as speaking understandable words 'to men for their strengthening, encouragement and comfort... He who prophesies edifies the church... I would rather speak five intelligible words to instruct others...' (1 Cor. 14:3,4,19) Failure to test the content of those who preach quenches the Spirit! Failure to give preaching its rightful place does the same! This is very different from the way some people are using the phrase.

Grieving the Spirit

The only other verse of a similar nature is: 'And do not grieve the Holy Spirit of God, with whom you were sealed for the day of redemption' (Eph. 4:30). This verse, like the previous phrase, is set in the midst of a series of exhortations urging the Ephesians to live holy lives free from deceit, evil desires, anger, violence, stealing, etc. The immediate context concerns harming others by unwholesome talk that arises from bitterness and anger accompanied by a failure to forgive. We grieve the Spirit when we hinder relationships by harbouring bitterness or spreading slander.

If what we say about the Toronto Blessing and the Vineyard movement is untrue and inaccurate — yes, that would grieve the Spirit. For this very reason I want to be extremely careful to quote extensively and to give both sides of the issue.

Testing all things

Overwhelming these two cautions are a host of exhortations urging believers to test all who claim to be apostles, prophets, preachers or teachers. By way of example, the Bereans are commended for their investigative approach to the preaching of Paul: 'These were more noble than those in Thessalonica, in that they received the word with all readiness of mind, and searched the scriptures daily, whether those things were so' (Acts 17:11, AV). When the Holy Spirit commends the Bereans for testing the teaching of the great apostle, why should we be condemned for expressing concern about teachers in the Vineyard movement?

Even Apollos, although he was 'a learned man, with a thorough knowledge of the Scriptures', was corrected in his erroneous views on baptism by Priscilla and Aquila (Acts 18:24-26).

Protestantism maintains a heritage of freedom of conscience — a freedom that allows any believer to question any teacher or preacher. Each believer has been entrusted with the Scriptures and the truth they enshrine. No man has authority higher than the Scriptures, our rule of faith and practice. It is our individual responsibility as believers to 'contend for the faith'.

In my own pastoral experience I have sought to encourage members to bring to my attention anything that I say that cannot be proved by Scripture. Down through the years a number have corrected me or discussed possible differences of interpretation. If carried out in the right way this process is healthy.

Nothing angers me more than manipulation, mind control, or any kind of attempt by someone to use his position or authority to demand unquestioning acceptance of what he says. Pastors have no right to enforce their opinion upon their congregation; they are called, rather, to expound the Word. Under Christ as the head of the church, the Word of God remains the final authority.

This freedom to question is characteristic of any church that seeks to live under the Spirit. Indeed, one common characteristic of groups that become cultic is the discouragement of freedom of thought, the urging of members to accept uncritically what is taught.

This responsibility to contend for the truth involves the gracious but firm exposure of error. In the same chapter in which Christ commands us, 'Do not judge, or you too will be judged,' he says, 'Watch out for false prophets. They come to you in sheep's clothing... By their fruit you will recognize them' (Matt. 7:1,15,16). His warning about being judgemental is an exposure of the hypocrisy of criticizing our brother for a speck in his eye while we have a plank in our own. This exhortation warns us against condemning others on a personal basis.

As soon as a person steps into a position of leadership in the church, he assumes a mantle of group responsibility, not to lord it over the saints, but to be accountable to them, and to Christ.

As you will see in the next chapter, I have no desire to judge John Wimber, John Arnott, or any in the movement, on a personal level. I trust their motives are sincere. It is my responsibility, however, and yours, to hold their teaching and practice up to the scrutiny of the Word of God — just as we do our own. This is especially important in the case of a movement whose influence is international and interdenominational.

Why? Because Scripture commands us to do this very thing: 'Test all things.' Concerning signs leading up to the end of the age, Christ says, 'Watch out that no one deceives you... Many false prophets will appear and deceive many people... For false Christs and false prophets will appear and perform great signs and miracles to deceive even the elect — if that were possible. See, I have told you ahead of time' (Matt. 24:4,11,24) Yes, the false prophets will perform signs and miracles! No wonder many of us are sceptical. We are supposed to be sceptical. Christ warns us that near the end of time teaching will appear that is so seductive and so deceptive that it will almost deceive even the elect.

In Acts 20 Paul appeals to the Ephesian elders to 'Keep watch over yourselves and all the flock ... savage wolves will come in among you and will not spare the flock. Even from your own number men will arise and distort the truth in order to draw away disciples after them. So be on your guard!' (Acts 20:28-31). In Romans Paul warns about 'smooth talk and flattery' that 'deceive the minds of naïve people' (Rom. 16:18). To Timothy he writes, 'In later times some will abandon the faith and follow deceiving spirits' (1 Tim. 4:1). Peter tells his readers, 'There will be false teachers among you' (2 Peter 2:1). These multiplied warnings, of which many more could be cited, make the evaluation of all movements and teachers an absolute duty for all Christians. If we fail to 'test all things', we fail Christ and hinder the extension of the kingdom.

Careful evaluation is especially important of a movement whose leaders claim that 'signs and wonders' are the key to end-time evangelism (see chapters 16 and 17). Jesus warned of a tendency common in his day. It is common in ours as well. 'A wicked and adulterous generation asks for a miraculous sign! But none will be given it except the sign of the prophet Jonah' (Matt. 12:39). All of us have an innate propensity within us that must be subdued — the propensity to seek the spectacular. As human beings we love circuses and sports events. We follow fire engines and gather at disasters. This is natural. But the kingdom is spiritual. We should celebrate, rather, the sign of Jonah — the resurrection of Christ.

Every apostolic writer, with few exceptions, warns about doctrinal or behavioural aberrations. In their day they did not wait for months or years to test some distant fruit of a new idea. The instant they recognized a danger, a tendency, a heresy, they fired off a letter to the infected church. Today, however, some evangelical leaders outside of the movement join voices from within the movement in appealing to us to suspend judgement. This would be akin to believers in the early church being told to suspend judgement on legalism or Gnosticism, etc. Many of our epistles would never have been written under that scenario. This appeal is in effect asking us to suspend our critical faculties, to forget discernment, to become naïve and trusting, to value tolerance above truth and to curtail the 'renewal of our minds' that is part of sanctification. We cannot do that.

The apostles urge us to think critically: 'The spiritual man makes judgements about all things…' (1 Cor. 2:15). 'Do you not know that the saints will judge the world? And if you are to judge the world, are you not competent to judge trivial cases?' (1 Cor. 6:2) 'I speak to sensible people; judge for yourselves what I say' (1 Cor. 10:15). 'Do not believe every spirit, but test the spirits to see whether they are from God, because many false prophets have gone out into the world' (1 John 4:1).

Although many Christian leaders have gathered around this 'strange fire', we must speak out kindly, humbly and carefully. The appeal to stop making any critique of the movement or run the risk of quenching the Spirit is a subtle form of spiritual blackmail that must be rejected out of hand.

Fortunately, some leaders in the Vineyard movement are recognizing the need to be open to criticism. In the autumn of 1994 the Board of the Association of Vineyard Churches listed nine areas of consensus about the phenomena occurring in the 'current renewal'. The eighth point states: 'While we will listen to our critics and learn from them, we do not want to be governed by them. If they can prove to us by sound exegesis and logic that we are wrong, we will change. By the nature of our movement (renewal of things of the Spirit) we have always had, and always will have, critics; let's interact with them as godly men and women without becoming reactionary, bitter, unteachable or controlled by them.'[12]

Statements such as these give us some reason to believe that the movement will progress towards, rather than away from, the historic faith once and for all delivered to the saints.

6.
The Vineyard pro and con — a summary of concerns

Every church I know, every Christian I have met, and every Christian I have read about all share one thing in common. All struggle with practical or doctrinal imperfection of one kind or another. New Testament churches all reflected this reality. The squabbles of two women in Philippi disturbed that church. The Thessalonian church had a naïve view of the Second Coming. The Colossians struggled with Gnosticism. Legalistic Judaism threatened to derail the work of God in Galatia. Corinth had multiple problems.

As a missionary in Pakistan I struggled to maintain balance in my own life and in my family. I sought to encourage balance in the Pakistani church. Upon return to Canada I faced the same challenges. Wherever I have pastored, I have found imbalance of one kind or another: resistance to constructive change; anti-intellectualism; legalism; lack of commitment to prayer; lethargy in worship; weakness in Bible knowledge; misunderstandings about doctrine; laziness in reading; resistance to meeting in homes; unconcern about missions. We all struggle to remain balanced. As John Wimber has himself pointed out, 'We spend a lifetime sorting out the fleshly, and devilish influences in our lives from the things of the Spirit.'[1]

We should not be surprised then, that the Vineyard movement is in the midst of a theological and practical struggle to achieve balance. If its divergence from evangelical norms was merely a temporary aberration in the pilgrimage to maturity, we ought to overlook their peccadilloes. We would do the same for any sister church. If, however, these divergences foreshadow serious departures from biblical Christianity a note of alarm must be sounded.

Certainly the Vineyard board recognized in the Toronto Blessing just such a danger. Their actions on 5 December 1995 demonstrate this fact. Unfortunately, pruning this aberrant branch has not purged Vineyardism of alarming tendencies. The Toronto Blessing grew out of hardy Vineyard stock and it illustrates the natural direction believers in the movement are bound to go if left unchecked. Exclusion of Toronto has not changed Vineyardism.

In my view, neither the Vineyard movement nor its Toronto expression is, at this time, heretical. Although its Statement of Faith is skimpy and charismatic, it asserts belief in the inerrant Word, the Trinity, the deity of Christ, the atonement, ascension and return of Christ, the new birth, the eternal destiny of all men and the unity of all believers (see doctrinal statement in notes).[2]

In deciding if the Vineyard is a cult, we must ask, 'Do they deny any cardinal Christian doctrine such as the Trinity or the inerrancy of Scripture?' The answer seems to be no. According to Grant Hochman cults can also be identified by exorbitant claims, misuse of Scripture or express intolerance of other Christians.[3] As we shall see in the chapters to follow, their exorbitant claims about signs and wonders, their imbalanced use of Scripture and their élitism might identify the Vineyard movement as resembling a cult. However, John Wimber and others in the movement seem to be struggling against this tendency. While some Vineyard meetings and some of their leaders do manifest cultic tendencies, in my opinion, the movement as a whole cannot be classed as a cult at this time. However, the serious imbalance present in the movement will inevitably lead that way if not corrected.

Bob Hunter, after transcribing scores of Vineyard sermons writes, 'Do, I believe that the Vineyard Church *as a whole* is a cult? No, I don't, but there are many cultic elements within it and the church is headed at full speed in that direction... Many Vineyard churches don't want to have anything to do with the things that we are hearing about.'[4]

They are not alone in majoring on secondary isues. The whole evangelical church is in a state of flux. It seems to be drifting steadily downstream away from the sources of its life and vibrancy. This drift is reflective of tendencies in the culture at large. Around us we see an obsession with entertainment, an anti-intellectualism, a frenzied mysticism, an emphasis on the visual and tactile, a proud self-centredness and a demand for one's needs to be met now. Tolerance has scrambled onto the throne as the king of virtues while those who promote absolute standards and ultimate truth are vilified.

Paul Friesen, professor at Ontario Bible College, believes that the Vineyard is a typical reflection of what happens in the church during a time of great cultural change. The same occurred, he believes, at the turn of the century in the Azusa revival that initiated modern Pentecostalism.[5]

David Reed, of Wycliffe College in Toronto, admits that the Vineyard has problems but views them as a spiritual casualty department that signals a church in crisis. In this capacity, he believes that they serve as a prophetic bridge movement for those anxious about the future. He lauds their role as gadflies raised up to protest against apathy, warn that something is wrong and provoke people to turn to God at a cultural turning point in our history.[6]

As a boy I loved to swim, especially where a wooden float was anchored in water deep enough for diving off. Sometimes, when too many of us scrambled onboard and all moved over to one side, the float would tip up and throw us in the water. The Vineyard, along with other evangelicals, is balancing on a religious platform over deep and dangerous water. Emotions are a gift of God. The Holy Spirit does give us amazing experiences. But too many are rushing to embrace experience and emotion. Too many are following impressions. The float is seriously tilted. Too many have no biblical lifejacket to preserve them in the midst of troubles and suffering, persecution and disappointment.

The positive aspects

In the Vineyard movement, we face a dangerous imbalance. But before I address the dangers, let me mention some positive aspects of the Vineyard movement.

Their emphasis on *the supernatural* reminds us that we are called to walk with Christ in the power of the indwelling Spirit. While we may not accept their emphasis on power evangelism as manifest in signs and wonders, we do need, as Daniel Lundy comments, 'a sense of God's presence and power... Our Baptist churches cannot recover fresh spiritual vigour without a determined effort to make prayer a priority in our private and corporate life... One reason for the attraction of the Vineyard is undoubtedly the sense of being in touch with God on a moment-by-moment basis. There is an expectation of receiving guidance and power from God that is tailor-made to one's situation.'[7]

Their emphasis on *revival and renewal* should strike a responsive note in our churches. Too often complacency with the status quo cuts the nerve of passion for revival. The plethora of books and conferences on how to manage and plan and prod the church into dynamic growth often fail to acknowledge the sovereign hand of God.

We could also learn something from their emphasis on *spontaneity*. Their leaders' openness to modifying worship services and scrapping their planned messages reminds us to be more flexible. In many of our churches things are planned ahead of time so rigidly that if God did come in revival power, there would be no flexibility to allow his entrance.

Unfortunately, their spontaneity too often seems to cover, on the one hand, a lack of exegetical preparation, and on the other, a carefully orchestrated agenda below the surface. As we shall see in chapter 15, their services tend to disguise a framework of rigidly planned informality. Nevertheless, many of us need to be more flexible and open to the leading of the Spirit in our meetings.

I have tried in my own ministry to prepare my sermons carefully and thoroughly plan the services. At the same time, I have sought to be open to stopping the service for prayer, or to adapting my message to changed circumstances.

Their emphasis on *personal ministry to needy hearts* deserves consideration. I disagree with their method of ending each service with an extended 'ministry time'. At this point, the 'ministry team' moves from person to person praying for people to be 'slain in the Spirit' or to 'soak in the Spirit'. However, I must admit that the typical evangelical church with its formal services in which people sit shoulder to shoulder leaves little opportunity to get personal about individual needs. The Vineyard does allow time for individual attention, however bizarre that may seem.

I believe that preaching and teaching the Word of God is consistently the best method of counselling people. But I do not believe it is the only way. In too many of our churches, shepherding is the duty of the pastor alone. There is little recognition of the importance of coffee-cup counselling and encouragement. There is resistance to small-group Bible studies where people can get to know each other and to pray for each other in specific ways. Perhaps the Vineyard's emphasis on 'ministry times' will jolt us into taking more seriously the Scripture's injunction to 'Bear one another's burdens,' 'Love one another,' 'Encourage one another,' 'Pray for one another.'

Another thing that strikes one about a Vineyard meeting is the sense of *exuberance and celebration*. The hour or so of singing seems much too repetitive and manipulative to me. The accompaniment on drums and guitars submerges sensitive eardrums in crashing waves of sound. But on the other side of the coin, many of our churches are too stodgy. Sometimes our singing is like a dirge. I believe we need times of quiet reverence and thoughtful, slow song. (The typical Vineyard meeting does not often allow this option.) But while serious themes such as repentance, commitment and suffering with Christ should engage our minds, joyful themes should also echo often from our lips. I therefore see nothing wrong with songs of celebration being upbeat.

For worship to be worship, it must engage our emotions as well as our minds and wills. While our intellect should drive our emotions, I have the impression that too often our responses are emotionless. Daniel Lundy asks, 'Are we so concerned with orthodoxy that we have an unwarranted wariness about emotion? Genuine response to the gospel involves the whole being.'[8] Personally, I would welcome a spirit of celebration invading our churches, as long as it was not accompanied by a plague of trite lyrics disguised by vocal gymnastics.

The emphasis on the joy of our relationship with God should not be discounted. Throughout my Christian life I have been struck repeatedly by the frequent encouragements in the Psalms to 'Rejoice in the Lord.' I have read and reread John Piper's book *Desiring God — Meditations of a Christian Hedonist*, with much profit.[9] His thesis, that we can best glorify God by enjoying him for ever, is not new but it needs re-emphasis in our midst.

The Vineyard has also evolved *a relaxed style*. Their Toronto cousins reflect this emphasis. James Beverley writes, 'The Toronto Blessing is nonlegalistic in its ethos and style. Jesus warned against mean and uptight religion in his rebuke to certain Jewish leaders of his day (Matt. 23:1-36). One of the appeals of the Vineyard movement is its relaxed style. This ease of spirit must be applauded and should not be dismissed as indifference, laziness, or antinomianism.'[10] Those who lead the services wear sport shorts or teeshirts and slacks, including jeans. Women dress modestly, but informally. It wouldn't hurt most of us to relax a little our tradition of wearing dark suits and ties in church. Even banks are beginning to urge their employees to dress informally one day a week!

Main concerns about Vineyardism

Having listed some positive elements in Vineyardism, let me return to my main concerns. My earlier illustration of the diving float stressed the importance of balance. It is here that I feel the greatest disquiet. John Wimber himself addressed the problem of imbalance in an article in the Vineyard magazine *Equipping the Saints* back in 1989. In warning about the danger of an over-emphasis on prophecy he explains, 'When God introduces something new, the church usually responds by overemphasizing it. That's human nature. But this is only a *temporary* imbalance.'[11]

However, Wimber goes on to document a series of other examples of imbalance in the Vineyard: 'Early on being "baptized in the Spirit" — accompanied by speaking in tongues — became a major focus... Later on we added praying for the sick to worship, and that became *all* we did. Our focus at every meeting was on healing — to the exclusion of other significant practices of the Christian life... In time we outgrew our myopic practice... Prophecy is now assuming center stage in the Vineyard, and — as we have done in the past with other moves of God — it is almost all that is talked about.'[12]

This fixation with prophecy did not last long. In 1991 Wimber became disillusioned with prophecy and put 'some separation and distance from Bob Jones, Paul Cain and Jack Deere', the Kansas City Prophets.[13] Prophecy is again on the front burner at the Toronto Airport Christian Fellowship, as we shall see in later chapters. The meteoric rise of the physical phenomena in January 1994 is just one more of these emphases.

Throughout the brief history of the Vineyard movement one exotic wonder after another has risen to prominence and then declined. Those involved welcome this as evidence of the dynamic nature of the Spirit's work in their midst. In reality, it seems more like a volatile and erratic movement engaged in a restless search for something novel to justify their 'Messianic complex'. The instability of the Vineyard can be traced directly to the movement's defective doctrinal moorings, which we shall discuss in chapter 12. Unfortunately, the heady wine of exotic experience and quixotic phenomena has proved intoxicating to many from other churches.

Before going on to consider these issues in detail in the following chapters let me briefly summarize some of the tendencies that threaten to plunge Vineyard members and their friends into dangerous waters.

1. Biblical authority

In the mightiest revival of history, outside the era of the early church, the Reformers cried, *'Sola scriptura* — Scripture alone!' Reformation fire swept across Europe fanned by the wind of the Spirit unleashed by a Bible unchained. Those flames swept away tradition and superstition, igniting a new fire of devotion to the absolute authority of the Word of God on all matters of faith and practice. In that Word the Reformers had rediscovered the authentic gospel of free grace. No wonder they also cried, *'Sola fide* — Faith alone!'

Like many others in our day, the Vineyard is eroding biblical authority and sufficiency. An emphasis on pragmatic experience, physical manifestations, inner impressions of guidance, testimonies, words of revelation and prophecy has usurped the place of Holy Writ. They have reversed the classic order in which Scripture produces, interprets and controls experience. As a result the role of preaching and teaching the Word has been seriously undermined. Doctrine is decried, in many instances, as the barren words of modern-day Pharisees. Emotion and impression are exalted to the detriment of the intellect. (We shall analyse these issues in detail in chapters 7, 11,12 and 13.)

2. The role of Christ

No one in the Vineyard movement would deny the deity of Christ. Indeed many who 'receive the blessing' testify that it made them love Christ more. In the Toronto Blessing, however, Christ appears in the background as an ethereal, undescribed figure. The focus is on the Spirit and manifestations. Most seriously, the cross is seldom mentioned. (We shall address this issue in chapter 14.)

3. The role of the Holy Spirit

While the Holy Spirit is mentioned much more often than Christ, the view presented is shallow. True, his power is emphasized, but his quiet, providential care for all God's people is largely ignored. One gains the impression that they feel that they have a corner on the Holy Spirit. Their leaders claim to be able to pass on the 'blessing of the Spirit' through prayer and the laying-on of the hands of the 'ministry team'. Without any biblical description of what they mean, they offer to 'soak people in the Spirit'. Of course, one of the most serious objections to their typical 'renewal' meeting is its disorder. Is the Holy Spirit a spirit of disorder? (We shall deal with this in chapter 11.)

4. Evangelism

One of the main emphases of the Vineyard is the belief that power evangelism will occur through signs and wonders. I would vigorously debate this thesis. But even without such debate the 'miracles' of healing they affirm seem far from impressive. The manifestations they point to as 'signs and wonders' appear to be more the result of psychological suggestion than spontaneous outpourings of the Spirit. Most seriously, from what I have read and the meetings I have attended, the gospel — God's evangelistic means — is scarcely mentioned or inadequately explained. Repentance, as evidenced by deep conviction and weeping, is little emphasized. The multitudes they claim to have seen come to Christ represent a dangerous 'broad gate' of easy-believism.

5. Harmony with other churches

While Vineyard churches claim to be mainstream evangelicals they are really a charismatic denomination with their own distinctives. Although they express concern about promoting unity and blessing in the body of Christ, we find, instead, increasing confusion and division. While they profess that they are humble servants of the whole church, others are expected to warm themselves at their fire. Since I shall not be dealing with this subject at any length in the rest of the book, let me pause on this subject briefly.

No matter how hard leaders of 'Third Wave Churches' try to declare their love for the whole body of Christ, it is clear that those of us who are not on their wavelength represent an inferior brand of the Christian faith. They imply that we have a defective relationship with the Spirit. We don't have 'the anointing'. We don't have 'power'. We cripple evangelism by failing to promote 'signs and wonders'. This movement fosters the classic charismatic caste system.

This attitude goes back a long way. In 1985 Professor Don Lewis of Regent College attended a conference on signs and wonders in Vancouver at which John Wimber was the featured speaker. Dr Lewis felt that Wimber had a 'love-hate relationship with the church. He professes to love it in all of its expressions and is strong in his denunciations of divisions within it. Almost in the same breath he is devastating in his criticisms... He is also frequently cynical and disparaging in his references to other churches (including churches which major on Bible study and even on the charismatic gifts) and went as far as to compare the church to the relationship between David and Bathsheba. None of these devastating criticisms were applied to Wimber's own Vineyard Fellowship [which he believes] is the vanguard' of what Christ is doing in the last days. Dr Lewis sensed a 'strong us-them mentality: those who are for signs and wonders and those who were just ordinary evangelicals (or even just run-of-the-mill charismatics).'[14]

Let's skip ten years to 1994. When I attended the Toronto Airport Vineyard I heard comments giving a similar impression: 'God is wooing us from our denominations. Are you ministering from dry wells, playing church? What's missing? ... The river of blessing [as in the Toronto Blessing]. He is breaking the status quo. Aren't you tired of pop-up-and-down church services?'[15]

Pentecostal minister Gordon Williams has found that 'Many people who have attended Vineyard meetings become hyper-critical, judgmental, and disruptive in the churches from which they have come and especially so in churches that ... allow the gifts of the Holy Spirit to be used by their people [i.e., charismatic churches].'[16]

Cheryl and Steve Thomson speak from their personal experience of having been part of a Toronto-area Vineyard church until 1989. They believe that the Vineyard churches have pursued a policy of enhancing their credibility in the larger evangelical world by presenting themselves as 'helpers and facilitators for interdenominational dialogue'. They involve themselves in 'Marches for Jesus' and conduct workshops on a variety of subjects, including contemporary music and worship. The Thomsons claim that, through these and other means, they are 'steadily gathering new members from other churches. They are also given a platform for their own leaders, and the teachings of their leaders, which over time are accorded greater and greater respect.'[17]

Whether or not the Vineyard movement approaches the rest of the church with such self-conscious tactics, Rick Joyner certainly gives that impression. In an article published in 1992 in *The Morningstar Journal*, of which he is the editor and to which Mike Bickle also contributes, he laid out the strategy: 'Conferences are a basic part of the Lord's end-time strategy. They are comparable to the Lord's command for Israel to go up to Jerusalem three times a year for His feasts.'[18]

Cheryl Thomson summarizes the approach: 'Each general conference "will spawn" local conferences for pastors, prophets, intercessors, etc., to be held throughout the year in each region. At the local level, "city-wide weekly prayer and leadership meetings would also begin... This strategy is not to in any way become a separate stream of influence in the church, but be a vehicle for the differing streams which already exist to interchange and begin flowing together."'[19] Obviously, this is a reflection of their view that the Vineyard is in the vanguard of God's end-time purposes.

Without charging them with conspiracy, it is interesting to note how closely what Rick Joyner wrote corresponds to what happens. In the autumn of 1995, the Toronto Airport Vineyard held three major conferences: the Toronto Alpha Conference on evangelism in the local church; Catch the Fire Again, at which 5,000 people gathered to interact on the Toronto Blessing; and the Healing School, on developing a healing ministry. By March 1996 five had already been scheduled for the first half of the year. Costs are nominal, and very attractive when compared to other conferences. The Toronto Airport church also has a meeting every Wednesday for area pastors from any denomination. Team members fan out across North America, and indeed the world, to spread the 'renewal'.

Obviously, inroads are being made into the evangelical psyche. The growth of Vineyard churches is mushrooming — almost exclusively from the transfer of believers from other communions. A former Southern Baptist testified one evening when I was there about his lack of success in influencing his whole church to accept the 'blessing'. Then he described how he took some members with him to start a new Vineyard church-plant.[20]

Now, just as those enamoured by the Toronto Blessing tell us that it will usher in a new age of mutual love and co-operation across denominational lines, the Vineyard movement is rent from within! The breach between the Association of Vineyard Churches and their Toronto church gives practical and visible expression to something endemic in the movement. The separation has sent a signal so diametrically opposed to all they profess to stand for that parties on both sides have rushed to try to repair the breach. Whether or not that will be possible will become evident as time goes by. In the meantime the Toronto Airport Christian Fellowship devoted the whole of the February 1996 issue of their magazine to exploring unity and division as they tried to put a positive slant on a shattering event.

6. Church history

They present a revisionist view of history. They appeal to the precedent set by the Montanists and Jonathan Edwards in the Great Awakening. The Montanists, however, were heretical and Jonathan Edwards believed in the cessation of the miraculous gifts!

If allowed to go unchallenged, their attempts at rewriting history call into question the spirituality of the vast majority of the great reformers, revivalists, preachers and missionaries of pre-modern history. Luther and Calvin, Knox and Bunyan, Whitefield and Edwards, John Newton and Charles Wesley, Carey and Judson would be discounted. (We shall consider this subject in chapters 9 and 10.)

7. Worship

Their manner of worship generates a powerful atmosphere of emotion through repetitive choruses with weak content sung to a loud and fast beat. The congregation becomes an instrument to be played by the leader. Emotion and exuberance come to the fore, with no opportunity for individual Christians to blend their minds — as well as their emotions — in the united worship of God.

Apparently, in the view of many in the movement, non-charismatic worship is a dead wasteland! Evidently thoughtfulness and quiet reverence, order and content cramp the style of the 'new gurus of worship'. Are we to believe that no hymn older than 1980 is worth its salt?

Guy Chevreau claims that 'The worship of the early Church is characterized by an openness to, and a dependence on, the immediate inspiration of the Spirit, be it through prophecy, spontaneous prayer and extemporaneous preaching, spiritual songs, and perhaps above all, an unfettered enthusiasm and joy.' He then quotes Johannes Weiss to state, without any basis in biblical texts, that primitive Christianity was characterized, among other things, by 'a tempestuous enthusiasm'.[21]

Separating the wheat and the chaff from Chevreau's analysis is no mean task. Some of what he says is true. We should be open and dependent on the Spirit as we worship. We should have opportunity for spontaneous prayer. We ought to 'enter his gates' with enthusiasm, devotion and boundless joy. This does not mean, however, that preachers who prepare their sermons are failing to trust in the 'immediate inspiration of the Spirit'. What a fallacious notion! To think that the God who planned redemption before the foundation of the earth cannot guide his servant ahead of time is blasphemy! (We shall discuss the fallacy of his belief in 'immediate inspiration', which is nothing more than a trust in fallible human impressions, in chapter 19.)

Especially grievous is the idea that worship ought to be 'tempestuous'. Paul corrected the Corinthians on this very point: 'For God is not a God of disorder but of peace' (1 Cor. 14:33). I certainly did not find peace to worship the Lord Jesus Christ in the midst of the cacophony at the Toronto Airport Vineyard, with the exception of certain periods of good singing. I do not believe the early church was tempestuous in its worship. The pattern of Old Testament worship that carried on into the early church denies this claim. As Gordon Fee brings out, pagan worship in Corinth and other places was 'characterized by frenzy and disorder. The theological point is crucial: the character of one's deity is reflected in the character of one's worship.'[22]

Should not our worship reflect our triune God? Of course it should. And while the opinions of evangelicals on worship vary greatly there are wide areas of agreement. Few today believe that stodgy, dead services glorify God. But surely most would agree that worship requires a mix of prayer, joyful celebration, quiet reverence, thoughtful contemplation, orderly progression and challenging preaching. Unfortunately, worship is another crucial area that deserves thorough treatment, treatment I am not going to be able to give in this book.

8. Christian living

As some have pointed out, the Vineyard view of the Christian life seems to be an 'over-realized eschatology'. They yearn for God to give them in full measure now what he has promised only in heaven. In the place of the classic disciplines of Christian living — Bible study, meditation, prayer, fellowship, service, etc. — they have substituted an event taking place in a geographic location. The message is: 'Come to Toronto (or wherever the practitioners of this experience are speaking) and get the blessing.' This is just one more in a long line of emphases on some kind of 'second blessing'. Like others which have been made before this event, it promises an experience that will translate us beyond our problems to a higher level of Christian living. In that rarefied atmosphere the inner struggles, the temptations of life, the disappointments and problems, the sufferings and self-denial all become things of the past. The living is easy, 'in the Spirit'.

Christian warfare, as perceived by the movement, is a series of crises, a sudden 'power encounter', an 'instantaneous deliverance', or an 'inner healing', rather than the result of disciplined and progressive training in the use of the Christian armour. One gets the impression that problems of Christian living will disappear in a burst of 'holy laughter'. Every genuine believer has been 'set free' and truly 'lives in the heavenly realms in Christ Jesus', but he or she still faces a lifetime of victory in progressive doses. In close on forty years of ministry I have seen the Vineyard type of formula produce untold damage.

But another discrepancy must engage our attention as well. For adequate Christian growth we need a strong local church that equips the saints to do the work of ministry in all its facets. The excitement the Toronto Blessing generates about physical phenomena and charismatic gifts detracts from the pursuit of more humble gifts such as evangelism, preaching, teaching, shepherding, mercy, encouragement and administration. I have in my possession a brochure from the Toronto Airport Vineyard advertising classes on the gifts of the Spirit.[23] Seven sessions deal with tongues, interpretation and prophecy. Ten sessions deal with words of knowledge, words of wisdom and discerning spirits. Six sessions deal with faith, miracles and healing. The other gifts are totally left out! How can an emphasis such as this produce balanced, ministering disciples?

9. Elitism

My earlier chapter on quenching the Spirit highlights a troubling tendency in the Vineyard. Too many Vineyard leaders give the impression that they have a monopoly of the Holy Spirit. James Beverley comments: 'The fundamental but pathetic posture of the Toronto Blessing is that God is doing *only one* thing in Toronto: His Spirit is being poured out at the Airport Vineyard. Period. End of story. Of course, no one in leadership ... is going to admit this reductionistic view... they may deny my criticism... Even a casual glance through transcripts of evening messages illustrates a self-absorbed ideology... Vineyard leaders are also too ready to bless everything they do and expect that the rest of the Christian church will fall in line... The Spirit of God landed in Toronto long before January 20, 1994. In thousands of churches and in a million ways, the Holy Spirit has been working in this great Canadian city.'[24]

To discount the work of the Spirit in those who do not subscribe to the Vineyard way is a serious flaw. Every day, almost without fail, I give thanks for the indwelling presence of the Comforter. On Sunday, as I approach the pulpit, I breathe a prayer to the Spirit for his anointing to attend my preaching. I appeal for the Holy Spirit to make real to me the presence of Jesus Christ.

The Holy Spirit has not restricted his gracious influences to those who have experienced the 'blessing'. Anyone who has taken the Scriptures seriously rejoices that he or she has been sealed by the Spirit and has received the Spirit as a guarantee of his or her final salvation (Eph. 1:13-14). All true believers celebrate the Spirit of adoption that enables them to cry to the Father, '*Abba* — Daddy!' Every serious believer knows that he or she cannot live the Christian life without the indwelling work of the Spirit as outlined in Romans 8. Indeed 'If anyone does not have the Spirit of Christ, he does not belong to Christ... Because those who are led by the Spirit of God are sons of God' (Rom. 8:9,14)

Vineyard élitism seems to lead those in the movement to discount the fact that God supernaturally works outside the Vineyard. In later chapters we shall examine the whole issue of the miraculous. Like many critics of the Vineyard, I believe that God used signs and wonders to attest the ministry of biblical apostles and prophets, but with the conclusion of the canon their occurrence ceased. This understanding of biblical history does not mean that critics of the Vineyard doubt God's ability to work supernaturally.

God is intimately involved with all the affairs of our lives as believers. We get up in the morning, open our Bibles and seek the face of God in his Word. We ask him to speak to us and teach us. He does. I have noted repeatedly in the margin of my Bible the amazing way he has met a particular need out of a seemingly chance devotional reading of the Scriptures. He is supernaturally speaking to me, as to others, through the Word.

He is supernaturally caring for each of his children through providence. I recall protection as a missionary in Pakistan in the turmoil of two wars with India, when caught up in an angry mob in a bazaar and when my office was wrecked in an anti-American riot. I recall many answers to prayer when medical help was unavailable for our family. In the more recent past I was saved from disaster by God's protection when a car raced through a red light on a rainy highway right into my path! I remember a concrete chimney cap, knocked loose by my ladder, plummeting to the ground scant milimetres from my head. More recently I think of a colonoscopy in which the surgeon removed quite a large polyp with cancer on the tip but not at the base.

Serious disciples, who have not received the Toronto Blessing, rejoice daily in the supernatural presence of the triune God. We believe in God's supernatural provision of our needs. We believe that God guides us. We believe that God answers prayer. When I was writing this I went to a prayer meeting one evening. That evening one of the deacons reported how the tumour on his brother's leg has disappeared over a period of several weeks as people prayed. One brother spoke of God's leading him to find work. Two different saints talked of God's intervention with car problems. Another brother told how the total paralysis of a friend with whom he is seeking to share the gospel has been subsiding.

Some of our prayer requests, of course, were not answered then. Some of them we have been making for quite a while. Prayer calls for openness to the will of God and patience. No doubt, we all sometimes get careless in our prayer lives. Surely all of us, whether we believe in power healing and power evangelism or not, believe that God supernaturally answers prayer!

The differences that I have summarized above constitute a substantial shift away from evangelical fundamentals. The shift is serious enough to plunge the whole evangelical church into confusion and controversy just when we need to join hands in world evangelization. Ultimately these emphases will stretch the fibre of evangelical life until it snaps. The result will be impotence and further division.

7.
Supreme court or round-table discussion?

In order to evaluate the Vineyard movement accurately, along with its Toronto transmutation, we need an impartial and objective court of appeal. We cannot just toss opinions out at a round-table discussion. No, we need something completely free from taint of denominational prejudice. Whatever court we choose must have sufficient insight to gauge emotions and experiences as well as beliefs and practices. Fortunately God has placed in our hands the jurisprudence of just such an infallible court of appeal. We have the inspired canon of Holy Scripture.

We shall move on in the chapters ahead to evaluate the Vineyard movement by comparing it with this changeless standard. We must be clear at the outset that the differences we find are not just matters of temperament. They are not differences between an emphasis on reason and an emphasis on feelings of faith and joy. Actually, there is no dichotomy here.

From the beginning the Lord has expected his people to respond to him with deep emotion: 'Love the Lord your God with all your heart and with all your soul and with all your strength' (Deut. 6:5). This involves no dichotomy between emotion and intellect. Christ interprets this command as: 'Love the Lord your God with all your heart and with all your soul and with all your mind' (Matt. 22:37). Christ's interpretation takes into account the context in Deuteronomy. The heart is sustained by the mind because 'These commandments that I give you today are to be upon your hearts' (Deut. 6:6).

The foundational role of the Word of God in illuminating the mind and warming the heart is woven into the very warp and woof of Scripture. In Psalm 19 David waxes lyrical about the part Scripture plays in reviving our souls, making us wise, giving joy to the heart and light to the eyes. He compares God's revealed will to gold and to honey. He concludes the psalm with a poignant admission, 'Who can discern his errors?' and continues: 'Forgive my hidden faults. Keep [me] ... from wilful sins' (Ps. 19:12-13). David knew that without the Scriptures discernment of our spiritual condition would be impossible and personal holiness unattainable.

In the first verse of Psalm 119, the psalmist outdoes himself in describing how 'Blessed are they ... who walk according to the law of the Lord,' a theme he develops to an unparalleled extent in the rest of the psalm.

Christ was the supreme example of victorious living. He repeatedly used Scripture to fend off the devil's temptations. Quoting Deuteronomy he replied to the first temptation: 'Man does not live on bread alone, but on every word that comes from the mouth of God' (Matt. 4:4). He later identified the error of the Pharisees: 'You are in error because you do not know the Scriptures or the power of God' (Matt. 22:29).

Jesus' title 'Master' reflects his astounding teaching ministry. He repeatedly emphasized the importance that teaching (doctrine) would play in the lives of his disciples: 'If you hold to my teaching, you are really my disciples. Then you will know the truth, and the truth will set you free' (John 8:31-32). The night before his crucifixion Christ prayed to the Father for the protection and development of his disciples. He prayed, 'Sanctify them by the truth; your word is truth' (John 17:17).

After Pentecost the apostles continued to hold forth 'the Word of God'. On his way to Jerusalem, Paul called the Ephesian elders to his side for some final instructions. He warned them about 'savage wolves', false teachers, who would 'arise and distort the truth in order to draw away disciples after them' (Acts 20:29,30). He summarizes his ministry by asserting, 'You know that I have not hesitated to preach anything that would be helpful to you but have taught you publicly and from house to house... I am innocent of the blood of all men. For I have not hesitated to proclaim to you the whole will of God. Keep watch... Now I commit you to God and to the word of his grace, which can build you up and give you an inheritance among all those who are sanctified' (Acts 20:20,26-28,32).

No wonder Paul urged Timothy and Titus again and again in the Pastoral Epistles: 'Until I come, devote yourself to the public reading of Scripture, to preaching and to teaching... Watch your life and your doctrine closely' (1 Tim. 4:13,16). 'What you heard from me, keep as the pattern of sound teaching, with faith and love in Christ Jesus. Guard the good deposit that was entrusted to you — guard it with the help of the Holy Spirit who lives in us' (2 Tim. 1:13-14). 'Preach the Word; be prepared in season and out of season; correct, rebuke and encourage — with great patience and careful instruction. For the time will come when men will not put up with sound doctrine' (2 Tim. 4:2-3). 'You must teach what is in accord with sound doctrine' (Titus 2:1).

The role of the Scriptures in the life of a believer is clear: they are God's word to his heart and life. They are the truth. Their teaching is doctrinal and practical. The divine Spirit takes teaching and uses it to sanctify redeemed sinners by conforming them to the image of Christ. We can be sure that wherever the Spirit is working in power, the Word of God is exalted and expounded. Paul, looking back over several generations in Timothy's life, could say, 'From infancy you have known the holy Scriptures, which are able to make you wise for salvation through faith in Christ Jesus' (2 Tim. 3:15). Timothy's discipleship could be traced back to the biblical 'faith which first lived in your grandmother Lois and in your mother Eunice' (2 Tim. 1:5).

Paul summarized the origin of the Scriptures and their importance for our lives by saying, 'All Scripture is God-breathed and is useful for teaching, rebuking, correcting and training in righteousness, so that the man of God may be thoroughly equipped for every good work' (2 Tim. 3:16-17).

Therefore anyone who accepts the Bible for what it is can relate to what the Westminster scholars wrote:

4. The authority of the Holy Scripture, for which it ought to be believed and obeyed, dependeth not upon the testimony of any man or church, but wholly upon God (who is truth itself), the author thereof; and therefore it is to be received, because it is the word of God.

6. The whole counsel of God, concerning all things necessary for his own glory, man's salvation, faith and life, is either

expressly set down in Scripture, or by good and necessary consequence may be deduced from Scripture: unto which nothing at any time is to be added, whether by new revelations of the Spirit, or traditions of men. Nevertheless we acknowledge the inward illumination of the Spirit of God to be necessary for the saving understanding of such things as are revealed in the word; and that there are some circumstances concerning the worship of God, and government of the church, common to human actions and societies, which are to be ordered by the light of nature and Christian prudence, according to the general rules of the word, which are always to be observed.

10. The Supreme Judge, by which all controversies of religion are to be determined, and all decrees of councils, opinions of ancient writers, doctrines of men, and private spirits are to be examined, and in whose sentence we are to rest, can be no other but the Holy Spirit speaking in the Scripture.'[1]

'The Supreme Judge' of 'holy laughter', the Toronto Blessing, the Vineyard movement and, of course, of ourselves, is 'the Holy Spirit speaking in the Scripture'. This movement cannot be truly evaluated by opinion, by appeal to new revelations or dreams, impressions or words of prophecy. It is not even the court of evangelical opinion that must be satisfied. Rather, the Scriptures stand as judge and jury.

In common with the followers of Christ throughout the ages, I affirm my belief and confidence in the inerrancy, authority and sufficiency of the Holy Scriptures. On the surface the Vineyard movement does the same. They affirm their commitment to the Word of God in their doctrinal statement: 'The Bible is God's Word to the world, speaking to us with authority and without error.'[2] In practice, however, they fail to demonstrate their commitment to its authority and sufficiency.

The crucial questions we face concern the authority of the Scriptures — in these matters, as in all matters of faith and practice. Are the Scriptures complete, or do we need further revelation? Has the Holy Spirit inspired a complete or incomplete guide to Christian living and worship? As the following chapters will show, the

Vineyard affirms their commitment to Scripture on the one hand. But on the other hand they depart from it — and expect us to follow their lead.

The first area we must evaluate about the Toronto Blessing concerns the manifestations that take place night after night in their 'renewal' meetings.

8.
Phenomena —
biblical or bizarre?

Although the Vineyard board urged their members in September 1994 not to stimulate or proof-text the physical manifestations, they were willing to allow them to happen. And well they might, for exotic phenomena are not new in the Vineyard. David Lewis documented their frequency of occurrence in some of John Wimber's meetings in a book published in 1989. He found that falling down — being 'slain in the Spirit' — was common. In a sample of those who participated 27% experienced spontaneous laughter, 11% reported feelings of heaviness, 45% shook, 40% had changes in breathing, 52% felt tingling, 38% felt hot areas on their bodies.[1] Why then has Wimber come down so hard on the Toronto Blessing? Has he realized the harmful nature of what he encouraged earlier? Has he changed his position? His response is puzzling.

In a major position paper on the phenomena, Bill Jackson, an Illinois Vineyard pastor, affirms their biblical basis. His writing reflects what many others in the movement say. He does admit that there is no primary text, a 'proof text when the writer clearly states what God wants us to believe, do or practise'.[2] Using baptism by immersion as an example, he asserts that other 'secondary' texts imply truths in principle form. 'Texts that illustrate that these [falling down, shaking, looking drunk] were some of the responses people had during moments of divine visitation.'[3]

I generally agree with Jackson's statements about primary and secondary texts. The *Westminster Confession* affirms: 'The whole counsel of God, concerning all things necessary for his own glory, man's salvation, faith and life, is either expressly set down in Scripture, or by good and necessary consequence may be deduced from Scripture.' There are truths and commands expressly stated in

Scripture, proof texts and principles derived from Scripture. I would radically disagree, however, that there is any principle in Scripture affirming that shaking, laughing, pogoing, roaring, jerking or acting as if drunk signify a revival or renewal of the Spirit.

Among those closely associated with the Toronto Blessing, there has been a gradual change in their interpretation of the phenomena. At first they viewed them as marks of revival. They sought to demonstrate each manifestation's divine credentials by using biblical and historical criteria. Before long they came to realize the difficulty of such an endeavour and they began to admit the presence of the flesh in some of what was going on. Leaders began to urge participants to look beyond the manifestations to Christ.

At the same time, however, they continued to encourage the phenomena by programming their services to lead up to 'ministry time', a term which refers to the climax of their three-hour services, when those who want 'the blessing' come forward to be prayed for. 'Ministry time' may go on for hours after the main part of the service is over. During this period it is expected that the manifestations would recur.

The 'anointing', as manifest in the phenomena, is also sown in churches all over the world by speakers and visitors to Toronto. This demonstrates an obsession with phenomena. No matter how often they declare that the manifestations are relatively unimportant, the facts are otherwise. Their meetings, their messages, their magazines and their testimonies all revolve around the phenomena. The Toronto Blessing stands or falls on whether these visible evidences are genuine marks of a 'time of refreshing from the presence of the Lord'. With physical phenomena occupying centre stage we need to look closely at each one.

Shaking, pogoing, etc.

Many participants shake back and forth, sometimes violently. Often those who give testimonies jerk up and down. Guy Chevreau writes that they commonly saw people 'waving their arms around, in windmill-like motions, or vigorous judo-like chopping with their forearms'.[4] Some bang their heads against the floor. 'Pogoing' occurs when 'those affected jump up and down on one spot, sometimes for extended periods of time'.[5]

Jim Paul of the Toronto Airport Christian Fellowship described what happened to a Texan at the Toronto meetings: 'The Texan had shaken so violently that his watch had flown off. After that, first one and then the other of his big cowboy boots had shot off. Mr Paul explained that "The Father came to play with him."'[6]

Bill Jackson, in the Vineyard position paper already mentioned, lists as 'secondary texts' the shaking that came over the men with Daniel when he saw a vision (Dan. 10:7); the predicted shaking of the nations in Psalm 99:1; the exhortation in Psalm 114:7 to 'Tremble, O earth, at the presence of the Lord'; instances of trembling and shaking in Jeremiah and Habakkuk; the shaking of the guards at the tomb of Jesus (Matt. 28:4); the shaking of the church's meeting-place (Acts 4:31); and the trembling of devils in James 2:19. He concludes his summary of evidence by pointing to the historical precedent of George Fox, founder of the Quakers.[7]

One gains the impression that proponents of the Toronto Blessing use isolated verses, wrenched out of context, to prop up a theology of 'renewal'. Notice how in most of the texts quoted there is a description of people afraid — so afraid that they quake in the presence of God. Most of those mentioned tried to hide from God. They didn't engage in a public spectacle. With no biblical warrant Jackson claims that 'The shaking we are experiencing seems to be related more to prophetic ministry and impartation of spiritual gifts … empowerment. [But] certain body movements [are] indicative of demonic presence.'[8] (These distinctive demonic marks are not explained.)

Explanations, however, multiply. A speaker I heard at the Toronto Airport Fellowship said, 'God is shaking us, shaking our status quo, shaking our prison — freeing us. Everything not built on the rock will shake and crumble. Shaking our programmes. Cleansing the temple from the leadership down.'[9]

While it is laudable to ask God to shake us out of self-dependence, lethargy and complacency, we must remember that the central shake-up occurs in the heart and in the mind — not in the body. The examples that are cited are either metaphorical or describe extremely rare and isolated incidents in the lives of individuals. There is no precedent for their repeated occurrence in a whole congregation. This use of isolated and unrelated examples to buttress a shaky theology of phenomena is highly objectionable.

Being 'slain in the Spirit', or 'doing carpet time'

These expressions are used to describe the most common phenomenon in the movement. People fall backwards and remain prone, sometimes for hours at a time. Bill Jackson explains that this is commonly called 'resting in the Spirit': 'Often they feel weak and find it difficult to do anything but rest with God.'[10]

Jackson claims biblical precedent for the phenomenon by citing the following passages: the deep sleep that came upon Abraham (Gen. 15:12); how Saul 'walked along prophesying... He stripped off his robes and also prophesied in Samuel's presence. He lay that way all that day and night' (1 Sam. 19:23-24); the glory (*kabod* — weight) that filled the temple in 2 Chronicles 5:13-14; how Ezekiel fell face down in the presence of the glory of God (Ezek. 1:28; 3:23); the falling of Daniel in the presence of Gabriel (Dan. 8:17; 10:9); the falling of the disciples on the Mount of Transfiguration (Matt. 17:6); the soldiers who came to arrest Jesus and the guards at the tomb (Matt. 28:4, John 18:6); the falling of Paul on the road to Damascus (Acts 9:4,6; 22:7; 26:14); Peter falling into a trance on the roof of Simon the tanner (Acts 10:10); Paul's vision of paradise (2 Cor. 12:1-4); and John's falling at the feet of Jesus (Rev. 1:17).

As quoted in an earlier chapter, Jim Paul interprets the floor as 'God's operating table'.[11] Bill Jackson conjectures that since the Hebrew word for glory (*kabod*) means a 'weight', 'Falling in God's presence might be understood as being overcome by the weight of God forcing them to the floor.'[12] He concludes his study: 'The kinds of falling we are seeing now seem to parallel more the action of God to put to sleep for the purpose of divine intervention, rest and healing rather than contrition. While some fall face down, the great majority fall backwards. John Wimber believes that falling face down is some kind of indication of a man's stature in the Lord.'[13]

When we examine the biblical evidence we find that Daniel, Moses, Job, Saul, John, etc., fell *forwards* not backwards. Their falling signified that they were overwhelmed by God's glory. Through the ages many believers have fallen at the feet of God in private moments of devotion. However, some of the examples cited concern the falling of unbelievers. With the possible exception of the deliberate bowing of the congregation in Ezra's day, all examples concern private and individual encounters with God. We have no precedent for large-scale congregational 'carpet time', nor for any repeatable external phenomena that may prove to be an infallible sign of refreshing from the presence of God.

'Holy laughter'

The Toronto Blessing has been called the 'laughing revival' because laughter has been associated with it from the beginning. This is to be expected since Randy Clark and John Arnott were affected by Rodney Howard-Browne. Howard-Browne calls himself 'the Holy Ghost Bartender', because of his supposed ability to dispense the 'new wine of laughter'.

Outbursts of uproarious laughter almost invariably characterize meetings affected by the Toronto Blessing. Leaders often refer to the 'renewal' as 'party time'. John Arnott explained in a pastor's meeting: 'We didn't think it was going to look like this... We didn't think He would come and throw a massive party, where people are laughing and rolling and crying and getting so empowered that emotional hurts from childhood were just lifted off.'[14]

In a meeting I attended, the speaker explained that several who had been laughing during their 'carpet time' told him that 'God was telling us jokes on the floor.'[15]

Nick Needham describes a meeting he attended in Edinburgh: 'Several people were laughing hysterically. This reminded me of one of those "laughing policeman" machines at an amusement arcade. The laughter was very infectious and I had to restrain myself from laughing: not because I was receiving the Toronto Blessing... It was the sheer infectious quality of uproarious laughter.'[16]

Wes Campbell reports a pastor's daughter who received 'the joy of the Lord' when Vineyard 'prophet' Marc Dupont 'just pointed at her, she went ha! ha! ha! She went down. She laughed for 23 hours straight... She had fits of sleep and would wake up laughing. She went to work, and she worked at this Christian school. She laughed so much she got all the secretaries laughing. Before long, all the students. It was breaking out in the school. They had to shut down classes at Kelowna Christian Centre. All the kids came back. They all came back. More. I tell you, we would just take them and throw them into this area. They would hit this epicentre of power. They would laugh.'[17] This talk of an 'epicentre of power' is all too reminiscent of New-Age mysticism!

Randy Clark, speaking in a conference in Anaheim, referred to some New Yorkers who came to the Toronto meetings. They laughed so uproariously during his preaching that he told them, "'I don't want you to quench the Holy Spirit, I don't want you to stop laughing, just please dial the decibels down a little bit." And you really have that ability to do that, and still can enter into the joy.'[18] But if this is really produced by the Holy Spirit, how can people dial it up and down? And why would the Spirit want to drown out the message? None of this makes any biblical sense whatever!

The laughter, and other manifestations, have often interfered with preaching. Rodney Howard-Browne, the main initiator of the phenomenon says, 'One night I was preaching on hell, and [laughter] just hit the whole place. The more I told people what hell was like, the more they laughed.'[19] What a contrast to the weeping and conviction that attended Jonathan Edwards' famous sermon on 'Sinners in the hands of an angry God'!

Bill Jackson quotes John Wimber as believing 'that laughter accompanies revivals because it represents God's sovereign activity to heal the barrenness of his people'.[20]

Seeking to establish some biblical basis for 'holy laughter', Jackson mentions Abraham and Sarah's initial laughter of unbelief that led them to name their son Isaac (which means, 'He laughs"); Psalm 126, which says that 'Our mouths were filled with laughter'; and the statement in Ecclesiastes that there is 'a time to weep and a time to laugh'.

Since textual precedent is so slim, Jackson and others in the movement assume that joy and laughter are synonymous. He notes Jesus' concern that his disciples should have 'the full measure of my joy within them' (John 17:13). He then comments: 'Certainly the full measure of joy within the Trinity is full of laughter.'[21] How does he arrive at that conclusion?

All genuine believers aspire to knowing the joy of the Lord, which is our strength. Joy is an important fruit of the Holy Spirit. I do not question our need for a spirit of celebration bubbling up from a contemplation of Christ and our adoption into God's family. However, this equating of joy with uncontrollable laughter is unwarranted. Joy is a deep sense of well-being. I have no doubt that God has a sense of humour. I do question the centrality of laughter in a renewal movement, when tears seem more appropriate in the face of the sins of the saints.

Pentecostal Ken Birch writes, 'We laugh when confronted with ideas or pictures that are out of sync with normal reality. Yes, God uses humour to drive home certain truths. But that's quite different from *charismaniacal* silliness… Holy Spirit inspired laughter? Hardly. It was pure, suggestive manipulation.'[22]

I am inclined to agree with Birch, especially when we see this phenomenon interfering with preaching and being imparted through the touch of 'anointed' men in the movement.

Warren Smith studied laughter in the Bible. He found forty references, with only six of these in the New Testament. Twenty-two referred to scornful laughter; seven were related to the laughter of Abraham and Sarah; Bildad wrongly advised Job 'that if he were in right standing with God he would be prosperous and full of laughter' (Job 8:21); Psalm 126:2 relates to Israel's laughter upon deliverance from their captivity; Ecclesiastes gives five references: 'I said of laughter, It is mad'; '… a time to weep, and a time to laugh'; 'Sorrow is better than laughter: for by the sadness of the countenance the heart is made better … the heart of fools is in the house of mirth… For as the crackling of thorns under a pot, so is the laughter of the fool,' and 'A feast is made for laughter, and wine maketh merry' (Eccl. 2:2; 3:4; 7:3-4,6; 10:19, AV) Out of these references in Ecclesiastes three warn against laughter! (See also Luke 6:21,25; James 4:9).[23]

These warnings in Ecclesiastes should be taken to heart. First comes sadness for sin; then comes laughter. There is no precedent whatever for a 'laughing revival'. Real revival brings sorrow and conviction, weeping and repentance. No wonder those in the movement term the Toronto Blessing a 'renewal', not a revival.

Crying

Some in the movement, but relatively few, weep. Guy Chevreau writes that after Randy Clark prayed for him he went over and 'As I lay there, I started weeping. Wailing, if the truth be told, for something like forty minutes… A long-standing bitterness and resentment was lifted in the process.' At another time he fell on his face and 'began to weep, and did so for the next three-and-a-half hours'.[24]

The only problem I have with Chevreau's testimony is that he explains his experience as receiving the new heart mentioned in Ezekiel and having the old things of 2 Corinthians 5:17 pass away by 'a deep restoration within me ... a new sense of intimacy with Jesus'. He goes on to say, 'I keep coming to the Airport meetings because there's a gap. A gap between the way the Apostle Paul brought the Gospel, and my experience of ministry.'[25]

Chevreau's experience of weeping sounds suspiciously like conversion to me. It highlights the huge problem of sorting through the experiences of people infected by the 'easy-believism' of our age.[26] The gap in his ministry may very well have been that he professed Christ but did not possess the new birth. (I don't know. I am merely conjecturing on the basis of how Scripture defines the process of conversion.) The new heart spoken of by Ezekiel and the experience mentioned in 2 Corinthians are the new birth. Conversion comes out of deep conviction, often with tears. Many people profess faith in Jesus Christ and have gone forward in meetings who have no real conversion experience. Quite a few professing Christians go into ministry without possessing salvation.

On the question of weeping, I have no problem with Bill Jackson's conclusion: 'Crying is a natural and normal response to the movement of the Holy Spirit.'[27] Conviction commonly brings weeping. When Ezra read the neglected Scriptures, 'All the people had been weeping as they listened to the words of the Law' (Neh. 8:9). God commended the Israelites for responding to the rediscovery of the Law under Josiah by weeping (2 Chron. 34:27). Those who heard Peter preaching about Christ at Pentecost 'were cut to the heart' (Acts 2:37).

The Toronto Blessing, however, demonstrates a paucity of tears and an abundance of laughter. The impression is given, and often expressed, that God is healing people's deep inner hurts instantaneously. This implies that God heals people spiritually without them going through the process of sorrow, confession and repentance. Of course, God may do gracious and transforming things in a spiritual crisis. But it is contrary to all we know from Scripture about the spiritual healing process for people to come to abiding peace without any process of self-examination or conviction. Sanctification occurs *after* conviction, confession and sorrow, as sins are recognized and relinquished.

The process of personal or corporate revival is so repeatedly reiterated in Scripture that marshalling a regiment of texts seems pointless. But the following passages should serve to illustrate the point: 2 Chronicles 7:14; David's penitential Psalms (32, 51, etc.); the beatitudes of Christ (Matt. 5:3-4); the response to Peter's sermon at Pentecost in Acts 2; James' warnings in chapter 4 of his epistle; and the instructions to the defective churches in Revelation chapters 2 and 3. James writes what seems particularly appropriate to our selfish age: 'You adulterous people, don't you know that friendship with the world is hatred towards God? ... Come near to God and he will come near to you. Wash your hands, you sinners, and purify your hearts, you double-minded. Grieve, mourn and wail. Change your laughter to mourning and your joy to gloom. Humble yourselves before the Lord, and he will lift you up' (James 4:4,8-10).

Acting as if drunk

The first newsletter issued by the Toronto Airport Vineyard said that 'Some are so drunk with the Spirit that they have to be helped from the meeting and driven home. One man, returning home from a meeting, was stopped by the police and asked, "Have you been drinking?"; he replied, "I am not drunk as you suppose"!'[28]

'In the wake of physical manifestations sweeping through churches in the United Kingdom, a Christian doctor in England has warned against driving under the influence of the Holy Spirit, according to the *Anglican Journal*. Dr Patrick Dixon said that the mental state induced by experiences of the "Toronto Blessing" is similar to drunkenness. "Although police breathalysers won't show the signs of the Spirit, church leaders should encourage people to sober up before they drive home," he said.'[29]

Randy Clark explains that being 'drunk in the Spirit' ushers people into a more exalted experience. 'Before I knew it I was laughing and I couldn't stop laughing. And then I was drunk, and so was my worship leader. You have to understand, I've only been drunk ... two or three times, because I think it's my Baptist background. We took these covenants we'd never drink and there's this thing about drunkenness and so I'd almost never drunk in my whole life, and I think subconsciously it's really hard for me to enter into that level, but my worship leader's a recovering alcoholic. Man, he can get right in there.'[30] Are we to assume from this that a recovered alcoholic can experience a higher level of the Holy Spirit? It seems preposterous, and almost blasphemous, to credit this kind of behaviour to the Holy Spirit!

Spokespersons for the Vineyard usually use Peter's statement to the onlookers at Pentecost, 'These men are not drunk, as you suppose,' to assert that the anointing makes people act like typical drunks. Bill Jackson writes, 'Compare Acts 10:44-46 where apparently the same kinds of phenomena occurred with the Gentiles. That the 120 newly filled believers were acting in a "drunken" manner is what is known as an argument from silence. The text never says that they were but it is obviously inferred. They would not be accused of being drunk because they were speaking in different languages. They would have been accused of such because they were acting like drunks; i.e., laughing, falling, slurred speech by some, boldness through lack of restraint, etc. The analogy of the gift of the Spirit being "new Wine" would lend itself to the connection.'[31]

What an incredible inference from silence! A crowd gathered at Pentecost 'when they heard this sound' — presumably 'a sound like the blowing of a violent wind' (Acts 2:6,2). They were bewildered and perplexed, 'because each one heard them speaking in his own language' (2:6). From verse 5 to verse 12 Luke describes the diverse linguistic backgrounds of the Jews in Jerusalem of Pentecost. He concludes this section by saying, 'Amazed and perplexed, they asked one another, "What does this mean?"' (2:12). Obviously the noise and babble of voices in different languages created a strange effect. We read that most of the crowd were amazed because they could understand the speakers 'declaring the wonders of God in our own tongues' (2:11).

This response hardly supports the thesis that the disciples had the slurred speech or staggering manner typical of drunkenness. Just the opposite. Order prevailed in spite of the confusion of tongues. Indeed the gathering was so orderly that Peter was able to preach his Pentecostal sermon and see 3,000 people hearing it so clearly that they were convicted and converted without being interrupted by laughter or shrieks!

As in any crowd, there were some sceptics and mockers. We read, 'Some, however, made fun of them and said, "They have had too much wine"' (2:13). Denying the wonder and amazement at seeing a real miracle, as was recognized by the majority of those present, this smaller group of sceptics looked for some basis for mockery. They hit on drunkenness, although there is nothing whatever in the text to indicate drunken behaviour on the part of the disciples. To assert, as Jackson does, that 'They would have been accused of such because they were acting like drunks, i.e., laughing, falling, slurred speech by some, boldness through lack of restraint, etc.,' is to do absolute violence to the text![32]

Proponents of this phenomenon also point to Ephesians 5:18:
'Do not get drunk on wine, which leads to debauchery. Instead, be
filled with the Spirit.' Jackson writes, 'Being filled with God's
Spirit is similar to being drunk on wine. The difference is that the
former is holy while the other is sinful.'[33]

Again, I am appalled at this approach to Scripture. Clearly, Paul
is not comparing the filling of the Spirit with drunkenness, but
contrasting the two. In the fourth and fifth chapters of Ephesians
Paul has been repeatedly contrasting the debauchery and ignorance
of the Gentile life-style with the enlightenment and holiness of
walking with Christ. In the immediately preceding verses, Paul
warns about being unwise and foolish by failing to 'understand what
the Lord's will is'. This foolishness leads to self-centred drunkenness and debauchery, while a life 'filled with the Spirit' leads to
speaking, singing, giving thanks and submitting to one another in
love (see verses 15-21). The contrast could not be clearer. (We shall
consider the whole matter of self-control and the Holy Spirit in
chapter 11.)

Animal noises

'Two people started barking loudly like dogs. The barks were
interspersed with howling noise like wolves, or possibly dogs
baying at the moon. I also heard one person screeching like a cat at
night.'[34]

Robert Hough did an article for *Toronto Life Magazine* in which
he writes, 'The man sitting beside me, Dwayne from California,
roared like a wounded lion... They howled like wolves, brayed like
donkeys and — in the case of a young man standing near the sound
board — started clucking like a feral chicken.'[35]

James Beverley reports: 'Still others roared like lions or barked
like dogs. I have personally heard both in various meetings. I also
heard one man making noises like a cow. Others have reported
people oinking like pigs and crowing like roosters... The lion
roaring is said to be a prophetic action to signal a powerful word
from Jesus, the lion of the tribe of Judah.'[36]

Randy Clark credits someone oinking like a pig near him with
ushering him into 'holy laughter' and being 'drunk in the Spirit'.
'One person about two people down that had the "anoinking". The
"anoinking", and I explained this the other night, you know when

you [sound of a pig grunting]… And I start laughing … then I was drunk.'[37]

Different Vineyard spokespersons concluded that the 'roaring' indicated 'God's indignation at the state of the church and the impact of the enemy's presence in the church … sort of an "announcement" of God's intention to take back territory'. Some sensed the authority and power of God. Most equated it with a prophetic experience.[38]

A year later the Vineyard was still trying to interpret animal noises. In an article in the October 1995 issue of *Spread The Fire*, Steve Long presents two sides to the phenomenon. He says that 'roarers' often mention visions, images and feelings they have had from God that often encourage boldness to evangelize or to intercede against enemy strongholds. Gideon Chui, a Vancouver-based Cantonese pastor, was the first to act like a lion at the Toronto Airport Vineyard. He interpreted his experience in the folowing way: 'Jesus, the Lion of the tribe of Judah, was going to free the Chinese … from the domination of the dragon.' Long mentions that 'People from countries in which the lion is a symbol, such as England and Japan, are the ones most likely to roar.' Then he cautions, 'It is better to speak in clear words rather than roaring,' and to beware of Satan who imitates the lion to frighten believers.[39]

Confusion and subjective interpretation reign! Bill Jackson makes no mention of these phenomena in his position paper on the manifestations. Wes Campbell does not deal with them in his paper either.[40] The silence on their part reflects the silence of Scripture.

The way domesticated animals, such as the ox and the donkey, know their master is commended by Scripture, but there the comparison ceases (Isa. 1:3). There is nothing whatever in Holy Writ to lead us to believe that the Holy Spirit goes about making us sound and act like animals. By contrast, Scripture pictures a God who heightens our human capacities, restoring the image of God within us that was marred at the Fall. Paul urges us to offer ourselves as living sacrifices, with the end in view that we may be 'transformed by the renewing [not the debasing] of your mind' (Rom. 12:2). The psalmist compares the arrogant rich with animals because both lack understanding: 'A man who has riches without understanding is like the beasts that perish' (Ps. 49:20; see also vv. 12,14).

I agree totally with Nick Needham when he says, 'It seems to me to contradict Scripture teaching about spiritual renewal to claim that the Spirit's sanctifying presence can reduce human beings to the

level of animal behaviour. The Holy Spirit unites us to the Lord
Jesus Christ so that we may be conformed to his perfect humanity.
To say that the Holy Spirit makes us gibber like monkeys is a
travesty of his blessed work.'[41]

Healing

Supernatural healing has been part of the Vineyard agenda since the
beginning. In meetings at the Toronto Airport Christian Fellowship
testimonies are frequently given of healings. When I was there in
July 1995, the speaker announced that the next evening all who had
joint pains of any kind would be healed. Since I deal with this issue
at more length in chapters 16 and 17, where I consider the role of
signs and wonders, I will limit myself here to a brief comment.

James Beverley has interviewed a number of the leaders in the
Vineyard, attended many meetings and read extensively in their
literature. While he was researching the material for his current
book, John Arnott invited him to investigate some of their claims
about miraculous healing. His findings demonstrate to me that
miraculous healing as practised by the apostles and that claimed by
the Vineyard are two totally different things.[42]

Manifestations of the presence or touch of God

This movement, like the Quakers, Pentecostals and charismatics,
believes that God speaks directly to his people today just as he did
in the early church. They claim that the vast majority of evangelicals
have been robbed of an intimate relationship with God by
bibliolatry.

Leaders in the movement testify that the manifestations often
transform people who 'know God is present in their minds' into
laughing believers who have experienced God's presence to such an
extent that they revel in his love. Guy Chevreau explains what has
been happening: 'They have been experiencing the presence of the
Lord, and they're so sure of the encounter, the revelation, the
"touch", there is absolutely no doubt in their minds. Some of them
have *seen* the Lord, or something of His glory; there has been given
them a dream or an open vision. Some of them have *heard* audible
words; some have heard words only with their hearts, but words,

nonetheless; words that left them with no doubt as to Who pronounced them. Some have *felt* the Lord's touch, physically. Some have felt the Lord's healing hand upon them, or the hand of blessing. Not until I came to the Airport had I heard of anyone *smelling* the presence of God, but having personally ministered on an occasion where that was the case, that's part of the experience of the presence of God too!'[43]

The yearning for a sense of God's nearness ought to be normative in the lives of genuine disciples. But many are not satisfied with that. Chevreau asserts that 'There is long, and strong *biblical* precedent for this kind [the kind noted above] of direct, personal encounter with God.'[44] He goes on to assert that this is both scriptural and historically normative. The Scriptures do record how God spoke to Adam and Eve, to Abraham, to Moses, to the prophets, to Paul and others. Verbal and visual encounters, such as these, however, are rare even in the Scriptures. If they had been the common heritage of all believers, why would the Scriptures call us to 'walk by faith and not by sight'? Why would Hebrews contain a great picture galley of men and women of faith in the context of such statements as: 'Now faith is being sure of what we hope for and certain of what we do not see,' and "Moses ... persevered because he saw him who is invisible'? (Heb. 11:1,24,27). The whole point of the chapter is to prove that 'We walk by faith and not by sight'! We are to 'fix our eyes on Jesus, the author and perfecter of our faith' (Heb. 12:2).

Chevreau tries to establish credibility for strange manifestations of God by rehearsing the experiences of Thomas Aquinas, Blaise Pascal and David Brainerd. He fails to prove his point. If they saw God at all, they saw the glory of God with the eyes of faith. Brainerd wrote, 'I was walking in a dark thick grove, unspeakable glory seemed to open to the view and apprehension of my soul. I do not mean any external brightness for I saw no such thing; nor do I intend any imagination of a body of light, somewhere in the third heavens, or any thing of that nature; but it was a new inward apprehension or view that I had of God.'[45]

This is a far cry from the bizarre experiences described by Bob Jones of Kansas City fame. He claimed to have journeyed to heaven and hell and to have talked with the apostle Paul.[46]

Would that all of us had an overwhelming impression of God in our souls! Many of us can testify, without being charismatic, that from time to time God has overwhelmed us with the a sense of his love and glory. Sometimes we were compelled to weep or bow,

speechless, in his presence. I well remember the sense of God I felt
in a secluded nook on a mountainside in Pakistan.

But this quickening of our souls occurs in the area of the spiritual
perception entitled 'faith'. It is very far from being a physical touch
from God, the smell of God, the heard voice of God, etc. Interest-
ingly enough, Brainerd, like all Calvinists of his day, believed
firmly in the cessation of the sign gifts, including prophecy.

Summary

Biblical warrant cannot be found for shaking, being 'slain in the
Spirit', 'holy laughter', 'being drunk in the Spirit', making animal
noises or experiencing physical evidences of God's presence in an
ongoing congregational context. There is precedent for weeping.

This is not the end of the catalogue of phenomena. Proponents of
the Toronto Blessing add further experiences as the movement
spreads. I have even read about feelings of nausea associated with
prophecy![47]

There is no compelling reason to believe that these phenomena
are produced by God. The following survey of some non-Christian
movements establishes this very point.

Phenomena among non-Christian groups

Some New-Agers talk of 'Kundalini energy', a dormant energy
source supposed to be in all of us in the form of 'a coiled serpent at
the base of the human spine'.[48] 'Christina and Stanislav Grof, New
Age authors of the book *The Stormy Search for the Self*, describe
how the awakening of the Kundalini energy can be triggered by an
advanced spiritual teacher or guru ... bring up memories of past
psychological and physical trauma' with the result that 'They emit
various involuntary sounds, and their bodies move in strange and
unexpected patterns ... unmotivated and unnatural laughter or
crying, talking in tongues ... imitating a variety of animal sounds
and movements... Careful study of the manifestations of Kundalini
awakening confirm that this process, although sometimes very
intense and shattering, is essentially healing.'[49]

The former guru of Oregon, Bhagwan Shree Rajneesh, urged his
followers to 'just be joyful... God is not serious ... this world cannot

fit with a theological god.' His touch would send many of his followers to the floor in 'ecstasy'.[50]

Ramakrishna, an Indian 'saint', routinely fell into a trance-like state *(samadhi)* in which he would fall unconscious on the floor for minutes or days. He could send others into this state by a touch. This *samadhi* is described as a 'rapturous state of super-conscious bliss *(ananda)* complete with beautiful visions' and 'astral projection', 'often accompanied by uncontrollable laughter or weeping'.[51]

Likewise, Swami Baba Muktananda could transfer 'what was called "guru's grace" to his followers through *Shakipat* (physical touch). This "grace" triggered the gradual awakening of the *Kundalini* which in turn produced ... uncontrollable laughing, roaring, barking, hissing, crying, shaking, etc. Some devotees became mute or unconscious.'[52]

Strangely enough, similar effects occur among the African Kung Bushmen of the Kalahari and among the thousands of followers of Qigong Yan Xin. The *San Francisco Chronicle* describes what happened minutes after Xin began talking: 'Before long the scene began to resemble a Pentecostal prayer meeting with many people waving their arms and making unintelligible sounds.'[53]

Vineyard leaders admit that there are some evidences of the flesh in what is going on. Nevertheless, John Arnott often asserts, in the face of comments critical of the movement, 'God's desire to bless us is far greater than Satan's ability to deceive us.' Knowing our human propensity to gullibility and suggestibility and Satan's ability to go about 'as an angel of light', that seems dangerously naïve to me. Guy Chevreau adds: 'It is far healthier to focus attention on the wheat, and not the chaff, nor on the enemy sowing weeds.'[54]

While some Vineyard leaders have expressed concerns about the phenomena, the majority of those who have experienced the Toronto Blessing are absolutely convinced that the phenomena are from God. Our studies have shown that they are not just skating on very thin ice, but on non-existent ice! With little to go on scripturally, apologists for the movement delve back into church history to try to establish precedents for their experiences.

9.
A needle in a historical haystack

Our beliefs and practices need to be viewed first in the light of Scripture, and then against the panorama of church history. The events of 1994 and 1995 in Toronto may seem momentous — until we bring in the historical context.

Vineyard apologist Bill Jackson admits that there are no clear biblical texts that describe Christians falling down, shaking or acting as if they were drunk. But he does assert that there are 'numerous examples of similar phenomena in church history, especially in seasons of revival'.[1] If so, we need to find them — even if it looks a bit like searching for a needle in a haystack.

In this chapter and the one following, I want to take a quick tour of church history. We want to look for evidence of the following:

> Phenomena such as being slain in the Spirit, shaking, crying out, etc.;
> Inspired prophecy;
> Charismatic gifts such as miracles, healing, speaking in tongues and interpretation of tongues;
> Exorcism of demons.

The last three constitute the 'signs and wonders' that the Vineyard movement claims are the heritage of any spiritual church. According to their view, called 'power evangelism', these signs and wonders create a powerful witness that draws people to Christ. They believe that their absence is a mark of a weak and worldly church. Traditional evangelicals, however, believe (with a few qualifications) that these kinds of signs and wonders have ceased.

I am connecting a historical search for the physical phenomena with a search for signs and wonders because together they comprise part of the charismatic, and Vineyard, frame of reference. They stand or fall together. And where scriptural evidence is scanty, proponents of this view appeal to historical precedent.

Cessationism

The view that the charismatic gifts were confined to the apostolic period is called 'cessationism'. It is rejected by Pentecostals, charismatics and those in the Vineyard movement. With the world-wide rise of the Pentecostal movement, cessationism has become unpopular even in some non-Pentecostal circles. I was astounded recently to read in the doctrinal statement made by a candidate for ministry in my own denomination a denial of cessationism. Fellow-ship Baptists in Canada have been historically, I thought, cessationist. Without demur, however, this candidate was ordained in one of our larger churches.

The view that the sign gifts have ceased should not be discarded so quickly. While we shall look at this in more detail in chapters 16 and 17, let me briefly summarize what is meant — and what is not meant — by this interpretation of Scripture.

Cessationists believe that miracles were historical redemptive signs that appeared intermittently in history. God used them to introduce special periods of revelation and to confirm the prophetic messages he gave. We have only one innerrant record of history — the Bible. It records the occurrence of signs, wonders and miracles during three main periods of history: during the Exodus, during the era of the Old Testament prophets and in the gospel period. The gospel era includes the incarnation of Christ, the birth of the church and the completion of the canon of Scripture. In this latter era, when the veracity and credentials of Christ and his apostles had been established, miracles ceased. With the church established and the canon complete, the need for signs and wonders vanished.

So cessationists believe that sign gifts such as healing, miracles, tongues and the interpretation of tongues ceased when the apostles died. They believe the same about the gift of inspired and predictive prophecy and the abundant exorcisms that occurred at the time of Christ. This does not mean that cessationists reject the possibility of miracles, healings, or the casting out of demons. Every conversion is a miracle and the new birth is the main miracle in view in this gospel age. God can and does heal in this age, but not through any one person, or through the laying on of the hands of 'healers'. The procedure to be used in healing today in prescribed is James 5. Demon possession does occur today, but even while I was a missionary in the spiritually oppressive country of Pakistan for sixteen years, I did not find it common. Cessationists realize that demonic activity must be discerned and demons cast out wherever they appear during this period of church history.

Biblically, a miracle is an extraordinary work of God's power, in which God supersedes the natural laws of the universe to effect an action which is wholly supernatural. A miracle occurs when something happens that is inexplicable by natural law. God, of course, providentially works through the events of day-to-day life to provide for and protect his children. Technically, however, neither providential circumstances nor answers to prayer qualify as miracles. Crossing the Red Sea on dry land, the collapse of the walls of Jericho, water from a rock, manna in the desert, fire from heaven on Elijah's altar, the feeding of the 5,000, the healing of a man born blind, the raising of the dead — these are miracles.

When I claim that the gift of miracles has ceased, I am not saying that God cannot work miracles. Rather, I am claiming that God does not now endue men with special power to effect miracles, as he did to Moses, Elijah, Peter, Philip and Paul. With the exception of regeneration, miracles are now rare.

The premier scholar writing in this field has been B. B. Warfield. His studies of Scripture and church history led him to unassailable conclusions. In his classic work *Counterfeit Miracles* he writes, 'Only in the two great initial instances of the descent of the Spirit at Pentecost and the reception of Cornelius are charismata [the sign gifts] recorded as conferred without the laying on of the hands of Apostles... The power of working miracles was not extended beyond the disciples upon whom the Apostles conferred it by the imposition of their hands... Miracles do not appear on the page of Scripture vagrantly, here, there, and elsewhere indifferently, without assignable reason. They belong to revelation periods, and appear only when God is speaking to His people through accredited messengers declaring His gracious purposes.'[2]

Some modern evangelicals dismiss his book as out of date. Those in the Vineyard regularly make derogatory comments about it. John

Wimber comments about cessationism: 'This theory finds no warrant in Scripture. Nowhere in his book does Warfield use any Scripture to support his contention that divine miracles ceased upon the death of the apostles and their generation. There are no Scriptures either stating or implying this position.'[3] But no one has been able to disprove his basic contention. Miracles occurred periodically and for a specific purpose.

Jonathan Edwards, whom those in the Vineyard movement regularly quote in an attempt to buttress their position, believed in cessationism. In his work *Charity and its Fruits* Edwards wrote, 'There seems to have been an intermission of the communication of the extraordinary gifts of the Spirit until Moses' time; and from his time they were continued in a succession of prophets, which was kept up not without some intermission till Malachi's time. After that there seems to have been a great intermission of several hundred years, till the dawn of the days of the gospel, when the Spirit began to give his extraordinary gifts... So that the first hundred years of the Christian era, or the first century, was the age of miracles. But soon after that, the canon of the Scripture having been completed ... the miraculous gifts of the Spirit ceased ... as being that for which there was no further occasion.'[4]

We shall deal later with the biblical teaching on this subject. For the present let's move through history as we search for evidence, or the lack of it, to back up either the cessationist or the charismatic interpretation.

The apostolic church

We have already established that the phenomena associated with the Toronto Blessing, with the possible exception of weeping, were absent from the early church. Obviously, healing, miracles, prophecy, tongues and the interpretation of tongues were present during that period. However, only Stephen and Philip, apart from the apostles, performed miracles — and they were part of the apostolic circle. Mention of tongues and their interpretation is confined to an early epistle, 1 Corinthians, which was written to a church having problems with the charismata.

Encouragement to extend the kingdom through signs and wonders is absent from the Pastoral Epistles. Predictive prophecy is rare, although it is mentioned in the book of Acts. The essence of the

continuing gift of prophecy, as preaching, is speaking 'to men for
their strengthening, encouragement and comfort … he who prophesies edifies the church' (1 Cor. 14:3,4).

The post-apostolic church

The memory of miracles remained fresh in the minds of post-
apostolic leaders. In a letter to the church of Smyrna about the
martyrdom of Polycarp in A.D. 155, there are some general asser-
tions about the presence of miraculous powers. Likewise Justin
Martyr mentions healing and prophecy in an enumeration of the
supernatural gifts of the Spirit. Irenaeus, Bishop of Asia around
A.D. 160, 'ascribes miracle-working to "all who are truly disciples
of Jesus",' and lists 'exorcism, prediction, healing, raising the dead,
speaking with tongues, insight into secrets, and expounding the
Scriptures'.[5] Irenaeus is the sole witness who mentions speaking
with tongues and raising the dead during the early centuries. He had
studied under the martyr Polycarp, who in turn was a disciple of the
apostle John.

Although we find these references in the so-called Apostolic
Fathers, they are problematic. They are not eyewitness accounts, but
statements about what others had witnessed or said. For example,
when an enquirer asked for proof concerning the miracle of raising
the dead, none could be given. (We find the same situation today.)
Autolycus asked Theophilus of Antioch to produce 'one dead man
who had been raised to life'. Theophilus 'discovers by his reply that
there was none to produce and "no instance of this miracle was ever
produced in the first three centuries".'[6]

Warfield quotes Gibbon about this incident: 'A noble Grecian
had rested on this important ground the whole controversy and
promised Theophilus, bishop of Antioch,' that he would 'embrace
the Christian religion' if only he could meet 'a single person who
had been actually raised from the dead'. Gibbon concludes, 'It is
somewhat remarkable that the prelate of the first Eastern church,
however anxious for the conversion of his friend, thought proper to
decline this fair and reasonable challenge.'[7]

Warfield summarizes his findings: 'The writings of the so-called
Apostolic Fathers contain no clear and certain allusions to miracle-
working or to the exercise of the charismatic gifts, *contempor-
aneously with themselves*.'[8] That is, none of the Apostolic Fathers

claimed to have the gift of miracles himself. Nor did they claim to have personally witnessed miracles. Their testimonies were hearsay.

Montanism

During the time of Irenaeus, Montanus used passages in John's Gospel (John 14:26; 16:12-13 — verses repeatedly used for the same purpose today) to claim that the Holy Spirit was giving new revelation through him. Two women, Priscilla and Maximilla, fell under his spell. Having left their husbands, they became his two main prophetesses. Soon they surpassed their new teacher. He gave them the rank of 'virgins in his church'. 'These women fell into strange ecstasies, delivering, while in this condition, what Montanus and his followers regarded as divine prophecies.'[9] As a result of these 'new revelations' virginity was exalted. Second marriages after the death of a spouse were rejected, in contradiction of the apostle Paul. Chastity as a preparation for ecstasy was advocated. The teaching that serious sins after conversion could not be forgiven was introduced.

The church declared Montanus a heretic about A.D. 160. Eusebius wrote, 'Montanus by name ... gave to the Adversary access to himself, and became obsessed, and, falling suddenly into a kind of frenzy and distraction, raved and began to babble and utter strange things, prophesying contrary to the custom of the Church... Some of those who at that time were within hearing of the bastard utterances were angry ... censured him, and forbade him to talk, remembering the distinction made by the Lord and his warning to be on guard against the coming of false prophets.'[10]

Tertullian

Although Tertullian had been a great defender of the faith, about A.D. 201 he became a Montanist. He claimed that 'He had the fullness of the Spirit and received, via his prophetesses, prophecy and visions, and since they were from God, they were binding on all Christians.'[11]

Many of Tertullian's beliefs, fed by this new stream of 'prophecy', began to diverge from the faith. He promoted baptismal regeneration. He claimed that there was no remedy for 'post-baptismal sin except martyrdom'. He asserted that 'The Holy Spirit in him was greater than that of the Apostles and thus, Paul allowed for remarriage because of the weakness of the flesh.'[12] The churches declared Tertullian a heretic in his own day. The charge was reviewed and confirmed in the fifth century.

One other reference from the third century needs to be mentioned. A letter of Bishop Cornelius of Rome in 251 mentions exorcists in a list of the minor orders present in the church. This indicates a belief in the church at that time about the need for casting out demons.

Early martyrs

Gary McHale makes the point that the early 'Christians were empowered by the Holy Spirit, not for signs and wonders, but to endure martyrdom with boldness and courage'.[13] Indeed our word 'martyr' comes from the Greek word *martures*, which means 'witnesses'. Eusebius does record the claim that a miracle occurred when Polycarp was committed to the fire. He alleges that the flames encircled Polycarp but did not burn him. It sounds apocryphal. In reality it was the *witness* of men such as Polycarp that constituted the real miracles. Their serenity and courage, the testimony the martyrs gave to the message of Christ in court, and particularly the way they died profoundly touched untold thousands.[14]

The early martyrs didn't appeal to their accusers for exemption from prosecution by doing miracles or prophesying. They didn't try to escape by miraculous means. They spoke of Christ as they died. McHale comments, 'With over two hundred years of martyrdom, the theology of evangelism was completely different from today. The power of the Holy Spirit was not signs and wonders, but the ability to publicly profess your faith boldly while being tortured.'[15]

The patristic fathers

Augustine

Augustine has been justly regarded, by both Roman Catholics and Reformers, as one of the greatest Christian thinkers. He became the

Bishop of Hippo, in present-day Algeria, in A. D. 396. In *Power Evangelism*, John Wimber lists eighteen examples of miracles mentioned by Augustine in his book, *City of God*. For example, a nun is supposed to have come back to life after her dress was taken to the shrine of St Stephen and then wrapped around her corpse; a man was delivered of evil spirits after a piece of dirt from Jesus' grave in Jerusalem was placed in the home; a blind man received sight by some martyrs' bones.

Wimber himself quotes Augustine as saying, 'For even now miracles are wrought in the name of Christ, whether by His sacraments or by the prayers or relics of His saints.'[16] Augustine goes on in his *City of God* to admit that 'They are not so brilliant and conspicuous as to cause them to be published with such glory as accompanied the former [biblical] miracles.'[17]

Is Wimber asking us to sanction the use of relics, holy water, tombs, the communion host, or prayers to the saints and martyrs to effect miracles? This was the practice of Augustine and other church fathers of his era such as Basil, Chrysostom and Jerome. However much we may appreciate Augustine's classic writings, *Confessions* and *The City of God*, we must realize that he was a product of his day — a period when mysticism and superstition abounded.

If we claim that the miracles described by Augustine and others are true, we must also accept the erroneous teachings linked with these superstitions. Warfield points out that these men, great as they were, 'inferred that celibacy was superior to marriage, that saints were to be invoked, prayers for the dead said, and the real presence believed in'.[18] You cannot have patristic miracles without patristic heresy!

Warfield makes an extremely important point here. He wrote, 'There is little or no evidence at all for miracle-working during the first fifty years of the post-Apostolic church; it is slight and unimportant for the next fifty years; it grows more abundant during the next century [the third]; and it becomes abundant and precise only in the fourth century, to increase further in the fifth and beyond.'[19] This leads us inescapably to the conclusion that claims about miracles increased in proportion as the church departed from the apostolic faith. The medieval church became a veritable hotbed of magical miracles, but at the same time it degenerated into a 'synagogue of Satan', requiring God the Holy Spirit to visit it with revival in the form of the Protestant Reformation!

The reliability of these primitive claims is another problem.

Warfield comments, 'And so we pass on to the fourth century in an ever-increasing stream [of miracles], but without a single writer having claimed himself to have wrought a miracle of any kind or having ascribed miracle-working to any known name in the church, and without a single instance having been recorded in detail. The contrast of this with the testimony of the fourth century is very great. There we have the greatest writers recording instances witnessed by themselves.'[20]

In other words, for three centuries we have miracles by hearsay without evidence or corroboration. In the fourth century and beyond we have 'the greater proportion of the miracles ... wrought in support of distinctively Romish teaching, which, it would seem, must be accepted, if their attesting miracles are allowed'.[21] If we denounce prayers to the saints or to relics as unbiblical, we must also reject the miracles linked to them. Both are bogus.

Contrary to the facts, Bill Jackson takes the opposite tack. In a Vineyard document seeking to disprove cessationism, he states that miracles waned in frequency when belief in cessationism came to the fore and when the church became weak. He notes that the early church was zealous and pure until the edict of Milan in A. D. 313 granted toleration to the church. After Christianity was legalized by Constantine the sudden freedom from persecution flooded the church with converts — but it became 'worldly and compromised. Miracles became less frequent, therefore, because of the resulting lack of faith.'[22] His comments about the nature of the church following the Edict of Milan are true, but his conclusions are erroneous. In fact, lack of *biblical faith*, as Warfield and others have shown, produced a *superstitious faith* that laid claim to more miracles than at the time when the church was zealous and pure.

In 1748 Conyers Middleton, a controversialist with a somewhat sceptical temper, published a book whose title says it all: *A Free Inquiry into the Miraculous Powers which are supposed to have subsisted in the Christian church from the earliest ages through several successive centuries. By which it is shown that we have no sufficient reason to believe, upon the authority of the primitive fathers, that any such powers were continued to the church, after the days of the Apostles.* Although it created a storm of controversy and many sought to disprove his researches it proved irrefutable, up to and including Warfield's day.

Revivals in the medieval church prior to the Reformation

The Waldensians

In the late twelfth century Peter Waldo, a merchant of Lyons, 'came to such an overwhelming sense of spiritual need that only the Scriptures could satisfy his soul'.[23] He persuaded some priests to dictate the Gospels in the vernacular so he could copy them down. In this way many of the books of the Bible were translated. Deeply moved by his new acquaintance with the gospel, Waldo gave up his trade and began to preach. The Holy Spirit touched many lives but before long persecution broke out. He and his followers were excommunicated in 1184. In the centuries that followed they spread the faith quickly into communities on both sides of the Alps: Piedmont and Lombardy, Naples and Provence, and even as far as the Netherlands, Rhineland, Bohemia and England.[24] The fires of persecution, and later the Inquisition, forced them back into their mountain valleys, but they never disappeared.

The Waldensians 'held to the authority and supremacy of the Scriptures, the right of the laity to read the Word and the urgency to preach it, justification by faith, and a life of good works together with stout denial of the value of priestly absolution or intercession of saints or angels ... their piety, poverty, sobriety, simplicity, and austerity made them very attractive to many of their contemporaries so that "The number of their disciples and followers increased from day to day." They could not be silent, for "The love of the Word of God moved them all, even the women, if not to preach, at least to testify."'[25] Revival came without signs and wonders except the miracle of transformed lives!

The Lollards

In 1378, long before the Reformation, John Wycliffe translated the Bible into English. He asserted that the Bible contains 'the whole of God's revelation. There was no need for any further teaching to be supplied by church tradition, the pope, or any other source.'[26] Wycliffe gathered around him a group of godly priests who were nicknamed 'poor preachers'. Wycliffe personally was protected during his lifetime by the English Crown. The fury of the Roman Catholic Church, however, fell upon the Lollard preachers who followed him. Under the Fire Act in 1401 whereby heretics could be burnt alive, many Lollards perished and the Wycliffe Bible became a hunted treasure. But the light lit by this 'Morning Star of the Reformation' ignited a fire that would not be extinguished. Wycliffe used *only* the tinder of Scripture — no signs and wonders! From it John Hus and his followers in Bohemia lit their torches.

Instead of pursuing the phantom of supernatural phenomena, why don't we let a hunger for the Word of God like that of Peter Waldo, John Wycliffe and John Hus smoulder in our breasts?

Theresa of Avila

John Wimber seeks to use this noted mystic, who was canonized by the Roman Catholic Church, to discredit cessationism. John White also quotes her in his book *When the Spirit Comes with Power*. After unsuccessful medical treatment for a serious illness contracted soon after she became a nun, Theresa was supposedly healed by the intercession of St Joseph. Thereafter, 'God used to visit her with "intellectual visions and locutions", where no outward manifestations were seen but the "things seen and the words heard [were] being directly impressed on her mind". In 1565 she had "such extraordinary manifestations as the piercing … of her heart, the spiritual espousals, and the mystical marriage" along with a vision of her place in hell in case she was unfaithful.'[27] Surely, our Vineyard friends do not want us to revive the medieval mysticism from which the Holy Spirit rescued us in the Reformation?

The Protestant Reformation

The greatest revival in all of history came to be called a reformation instead of a revival because it totally reformed European society from 1517 onwards and swept untold millions into the kingdom. Unfortunately, this title has led many, including those in the Vineyard movement, to overlook its revival power.

Martin Luther nailed his protest against indulgences to the Wittenburg church door on 31 October 1517. He denied church authority in 1519, separated from the Roman Catholic Church in 1520 and prepared the *Augsburg Confession* in 1530. His watchwords, *Sola fide* (faith alone) and *Sola Scriptura* (the Scriptures alone), lit a revival fire that began to spread from northern Germany to Denmark, Norway and Sweden.

John Calvin was converted in 1529 and his *Institutes* further spread the reformed faith to Switzerland, France, Netherlands, Scotland, Germany, Hungary, Poland and England.

The Anglican Church, formed during King Henry VIII's revolt against Rome, was confirmed as England's state church under Elizabeth (1558-1603).

The Catholic Counter-Reformation and the dreaded Inquisition could not stamp out the revival of faith in Christ alone for salvation. Wars and strife thrashed Europe until the Treaty of Westphalia in 1648 brought an exhausted peace. Finally, Protestants could regroup and look beyond their own survival.

Failure to recognize the power and extent of the Reformation and the political and religious climate of the time has led many to overlook it as a revival. It has also been criticized for failing to initiate a cross-cultural missionary movement. How could the Reformers, whose Spirit-led goal was no less than the reconversion of Europe from the superstition of Romanism, lift their eyes beyond the millions of lost French, German, English, Swedish and Italian souls? They turned men and women back to the Scriptures, back to justification by faith, back to Christ and his atonement. This message of the gospel transformed Europe without any appeal to signs and wonders! God used the Reformers to bring about the most powerful revival in history.

Bill Jackson echoes the classic Vineyard position fostered by William DeArteaga and others. Without any proof he claims that 'Luther later recanted of his cessationist position.' He states that John Calvin developed a radical doctrine of cessationism 'that doomed Protestantism to a state of long-standing powerlessness'. He accuses Calvin of believing that spiritual experience is invalid. He states that cessationism led to the liberalism that doomed Europe. Further he says, 'Not only was healing curtailed by Cessationism, but so were missions. Since God was no longer calling men into the apostolic ministry, and that ministry was cross-cultural, then God was no longer calling men to move cross-culturally. Protestant missions would have to wait almost 300 years for William Carey … in 1793.'[28]

That there were flaws in the Reformers and their work is not in question. There were serious divisions between Lutherans and Zwingliites. The Calvinists took the middle ground and tried to promote harmony. Lutheran doctrine did misinterpret the Great Commission. Too often the political fortunes of various princes impinged on church matters. And, sadly, Anabaptists were persecuted by all three groups.

But the oft-repeated half-truth about John Calvin's theology and anti-missionary bias needs to be corrected. True, for the first century or so, the Reformers sent few missionaries to America, Africa or Asia. They were devastated by wars and consumed by the need to evangelize Europe. This was the time of the great explorers. These seafaring Catholic adventurers ruled the seas and prevented Protestants from any contact with the world beyond Europe. It was only after the Peace of Westphalia that Protestant merchants began to sail the seas and bring back news of heathen lands.

As to his theology, Calvin's high view of God's sovereignty recovered for unborn generations of preachers and missionaries a confidence in God's presence and power that energized them. Roland Bainton writes, 'For Calvin the doctrine of election was an unspeakable comfort because it eliminated all such worries [Luther's lifelong agonizing for faith] and freed man from concern for himself in order that he might devote every energy to the unflagging service of the sovereign Lord. Calvinism bred a race of heroes.'[29]

From Calvin's time until the triumph of Arminianism in the nineteenth century most of the famous preachers, revivalists and missionaries shared a common faith. They were Calvinists, cessationists and ardent students of the Word — from John Knox, through the Puritans, Richard Baxter, John Owen, John Bunyan, George Whitefield, Jonathan Edwards, Gilbert Tennent, Howel Harris, John Eliot, David Brainerd, William Carey, Robert Murray M'Cheyne, Adoniram Judson, Henry Martyn, J. C. Ryle, John Paton, Charles H. Spurgeon. (The exception to this list would be the warm-hearted and missionary-minded Moravians and the pietistic Lutherans of the seventeenth and eighteenth centuries.) Far from rendering the church powerless, Calvin's recovery of the biblical view of God's sovereign glory filled the church with power. It is this power we desperately need to help battered Christians to recover from the clutches of an Arminian, man-centred, consumer Christianity.

Calvin's missionary concern has also been vastly underrated. Far from negating the essential apostolic gift, John Calvin followed the ancient *Didache* in distinguishing between the twelve original apostles and those called out to continue the apostolic ministry of the gospel. He said, 'According to the meaning and etymology of the word, all the ministers of the Church may be called apostles, because they are all sent by the Lord, and are His messengers.'[30]

In fact Calvin sent out over 300 evangelists [missionaries] to France and trained men from many countries in Europe. Atkinson writes, 'The men that Calvin established in sound learning and godly discipline came from many lands and went back as ministers of the struggling Protestants in the Netherlands, England, Scotland, the Rhineland and France. They were learned and godly, fearless and devoted, and what these unnamed *apostles* did for the cause of reform [read, evangelism] may never be known.'[31]

In 1555 Calvin commissioned four missionaries, along with a number of French Huguenots, to evangelize the Indians in Brazil. Unfortunately, the leader defected to the Portuguese. The small colony was plundered and any survivors slaughtered by the Jesuits.

In my library I have almost a dozen books on history and missions that repeat this fallacy about Calvin's supposed disinterest in missions. Why have they so twisted history? Was Europe not doomed by ignorance and superstition at the time of the Reformation? Were millions not saved in Europe through the Reformation? Was the spread of the gospel from Germany to France to Switzerland to Sweden to Britain not cross-cultural? Can this not be considered missions? Without a doubt. Doug Adams, professor of church history at Toronto Baptist Seminary, concludes from his researches that Calvin was the greatest missionary since the apostle Paul.

It is only by virtue of our myopic twentieth-century view of missions that we fail to see that Europe at the time of Luther was a dark continent crying out for salvation. John Wycliffe, John Calvin and many others lit the fires of evangelism, not with signs and wonders, but the Word of God.

Martin Luther faced the church council *(Diet)* at Worms, in Germany and, while defending his theses said, 'Necessity forces us to run to the Bible with the writings of all teachers, and to obtain there a verdict and judgement upon them. Scripture alone is the true lord and master of all writings and doctrine on earth.'[32]

Like all great movements, the new reformed churches lost their first love and became imbalanced. But we cannot blame the inevitable deterioration of the European church on Calvin any more than we can blame the decline of the Ephesian or Corinthian churches on the apostle Paul. As the Puritans so clearly recognized, purity of life and doctrine must be continually sought. The truly reformed church must be always reforming.

The Puritans

Puritanism began with a desire to complete the stalled reformation of the English church. In 1559, Queen Elizabeth I, in her efforts to control all areas of society and suppress discontent, imposed 'conformity to her Anglican model by the Acts of Supremacy and Uniformity'. Having failed politically, the Puritans went underground. Thus began a hundred-year period during which Puritans sought to demonstrate a vision of a holy life of fervent devotion to Christ. They emphasized 'personal piety, sound doctrine and a properly ordered Church-life'.[33]

For the Puritan, 'Each day began and ended with searching, unhurried and devout personal and family prayer. Each task ... was done to the glory of God... The "great business of godliness" dominated the ardent believer's ambitions and called forth all his energies... Puritanism succeeded where other more cloistered ideologies failed, because here men *embodied* true doctrine so that Puritanism was made visible before men.'[34]

The Puritans combined warmth and heart-stirring devotion with a profound commitment to understanding the Scriptures through diligent study. The great Puritan Richard Baxter wrote, 'Sound doctrine makes a sound judgement, a sound heart, a sound conversation [life] and a sound conscience.' Peter Lewis explains, 'Piety does not grow out of the ground nor does it materialize out of the air. True godliness is born, not of mystical experience, nor of educated nature, but of the royal marriage of Truth and Grace.'[35]

The Puritans enjoyed a short zenith of expression under Oliver Cromwell's enlightened rule between 1654 and 1658. Then persecution from the established Anglican Church broke out again. The 1662 Act of Uniformity required the total conformity of all clergy to the episcopal system. In the Great Ejection of 1662 almost two thousand ministers were cast out of their churches without any means of livelihood. In the providence of God this ejection created nonconformity, a vigorous new branch of the church, which was to feed the massive missionary movements just around the corner. It ultimately laid the foundation for the freedom we know in evangelical nonconformity today.

Puritanism, pure and simple, was a pervasive and lasting renewal in the Anglican Church that smouldered for a hundred years without benefit of signs and wonders but with the passion and fervour of biblical devotion to Christ. The writings of the Puritans (many have been reprinted in our day) still inspire a unique vision of godliness.

The Moravians

John Hus, martyred in 1415, became the precursor of the Moravian Brethren, first called *Unitas Fratrum* (Unity of Brethren) in Bohemia. Their testimony spread through Moravia, Poland and Prussia. By 1609, when they were granted legal recognition, they had 'five hundred clergymen, hundreds of meeting places, and thousands of converts'.[36] However, political events — including the Thirty Years War (1618-1648), propelled Roman Catholic leaders to power, and persecution fell. The seventeenth century became a time of harried underground meetings and exile. In 1722 Moravians began to flee to Count Zinzendorf's estate in Germany and a new era of revival and missionary fervour began.

At first, discord marred the atmosphere in Herrnhut (the Watch of the Lord), the name they gave to their new community. Then at a communion service on 13 August 1727 a great revival fell. It produced a new unity, a dependence on God and a passion for missions. 'A prayer vigil was begun that continued around the clock, seven days a week, without interruption for more than a hundred years.'[37] The Moravian church sent out thousands of missionaries in the years to follow.

Count Zinzendorf had rightly placed great emphasis on the death of Christ but, wrongly, little emphasis on doctrine. Tucker explains, 'Their message was the love of Christ — a very simple message — with intentional disregard for doctrinal truths until after conversion and even then, an emotional mysticism took precedence over theological training.' Unfortunately, as time passed the emphasis on the death of Christ became 'gruesome obsession, and the whole church seemed to be carried away in a radical form of mysticism ...

they morbidly depicted the death of Christ', and talked of being worms or fish or bees 'swimming in the blood of Christ or sucking at his wounds'.[38]

As they became more mystical they became more introspective and less concerned about missions until Zinzendorf recognized their error and called them back to a more balanced view of the cross. There were aberrations — yes; signs and wonders — no.

The Quakers

Another group arose in the early 1650s to which many in the Vineyard movement claim affinity. During the confusion that occurred upon the splintering of Puritanism a number of mystical sects were formed: the Seekers, the Ranters and the Society of Friends. George Fox, the leader of this last-named group, went about on foot dressed in leather clothes. He often slept out of doors. His unorthodox ways and powerful preaching led to persecution and imprisonment, but his movement grew. He introduced plain speech and dress, refusal to pay tithes, take oaths and use pagan names for days and months.

George Fox described what happened where he preached: 'The Lord's power began to shake them, and great meetings we began to have, and a mighty power and work of God there was amongst people to the astonishment of both people and priests.' Because of the shaking that came over many, they were nicknamed 'Quakers'.[39]

Their belief that the Holy Spirit must lead their meetings meant that sometimes they would wait in silence for hours before the Spirit 'manifested' himself. Their emphasis on an 'inner light' led to their playing down Scripture. George Fox was wont to say, 'Christ is come to teach his people himself.' In his study on Fox, Christopher Rule writes that 'Fox sometimes seemed to think himself infallible.'[40]

The *Perennial Dictionary of World Religions* defines the Quakers as follows: 'A form of radical Christianity ... marked by its belief in the divine light of Christ in all people, its meditative form of worship or group Mysticism in reliance on the Holy Spirit, and its humanitarian social witness. Known as Quakerism, the Society of Friends can be understood as either a radical form of Protestantism or as a third form of Western Christianity, relying on the inner light as its main authority... It was marked by the belief that the divine light within all people brought true religion by enabling one to experience a radical rebirth and to cultivate a style of living that culminated in perfect obedience to God... The central Quaker conviction is that the saving knowledge and power of God are present as divine influences in all human beings through what is variously called the inner light, the light of the eternal Christ within, or "That of God". This belief has inevitably produced distinctive approaches to, and often de-emphasis on, the doctrine of the Trinity, the person and work of Christ, bondage to sin, and the uniqueness of Christianity.'[41]

Various groups of Quakers have survived, some rescued from liberalism by their Puritan roots but some, for example, the Friends' General Conference, are very liberal. Whatever their profession, their belief in the 'inner light' in all peoples and their perfectionism place them on the fringes of Protestantism.

The French Prophets

Following the revocation of the Edict of Nantes in 1685, Protestants in southern France faced vicious persecution. In this atmosphere a movement arose claiming visions, prophecies, tongues and trances. Some of this group came to London. By 1707 their charismatic manifestations had begun to attract attention. Their influence waned, however, when they prophesied that Thomas Emes would be resurrected on 25 May 1708. Emes did not rise.

When the Evangelical Revival burst upon the scene in the mid-1730s they sought again to win converts to their beliefs. George Whitefield and all the great revival preachers of the period rejected the unbiblical emphases of the French Prophets, a group whose beliefs were close to that of modern Vineyardism. They gradually faded into obscurity.

Summary

1. Physical phenomena such as shaking, falling down, crying out, roaring, etc., are not found in church history except among questionable groups such as the Montanists, Quakers and French Prophets, and among some Roman Catholic mystics.

2. Only heretical groups such as the Montanists and French Prophets believed in the continuation of revelatory prophecy. The Quakers' emphasis on 'inner light' opens the door to imaginations and impressions of any kind and discredits the sufficiency and authority of Scripture. Insisting on continuing revelation has inevitably led to heresy.

3. Miracles were claimed in inverse proportion to the purity of doctrine found in the group. For example, the medieval church promoted a whole range of mystical and magical claims about miracles at the same time as they departed progressively farther from biblical faith. Medieval miracles rested on the mystical power of relics, shrines, visions of the virgin, stigmata, etc. In our day Lourdes and St Anne de Beaupré carry on this sad tradition.

4. The rediscovery of the Scriptures, and the person of Christ as portrayed there, fuelled genuine revivals among the Waldensians, Lollards, Puritans and during the Protestant Reformation. Rediscovery of great truths (doctrines) such as justification by faith promoted holiness of life and power in evangelism. Where doctrine was bypassed, as in the case of the Moravians, imbalance ensued. Signs and wonders played no role in genuine movements of God during the first sixteen centuries of church history.

5. Unless one accepts Roman Catholic doctrine and miracles, church history supports cessationism.

10.
The great evangelical revivals

Revival — how we long for it! No wonder news of a revival in Toronto electrified the evangelical world. But events in Toronto fail to mirror the great evangelical revivals of history. Proponents of the Toronto Blessing claim otherwise. In doing so they appeal to Jonathan Edwards, who is accepted by both sides of the debate as 'the theologian of revival'. Guy Chevreau gives over at least a third of his book, *Catch the Fire*, to arguing that Edwards would have been happy with the Toronto Blessing. I heartily dispute his view.

Obviously, we need to look closely at the events surrounding the revival in Northampton where Edwards served as pastor. But before we do, we need an overview of people and happenings on both sides of the Atlantic. Revival was not confined to America and it did not end in the 1730s. Three great revivals swept over society in the eighteenth and nineteenth centuries.

1. The Great Awakening

Dr Michael Haykin has done considerable study in this field. I acknowledge the immense help his writings have been in summarizing this period.[1] In the 1730s and 1740s a wave of revivals spread through the English-speaking world on both sides of the Atlantic. God swept thousands into the kingdom. In New England, God used Jonathan Edwards (1703-1758) to ignite revival fire from his parish of Northampton. Thirty or forty thousand were converted in a three-year period as the revival spread. In Great Britain, George Whitefield (1714-1770) began to preach in the fields. Huge crowds of 10,000 or more thronged his meetings. In the thirty-four years between his ordination in 1736 and his death he preached around 18,000 sermons, visited Scotland fifteen times, crossed the Atlantic thirteen times and preached all over England and Wales. John Wesley (1703-1791) and his brother Charles (1707-1788) soon joined him. The Arminian Methodists grew to 88,000 by 1800. In Wales the preaching and spirituality of Howel Harris (1714-1773) and Daniel Rowland (1711-1790) set the hillsides aflame. (For a summary of events during this period see Appendix I.)

George Whitefield

In 1737 George Whitefield became a reluctant preacher. He felt, 'I am undone, I am unfit to preach in thy great name! Send me not, I pray, Lord, send me not yet!'[2] However, God sent him to London where he preached for two months. Then, 'At Bristol, after preaching once, he found it necessary to preach every day of the week and twice on Sundays. Churches quickly became crowded, often to overflowing, with many turned away for lack of room. People under spiritual concern sought him continually.'[3]

People were not used to a preacher whose sermons were full of life and power. In Bristol he preached five times a week to throngs of awakened listeners. He writes, 'It was wonderful to see how the people hung upon the rails of the organ loft, climbed upon the leads of the church and made the church itself so hot with their breath that the steam would fall from the pillars like drops of rain... Multitudes, after sermons, followed me home, weeping and the next day I was employed from seven in the morning till midnight, in giving spiritual advice to awakened souls.'[4] In Wales God had already been using Howel Harris to mighty effect.

From this point onwards Whitefield became immersed in preaching until he sailed for Georgia. Dallimore writes, 'London — a city then of about five hundred thousand inhabitants — was stirred by Whitefield's ministry ... the mass of people were drawn by a deep spiritual hunger... He preached nothing but the basic doctrines of the Church of England; in glowing contrast to the majority of the clergy, his life was marked by personal holiness and everything about him seemed ablaze with zeal.'[5] His preaching differed greatly from the rhetorical and elegant sermons embellished by flights of fancy that characterized other preachers. 'Its chief characteristics are its Biblical content, its doctrinal emphasis and its simplification.'[6] He preached on the new birth, the evils of sin, justification by faith, that salvation is a work of God, the preservation of the believer, particular redemption and many other biblical themes.

Whitefield soon left for Georgia, where he stayed for most of 1738. Meanwhile his friends John and Charles Wesley had returned to England from Georgia. Before long, both were soundly converted. Upon his own return to Britain in 1739 Whitefield rejoiced to find the earlier work showing evidences of a continuing grace. However, some clergy began to close their churches to him. On a bitterly cold February day he began his famous 'field preaching'. He called the Kingswood coalminers into the open fields to hear the gospel. Of one of these meetings he writes, 'Having no righteousness of their own to renounce, they were glad to hear of a Jesus who was a friend of publicans, and came not to call the righteous, but sinners to repentance. The first discovery of their being affected was to see the white gutters made by their tears which plentifully fell down their black cheeks, as they came out of their coal pits. Hundreds and hundreds of them were soon brought under deep convictions and thorough conversion.'[7]

In the years following, the revival flourished and spread throughout England, Scotland and Wales. Charles Wesley, the poet and musician of the movement, wrote this elegy at Whitefield's death:

Roused from the sleep of death, a countless crowd,
Whose hearts like trees before the wind are bow'd...
Press to the hallow'd courts, with eager strife,
Catch the convincing word, and hear for life,
Parties and sects their endless feuds forget,
And fall and tremble at the Preacher's feet...
While yet he speaks the Lord Himself comes down,
Applies and proves the gracious word His own,
The Holy Ghost to thirsty souls imparts,
And writes forgiveness on the broken hearts.[8]

With only the rare outbreak of physical phenomena, with no supernatural sign gifts — with *only* the mighty gospel of grace, a whole era was changed! But since physical manifestations did occur occasionally here and there, let me turn to that issue at this point.

Phenomena in Britain

As an example of physical manifestations in meetings, consider the little town of Cambuslang, a few miles south-east of Glasgow in Scotland. The local minister, a somewhat dry preacher by the name of McCulloch, began to see an unusual stirring of God among his rather disinterested parishioners. In February 1742 about 130 people were awakened. George Whitefield arrived in July and continued to preach for some weeks. In August 30,000 attended an outdoor communion service. Philip Doddridge wrote that 'During the time of divine worship, profound reverence overspread every countenance. They hear as for eternity... Thousands are melted into tears. Many cry out in the bitterness of their souls. Some ... from the stoutest man to the tenderest child, shake and tremble and a few fall down as dead. Nor does this happen only when men of warm address alarm them with the terrors of the law, but when the most deliberate preacher speaks of redeeming love.'[9]

As we shall see later, when the phenomena were expressions of genuine conviction, repentance and joyful faith, they were received as from God. Dramatic evidences such as these were not common, but they were not unknown. Howel Harris writes in March 1743 to Whitefield about the effect of the preaching of his fellow Welshman, Daniel Rowland: 'Such crying out and Heart breaking groans, Silent Weeping and Holy Joy, and shouts of Rejoicing I never saw... 'Tis very common when He preaches for Scores to fall down by the Power of the Lord, pierced and wounded or overcom'd by the Love of God and Sights of the Beauty and Excellency of Jesus, and lie on the Ground... Some lye there for Hours, Some praising and admiring Jesus, free Grace, Distinguishing Grace, others wanting the words to utter ...'[10]

How did Whitefield interpret these manifestations? He declared, 'To say we may have God's Spirit without feeling it ... is, in reality, to deny the thing itself.'[11] Profound emotions of conviction or joy usually manifest themselves outwardly. The Lollards, the Waldensians, the Moravians and the Puritans all had a passion for God. In our discussions concerning manifestations, I would not want to give the impression that I do not believe that genuine faith fosters the most intense feelings possible by mankind. All great movements, all lovers of God, know times of overwhelming emotion.

As early as 1739 Whitefield had concluded that it was 'tempting God to require such signs. That there is something of God in it I doubt not; but the devil, I believe, does interpose. I think it will encourage the French Prophets, take people from the written word, and make them depend on visions, convulsions, etc., more than on the promises and precepts of the Gospel.'[12]

As we have already noted, the mystical French Prophets provided an abhorrent example of what eighteenth-century Christians called 'enthusiasm'. Enthusiasm was defined as 'a vain belief of private revelation; a vain confidence of divine favour or communication.'[13] Whitefield felt that to use external phenomena as a criterion of revival was to tempt God. It encouraged the devil to tempt people to mimic the signs while minimizing the importance of the Bible. In a sermon published in 1746 he warned that enthusiasm would lead people 'to pretend to be guided by the Spirit without the written word'.[14] Michael Haykin explains Whitefield's position: 'All inner impressions must be tried by "the unerring rule of God's most holy word," and if found incompatible, rejected as "diabolical and delusive."'[15]

Whitefield, in common with all the preachers of the Great Awakening except John Wesley, believed in the cessation of charismatic gifts and signs. Haykin writes, 'He was adamant that the extraordinary gifts of the Spirit, such as prophecy, glossolalia, and miraculous powers, had ceased with the passing of the apostles.' In a sermon that Wesley helped him edit for publication in 1739, 'Whitefield declared that Christ's promise of the Spirit in John 7:37-39 has nothing to do with receiving power "to work miracles, or show outward signs and wonders,"' since 'Such signs and wonders occurred only when "some new revelation was to be established, as at the first settling of the Mosaic or gospel dispensation".'[16]

In that sermon Whitefield continued, 'I cannot but suspect the spirit of those who insist upon a repetition of such miracles at this time... There need not outward miracles, but only an inward co-operation of the Holy Spirit with the word, to prove that Jesus is the Messiah which was come into the world.'[17] No one could more firmly hammer a series of nails into the coffin of modern signs and wonders than Whitefield did.

John Wesley

John Wesley differed from Whitefield, and indeed all the other great preachers of the eighteenth-century revivals, in rejecting many aspects of the faith held by his contemporaries. He differed also in denying the cessation of the miraculous gifts. In his view the gifts ceased in the middle of the fourth century when the love and faith of the church waxed cold due to the increase in its wealth and influence after Constantine came to power.

Although Wesley approved of displays of emotion more than Whitefield did, he did not encourage a recovery of charismatic gifts. A man called George Bell 'claimed that he and a coterie of London Methodists possessed the power to regularly heal the sick ... and to raise the dead'.[18] When Bell claimed prophetic powers and the gift of discernment of spirits, and when he predicted the end of the world on 28 February 1763, Wesley stepped in and disowned him.

While Wesley granted that God on rare occasions speaks through visions and dreams, yet he warned that 'Pride and "warm imagination" frequently mislead people into ascribing visions, dreams, and mental impressions to God's authorship.' He said that those who imagine they are 'endued with a power of working miracles, of healing the sick by a word or a touch, of restoring the sight to the blind' were 'enthusiasts', the derogatory term often used in this period for ungrounded mysticism.[19] Wesley's position was very far from that of those caught up in the Toronto Blessing!

The role of John Wesley in the revival and in subsequent church history is paradoxical. In his marvellous duo of volumes on George Whitefield, Arnold Dallimore establishes how John Wesley introduced division into the movement by preaching against the reformed faith. He gradually won away many followers to his Arminian views.[20]

Not content with rejecting the reformed faith that God had used to transform Europe in the Reformation, revitalize England under the Puritans and revive it again under Whitefield, Wesley improvised another novelty — 'Christian perfection'. 'He began to associate the overpowering emotions that he had witnessed with the experience of entire sanctification. Of one man, in whom physical phenomena were displayed, he said, "He received a full, clear sense of His pardoning love, and power to sin no more."[21]

By 'perfection' Wesley did not mean maturity, or a high degree of Christian discipleship. Without clearly defining sin, he taught 'an attainable condition in which the sin nature is eradicated and the soul entirely sanctified'.[22] Leaders in the revival such as Howel Harris and John Cennick sought to dissuade Wesley from this teaching. Even Count Zinzendorf, leader of the Moravians, remonstrated with him, but to no avail.

John Wesley propounded doctrines that have laid the foundation for a whole series of errors that have become compounded down to our day: entire sanctification, sinless perfection and falling from grace. He used these novel doctrines to consolidate his position as a leader of the revival in his own right. Since emotional phenomena furthered his purposes, he encouraged them at Bristol.

In 1739 violent trembling, sinking to the ground as dead, cries and tears, groanings and shrieks began to appear in Wesley's congregation. Dallimore comments, 'It is significant, however, that this phenomenon, in its manifestation in England during 1739, was almost entirely limited to the ministry of John Wesley. Howel Harris' preaching was accompanied by tremendous conviction of sin and, at times, by outcryings, but not by these extreme effects. Tyerman ... stated, "No such results attended Whitefield's ministry, and Whitefield himself regarded them with suspicion and dislike." Whitefield's audiences were often moved to weeping and there were times when the sobbing became ... loud ... but the effect was not such as to overwhelm the hearers, either in mind or body. Only on certain rare occasions on which Whitefield or Charles Wesley preached *where people had learned to induce this kind of thing under the ministry of others* did it occur under their own.'[23]

One might suppose that these phenomena occurred because John Wesley was a stronger or more emotional preacher. To the contrary, Dallimore comments, 'In the preaching of Harris, Charles Wesley and Whitefield, emotion was freely expressed, while in that of John Wesley it was largely pent up.'[24]

At first the phenomena were undoubtedly the result of God's convicting work, but soon 'The original experience began to be imitated, for certain of Wesley's hearers learned to make a practice of effecting a self-induced paroxysm during his services.'[25] Thinking they were genuine marks of a divine work, Wesley encouraged them.

Charles Wesley, his brother, narrates several occasions when he caught people imitating the phenomena. A girl at Kingswood 'confessed that her fits and cryings out (above thirty of them) were all feigned that Mr Wesley might take notice of her.'[26] Four years later in the north of England Charles wrote about a girl crying out with violent convulsions who was carried out, but as soon as she was outside the door to the meeting immediately got to her feet and quietly walked off. Several other girls who vied with each other to shriek the loudest became as quiet as lambs after they were carried out of the meeting.[27]

Things grew more violent under Wesley's ministry in Kingswood. At first people recovered after Wesley prayed for them. But Cennick, his companion at this time says, 'Often-times the same persons were seized again and again and grew intolerable, and though he prayed with them whole nights, they grew worse and worse.'[28] In his *Journal* Wesley admitted 'that matters were getting out of hand that he too was becoming afraid. His journal of the latter half of October depicts scenes of hysteria and seemingly-Satanic possession.'[29]

In the midst of this situation he set out for London. 'With his departure the hysteria began to abate and, within a few months had all but ceased in the Bristol and Kingswood area. Such experiences very seldom occurred under his ministry throughout the rest of his career.'[30]

In our own day men such as Benny Hinn, Rodney Howard-Browne, and now the team from the Toronto Airport Fellowship, encourage physical phenomena, but the great revivalists Charles Wesley, Howel Harris and George Whitefield all discouraged their occurrence. John Wesley himself finally turned away from emotional excesses. Ralph Erskine, out of an intimate acquaintance with the circumstances, wrote to John Wesley, 'But I make no question, Satan, so far as he gets power, may exert himself on such occasions, partly to hinder the good work in the persons who are thus touched with the sharp arrows of conviction, and partly to disparage the work of God, as if it tended to lead people to distraction.'[31]

Charles Wesley also attributed the disruptive aspects of the phenomena to Satan. In his *Journal* he wrote, 'The power of the Lord was present in his word, both to wound and to heal. The adversary roared in the midst of the congregation; for to him, and not to the God of order, do I impute those horrible outcries which almost drowned my voice, and kept back the glad tidings from sinners.'[32] Note the contrast between preachers involved in the Toronto Blessing and Charles Wesley: they assume it is of God; Charles Wesley knew that anything that hindered the gospel was of the devil.

Dallimore concludes his record of signs and wonders by saying, 'Nevertheless, during the short time that it lasted, the phenomenon served John Wesley's cause. Many people looked upon these experiences as an unmistakable sign of the supernatural — a demonstration of the mighty working of God — and viewing

Wesley as the one Divinely used channel of this power, they found him raised to extraordinary heights of esteem in their minds.'[33]

I cannot help drawing an application to our own day from this situation. John Arnott and others of the Toronto team, regardless of their own personal humility — which I have no reason to judge — have been placed on the Christian world stage as 'men of power, of signs and wonders', *not because of their preaching* but because of the *phenomena* attending their ministries. The same can be said of John Wimber's earlier ministry.

This Wesleyan approach to phenomena was allied with a promise of a second experience of grace. From this soil Pentecostalism and, eventually, Vineyardism germinated. Michael Haykin writes, 'Undoubtedly, Pentecostalism emerged from a theological matrix which owed its shape and structure to the theology of Wesley. But it is one thing to admit this indebtedness of Pentecostalism to Wesley's theology: it is quite another thing to argue that Wesley was a proto-Pentecostal.'[34] Wesley was not Pentecostal — but he was a fellow traveller! Meanwhile revival had been gripping America.

Jonathan Edwards

In the early years of the eighteenth century a number of men began to raise their voices in the American colonies against unconcern and lethargy in the churches. Scattered ingatherings of souls followed the labours of the Tennents, John Rowland and others in Pennsylvania and New Jersey. Gilbert Tennent reported 'signal displays of the Divine power and presence' as he preached 'much upon original sin, repentance, the nature and necessity of conversion' and the judgement of God.[35] (Note the summary of events during this period and the list of books written by Edwards in Appendix I.)

In Northampton, Massachusetts, a town of about 1000 people, Jonathan Edwards served as pastor. 'In 1734, fearing the growth of Arminianism, Edwards preached a series of sermons on "Justification by Faith Alone". This was followed by another on "God's absolute sovereignty in the salvation of sinners". Using such Scriptures as "I will have mercy on whom I will have mercy", and "That every mouth may be stopped",' he showed that God could justly cast off all unrepentant men.[36] He stressed the hellish peril of men unless God brought them to faith and repentance. The Holy Spirit began to powerfully touch people through his preaching.

Edwards comments, 'The work of *conversion* was carried on in a most *astonishing* manner, and increased more and more. Souls did, as it were, come by flocks to Jesus Christ.'[37] In half a year over 300 had been swept into the kingdom.

'He did not (as so many do today) "take every religious pang and enthusiastic conceit, for saving conversion"... He looked for evidence of a deep and abiding work of the Spirit of God in the heart ... a weighty conviction of sin, an utter rejection of all trust in things human, and finally, a very definite experience — that which he referred to as "a saving closure with Christ"... In many of these persons, so exalted was the view of Divine holiness and so black the concept of their own sinful hearts that they declared, "The glory of God would *shine bright* in their own condemnation." In this bitter sense of need they cried out to God for mercy.'[38]

Preaching that exalted God, warned of hell, probed the human heart and held out hope in conversion to Christ engaged the minds and hearts of Edwards' hearers. Distress of soul was deep and thorough. Joy followed, when those convicted discovered mercy. 'Their joyful surprise has caused their hearts as it were to leap so that they have been ready to break forth into laughter, tears often at the same time issuing like a flood, and intermingling a loud weeping, Sometimes they have not been able to forbear crying out with a loud voice, expressing their great admiration.'[39]

In his *Narrative of Surprising Conversions*, Edwards describes the spiritual ecstasy of many and stresses the genuine marks of conversion that followed: 'humility of mind, gentleness, self-control and prayerfulness'.[40]

Although the revival spread into other parts of Massachusetts and Connecticut, 'By the summer of 1735 the revival in the Northampton district began to lose its original force.'[41] Through the 1730s and into the first half of the 1740s, however, the devotion to spiritual things remained intense and widespread. In November 1739 George Whitefield arrived on one of his many visits to America to help spread the flame. He preached from New York in the north to Savannah in the south.

From 1736 onwards Edwards' wife Sarah enjoyed a remarkable sense of the glory of heavenly things. Contemplations of God as her loving Father, Christ as her Saviour and Lord, and of the Comforter filled her mind to overflowing with joy unspeakable and full of glory. These thoughts would overwhelm her, sometimes causing her to want to leap for joy and at others to sink down in weakness.

In a section in his *Some Thoughts concerning the Present Revival of Religion in New-England* (1743), Edwards, without naming her, detailed seventeen amazing days in her life.

Many in the Vineyard movement turn to these overwhelming experiences of Sarah Edwards to find precedent for what they experience. Guy Chevreau spends some time in his book on detailing her experiences. He believes that 'The expressions [used in Edwards' book to describe Sarah Edwards], "took away my bodily strength", "overbear the body", and "fainting" seem to be eighteenth-century equivalents to falling, resting and "slain" experiences at the Airport Vineyard.'[42] Mrs Eleanor Mumford in describing her experiences in Toronto mentions Sarah Edwards as having had 'intimate acquaintance with her carpet for 17 days'. She indicates that she was 'insensible' for this period and 'unable to get the meals' etc.[43]

Let me quote extensively from Sarah's experience to establish the fact that she was neither insensible during this time, nor flat out on the carpet, nor unable to talk; nor did her experiences parallel those seen in the Vineyard today. These events took place between 19 January and 4 February 1742.

We remained in the meeting house about three hours after the public exercises were over... *During most of the time my bodily strength was overcome and the joy and thankfulness*, which excited my mind, as I contemplated the great goodness of God, *led me to converse with those who were near me in a very earnest manner*.

[Later] the intenseness of my feelings again took away my bodily strength... I could with difficulty refrain from *rising from my seat and leaping for joy*.

[Thursday, 29 January]. My bodily strength was much weakened and it was *with difficulty that I could pursue my ordinary avocations*... About 11 o'clock [the next day], as I accidentally went into the room where Mr Buell was conversing with some people, I heard him say, "O that we, who are children of God, should be cold and lifeless in religion!" and I felt such a sense of the deep ingratitude manifested by the children of God, in such coldness and deadness, that my strength was immediately taken away, and I sunk down on the spot. Those who were near raised me and placed me in a chair and from the fullness of my heart I expressed to them in a very earnest manner, the deep sense I had of the wonderful grace of Christ towards me... At length my strength failed me and I sunk down, when they took me up and laid me on the bed where I lay for a considerable time, faint with joy, while contemplating the glories of the heavenly world... These anticipations [of the resurrection] were renewed over and over while I lay on the bed from twelve o'clock till about four, being too much exhausted by emotions of joy to rise and sit up; and *during most of the time my feelings prompted me to converse very earnestly with one and another* of the pious women who were present on those spiritual and heavenly objects of which I had so deep an impression. A little while before I arose, Mr Buell and the people went to meeting [italics mine].

Sarah Edwards' experiences of the wonder and glory of God were marvellous. Clearly, she was not insensible for seventeen days. She was not 'slain in the Spirit', or 'doing carpet time', for seventeen days. She remained conscious throughout. Even when most overpowered she talked earnestly with those around. Sometimes she wanted to leap up for joy. All this is hardly consistent with the Toronto Airport Fellowship experience of 'falling out' insensible for long periods of time.

Apparently, Sarah Edwards had a rich emotional nature. Jonathan Edwards explained that she 'had formerly ... been subject to unsteadiness and many ups and downs in the frame of mind, being under great disadvantages through a vaporous habit of body, and often subject to melancholy, and at time almost overborne with it, having been so even from early youth'. After 1742, 'Vapours have had great effects on the body, such as they used to have before, but the soul has always remained out of their reach.'[44]

Evidently, Edwards viewed these 'vapours', or faintings, as a disadvantageous aspect of his wife's constitution. While her soul remained full of the glory of Christ, her bodily weaknesses continued after the revival, as before. We cannot draw the inference that these physical manifestations were exclusively produced by the Holy Spirit. God met her in revival power — but she responded in accord with her own constitution and temperament.

This revival did produce bodily effects in some. I am not denying this. The question we must ask is whether such effects are an *essential part of revival*, or *incidental* side-effects that may or may not take place. What we have already seen about revival in England proves the latter. But even in the time of Edwards, some extremists began to substitute the *incidental effects* for the *essentials*. As the intensity of the revival abated, 'Some of the people ... looked upon such outcryings [the extreme emotional experiences that had occurred in some instances] as an essential feature of revival and developed the idea that the way to reawaken the revival fervour would be to make loud outcryings in the services. This became the practice in some locations in New England and in others in [New Jersey] — a practice similar to the self-induced paroxysms of the people of Bristol and Kingswood [under John Wesley].'[45]

In the early 1740s James Davenport of Long Island and Andrew Croswell of Connecticut began to assure 'individuals who either fell to the ground, or experienced bodily tremors, or saw visions during the preaching of God's Word that such experiences were a sure sign of the Spirit's converting work. In Croswell's words, only those who have had such "divine Manifestations ... know what true Holiness means". He asserted that "God never works powerfully, but men cry out disorder; for God's order differs vastly from their nice and delicate apprehensions" of him... Prominent also in Davenport's ministry was a devotion to loud, boisterous songs'[46] with questionable lyrics. There is certainly nothing new under the sun!

James Davenport and Andrew Croswell became leading figures among the group that was known as the 'New Light Prophets'. They thought they had rediscovered the supernatural spiritual gifts. They would fall '"to the ground, or experience bodily tremors, or see visions during the preaching of God's Word". Davenport claimed that he was given the gift to discern who were the elect of God. And like any other gift he sought to exercise it by going from town to town and splitting congregations that he stated had ministers leading them that were not Christian.'[47]

Davenport organized a crowd to burn Puritan books and taught that they had no need of books or the Bible since the Holy Spirit would teach all truth as predicted in John 16. Thousands followed his exhortations to walk by 'inner light'. When his extremism led Davenport to throw his clothes in the same fire that was burning the books, a bystander 'accused Davenport of having the "Devil in him"'. He was deeply convicted, accepted the charge and explained that he had been influenced by an evil spirit. He issued a series of retractions confessing his faults.[48]

Both Davenport and Croswell repudiated much of what they had said and done, but 'They had helped spark a "wild-fire" spirit, which in many places made havoc of the revival.'[49] The ammunition these men and others gave to critics of the revival led Edwards to write a series of treatises defending the revival and distinguishing the wheat from the chaff. 'Edwards himself was convinced that Davenport did more "towards giving Satan and those opposers [of the revival] an advantage against the work than any other person".'[50]

In a footnote, Iain Murray notes that 'These phenomena do not appear to have been present at the beginning of the Great Awakening. Thomas Prince remembered nothing of the kind under the preaching of Whitefield or Tennent.'[51]

In his first writings Edwards described and defended much of what happened. But in his later work, *A Treatise concerning Religious Affections,* he stated that 'Great effects on the body certainly are no sure evidences' that 'the affections' come from God, 'for we see such effects oftentimes arise from great affections about temporal things, and when religion is in no way concerned.'[52] That is exactly the point I am trying to make! People can be overwhelmed by football games, or the Northern Lights, or the death of a spouse.

Guy Chevreau takes up over a quarter of his whole book *Catch the Fire* to describing phenomena in the Great Awakening and Edwards' evaluation of them. Chevreau tries to prove that the manifestations occurring in Toronto are similar to those that Edwards knew. A few may bear some distant resemblance, but identity is missing. He also tries to use Edwards to warn those who are slow about accepting this 'renewal' to beware of fighting against God. He claims that Edwards would have no problem with the Toronto Blessing. Much of what Chevreau says is accurate if taken in isolation. However, it is incomplete and unbalanced because it fails to give proper credence to Edwards' own statements about the phenomena. Nor does it take into account what was happening across the Atlantic in England.

James Beverley in his book, *Holy Laughter and The Toronto Blessing*, points out the errors in Chevreau's thesis: 'Many of the manifestations connected with The Toronto Blessing were *not* experienced during Edwards' day. Likewise, rounds of Holy Laughter did not interrupt his preaching! ... Chevreau's points here are misleading, not only about history, but also as a guide to the debate today... I suggest that Edwards' Calvinism, his high regard for intellectual and theological analysis, and his esteem for careful, biblical preaching would have led him to have some serious hesitations about Holy Laughter and The Toronto Blessing.'[53]

Iain Murray, in a review of Chevreau's book, commends him for his long chapter on Edwards. Then he raises a query. Chevreau claims to accept Edwards' point that 'Physical actions can never of themselves provide any proof of the power of the Spirit. But while asserting this, Guy Chevreau contradicts it by constructing his book very largely *around* the physical phenomenon. We fail to see how this is consistent with what he quotes from Edwards. If [the physical manifestations] ... are not *the* vital thing, why should they be given such prominence?'[54] Why do those involved in the Toronto Blessing continually insist that the manifestations do not matter that much while at the same time encouraging them?

As we have already seen, William DeArteaga, in his book *Quenching the Spirit*, is even further from the mark. He tries to use Edwards to support anti-Calvinist and anti-theological views. But Edwards was Calvinistic. He was a great preacher. He was one of the greatest theologians America has produced. And he clearly taught the cessation of the sign gifts. How DeArteaga can hope to use Edwards to defend views that Edwards himself strongly opposed defies reason!

Before we leave the subject of historical revivals, let me briefly mention two further outpourings of the Spirit that are much neglected by proponents of extraordinary manifestations.

2. The Second Great Awakening

Many of the English nonconformists (that is, those who did not conform to Anglicanism) had been passed over by the Great Awakening which began under Whitefield in Anglican circles. In 1784 John Ryland, an English Calvinistic Baptist pastor, received a copy of Edwards' *Humble Attempt*, written to promote prayer for revival. This led Ryland, with Andrew Fuller and John Sutcliff, to begin a concert of prayer in the English midlands. This in turn led to revival that lasted from the 1780s to about the 1820s among the nonconformists, including the Calvinistic Baptists. Stagnant congregations were revitalized and the modern missionary movement was born. William Carey went to India in 1792. Like earlier revivalists these men preached the Word and did not seek supernatural gifts of the Spirit. Haykin writes that the revival in the Calvinistic Baptist denomination occurred 'with remarkably few of the unusual manifestations which occurred in the early years of the Evangelical Revival [the Great Awakening)'.[55]

Iain Murray in his work, *Revival and Revivalism: The Making and Marring of American Evangelicalism*, points out in chapters 5 and 6 that the Second Great Awakening lasted much longer than the first — spanning a period of twenty-five to thirty years, as opposed to the four to five years covered by the earlier awakening. It also reached far more people and remained largely clear of phenomena such as faintings. Unfortunately much less is known about this revival.

We do know that, on the whole, its leaders were Calvinistic and believed in the cessation of the miraculous gifts. John Ryland preached that the gift of tongues has ceased, that there is 'no inseparable connection between the gifts and holiness', since the former are not evidences of salvation, while the fruits of the Spirit are. He 'regularly drew a contrast between the extraordinary gifts of the Spirit and his "ordinary (or sanctifying) influences". "The ordinary influences of the Holy Spirit are of far more importance to the individuals who partake of them, than his extraordinary gifts; that is, it is far better to be a saint than a prophet; better to be made holy, than to be inspired; better to be directed into the love of God, than into the knowledge of futurity."'[56]

Michael Haykin points out that while William Carey, the pioneer missionary, did not deny that unusual phenomena such as visions could occur, he maintained that they constituted no proof of genuine faith. 'Real religion' consists of 'repentance, faith, obedience, submission, zeal and consolation'.[57]

3. The Third Great Awakening — the prayer revival

In 1857-58 a spontaneous awakening occurred that spread throughout denominations in America and across the ocean. Iain Murray notes that J. Edwin Orr, the great student of revivals, believed that this awakening was the most thorough and wholesome movement ever known in the Christian church. Evidently, there were no revivalists and no revival machinery such as the 'anxious seat', which was soon to be introduced, to manipulate people into a state of professed revival.[58] Again we have much less information about this awakening, probably due to the fact that there were fewer great names associated with it.

4. Charles G. Finney (1792-1875) and modern revivalism

Some in the Vineyard view Finney as the greatest revival preacher of history. Jackson says he 'was one of the most powerful revivalists since the reformation'.[59] Jackson notes that while preaching in a place called Sodom in New York State, Finney found that after a short time, 'The congregation began to fall from their seats in every direction, and cried for mercy... Nearly the whole congregation were either on their knees or prostrate... Similar scenes were witnessed in many other places.'[60]

Iain Murray does not share this high opinion of Finney. Previous to Finney, the view that revival was a supernatural and sovereign intervention of God prevailed. In a review of Murray's book on *Revival and Revivalism*, Dr Joel R. Beeke summarizes Murray's analysis: 'It argues persuasively that most revivals in America were largely Spirit-wrought, Calvinistic, and sound in doctrine prior to the introduction in the 1820's and 1830's of "new measures" (such as the anxious seat and protracted meetings) designed to promote revivalism and "conversions". Charles Finney is viewed as the major catalyst who led America's major denominations from God-centred revivals to a "revivalism" grounded on human methodology and instrumentality.'

In Finney we see the full flowering of an Arminian break with Calvinist dependence on God alone. Murray underscores what we have already seen in our historical survey of revivals. He asserts that before 1830 revival was usually defined as 'a sovereign and large giving of the Spirit of God, resulting in the addition of many to the kingdom of God'.[61] Revivals could not be produced, since God brought them. Murray then distinguishes between 'revivals' and 'revivalism'. Revivalism from this time forward originated in the planning and promotion of men. Methods became more and more manipulative. A theology of conversion developed that embraced the Arminian teaching on the freedom of the human will. The depravity of man and the sovereignty of God were downplayed.

With conversion now viewed as an event in a meeting, 'The secret of a successful revival was to appeal to the reason, intellect and emotions of the individual. Thus conviction resulting from the preaching of God's Law was increasingly replaced with guilt-manipulation, emotional outbursts and appealing to the individual will. Sinful men could now be saved on their own terms, with a simplified gospel watered down for the masses.'[62]

How foreign this new approach to conversion was may be judged by Dallimore's comments on Whitefield: 'It must be explained that Whitefield made no appeal for people to make a public profession of salvation at his services. His practice (which had also been that of the Puritans) was one of making powerful application of the Gospel as he preached and of therewith leaving the Word to become operative in the heart by the ministry of the Holy Spirit. He looked for the Spirit's work in arousing the sinner to deep, and even overwhelming, sense of his need, but this work he called, not *conversion*, but *awakening*.' Many awakened souls came to him in private. 'In these interviews he taught that the illumination of the mind and the implanting of faith in the heart are entirely the work of the Holy Spirit. He urged the seeker to go directly to the Lord ... [with] Gospel promises.'[63]

Since Finney viewed revival as something that could be engineered, it is no surprise to find several chapters in his book, *Revivals of Religion*, devoted to describing how to promote a revival.[64] One of his sermons was entitled 'Make yourself a new heart'. He described how by a decision of the will, anyone could be converted. Murray observes, 'By asserting that man's only problem was his will, Finney had put himself among the Pelagians who denied the reality of man's fallen nature.'[65] Augustine, believing man to be dead in sins, had debated with Pelagius, who believed man had the moral and spiritual ability to change. While Augustine held Pelagius at bay as a heretic, by the time Finney had concluded his campaigns the Semi-Pelagians had taken over the camp!

As a result the churches were inundated with 'converts' who might not be 'converts', whose understanding of the gospel was limited and whose focus was on their own inner subjective experience. The foundation began to erode quickly. 'After Revivalism, religion increasingly became a matter of mystic imagination. Some Presbyterians (e.g., Hodge, Warfield, Machen) would fight a long and valiant rearguard action, but experience, rather than truth, became the centre of American Christianity.'[66] Is it any wonder that thinking Christians today view American Christianity as 3,000 miles wide and a fraction of inch deep?

The Vineyard movement is following in the logical footsteps of John Wesley and Charles Finney, and now has gone far beyond them. It has no affinity with Luther, the Puritans, Edwards, or George Whitefield. No wonder phenomena are so important and doctrine so irrelevant in the movement. Let me summarize some of the divergencies we have traced.

Contrasts between the great revivals and Vineyard practice

1. Reformed not Arminian

Up to the mid-1800s, all the great men God used were reformed in their faith with the exception of the Moravians, the Lutheran pietists and John Wesley. Wesley helped to foster the Arminianism that has become the majority view of the modern church. (By the reformed faith or Calvinism is meant Pauline theology as revived by Augustine, Luther, Calvin and the Puritans, among others. This interpretation of biblical faith is often called Calvinism, not because John Calvin originated it, but because he was one of its greatest systematizers.) These men preached the great doctrines of Scripture with a passion for the glory of God. By contrast, the present Vineyard movement and the Toronto Blessing, as we shall see in a chapter to follow, devalue doctrine and play down the importance of preaching.

2. Spontaneous not programmed

God sovereignly and spontaneously brought revivals to birth. The reliance on the Holy Spirit of the men involved is evident in their open invitation to sinners to repent without calling them to come forward. The invitation system, introduced later by Finney and others, was unknown.

All the reformed preachers followed this same pattern. They left the field free from human manipulation to allow God to work a genuine work of grace. By contrast, those involved in the current 'renewal' depend heavily on people knowing ahead of time how they should react, in calling people to come forward and line up, and in laying hands on seekers. Response is programmed. This manipulative process leaves little room for the spontaneity of the Holy Spirit.

3. Conviction preceding bliss

In the early stages of these revivals the Word penetrated so deeply that people fell under a profound sense of conviction. When they came through this, some taking more time than others, they burst out into a sense of the joy of Christ, of sins forgiven, of justification, of peace with God. They felt as if the sun had risen to shine in their hearts after a dark night of terror. By contrast, in the current 'renewal' we find conviction almost completely bypassed by the 'happy phenomena'. It is called a 'laughing revival'. How can people know real joy without experiencing heart-rending conviction?

4. Christ not phenomena

Physical phenomena, such as shaking, falling or crying, did not occur in the Third Awakening. They occurred only rarely in the First and Second Awakenings. George Whitefield and Charles Wesley discouraged them. John Wesley encouraged phenomena until events got out of hand. Fairly early in the Northampton revival under Edwards, physical phenomena did occur. In his later writings, however, Edwards laments the excesses that began to multiply and seriously discounts the value of external phenomena as any kind of credible mark of revival.

Phenomena related to deep conviction, such as weeping, crying out or even falling down, were usually accepted as genuine. Similarly, the profound joy that accompanies conversion created praise and even ecstasy — so much so, that sometimes people were overcome. Unfortunately, very quickly people seem to be drawn to mimicking these outward marks. For this reason, the great revivalists almost universally recognized that phenomena are unreliable indices of revival.

History shows that the devil quickly seeks to blunt the force of revival by introducing carnality and wildfire of one kind or another. In England John Wesley was swept away by the phenomena. Charles Wesley listed a number of cases where people put on the phenomena to draw attention to themselves. Whitefield concluded, 'All inner impressions must be tried by "the unerring rule of God's most holy word", and if found incompatible, rejected as "diabolical and delusive."'[67] In America, Davenport and Croswell introduced wildfire into the movement until they recanted.

In his *Treatise concerning Religious Affections*, published in 1741, Edwards listed five indispensable marks of a true work of God:

1. That the esteem of people for Jesus as the Son of God and Saviour of the world is raised;

2. That it moves them to turn away from sin towards holiness and moral excellence;

3. That it increases their love for the Holy Scriptures;

4. That it grounds them in the basic truths of the faith — 'Gracious affections arise from the mind being enlightened, rightly and spiritually to understand or apprehend divine things';

5. That it provokes greater love for God and his people and a desire to serve them.[68]

On at least three of these points, numbers 3, 4 and 5, the Toronto Blessing is seriously flawed.

Edwards also listed a number of marks that could *not* be used to either disprove or prove that a revival was a work of God. I have listed these 'no-signs', as he called them, in Appendix II.

History shows us that the encouragement of phenomena, the gift of revelatory prophecy and signs and wonders leads to confusion and carnality. The focus must be on the truths that set forth the glory of God in the face of Jesus Christ, our Lord, Master and reigning King. Unfortunately, the Vineyard movement promotes the very things that leave them open to serious delusion and promote carnal mimicry.

5. The cessation of sign gifts — not their recovery

With the exception of John Wesley and a few others, the leaders of the revivals believed in the cessation of the supernatural gifts, including prophecy. In describing his own wife's unusual experiences, Edwards very carefully asserted that she never showed an 'enthusiastic disposition to follow impulses, or any supposed prophetical revelations'. Edwards insisted that the Spirit of God always leads believers to view the Scriptures as 'the great and standing rule for the direction of his church in all religious matters, and all concerns of their soul, in all ages'. Enthusiasts, on the other hand, 'depreciate this written rule, and set up the light within or some other rule above it'.[69]

6. Wildfire within, not critics without, hinders a revival

As already noted in chapter 5, on quenching the Spirit, DeArteaga claims that Edwards believed that pharisaical critics outside the movement stopped the revival. He also asserts that the Calvinism of men like Chaucy hindered the work. However, Chaucy tended towards Arminianism, not Calvinism. He became Unitarian.

Iain Murray, in his scholarly new work on Edwards, writes that 'He [Edwards] came to believe that there was one principal cause of reversal, namely, the unwatchfulness of the friends of the Awakening who allowed genuine and pure religion to become so mixed with "wildfire" and carnal "enthusiasm" that the Spirit of God was grieved and the advantage given to Satan.'[70] In 1741 he spoke in rather general terms about the devil's work of introducing confusion but writing in 1742 he recognized the clear hand of Satan in hindering the current revival. He said, 'If we look back into the history of the church of God in past ages, we may observe that it has been a common device of the devil to overset a revival of religion; when he finds he can keep men quiet and secure no longer, then he drives them to excesses and extravagances … indiscreet zeal of Christians, to drive them into those three extremes of *enthusiasm, superstition,* and *severity toward opposers*; … in a time of revival of religion, his main strength shall be tried with the friends of it; … to mislead them.'[71]

The physical manifestations, boisterous music, lack of preaching and avoidance of doctrine that are associated with the Toronto Blessing are the very things that the devil used in other contexts and eras to destroy revival. The view of revival being accepted in Vineyard and Toronto Blessing circles is a pattern that finds no parallel in the great revivals of history. The danger the evangelical church faces is that this shift in emphasis will further insulate people from the genuine heaven-sent conviction that produces real revival.

The counsel of Dr Martyn Lloyd-Jones is severe. After examining revivals in history and studying Jonathan Edwards' conclusions about the Great Awakening, he writes, 'The phenomena should not be sought, they should not be encouraged, they should not be boasted… We must not seek phenomena and strange experiences... Anyone who tries to work up phenomena is a tool of the Devil, and is putting himself into the position of the psychic, and the psychological.'[72]

The dangers are multiplied, for not only do leaders of the Toronto Blessing promote the physical phenomena but they exhort people to empty their minds to receive them!

11.
Divine disorder or cultivated chaos?

An appeal to church history, like an appeal to Scripture, is unlikely to impress the enthusiastic apologists of the Toronto phenomena. In the view of many in the movement, a commitment to an orderly review of Scripture and history strikes them as a fetish — a fetish that hinders the freedom of the Spirit. Instead we are urged to just relax our critical faculties and open our minds to whatever happens. The result is often chaos.

Indeed, disorder and the surrender of self-control characterize this movement. Frequent references to being 'drunk in the Spirit' demonstrate that irrational behaviour is admired. Strange! From reading the Bible and observing nature, one would assume it to be self-evident that God is a God of order who teaches us self-control.

Those who have 'soaked in the Spirit' explain their chaotic actions in various ways. Even John Wimber defended the movement by comparing it to having a baby: 'The birthing of a child is a messy experience at best. Not many people want to hear about that part. The same thing applies to revival ... going through the birthing process of a revival, is ... messy.'[1]

Ron Allen, founding pastor of the Fort Wayne Vineyard and a regional overseer for the Association of Vineyard Churches, was profoundly smitten at Toronto. He explains his bizarre behaviour: 'Our meetings are messy and a little scary, but then we've moved from the order of respectability to the order of anointing.'[2]

We certainly don't want to become the slaves of an empty, but well-ordered programme. And we must admit that busyness and a passion for planning and order can produce sterility. We need to continually seek the face of Christ with the passion exemplified by David: 'As the deer pants for streams of water, so my soul pants for you, O God' (Ps. 42:1). But, surely, we don't need to fight the evil of unfeeling order by going to the opposite extreme of emotional disorder. Enthusiasts in the movement, however, often urge those who seem reluctant: 'Let yourself go.' Those who fail to manifest physical signs are designated as having the HTR condition — that is, 'Hard To Receive'. Is this not the same resistance that hypnotists encounter in some members of a given population?

Comments such as these illustrate the serious anti-intellectualism endemic to the movement. Supporters of the 'blessing' frequently assert the priority of feelings over understanding by repeating their mantra, 'God reveals the heart by offending the mind.'[3] This is another form of the old rubric, 'It's better felt than telt.'

Back in Argentina in November 1993 Claudio Freidzon, head of the Pentecostal Assemblies of God there, prayed for John and Carol Arnott. 'Carol went flying.' John fell down but began to analyse things and question what and why. He claims that he was not really 'empowered with God's anointing' until he 'dialled out a lot of analysis and said, "I don't care, I'm just going to take what God has to give." Something clicked in his heart at that moment... John realised then that there is a faith component.'[4]

Faith in what?

'Faith comes by hearing, and hearing by the Word of God' (Rom. 10:17, NKJV). Notice the progression here. John Arnott and others in the movement urge people to accept manifestations by faith. Faith in what? Not the Bible! We have already seen that there is no biblical precedent for these phenomena. No, it is faith in what Rodney Howard-Browne, Randy Clark, John Arnott and a host of others say about bizarre phenomena. It is faith in an experience that others have had. It is faith in the charismatic paradigm. This is really extrabiblical faith — a leap in the dark. It may be warm and cosy to experience what others of one's group experience, but is it of God? Well, surely one should pray for God to reveal his will?

What about prayer?

But no, according to John Arnott, it is better not to pray. Speaking at Holy Trinity in Brompton, England, Arnott sought to prepare people for 'ministry time', when chairs would be stacked and they would form lines to 'do carpet time'. He said, 'Another thing that hinders is, people pray all the time... Our experience is, that will hinder substantially your ability to receive... Pray on the way out; you can pray later. Don't take control; you can take control later. The whole deal is, you lose control, he takes control. He gets you out of your comfort zone, makes you feel vulnerable, right? You can analyse it later, can't you?'[5]

On another occasion John Arnott commented about what those may say who are reluctant to be open to the phenomena: '"Yeah, but I don't like the way he fell and shook and got stuck to the floor and everything!" Listen! Who cares whether he did or he didn't? Who cares? If he *thinks* it's God and he *likes* it, let him enjoy it! Because you can test the fruit later.'[6]

Is it rational?

Those who appeal for people to be open to the phenomena say things like, 'You can't explain this out of the Bible. He's chosen the foolish things of the world to confound the wise ... the world despises it when we lose control. The world loves intelligence. The world worships intelligence. And God is in the business today of bypassing our minds and doing something that cannot be explained in rational terms. And it offends the mind.'[7]

This anti-intellectual stance has become so entrenched in the movement that 'prophets' such as Bob Jones, of Kansas City, along with James Ryle and Wes Campbell, have brought prophecies predicting a future war between two groups of Christians — the 'blue coats and the grey coats'. The blue coats stand for those who believe in ongoing revelation — the Vineyard movement particularly. The grey coats represent other evangelicals, who they believe are stuck in a theological time-warp generated by their understanding of the Word of God. The 'grey coats' are infected by 'the wisdom of the world'. Wes Campbell stated, 'And in this context the north fought the south and the south fought the north, and the south wanted to keep people enslaved... As this becomes known throughout the entire Christian community of the world, there will come a polarization ... wars in your household... We're talking about Christians.'[8]

At this point in his 'prophecy' Campbell's wife, Stacey, came up to predict a great division in the church. She foresaw a time when Vineyard adherents would be accused of being cultic. (Such a warning is certainly the way most cults start!) Wes Campbell concluded his prophecy by warning, 'Do not allow your ears, do not allow your hearts to be turned to those that would say unto you "Be reasonable! Be rational! This is not logical." I say unto you, the natural man receiveth not the things of the Spirit of God, for they are foolishness to him.'[9]

With a bold stroke of 'prophecy' all those who question the movement are categorized as natural men ignorant of the realities of the Holy Spirit, blinded as they are by their own worldly wisdom! With a broad broom they sweep away two millennia of Christian scholarship. They equate spirituality with being irrational, un-reasonable and illogical! How should we answer such claims?

Intellect and experience

We need to admit that words can blind us to the truths and realities behind them. Knowing biblical truth intellectually is no guarantee that we experience it. Too many play with theological words while leading lives empty of passionate experience. But let's not throw the baby of intelligence out with the bath water of defective experience. For godly experience is not conceived in the womb of an empty mind. We are nowhere exhorted to empty our minds and close our ears with the expectation that God will, willy-nilly, drop some marvellous experience into our laps. Jesus prayed, 'Sanctify them by the truth; your word is truth.' Experiential faith and joy and peace come into our hearts through a channel. That channel is excavated by the Spirit driving the bulldozer of Scripture through the clogged passages of our worldly psyches. Every time a real disciple listens to a good preacher or teacher expounding the Word, the weeds and muck of his fallen nature are scoured out a little more.

I do not question that we need to experience God and his gracious love more and more as the days go by. Peter urges us to taste and see that the Lord is good. But this taste only comes to those who 'desire the sincere milk of the word that [they] may grow thereby'. The milk is offered to us in the glass (tumbler) of Holy Writ. The role Scripture plays in mediating genuine experience has already been established.

The appeal of proponents of 'the blessing' to become open and absolutely submissive to the Spirit is fine as far as it goes. Paul in Romans 12:1 urges this very thing. But there is a vast difference between *opening* our minds and *emptying* our minds. In verse 2 of this chapter Paul urges us to present ourselves to God ready for transformation through the *renewing* of our minds, *not* the *emptying* of our minds.

The Lord Jesus portrays the danger of having an empty mind: 'When an evil spirit comes out of a man, it goes through arid places seeking rest and does not find it. Then it says, "I will return to the house I left." When it arrives, it finds the house unoccupied, swept clean and put in order. Then it goes and takes with it seven other spirits more wicked than itself, and they go in and live there. And the final condition of that man is worse than the first. That is how it will be with this wicked generation' (Matt. 12:43-45). If we take this warning seriously, we must let our hearts become Christ's home and fill our minds with his words.

Astoundingly enough, the context leading up to this passage speaks exactly to the Vineyard appeal. Leaders urge people to become empty in order to be ready to receive 'signs and wonders'. Christ states that a key problem of 'this wicked and adulterous generation' is that it 'asks for a miraculous sign'! Then he firmly responds: 'But none will be given it except the sign of the prophet Jonah' (Matt. 12:39). The real sign that transforms our lives is the Jonah-like resurrection of Christ as preached in the gospel.

Proponents of the Toronto Blessing seem to seriously misunderstand how God has created the human personality. They apparently believe that the intellect is to trail along behind the emotions. In reality, the mind, not the emotions, is the doorway to the soul. The sinner who understands the rudiments of the gospel and puts his faith in Christ as described in the gospel experiences salvation. Later, as the believer continues in the Word, the truths of justification by faith, and not works, the nature of regeneration and the atonement become the conduits through which the Spirit deepens his experience. The sanctified emotions of peace and joy follow a mind renewed by truth. Emotions are the guard's van, not the engine that drives the personality of redeemed sinners.

Dr Martyn Lloyd-Jones, in his book on revival rightly says, 'And if emotionalism is bad, how much worse is a deliberate attempt to produce it. So any effort which deliberately tries to work up the emotions, whether by singing, or incantation, or anything else, or as you get in primitive people, in various dances and things like that, all this, of course is just condemned by the New Testament. The mere playing on the emotions is never right. It is something which is condemned right through the Bible. The emotions are to be approached through the understanding, through the mind, by truth.'[10]

The foolishness of the cross

Their anti-intellectualism goes further, however. Leaders in the movement urge people to become foolish in order to understand the things of the Spirit. This reflects a serious misinterpretation of Paul's teaching in 1 Corinthians. In the first two chapters of this epistle Paul contrasts the wisdom and intelligence of the world with the wisdom of God centred in the cross. He appeals for the worldly wise to become what they view as foolish. How can they do this? By accepting and understanding the gospel. What the world views as foolishness is, in reality, the wisdom of God.

Paul contrasts what saved and unsaved men and women call wisdom and foolishness. Proponents of the Toronto Blessing use this passage in a completely different way. Their appeal boils down to asking those who are professing Christians, because of accepting 'the foolishness of the cross', to now become mindless in order to accept 'exotic' (to use Wimber's term) experiences. If a segment of the Christian church had a defective view of the cross we could legitimately appeal to them to become foolish enough to accept it, but this is not the way they use the passage. Unfortunately the cross is almost invisible in their emphasis. Would that they would become 'foolish' in this Pauline sense!

Since this passage is used so frequently in support of the experiences of exotic phenomena, let me rehearse Paul's argument in 1 Corinthians 1 and 2. From verse 17 of chapter 1, Paul asserts that God sent him to 'preach the gospel — not with words of human wisdom, lest the cross of Christ be emptied of its power. For the message of the cross is foolishness to those who are perishing,' although 'The foolishness of God is wiser than man's wisdom' (1:17-18,25). Two kinds of wisdom and two kinds of foolishness are in view: that of worldly, unsaved, perishing men; and that of God.

Paul asserts that God will 'destroy the wisdom of the wise; the intelligence of the intelligent I will frustrate' (1:19), meaning the unredemptive ideas and philosophies that look upon salvation through the cross as foolishness. There is no appeal here to become stupid, to empty our minds or to stop thinking. If this was the appeal, what would we do with the book of Proverbs and the rest of Scripture? Indeed, why is Paul engaging our minds on such a high level to understand his argument?

Humility in accepting the scandalous message of the cross is required. Paul explains that it was for this reason that 'God chose the foolish things of the world to shame the wise... He chose the lowly ... the despised... so that no one may boast before him' (1: 27-29).

Paul's whole point is that 'I resolved to know nothing while I was with you except Jesus Christ and him crucified' (2:2). There is nothing in the context about *acting* foolishly, by barking like a dog, or being 'slain in the Spirit', or 'soaking in the Spirit'. The cross is the focus. This emphasis is sadly missing from meetings I have attended and material that I have read.

Paul then goes on to clarify his meaning further: 'We do, however, speak a message of wisdom among the mature, but not the wisdom of this age... No, we speak of God's secret wisdom' (2:6,7). The apostle explains that this secret 'cross-centred wisdom' is our glory. We rejoice in the cross — the instrument of our redemption. Had the Jewish rulers possessed this 'cross-wisdom' it would have kept them from crucifying Christ. But no one can understand this 'cross-wisdom' without the Spirit. Fortunately all believers have received the Spirit, 'that we may *understand* what God has freely given us. This is what we speak, not in words taught us by human wisdom but in words taught by the Spirit, expressing spiritual truths in spiritual words' (2:12-13).

Notice that the Spirit within us, far from expecting us to empty our minds, enhances our *understanding* so that we may appreciate what we have in Christ. Here is the correct order: understanding producing experience. An empty mind cannot produce an experience that will mystically impart understanding of God. Paul presents the gospel message in words, as the software God uses to revolutionize and run our muddled minds. God always uses our minds to help us appreciate the glory of the cross. 'Renewal' services, where there is such a paucity of teaching, preaching and Scripture reading and an overabundance of shallow choruses, with little or no mention of the cross, stand in stark contrast to Paul's practice.

Yielding control, no control and self-control

The exhortation to empty one's mind also carries with it the urge to yield up control of one's personality. As already noted, John Arnott counsels people not even to pray: 'Pray on the way out; you can pray later. Don't take control; you can take control later. The whole deal is, you lose control, he takes control.'

It is certainly valid to urge believers to yield control to Christ. But what does that mean? Christ explained in John chapters 13-16 that yielding to him means that 'If you love me, you will obey what I command... Whoever has my commands and obeys them, he is the one who loves me' (John 14:15,21). To *do* what he commands, we have to 'have' what he commands in our minds. We must *know* what he commands. In other words, yielding means a commitment to seek to know and do the will of Christ as defined by what he has revealed in Scripture. This in turn produces a profound experience: 'Whoever has my commands and obeys them, he is the one who loves me. He ... will be loved by my Father, and I too will love him and show myself to him' (John 14:21).

The process presented at the Toronto Airport Christian Fellowship, however, is quite different. In reality it is not yielding control to Christ that is urged. It is yielding up the control of one's mind and faculties so that one becomes 'out of control'. In this state one becomes open to whatever kind of bizarre physical phenomena may be occurring at the time. Leaders are really exhorting people to short-circuit their normal self-control mechanisms.

Abandoning self-control in this way is totally unbiblical for the following reasons:

> 1. One of the main purposes of the book of Proverbs is to equip us with the wisdom we need to be able to control our baser urges. Sin occurs when we yield to our over-extended desires, or lusts, in the heat of temptation (see James 1:14-15). Wisdom fortifies us against breaches in our self-control through which evil pours into our personalities: 'Like a city whose walls are broken down is a man who lacks self-control' (Prov. 25:28).

2. Along with love, self-control is one of the most important evidences of the Spirit's work in us (see Gal. 5:22-23). Everything in the universe manifests the Creator's pattern and order. Confusion, randomness, chaos and disorder are marks of the Fall. So are carelessness and lawlessness. God is a God of order, not chaos. To ask us to be open to *anything* that may happen, including chaos and disorder, is to ask us to turn our backs on everything we know about the God of the Bible.

3. This appeal is also contrary to discipleship. The Fall marred our personalities. God saves us in order to restore his image in us. The Holy Spirit undertakes this restoration process by conforming us to the image of Christ (2 Cor. 3:18). This process is called sanctification. Sanctification occurs as the Holy Spirit renews our darkened minds. He uses the light of Scripture to enlighten those gloomy recesses of thought. The renewed mind, in turn, directs the heart and will to apply this new light to the practical issues of daily life.

4. This process of developing maturity involves putting on the whole armour of God — a series of disciplines and endowments that have been recognized throughout church history by godly men and women. It involves becoming more self-controlled by putting to death the deeds of the body.

What proponents of the Toronto Blessing seem to be asking us to do is to go the opposite way: to stop thinking; to stop praying; to empty our minds; to become open to anything. How dangerous! One just has to ask oneself, 'Would Christ have adopted these measures? If he were here today would he ask us to act like animals, to laugh hysterically, to fall on the floor, to stagger around drunkenly?' The scenario is so foreign to everything we see of Christ in the Scriptures that it becomes blasphemous. One can imagine Muslim dervishes and Hindu sadhus and African witch-doctors making such requests, but not the Lord Jesus Christ.

Now, I admit that, on a personal level, God does stop us in our tracks by bringing trials, sicknesses and persecution into our lives to mature us or humble us. God has many ways of humbling us and training us. But asking us to go through, on a congregational level, what the Toronto Vineyard goes through at each meeting seems totally foreign to anything we read of God's ways.

A woman who had received the Toronto Blessing and who became a part of the 'ministry team' in a US church wrote about her experience. She recounted how her intoxication with the exotic phenomena eroded her spiritual restraints. Eventually, she fell into sexual sin. She watched her carefully nurtured Christian life fall apart until she became more 'unholy and unclean' than she had ever been. Her spiritual struggle back to the point where she could again lead a disciplined Christian life has been long and painful. She wrote, 'I can't understand why Christian leaders don't speak out about the danger of the Toronto Blessing.'[11]

Is it demonic?

It is for this reason — the emptying of minds — that some conjecture that the Toronto Blessing opens up the way for demonic activity. I would not personally class it as demonic. I think the leaders have convinced themselves that they are doing what God wants them to do. I think they are sincere, but wrong. I foresee disastrous long-term effects of this movement. People caught up in the Toronto Blessing leave themselves open to all kinds of weird and strange ideas and practices. Satan will certainly take advantage of any opportunity to spread confusion and distortion. The woman whose letter I just quoted mentions 'coming under an alien influence'.

The claims and prophecies put forward are becoming more mystical and magical as time goes on. In a recent meeting I attended, a prophecy by Howard-Browne was reiterated. He had prophesied that God would shortly be transporting people through the air. In one of his meetings Howard-Browne had gently chided some who were making a lot of noise by saying, 'How are you going to take it when God begins to transport people? If God transported some of you from one city to another, you'd scream all the way to your destination.'[12]

A hoped-for toning down of the more bizarre phenomena may not materialize. Toronto 'prophet' Marc Dupont has been reported as saying that 'The church has seen nothing yet and that there is going to be an even wilder sense of abandonment in worship.'[13]

Dr Martyn Lloyd-Jones, who wrote long before the Toronto Blessing, gives some advice in his book *Revival* that seems almost prophetic. He warns us about quenching the Spirit through fear of spontaneity or enthusiasm. Then he balances this warning by the caution: 'There are genuine Christian people, who ... regard confusion as a hallmark of Christianity, and feel that unless they are all shouting together at the same time, the Spirit is not present. But it is sheer confusion. So they need to read 1 Corinthians 14... "The spirits of the prophets are subject to the prophets" ... And as long as a man can control himself he must do so... Excitement, or a false sense of joy ... can be purely of the flesh.'[14]

12.
Theology —
modern whipping boy

The Toronto Blessing has sent the evangelical world a clear signal that doctrine hinders the freedom of the Spirit. This is the inevitable fruit of the anti-intellectualism documented in the previous chapter. In my first attendance at the Toronto Vineyard the speaker urged us to 'let God out of your theological boxes'.[1] Evidently this is typical. James Beverley, who has attended Toronto Airport meetings at least thirty times, comments, 'Proponents of The Toronto Blessing frequently complain about the theological traditions that put God in a box.'[2] This idea that evangelical theology is a strait-jacket that limits God pervades the whole Vineyard movement.

John Wimber's views on doctrine

While speaking on the healing of the paralysed man in Luke 5:18-24, John Wimber comments about the Pharisees: 'Jesus, knowing their hearts, said, "Why are you thinking evil in your heart?" ... I remember when the Lord spoke that word to my heart it was like an arrow in my heart. I said, "Lord they're not thinking evil... *They're just operating under sound doctrine...* These men aren't thinking evil; these men were under doctrine; they were under a dispensation; they were under the Old Testament. They're not being evil, Lord." But you see, it's evil when you don't recognize God. It's evil when you don't see Jesus in the things that are going on. It's evil when you hide behind doctrinal beliefs that curtail and control the work of the Spirit. It's evil when you don't recognize the Lord of glory in the work He's doing.'[3]

From these statements, made in 1981, it would appear that John Wimber fostered an idea that has become prevalent in the movement. The impression is projected that traditional evangelicals routinely hide behind sound doctrine in an effort to shield themselves from the works of the Spirit.

John Wimber's fluid approach to doctrine gave him the flexibility to develop his views on healing, prophecy and miracles as he went along. Dr Don Lewis of Regent College quotes him as saying, 'We are cataloguing all of our experiences so we can develop a theology.'[4] One wonders why Wimber would jettison twenty centuries of evangelical scholarship to strike out on his own.

Lewis, in a paper written in June 1985, questioned Wimber's anti-intellectualism. 'His insistence that "At some point critical thinking must be laid aside" is nothing less than dangerous. Wimber several times equated critical thinking with unbelief, and his apparent inability to distinguish the two is most disturbing.'[5] This anti-intellectualism discounts the importance of doctrine.

Lewis continues, 'At one point he asked: "When are we going to see a generation who doesn't try to understand this book [the Bible], but just believes it?" In effect, this is saying, "When are we going to see a generation that believes my interpretation of this book without question?" This anti-intellectual strain which shows through in Wimber is typical of nineteenth-century American revivalism and is just the sort of thing that evangelicalism has been trying to live down in the twentieth century. It disparages God's gracious gift of our mind and reflects ill on a Creator who chose to endow us with the ability to think critically.'[6]

Apparently, Wimber does not favour being bound by the body of doctrine that has historically guided the church, but he does want the freedom to develop his own doctrine. This approach has fostered the adoption by the movement as a whole of an experience-centred frame of reference that is presented in such a way as to itself become a dogma.

A similar approach on the part of the charismatic movement caused many to leave. One of them, G. Thomas Morton, wrote about some of the frustrations which led to their decision to quit the movement: 'Doctrinal errors, private and corporate, convince many of us that we must cease emphasizing these doctrines and experiences such as the baptism in the Spirit until changes are made... Another hallmark of the charismatic renewal has been that of anti-intellectualism... Such anti-intellectualism comes from a false spirit/mind dichotomy... Irrationality then evolves into a virtue. More than once I have heard, "Worshipping God is great so long as you don't use your mind." ... Even though charismatics have said the emphasis is to be on experience, not doctrine (1 Cor. 4:20), the experiential lifestyle usually is advocated dogmatically.'[7]

John Wimber and the Vineyard movement are recycling the same errors that caused many to become disillusioned with the charismatic movement. Now I realize that the Vineyard movement subscribes to a basically evangelical doctrinal statement. They affirm belief in the Trinity, the Scriptures, the deity and atonement of Christ, the sinfulness of man, the church and its two ordinances, salvation by grace, etc. From its beginning, however, the movement has nurtured a disparaging attitude towards doctrine. This has left them with a frayed link to the Christian fundamentals, while fostering a naïve acceptance of whatever experience happens to come along. In turn, others in the movement have become even less committed to doctrine than Wimber.

A selection of Vineyard statements

William DeArteaga, author of *Quenching the Spirit,* a book much heralded in the Vineyard, has said that 'We may be experiencing something that later on we may have a more sophisticated explanation for. That we don't have all the answers right now. Let it happen, don't be doctrinaire as to why it happens.'[8]

In mid-February 1994 Guy Chevreau looked around at the bodies all over the floor and commented to a new friend: 'All this makes apple sauce of a fellow's theological apple carts.'[9]

Chevreau wrongly equates Paul's Damascus Road conversion to the transformation that takes place when an evangelical seminary professor experiences the Toronto Blessing. Of Paul he says, 'He was the equivalent of a tenured position at the local seminary, his theology was circumscribed and systematic; he knew what he knew, and he knew what wasn't of God when he saw it ... until he got knocked off his high horse. The manifest presence of Christ undid him thoroughly!'[10]

Chevreau fails to emphasize that Paul was a non-Christian Jewish scholar with a false doctrinal view of salvation and the

Messiah. Erroneously, he chooses to use Paul's Damascus Road experience to illustrate the supposed change that comes over an evangelical theologian when he experiences 'the blessing'. But Paul's experience was conversion, not something like the Toronto Blessing, which is supposed to happen to people who are already saved. As a result of that conversion Paul became the systematic theologian *par excellence* of the early church. True conversion produces a love affair with truth in both its doctrinal and experiential dimensions. The Vineyard movement, by its stance, devalues the theological nature of Paul's subsequent epistles and fails to emphasize the terrible errors he had previously held as a Pharisee.

William DeArteaga has claimed that a concern for doctrinal purity, as manifest in Calvinism, hindered the revival under Jonathan Edwards. Why this vendetta against theology? Because, like so many in the movement, he fails to see that scriptural theology and doctrinal preaching contribute to the yearnings of the soul that feed genuine revival. Totally missing the point he says, 'Calvinist theology could not interpret the spiritual experiences that were to accompany the Great Awakening.'[11]

As established in chapters 9 and 10, this statement betrays a complete misunderstanding of the role of Calvinist theology in promoting and inspiring the Reformers and the revivalists. Obviously, the negative connotations which have become attached to the word 'Calvinism' keep him from realizing that it is only a name for the stream of theological thought that flows from Christ through Paul to Augustine and John Calvin. Calvin's name has come to be attached to it because he was a great systematizer of doctrine, not because he formulated novel doctrines. Assuming that Arminians and Pentecostals have a monopoly of discernment of the Spirit, he rashly comments that 'The reformers rejected the need for discernment when they threw out the whole of Catholic mystical theology.'[12] Is he advocating a return to indulgences, saints and relics? Or is he assuming, because the Catholics had a ritual of exorcism, that they truly discerned evil spirits?

This profound lack of understanding of doctrine and its development is also at the root of DeArteaga's claim that 'Calvin's expanded cessationism unintentionally destroyed the capacity for spiritual discernment in Reformed Protestantism,' and that this led directly to the destruction of Christianity in northern Europe.[13] Not only does he discount completely the penetrating discernment evident in reformers who probed the dark practices and beliefs of medieval Romanism to root out anything unbiblical, but no Reformers that I have read about rejected discernment, as *diakrino*, the ability to 'discriminate, discern, and hence to decide, to judge'.[14] It is precisely this faculty that we need today to evaluate the whole Vineyard movement. But what do we make of this aversion to doctrine?

Doctrine — beneficial gift of God or dangerous fabrication of man?

Unfortunately, in many Christian circles the theologian is *persona non grata*. Mental images of white-haired men consulting mouldy old tomes while they debate how many angels can dance on the head of a pin jaundice our view of theological learning.

The prevailing suspicion is so widespread that J. I. Packer piqued our interest by giving one of his books the intriguing title, *Hot Tub Religion*. Inside he further fans the reader's curiosity by entitling his first chapter, 'Danger! Theologian At Work'.[15] Only powerful curiosity can induce many of us to tackle a serious theological work.

But without theological moorings we are adrift in a sea of conflicting ideas without charts or compass, without any rudder and without any engine to give steerage. In the last few decades the voices of those who decry doctrine have become increasingly strident — and dangerous.

This period was predicted: 'The time will come when men will not put up with sound doctrine. Instead, to suit their own desires, they will gather around them a great number of teachers to say what their itching ears want to hear. They will turn their ears away from the truth and turn aside to myths' (2 Tim. 4:3-4). Clearly, sound doctrine fulfils a crucial function. It exposes urges that tempt us to substitute impressions and opinions for truth.

This is exactly where we are today. Liberals want to de-mythologize the Gospels. Kenneth Hagin tries to deify our humanity. Robert Schuller tries to de-Paulize the gospel with generous dollops of positive thinking. And the Vineyard seems to want to phenomenalize New Testament doctrine in order to baptize their own experiences, ideas and impressions with biblical legitimacy.

The idea that doctrine is the product of human ingenuity and subject to the ebb and flow of theological controversy is far from the truth. Doctrine is a gift of God. It basically means 'teaching' or 'truth'. Granted, theologians, teachers and preachers take what is revealed and arrange it systematically in order to present it simply and logically. But this is an honourable calling originating with the apostles, especially Paul — the great systemizer of truth. I admit that on secondary issues such as how we should worship, the details of the Second Coming, or church organization there are differences of opinion due to the lack of biblical specifics.

But our evaluation of the Vineyard involves much more crucial doctrinal issues than these. It concerns the sufficiency of Scripture, the nature of inspired prophecy, the role of the gospel in conversion, the depravity of man, the place of Christ and the preaching of the cross, the role of the Holy Spirit and the function of charismatic gifts — to name a few.

Let's look a little deeper at the role of doctrine. Truth sets us free (John 8:32). Truth sanctifies (John 17:17). Truth fosters genuine experience and exposes what is erroneous.

Concern for the future of the church led Paul to gather the Ephesian elders together so they could understand ministry. In Acts 20 we have the fullest description of Paul's ministry to be found outside 2 Corinthians. In his parting instructions to the Ephesians, he said nothing about the importance of signs and wonders or physical phenomena but he did emphasize the importance of teaching doctrine. He urged them to 'keep watch' and 'be on your guard' against 'savage wolves' that would come into the church. He warned about men already in the church who 'will arise and distort the truth' (Acts 20:28-31).

Truth is always under attack by those who would distort, replace, or water it down. To protect it from compromise, Paul urged the Ephesian elders to follow his pattern of preaching 'anything that would be helpful to you', teaching 'publicly and from house to house,' 'testifying to the gospel of God's grace,' 'preaching the kingdom' and proclaiming 'the whole will of God'. He concluded his exhortation by committing them 'to the word of his grace, which can build you up and give you an inheritance among all those who are sanctified' (Acts 20:20,24,25,27,32).

The August 1995 issue of *Spread the Fire* lists 'the wonderful spiritual tools [needed] to minister the life of the Spirit'.[16] What are these crucial spiritual tools produced by the present 'renewal'?

'Words of knowledge, words of wisdom, discerning of spirits; tongues, interpretation of tongues, and prophecy; faith, performing of miracles and gifts of healing.'[17] Why didn't they list evangelism, teaching, preaching, administration, mercy, etc.?

By contrast, the three Pastoral Epistles have been universally recognized throughout history as the key New Testament texts that give guidance to pastors on how to shepherd God's people. In these epistles we look in vain for guidance about the type of phenomena and 'spiritual gifts' associated with the Vineyard movement, with the possible exception of prophecy, discernment and faith. If the current renewal is of the Spirit, why is there no emphasis on the ministry tools Paul stressed in writing to Timothy and Titus?

What we do find in the Pastoral Epistles is a heavy emphasis on the teaching and preaching of doctrine. There is guidance on choosing leaders, on prayer, on how to promote peaceful relationships in the church and how to relate to political rulers, and there are warnings about false doctrine — all of which is very practical. Let me pick a couple of the verses that underscore the importance of doctrine. Many more could be quoted.

> I give you this charge: Preach the Word; be prepared in season and out of season; correct, rebuke and encourage — with great patience and careful instruction. For the time will come when men will not put up with sound doctrine (2 Tim. 4:1-3).
> An overseer ... must hold firmly to the trustworthy message as it has been taught, so that he can encourage others by sound doctrine and refute those who oppose it (Titus 1:7,9).
> You must teach what is in accord with sound doctrine (Titus 2:1; see also 1 Tim. 1:3-4; 4:1; 6:3-5; 2 Tim. 1:13-14; 2:14-15; 3:10-17).

Even a cursory glance at these verses reveals that doctrine is a gracious gift of God. It protects, corrects, inspires, teaches, encourages, trains — and leads us by faith into the very presence of its Giver. Every church must counter the perpetual tendency in human beings to drift away from the truth, to fabricate false doctrine and to invest human imagination with divine authority. This tendency is fostered by 'deceiving spirits' and can only be countered by emphasizing the teaching and preaching of doctrine.

The indispensable value of revealed doctrine resides in its objectivity. Yielding to the authority of 'words of knowledge, words of wisdom, impressions or words of prophecy' opens us up to serious human distortion. For this very reason the Association of Vineyard churches has warned against drawing theological conclusions from manifestations. 'No doctrine should be based on a prophetic interpretation of a particular manifestation.'[18] Unfortunately, this guideline was largely ignored by leaders of the Toronto Blessing.

We must have an objective standard judging us because, as Jeremiah so succinctly stated, 'The heart is deceitful above all things and beyond cure. Who can understand it?' (Jer. 17:9). He went on to explain that only God can recognize the deceitfulness of the human psyche with its proneness to substitute imagination for truth. God told Noah, 'Every inclination of [man's] heart is evil from childhood.' Men and women who trust their own impressions, ideas and feelings rather than revealed doctrine live in peril. This is how heresy originates.

No, doctrine is not a box to confine us, but a window through which we gain a panoramic view of the glories of God and his will. Let me summarize why doctrine is so crucial.

The importance of doctrine

1. God is incomprehensible in his invisible, infinite and eternal tri-unity. He is hidden from our sight and understanding by an infinite gap. 'No one has ever seen God' (1 John 4:12).

2. Men and women are finite, fallible, fallen, and thus biased in their understanding. Unaided, no one can comprehend anything about the incomprehensible God:

> For my thoughts are not your thoughts,
> neither are your ways my ways,
>
>   declares the Lord.
> As the heavens are higher than the earth,
> so are my ways higher than your ways
> and my thoughts than your thoughts
>
>   (Isa. 55:8-9).

To know God mankind needs an objective revelation from God. Even the individual interpretation of this revelation is suspect because of the deceitfulness of the human heart. Each of us needs to check our interpretation against that 'multitude of godly counsellors' who have recorded their conclusions in the evangelical creeds, confessions, commentaries and theologies of the church.

3. The visible things of creation bear witness to some of the most obvious things about God — his eternity, his divinity and his almighty power. Natural revelation, however, cannot in any infallible way communicate truth because those of us who read creation are both finite and damaged.

4. God chose to reveal all we need to know about himself and his will through the infallible words of the Scriptures. All necessary revelation is contained in the closed canon of the Bible.

5. These revelations are windows through which we see into the spiritual realm, love letters from God to us, portraits of God's divine attributes painted by God himself to illustrate what he wants us to know.

6. Theology is the art gallery where students of revelation have hung, in order, these different murals from God. Like an art gallery these paintings are arranged to communicate truth about God and his will for our lives in a logical order. One group of canvases depicts God's attributes. Another group portrays the Trinity. A third group pictures man's nature and depravity. Another group depicts Christ, and so on.

7. Theology, or doctrine, far from leading us away from God, leads us towards God. It helps us put together in logical categories the nuanced revelations God has given. The disciple who wanders through this theological art gallery finds his ability to walk by faith in the invisible God immeasurably enhanced. He finds his thirst for God quenched as he responds in wonder and love.

8. Those who paint their own pictures of the incomprehensible God based on their own impressions, dreams, ideas or conjectures, can seriously distort the truth God has revealed.

9. For this reason we are urged to protect the paintings (truth, doctrine, revelation) that have come from the divine artist against all forgeries — heresies, false teaching, imbalance, etc.

10. Our art galleries, i.e. our theology books, contain an order that is not inspired. They involve some extrapolations from God's revelation that are tentative and speculative. But no important

painting is incomplete. For example, the pictures we have of salvation and how to live the Christian life are as clear as snap shots. Our theology of God, the Trinity, the Holy Spirit, redemption, the incarnation, Christian living, etc. is not in a state of flux or development. These paintings are complete. On the other hand, our pictures of eschatology, man's bipartite or tripartite nature, etc. are like incomplete frescoes due to their somewhat speculative nature. God has not revealed everything about everything — only what is necessary.

Our understanding of God's revelation grows as we pursue an ever more thorough investigation of the actual content of the Bible. This explains why all churches that believe in the inerrancy, authority and sufficiency of the Scriptures commit themselves to a rigorous programme of preaching and teaching. They demand of their preachers and teachers careful exegesis using the universally accepted principles of interpretation.

John MacArthur writes, 'Any trivial, trite, whimsical, capricious treatment of Scripture that does not pursue the truth and the meaning of Scripture to get at exactly what God meant is to blaspheme His Word, and He holds His Word equal to His own name. Treating God with disrespect is a frightening thing, but treating the Word with disrespect is equally frightening, and the mandate for the church and the mandate for Christians is to know the Word, to study to be approved unto God, workmen who need not to be ashamed because they rightly divide the Word of truth.'[19]

A commitment to careful exegesis of biblical doctrine is essential. It is possible that our Vineyard friends may accuse us of sloppy or inaccurate exegesis in the whole areas of signs, wonders and the charismatic gifts. We must consider that challenge carefully. We shall do just that in chapters 16-19.

When we examine any movement or church we should not only listen to what is said, but also what is emphasized. Groups can be biblical in the statements they make, but unbiblical in their emphasis. The bias against doctrine discernible in the Vineyard movement and the lack of attention to teaching and preaching at the Toronto meetings are clearly unbiblical.

One of the main reasons why many in the Vineyard movement shy away from doctrine is their perception that it leads theologians to become theoretical and impractical. This view has led them to characterize those not on their bandwagon as Pharisees.

Claims that those who do not subscribe to the Third Wave are Pharisees

On doctrinal grounds, leaders in the movement commonly label those who oppose them as Pharisees. In this they follow an interpretation pioneered by Wimber. As we noted earlier, he indicated that it is common for evangelicals, like the Pharisees, to use sound doctrine as a shield to 'curtail and control the work of the Spirit', and thus fail to recognize Christ in a present work.[20]

In going through ninety-one pages of transcripts of messages given at the Toronto Airport Christian Fellowship, I noted dozens of references to Pharisees. William DeArteaga is an example of one who uses this accusation against critics: 'They sit themselves in the chair of Moses and they have right doctrine. Their ideas are okay. But don't follow their examples. Phariseeism is the heresy of orthodoxy that is basically correct ideas... They were evangelicals who ... resisted the liberals... So, ironically, the core problem with the Pharisee is that he cannot recognize the present work of the Holy Spirit because he's so enthralled with his past victories and past doctrine.'[21] DeArteaga accuses evangelicals of being pharisaical.

In a Prophetic School held in November 1994 at the Toronto Airport Vineyard, Marc Dupont warned that judgement would fall on Christian leaders who fail to respond to what he perceives the Spirit to be doing in the nineties. Leaders who take 'a strong Pharisaical stance and are going to attack what God is doing ... God is going to take them out of the ministry ... taking some leaders home to heaven.'[22]

Are critics of the Vineyard or the Toronto Blessing Pharisees? These are serious charges! Christ Jesus pronounces a frightening series of woes on the Pharisees in Matthew 23 for their obsession with externals and incidentals, for their love of the praise of men, for the legalistic burdens they imposed on others, for their greed and deceit, and especially for their hypocrisy. Being too orthodox or doctrinal was not their problem. They failed to maintain biblical balance, distorted biblical truth and neglected 'justice, mercy and faithfulness' (Matt. 23:23). Jesus did not condemn them for any biblical truth or practice they obeyed — but for *failing to practise what they preached*. A concern for biblical doctrine is not pharisaical because biblical doctrine always includes application — and requires obedience.

Now if I, or any others who have concerns about the Vineyard movement, should mask hypocrisy, disobedience, immorality, greed or malice by what we say — then we would be Pharisees. I would hesitate to make such a terrible indictment of another. In this allegation Vineyard leaders, perhaps unwittingly, accuse their critics of failing to be genuine disciples of Christ. True followers of the Master are committed to live godly lives by putting what they believe (doctrine) into practice.

The marriage of doctrine and practice in the lives of genuine disciples

Doctrine and practice, like love and marriage, go together like the proverbial horse and carriage. Other couplets could be added that express the biblical balance between knowledge and application. Christian living involves a balance of truth and spiritual freedom, trust and obedience, justification and peace, knowledge of Christ and love for Christ, faith in the indwelling Spirit and spiritual power.

No one denies that we always face the danger of over-emphasizing the doctrinal and under-emphasizing the practical. However, any disciple of Christ who spends even a modicum of time devotionally reading the Scriptures finds the Holy Spirit repeatedly correcting any such imbalance. Wherever the disciple goes he discovers this marriage of doctrine and practice. In Deuteronomy we read, 'Hear, O Israel: The Lord our God, the Lord is one [powerful theology on the unity of God]. Love the Lord your God with all your heart and with all your soul and with all your strength. These commandments ... are to be upon your hearts. Impress them on your children. Talk about them ... Fear the Lord your God, serve him only' (Deut. 6:4-7,13). The Scriptures always link truth and application.

One would have to be blind to miss the connection. All of us admit that sometimes our Bible reading becomes mechanical. But when we discover the words of life becoming just words, we bow in confession and prayer. We plead with God to apply the Word to our hearts and to change our lives. No sincere disciple of Christ wants to be a Pharisee or an ivory-tower scholar who has no passion for God!

This connection is maintained throughout the books of Old Testament history. In the New Testament sincere followers of

Christ absorb his doctrine in the Gospels and apply it to their lives. They seek to *do* God's will and thereby *prove the truth* of Jesus' doctrine. Jesus promised, 'If anyone chooses to do God's will, he will find out whether my teaching [doctrine] comes from God or whether I speak on my own' (John 7:17).

Throughout the epistles application follows doctrine. Even a cursory reading reveals that the doctrines of adoption, justification, redemption and identification with Christ have profound practical fall-out. Paul rejoices that though the Romans used to be slaves of sin, they wholeheartedly obeyed the form of teaching (doctrine) entrusted to them (Rom. 6:17). We are not to live the Christian life by listening to vague feelings about doing this or that. Rather we should walk in the light of revealed doctrinal truth. It is not experiences in limbo, but experience built on truth. All biblical doctrine is meant to produce godliness. Paul often points out that it is through godly and practical relationships that believers 'make the teaching [doctrine] about God our Saviour attractive' (Titus 2:10).

The Vineyard did not arrive at this aversion towards doctrine by themselves. They reflect a widespread perception that doctrine is boring and impractical. We are reaping decades of biblical and theological ignorance. Consumer Christians have come to expect instant benefits without the blood, sweat and tears of persevering biblical study. Discipleship has been at a low ebb for at least a generation.

It is no accident, in my opinion, that I searched the Toronto Vineyard bookshop and could not find the Bible study helps, commentaries, concordances, Bible dictionaries, etc. that have been the steady diet of another era. It was full of books on inner healing, recovery, revival, the Holy Spirit, testimonies, cassettes and videos.

The doctrinal moorings of the Vineyard movement seem seriously frayed. The chapters that follow will expose the extent of this danger. Dr Don Lewis comments on John Wimber: 'In the first place, his use of Scripture is highly problematic. His starting place seems to be his own experience and Scripture is drawn in to proof-text his own position. This was particularly seen in his teaching methodology regarding healing. People were taught a theology of healing based on the observation of phenomenological responses (shaking, stiffening, respiration, laughter, fluttering of eyelids, etc.) and were encouraged to use such subjective criteria as the basis on which to evaluate spiritual responses.'[23]

Dr Lewis continues: 'There are some serious difficulties in his theology for a thinking evangelical ... Wimber's radical

Arminianism (some might well argue it is Pelagianism). He seems to have little or no appreciation of the doctrine of the Fall and speaks of being involved in "restoring the Edenic state" in and through his ministry. He leaves no real place for an ongoing struggle with the old nature in the life of a Christian which the New Testament teaches the believer to expect. In the long run this can only lead to disillusionment because the promised state is not attained — or to a refusal to face reality by denying one's own experience of temptation and sin.'[24] One wonders whether the haze of happy hilarity associated with the Toronto Blessing is not an attempt to restore the Edenic state without the struggle. Although Wimber may react against the Toronto Blessing, in reality his presuppositions have fed the fire.

The foggy doctrinal landscape of the Vineyard is not caused by a minor eclipse of the biblical sun. The fires of their experiential aberrations have raised a pall of smoke that obscures truths clear to others. A chorus of concern has risen from many godly and discerning Christian leaders.

Dr John Armstrong expresses grave concern about the way they use experience to interpret Scripture, their misunderstanding of biblical signs and wonders, their downplaying of doctrine, their fascination with power and phenomena 'replacing a serious interest in the actual content of the gospel' and the danger that 'The anecdotal character of the movement runs the risk of justifying superstition.'[25]

Daniel Lundy is uneasy that their failure to make Scripture their supreme court leads them to a subjectivism in which they tend to define God according to their own experience. He also expresses concern about their failure to make the cross the central action of God that defines his love and the reality that defines Christian discipleship.[26]

As we saw earlier, James Beverley finds that the movement fails on five of his ten tests of truth.[27]

The missing link — lack of doctrinal discernment

This doctrinal drift has made the Vineyard movement unusually susceptible to heresy. Sound doctrine, as provided by the exegesis of the whole counsel of God, provides the raw material out of which the Holy Spirit crafts discernment. Without being rooted and grounded doctrinally their leaders are open to heretical influences that others might recognize. I am not saying they are heretical, nor am I seeking to tar them with the brush of guilt by association. But they are skating on very thin ice. Let me present several examples of dangerous liaisons.

We have already noted in chapter 9 their connection with Quakerism. John Wimber first pastored a Quaker church. According to Vineyard leader Todd Hunter, 'You don't get any more Evangelical than Quakerism. I mean that's true, blue blood Evangelicalism.'[28] While some modern Quakers are apparently evangelical, their root belief in a universal 'inner light' in all men 'enabling one to experience a radical rebirth ... perfect obedience to God,' is clearly unbiblical.[29] The shift from the authority of Scripture, fuzziness on the new birth and universalistic tendencies put Quakerism far from the evangelical camp. Their influence, however, pervades the Vineyard. A 'Quaker-like' reliance on inner impressions, believing them to be from God, has fed the whole movement and created the intense desire for the restoration of inspired prophecy.

As already mentioned, John Wimber embraced the prophetic movement of the Kansas City Fellowship in 1988. In 1990 Ernie Gruen, pastor of a large Pentecostal church in Kansas, issued a 200 page-exposé of the teachings and practices of Kansas City Prophets Paul Cain, Bob Jones, John Paul Jackson and Mike Bickle. He felt that the Kansas City Fellowship, pastored by Mike Bickle, was in danger of becoming a 'charismatic heresy'. Several in the Vineyard responded to the charges, including John Wimber. Although reconciliation with Gruen was effected, his charges were not answered satisfactorily.

Gruen warned of an élitist tendency. Bob Jones had talked of 'a new breed of "elect seed" [humans] created by God in 1973 to form a super-church that would be ten thousand times greater than the church in the book of Acts'. Jones and Paul Cain claimed that 'Kansas City was going to be headquarters for a group of super-Christians who would form "Joel's Army" and prepare for the final end-time harvest of souls to herald the return of Jesus Christ.'[30] Bob Jones claimed mystical journeys to heaven and hell, that the apostle Paul recognized him as an end-time prophet, as well as all kinds of mistaken and foolish prophetic speculations. Both Paul Cain and Bob Jones claimed to have had private, subjective miracles.[31]

The teaching of these 'prophets' reflects a belief in the 'latter rain' doctrine promulgated by a cultic group arising in North Battleford, Saskatchewan. In 1947 George Hatwin and Percy Hunt launched an independent Bible School and began evolving a teaching emphasizing local authority committed to a restored order of apostles who would in turn dispense spiritual gifts through the laying on of their hands. Many followed them in what they termed a fresh revival among 'apostatized Pentecostals'.[32] This heretical teaching is currently being revived.

Many in the movement see this present period in history as a time of latter rain, or revival, in which a new kind of Christian will be raised up to serve in 'Joel's army'. This end-time vision pictures a revitalized church with the offices of apostle and prophet restored. According to Bob Jones this group 'possesses the Spirit without measure' (as Christ did?), has believers moving consistently in 'every miracle, sign and wonder that has ever been in the Bible. They'll move in the power that Christ did.'[33] Many Christians will leave their denominations, because as Mike Bickle says, 'The majority of the church could not swallow the new thing coming... It is going to be so unusual you are not going to be able to look at the word for every manifestation and find one there because the Spirit of the Lord has so many manifestations that you and I know nothing about. This many-membered corporate body (corporate man) will take dominion over (conquer) the Earth for ultimate presentation to Christ at his second coming.'[34] I shall refer to the Vineyard's relationship with the Kansas City Prophets in more detail in a later chapter.

Apocalyptic teaching such as this seems to be coming more and more to the fore in writings and sermons in the movement. While its post-millennialism is not new, its élitism, fanciful prophecies and suggestions that end-time phenomena will not be governed by the Bible are very troubling. While John Wimber did bring significant order to the Kansas City Prophets, his relationship with them represents a live-and-let-live accommodation that took several years to move him to act. In my opinion the *laissez-faire* approach of Wimber and the Vineyard to doctrine accounts for the erratic nature of the movement. Their doctrinal naïvety kicks down the very walls they need to protect them from heretical and cultic influences.

The relationship that Rodney Howard-Browne, the main source of 'holy laughter', and some others have had with the overtly

heretical Word Faith movement displays serious lack of discernment. Kenneth Hagin, E. W. Kenyon, K. C. Price, Benny Hinn and
Kenneth Copeland belong to this group. In 1993 Hank Hanegraaff
wrote a powerful critique of the Word Faith movement, *Christianity
in Crisis*. In this work Hannegraaf documents his concerns about
their faulty view of faith, their erroneous teachings about the
deification of Christians, their misunderstandings about the atonement, their materialistic worldview and their dangerous ideas about
sickness and suffering.[35] This movement teaches that 'Faith is a
force, words being the container of the force. And through the force
of faith, you can create your own reality... When you're born again,
you not only have salvation, but you have unlimited health and
unlimited wealth. All you have to do is visualize it, speak it into
existence.'[36]

Word Faith preachers make some weird and blasphemous
claims. Kenneth Copeland alleges that Christ spoke through him,
saying, 'I didn't claim I was God; I just claimed I walked with Him
and that He was in Me.'[37] What a blasphemous attack on the deity of
Christ!

In spite of these serious problems, William DeArteaga chooses
to defend the Word Faith movement. He seeks to discount clear
evidence that Kenneth Hagin plagiarized the writings of E. W.
Kenyon. DeArteaga claims that it occurred innocently, due to
Hagin's 'almost perfect photographic memory'. Instead of taking
this opportunity to censure Hagin and dissociate the Vineyard
movement from clearly heretical teachers, DeArteaga says, 'Hagin
is a person of unquestioned integrity.'[38]

The movement also shows lack of doctrinal discernment in its
relationships with Roman Catholics. In my readings and attendance
at Toronto Airport Christian Fellowship meetings I have noticed an
imprudent approach to Roman Catholicism. In July 1995 I talked
with a Roman Catholic man from Ottawa who had been a member
of the charismatic renewal movement for twenty years. He had
recently received the 'Toronto Blessing' which, he stated, made him
a better Catholic. He explained how his parish priest had also been
'blessed'. Arnott and a team had been to his church, he claimed, and
many had been 'slain in the Spirit'.

I have no problem with going anywhere to preach the gospel —
but to go into a Roman Catholic Church to pass on a supposed
experience of the Spirit that Roman Catholics interpret as 'making

them better Catholics' strikes me as dangerous. It may serve to confirm them in their worship of Mary, belief in salvation through sacraments and other unbiblical ideas. We have already noted William DeArteaga's strange views of the Reformers: 'The reformers rejected the need for discernment when they threw out the whole of Catholic mystical theology.'[39] In making this absurd, and dangerous, comment, is he demonstrating an aversion to Pauline theology and an attraction to Roman mysticism with its advocacy of saints and relics?

We saw in chapter 9 John Wimber's propensity to accept the testimony of Roman Catholic mystics such as Theresa of Avila concerning mystical signs and wonders. In this search for historical precedent, he displays an uncritical willingness to accept their claims without questioning their basic commitment to truths as essential as justification by faith. This extends to crediting Lourdes as a place of miracles. This accommodation to groups beset with serious doctrinal and practical errors appears to reflect his Quaker heritage.

Even more serious is the assertion that the Toronto Blessing manifests many of the characteristics of New Age mysticism. If true, it would tip the movement into the cultic camp. Alan Morrison asserts, 'If I had been faced with the "Toronto Blessing" as representative of Christianity before I was saved, I would have viewed the church as simply one more of the many cults that I experienced in over twenty years of spiritual searching.' His concerns stem from counselling many hundreds of people 'who have been affected by this psycho-religious experience (which has often been extremely harrowing)'. He concludes that it displays all the marks of a cult: 'extra-biblical revelation, a false basis of salvation, arrogant personal claims of the leaders, doctrinal double-talk, defective Christology, defective pneumatology, unjustified scriptural proof-texting, vicious and threatening denunciation of those who disagree [and] syncretistic practices and associations'.[40]

Morrison believes that 'One could achieve the same fruits from attendance at Erhard Seminars Training, a course in Silva Mind Control or becoming a sanyassin in the Society for Krishna Consciousness.' He makes these claims 'as a veteran of the New Age movement and Eastern mystical sects'.[41] Morrison's allegations sound a serious note of warning about an area that requires further study and evaluation.

The great omission in the Vineyard — teaching and preaching

We have already noted in some detail the importance Christ and the apostles gave to the teaching and preaching of the whole counsel of God. The first time I went to the Toronto Airport Fellowship, the sermon was replaced (the lady speaker said by the leading of the Holy Spirit) with a homily and history of the phenomena interspersed by various exhortations. There was no Scripture read. The next time there was a message on the prodigal son, but no Scripture reading. On that occasion, two hours or more had elapsed before the message. As soon as the music and spectacular testimonies faded away the congregation gave the speaker almost no attention. People rested. Some let their heads fall on their chests as if they were dosing. Others talked to each other. When laughter broke out on one side, everyone craned their necks to look. Most were bored until the speaker got near the close of his message and began to lead up to the 'ministry time'.

These are not isolated instances. Sometimes messages are drowned out by shrieks and laughter. On 20 January 1996 R. T. Kendall was unable to preach for over fifteen minutes as a result of uproarious laughter.

Don McCallum chides his friend Jeremy Sinnott, music director at the Toronto Airport Christian Fellowship, for 'little emphasis on teaching — and when teaching is given, the Bible is sometimes abused rather than used'. He went on to cite several examples including an unwarranted assertion that the Pauline requirement that things be done 'decently and in order' does not apply. He also mentioned how the speaker in a meeting attended by a friend 'got up to announce the text and started laughing so hard that he could not continue. He tried to preach but could not because of laughter. Finally he asked if everyone didn't already know the text anyway and laughingly concluded without having said one intelligible word.'[42]

Ron Riff, a pastor from Cincinnati, Ohio, asked Randy Clark at the 1995 anniversary meeting at the Toronto Airport Vineyard, why he did not see in this renewal what was characteristic of historic revivals: 'a strong anointed preaching … an emphasis on holiness of God and depravity of man'.[43] Randy Clark answered that 'God threw a party first, and if we had got the heavy message of holiness to start with — I think one of the problems is most of the people in church already feel so icky about themselves … it's not so much His wrath but His goodness that brings us to repentance.'[44] In the light of both Scripture and historical revivals, the questioner is right and Clark is wrong.

James Beverley confirms my findings. He says, 'Something should be done about the *weak preaching* that typifies the nightly meetings. I have talked to hundreds of people who have been to the Airport Vineyard and have asked them about their perceptions of the strengths and weaknesses of the preaching they heard. Their chief complaint is the lack of clarity, exegetical skill, and focus that is brought to the biblical text during worship… A regular pattern has emerged since January 20, 1994 in that the messages usually consist of story-telling about "manifestations" or about the latest developments in The Blessing.'[45]

Our survey of the great movements of the past in chapters 9 and 10 points up a stark contrast. The revivals may have come spontaneously, but they were always associated with great preaching. As Charles Spurgeon cried, 'We want again Luthers, Calvins, Bunyans, Whitefields, men fit to mark eras, whose names breathe terror in our [foes] ears… They are the gifts of Jesus Christ to the Church, and will come in due time. He has power to give us back again a golden age of preachers, a time as fertile of great divines and mighty ministers as was the Puritan age, and when the good old truth is once more preached by men whose lips are touched as with a live coal from off the altar, this shall be the instrument in the hand of the Spirit for bringing about a great and thorough revival of religion in the land… The moment the Church of God shall despise the pulpit, God will despise her.'[46]

But instead of great expository preaching that turns our attention to the God of the Word, we find experiences and mystical messages that draw our attention away from the Word!

13.
Putting the cart of experience before the horse of Scripture

When the historical and doctrinal basis for the current 'renewal' proves shaky, its proponents inevitably turn to experience. They say something to the effect that 'It must be of God since it brought me nearer to God,' or 'It must be of the Spirit since it made me love Christ more.' This line of argument has become, more and more, the main 'proof' of the movement. In substance, they are claiming that a subjective feeling or impression that they have about the presence of Christ provides conclusive proof that the objective phenomena are of God. This reverses the way evangelicals have historically understood how God produces genuine experience. Before I examine this divergence, I want to assert the importance of subjective experience.

Genuine experience is to be sought

The Christian faith should lead us to live lives marked by authentic warmth and feeling. We ought to love the Lord with our emotions as well as our mind. We must know Christ in our day-to-day experience.

Experiences, of course, vary greatly. The Bible records authentic experiences as diverse as Jeremiah's weeping, Isaiah's awe as he fell before the thrice-holy God, David's flight for his life and his triumphal return as new king, Peter's ill-fated attempt to walk on water and his deliverance from jail. Some of these experiences were subjective; many were objective. However, from our perspective, all are recorded objectively in the Bible.

In Ephesians 1 Paul prays for the Ephesians and all believers: 'I keep asking that the God of our Lord Jesus Christ, the glorious Father, may give you the Spirit of wisdom and revelation, so that you may know him better … that you may know the hope to which he has called you, the riches of his glorious inheritance … and his incomparably great power for us who believe' (Eph. 1:17-19). Paul wants us to enjoy a profound experience of the hope, inheritance and power of the Father through the indwelling Spirit giving us wisdom and understanding of the revelation God has given. Authentic experience, whether objective or subjective, is mediated by the Spirit through the living Word. The Word is dead only to those who are dead and are not excited by the power of biblical revelation.

In chapter 3 Paul goes on to pray for us to experience the love of God through 'his Spirit in your inner being, so that Christ may dwell in your hearts through faith' (Eph. 3:16-17). Surpassing experiences of the love of Christ dawn as the Spirit who dwells within us enhances our faith in Christ. As our faith grows, the greatness of his love overwhelms us more and more. Faith, of course, comes not through looking around at circumstances, or at the experiences of others, or waiting for some overwhelming emotional experience in a meeting — but by looking at the picture of Christ recorded by the Spirit in the Word of God.

John explained, at the beginning of his first epistle, the purpose of his writing. He wanted to communicate what the apostles actually experienced and heard in the presence of Jesus Christ. Since Christ actually lived, taught, ate and died before their very eyes, the experience of the apostles can never be duplicated. But John wants his readers to experience Christ too. How does he plan to help them to do that? By setting up a meeting in which Christ will appear visibly, or by a dramatic sign or wonder? No! John says, 'We proclaim to you what we have seen and heard, so that you also may have fellowship with us. And our fellowship is with the Father and with his Son, Jesus Christ… This is the message we have heard…' (1 John 1:3,5). Experience follows proclamation! Before Christ ascended he commanded the disciples to 'preach the gospel to the whole creation'. God mediates genuine experiences of Christ through this proclamation of the gospel. John knew that people living subsequent to Christ's ascension could still have real fellowship with God. How? Through his proclamation of 'what we have seen and heard'. This experience of Christ is no less real than that of the apostles. It is real but spiritually different. As Jesus remarked to Thomas, 'Because you have seen me, you have believed; blessed are those who have not seen and yet have believed' (John 20:29). Experiences of Christ that occur without the aid of visible manifestations are not inferior. Indeed, faith in the apostolic message about the invisible Christ is far superior to a halting faith that depends upon external stimuli or manifestations.

Obviously, Scripture expects us to experience the presence and love of Christ. The agent who produces genuine experiences is the Holy Spirit. The means he uses is the message — in fact, the whole Bible.

Great experiences of God

When he was twenty-two, Whitefield had an intense but subjective experience of the presence and glory of God. About this time he wrote in his *Journal*, 'Sometimes, as I was walking, my soul would make such sallies as though it would go out of the body. At other times I would be so overpowered with a sense of God's Infinite Majesty that I would be constrained to throw myself on the ground and offer my soul as a blank in His hands, to write on it what He pleased. One night ... I and another, a poor but pious countryman, were in the fields, exulting in our God and longing for the time when Jesus would be revealed from Heaven in a flame of fire.'[1]

Throughout history the Spirit has graciously given believers transforming experiences of God. I hesitate to become personal, so close to the record of such a godly man as Whitefield. But I do want to assert that ordinary saints have genuine experiences of the indescribable glory of Christ. Let me give an example. I well remember a secluded nook on a hillside in Pakistan where I went to read and meditate on 1 Peter. That spot became hallowed ground for me as the Holy Spirit illumined Peter's writings. Tears flowed often as I pondered the mercy of Christ, the hope we have in his resurrection, the incorruptible inheritance kept for us, the power of the liberating blood of Christ, the challenge of holiness, the call to a royal priesthood. A thirst for the 'pure spiritual milk' of the Word burned within. Truly, for me at that time, 1 Peter 1:8 became my experience: 'Though you have not seen him, you love him; and even though you do not see him now, you believe in him and are filled with an inexpressible and glorious joy.' The Holy Spirit used Scripture to deepen my experience of Christ.

We all have differing experiences because we have differing temperaments and face diverse circumstances. But our experience of the living Christ is no less authentic because it is less dramatic! Through the years my experience of Christ has, admittedly, often ebbed, but I am thankful for a variety of experiences of his presence. I have been overwhelmed in sermon preparation by meditation on one of the attributes of God or a passage of Scripture. I have been moved to tears while preaching, forcing me to stop. I have been rendered almost speechless during the Lord's Table. No, please don't get the idea that I don't believe in experience! The problem occurs when we try to interpret experience by experience, or use one experience to produce others.

The source of real experience

Biblically and historically, Christians have understood that faith in scriptural truth produces genuine experiences. 'Everyone who calls on the name of the Lord will be saved' (Rom. 10:13). Being saved is a life-changing experience of grace in which a sinner experiences both the new birth and peace with God through having his sins forgiven in Jesus' name. This initial experience is the seedbed in which a host of other spiritual experiences flourish.

How does genuine experience originate? Paul makes essentially the same query: 'How, then, can they call on the one they have not believed in [since faith precedes the experience]? And how can they believe in the one of whom they have not heard [since hearing a message, in turn, precedes faith]? And how can they hear without someone preaching to them [since someone preaching about Christ precedes both hearing and believing]?' (Rom. 10:14). Paul explains that faith produces a genuine experience of saving intimacy with Christ. But faith does not grow in a vacuum. Ignorance about Christ must be dispelled by hearing about Christ in the gospel through someone preaching. Truth proclaimed produces faith. 'Faith comes from hearing the message' (Rom. 10:17).

What is true of the experience of conversion is true throughout our Christian lives. 'We walk by faith, not by sight.' The whole of Hebrews 11 demonstrates that men and women of God throughout history gained the strength to walk with God, to persevere in difficulties and to do exploits — by faith in unseen realities. 'Now faith is being sure of what we hope for and certain of what we do not see. This is what the ancients were commended for' (Heb. 11:1). They were not commended for trusting visible phenomena or signs and wonders. 'And without faith it is impossible to please God' (Heb. 11:6). Along with those who preceded him, and all the saints down through the ages to our own day, Moses 'persevered because he saw him who is invisible' (Heb. 11:27).

In the next chapter of Hebrews, the author exhorts us to run the Christian race by fixing our eyes, by faith, on the invisible 'Jesus, the author and perfecter of our faith' (Heb. 12:2).

The first step in the revealed pathway to deep and genuine experiences of Christ is the *presentation of the truth of God*. Under the influence of the Holy Spirit, this truth generates *faith in the invisible realities of God*, which in its turn produces *genuine experiences of God*.

Truth + faith = experience.

In all the great movements and revivals of history this same pattern emerges. Luther rediscovered scriptural truth and it transformed his own life. As he proclaimed it, people responded by putting their faith in Christ alone for salvation. As a result they experienced justification. Later Whitefield and Edwards preached the Word with power. Their hearers believed their messages and fell under great experiences of conviction, sorrow, conversion and joy.

Those propagating the Toronto Blessing, give some lip-service to this divinely revealed process. However, they devalue the role of truth by giving the highest place of all to physical experiences of the phenomena. In their movement, as in charismatic circles in general, the order becomes: perception of happenings in a meeting or testimonies of those slain in the Spirit produce 'faith' that the movement is of God. This 'faith,' in turn, generates an expectation of an objective physical experience. When one's 'expectation faith' does generate such experiences as falling, shaking, etc., or even a perceived closeness to Christ, then this is claimed to prove the validity of the movement. Personal feelings and physical experiences strengthen this kind of 'faith' in the happenings. By this circular method of reasoning those in the movement are confirmed and the questions of those outside are effectively silenced. It becomes a closed club of those who have 'experienced the blessing'.

Thomas Morton, formerly a charismatic, in an article examining why many have left the movement comments: 'The experiential lifestyle usually is advocated dogmatically... The freedom in the Spirit we wanted was subverted by our own zeal and dogmatism.'[2] Those in the movement become so dogmatic about the authenticity of their experiences that a doctrine of outward experiences develops.

When experiences are enthroned in this way it is no wonder that preaching and teaching are so abysmally neglected. The process that takes place where something akin to the Toronto Blessing is encouraged may involve one or more of the following steps:

> Attendance at an experiential *happening* (i.e. a meeting) produces a personal, and usually a physical *experience*, such as being slain in the Spirit.
>
> External *manifestations*, music, etc. produce internal *feelings*.
>
> One's personal *interpretation* or *perception* of one's feelings validates *one's visible experience*.
>
> Other people's *testimonies*, experiences, etc. generate an *expectation* of having similar experiences.
>
> This *expectation* generates some kind of *experience*.
>
> *Experiences*, feelings, perceptions, testimonies are put forward as '*proof*' of the renewing presence of the Spirit.
>
> Afterwards, support is sought in Scripture and history to buttress conclusions drawn from feelings and outward experiences.

Historically, evangelicals have held that God uses the proclamation or witness of the gospel to provoke emotions of conviction and faith that lead to an experience of grace. Testimonies and music may play a part. Being in a meeting may play a part. But the anointed opening of the Scriptures is the central means of grace God uses to mediate genuine experience. The Word is also the one, objective standard God uses to validate or correct inadequate or misleading experiences.

In response to his writing and preaching about *Charismatic Chaos*, John MacArthur received a letter that illustrates the approach many in the Vineyard share with charismatics, although the

Vineyard does not emphasize the importance of tongues. A woman wrote to him, 'You resort to Greek translations and fancy words to explain away what the Holy Spirit is doing in the Church today. Let me give you a piece of advice that might just save you from the wrath of Almighty God. Put away your Bible and your books and stop studying. Ask the Holy Ghost to come upon you and give you the gift of tongues. You have no right to question something you've never experienced.'[3] Evidently, she believes that experiences of her type are more authentic than Scripture.

Let me go on to illustrate from Vineyard writings how their view of the role of experience parallels this woman's stark statement.

Vineyard views on the role of experience

I want to begin by returning to comments John Wimber made in his July/August 1994 leadership letter. In discussing the whole issue of the phenomena and the apparent disorder present in 'renewal' meetings, he points out the importance of testing practices by the Word of God and of testing the fruit of the experiences. He admits that 'Some things occur because of overzealousness, emotional disorder, or the devil. And some occur because of God.'[4] He grants that the Word of God is important in testing even their experiences.

We might ask, 'How then should we distinguish between that which occurs as a result of mistaken zeal, emotional disorder, or the devil?' Wimber responds, 'So if someone comes to me after they've shaken, fallen down, or made a noise, my question is "Do you love Jesus more? Do you believe in him more? Are you more committed to him?" If the answer is "Yes!" then praise the Lord! I hope that from this day forward she will walk closer to God in a more accountable, more mature, and more godly way than she ever has before.'[5] In the same article he abandons his earlier commitment to Scripture! One's own perception of one's nearness to Christ and commitment to him becomes the criterion for evaluation.

Commenting on the same article I have quoted from John Wimber, James Beverley writes, 'Wimber's previously noted concerns about the human element should make him more cautious. As The Toronto Blessing sweeps the globe, the willing multitudes are being taught this ['Do you love Jesus more?'] as the standard defence to the manifestations. This too readily opens the door to the chaotic forces of human emotions and religious ecstasy. After barking like a dog in public, who is going to be self-critical and say that he or she does not feel closer to Jesus?'[6]

Beverley's point is well taken. How can we trust our own perceptions and emotions when we know that the human heart is both intellectually fallible and emotionally 'deceitful above all things and beyond cure'?

John Wimber's approach to experiences has actually fed the movement that he now seems so concerned about. In 1986 he wrote, 'So God uses our experiences to show us more fully what he teaches in Scripture, many times toppling or altering elements of our theology and worldview.'[7] Asserting the supremacy of experience over doctrine, he wrote, 'I have talked with many evangelical theologians who have undergone significant changes in their theology because of an experience.'[8] 'Don't worship the book. Evangelicals all over the country are worshipping the book. They have God the Father, God the Son and God the Holy Book. They took the very workings of the Holy Spirit and placed it in the Book.'[9] Wimber has certainly weaned his movement so far away from worshipping the Book that they now worship their own experiences as evidence of the fire of the Spirit.

Worshipping the Bible is, of course, wrong. But is Wimber contending that the Holy Spirit, the Author of the Bible, did not give us clear, dependable, permanent guidance in his book? If so, he is denying the authority and sufficiency of Scripture. To do that would be to imply that the Holy Spirit did not know what he was doing, and that he failed to foresee the kind of guidance we would need in this century!

If we fail to make the Scriptures the touchstone of experience, we shall end up worshipping God according to our own subjective interpretation of our experiences — something we should be very wary of in the light of the deceitfulness of the human heart. That is exactly how cults begin.

Later disciples in the movement seem to be even more radical. Wes Campbell said at the Toronto Airport Vineyard, 'The bottom line is, people measure according to their own experience, not the Bible. Not the Bible. And when all is said and done, here it is, the spiritual fruit that we have seen from six and eight years of phenomena has been overwhelmingly good ... some of the strongest Christians that I ever knew, have seen, are all shakers. They all have had phenomena happen... And the fruit is the test. This doesn't violate Scripture. It just violates the mind. It aligns itself with Scripture and it aligns itself with the fruit of Scripture.'[10] What kind of reasoning is this — that something can violate the mind but not the Scripture? Does Campbell consider the Scripture irrational? This kind of approach could be happily used by Mormonism or Christian Science. (Note also this admission that the phenomena occurred long before the Toronto blessing, while John Wimber exercised extensive oversight of the movement.)

In spite of the dangers, statements such as, 'It must be of God since it leads us to love Christ more,' have become the watchword of the movement. In one form or another I heard this whenever I visited the Vineyard. It surfaces repeatedly in the testimonies in Chevreau's book on the movement, *Catch The Fire.*

Chevreau reports that Ron Allen, pastor of the Fort Wayne Vineyard and a veteran church planter, came to Toronto and was 'slain in the Spirit'. His wife Carolyn soon followed to find out what was happening. Wisely, she said, 'I'm tired of having more *goose bump experiences* that really don't change the way I am or live.'[11] In the Third Wave this is exactly what leaders keep promoting, 'goose-bump experiences'.

In spite of her reservations, however, Carolyn soon 'felt his power so strongly in my body one night, I became fearful that I was going to die: I have also felt an incredible presence of peace like never before... Could this be about learning of the abiding presence of the living Lord within His tabernacle — His people?'[12]

Evidently, Carolyn was convinced by a 'goose-bump experience'. What will the long-term fruit of this experience be, two or ten years from now? That will be hard to discern and follow up. The fact is that those who give testimonies base their evaluation of the movement on their own *analysis* of their *feelings* and *experiences* and not on scripturally inspired records of experiences.

Loving God more, sensing his indwelling presence more, feeling at peace with him have certainly been the passionate goal of believers from Abraham's day down to ours. There is nothing wrong with the desire. It is that which is promoted to fulfil this desire that raises questions.

One cannot blame the Vineyard for highlighting what people say about how they feel. Testimonies have become the evangelical stock-in-trade, displacing truth as the primary focus of messages.

People would much rather listen to stories and testimonies about experiences than a careful, but passionate exegesis, of the Word of God. Go to any large meeting, listen to any popular speaker and you will usually find that stories take up an inordinate amount of space.

In Chevreau's book *Catch the Fire* his long list of testimonies is used to 'prove' the genuine nature of the 'renewal'. Let me interact further with Chevreau since his book has become phenomenally popular, and since he is one of the more moderate Vineyard apologists.

Chevreau majors on experiences because this is basic to his whole approach to the interpretation of Scripture. Overlooking the principle that 'The narrative portions of the Bible must be interpreted by the didactic or doctrinal portions,' Chevreau turns to the book of Acts to seek to prove that experiences attest the 'renewal'. He claims that Acts demonstrates that it was the '*experiences* of spiritual encounter, of visions, revelations, commissions, signs, wonders, and the other manifestations of the Spirit's presence and power that were the source and impetus for the mission in which the early Church engaged'.[13]

He is quite right in noting that the early church had a dynamic sense of the reality of the Spirit and the presence of the risen Christ. All genuine church life is experiential in this sense. But he is so anxious to prove the pre-eminence of physical, objective experience that he denigrates the role of the messages which the apostles brought about Christ. In the view of Chevreau, and of others in the movement, real church life is a pot-pourri of exciting happenings punctuated by the sparkle of signs and wonders.

I categorically deny that the early Christians were motivated by a bunch of exciting external signs and wonders. They were motivated by a dynamic encounter with the risen Christ — from that point on they were changed. What they carried with them was his evangelistic command and his teaching. They didn't wait for visions, or signs and wonders, to be motivated. The risen Christ motivated them. Any other motivation is suspect and subject to disappointment.

Chevreau goes on to say, 'For the apostle Paul, his understanding and expectation of the Spirit of the Risen Christ was always *experiential*. It was not *primarily* theological, doctrinal or speculative. The thinking about it all came after, secondarily. First and foremost it was experiential.'[14] Again, I would agree that Paul's

Damascus Road experience with the risen Christ was the life-changing event that turned him around. In his case the thinking did come after, but what of those to whom he wrote and preached? Did he try to thrill them with an experience before he talked to them? Chevreau would seem to want us to believe so, although the text clearly shows that truth came before experience.

Like others in the movement, Chevreau turns to the passage in 1 Corinthians in which Paul contrasts worldly wisdom with the message of the cross. He uses this passage to try to maintain the priority of experience over understanding. He calls it spiritual power 'coming to visible expression'. He writes, 'The issue is not rational persuasion, but life-engaging encounter.'

I have already shown in chapter 11 how proponents of the Toronto Blessing misunderstand this passage. They fail to see that Paul is appealing for the Corinthians to understand and accept 'cross-centred wisdom' rather than worldly wisdom. The cross produces powerful experience. But if the rational faculties of the Corinthians were not involved, Paul would not have bothered to write a letter. The epistle itself assumes the importance of understanding a message. It assumes that genuine experience is linked to spiritual words about the cross!

Chevreau goes on to quote Paul's description of his ministry to Thessalonica from the Revised English Bible: 'When we brought you the Gospel we did not bring it in mere words but in the power of the Holy Spirit and with strong conviction' (1 Thess. 1:5). He explains, 'It is not new head-knowledge that brought transformation to the Corinthians and Thessalonians, but the impartation of grace. Implicitly, he is giving witness to the experiential reality of being *grasped*. Grabbed. Zapped, Wowed. Awed, Overwhelmed. The demonstration of the Gospel is not due to Paul's ability as a preacher, a spell-binding speaker with intellectual powers of persuasion ...'[15]

The passage he quotes from 1 Thessalonians does not mean that the words of the gospel are irrelevant, but that they are *not enough*. These are not 'mere words', as translated in the version he quotes, but, as the NIV puts it (and this translation is in this instance, I believe, truer to the context), 'Our gospel came to you *not simply with words, but also* with power, with the Holy Spirit and with deep conviction.' What Paul really means is that a gospel presentation that comes in words — there is no other way — is incomplete without the powerful influence of the Holy Spirit. This is not a contest between words and experience, or mental activity and emotional activity! Nothing could be further from the truth. Indeed, the Spirit uses gospel words to produce experience. Notice the experiences that are mentioned: conviction, conversion and joy. Conviction first! And nothing about external signs, wonders or visions, nor about being overcome by experience.

Chevreau's statements devalue the importance of Paul's preaching. True, preaching was not enough, but without preaching the Corinthians and the Thessalonians would have had no experience. The proper formula is: a preacher, preaching gospel words, under the power of the Spirit. This is the method God used in Paul's day and throughout history, as we have already noted in previous chapters. With this connection so clearly made, why do we not see a passion for preaching in the Vineyard movement?

The way Chevreau and others question the value of 'new head-knowledge' in the conversion of the Corinthians and Thessalonians is very troubling. Certainly, it was not head-knowledge *alone* that transformed them; but they were not transformed *without* words — without their minds being engaged by the words Paul wrote in his epistles and preached in their presence. It was, precisely, the new words that Paul wrote in Corinthians and Thessalonians, as well as the new words he brought them in the gospel, that the Spirit used to transform them!

How can Chevreau and others who adopt the Vineyard position fail to see that the book of Acts and the epistles they quote are full of words — words inspired by the Holy Spirit, words that Luke and Paul wrote to influence the people who would read them? Obviously, the Holy Spirit has determined to use words to illumine the mind. Words and experience are not rivals; they are partners. Inspired words grasped by the mind transform the emotions of the heart and create powerful experiences of grace. Advocates of the Toronto Blessing seem bent on debunking completely the role of the mind in Christian experience in order to substitute their own experience-based frame of reference.

It should be noted, as well, that although Paul's experience came before his mental engagement with gospel truth, his experience was unusual. In his own preaching he did not expect people to experience what he had experienced. Rather he preached the message of the gospel in words given by the Spirit. The Spirit used those words to initiate experiences of deep conviction and solid conversion.

Chevreau not only puts ideas into the mind of the apostle, but he also misinterprets Jonathan Edwards. He rightly comments on Edwards' passion for 'practical and vital Christianity'. But then he interprets Edwards to mean 'religious knowledge as *experience*, held not in the head but in the heart'.[16] How can Chevreau misunderstand Edwards' position so abysmally? In his preaching Edwards appealed not for one or the other, but both *the knowledge of God* illuminating darkened minds and that illumination producing *emotional and practical experience*. Edwards was a great doctrinal preacher whose sermons assailed both the mind and the heart! It was never experience *without* doctrine, but experience *because of* doctrine.

The Vineyard is not alone in this tendency. Unfortunately, much of Christendom has accepted a view according to which experience becomes the judge and jury of what is true and false; in which feelings and opinions, instead of truth, have become the engine driving the train of supposedly genuine experiences.

During a 'groundbreaking conference' on Canadian evangelicalism at Queen's University in Kingston, Ontario, in May 1995, 115 participants examined thirty papers. They looked at both the historical development of the faith in Canada and its current condition. George Rawlyk and Andrew Grenville, pollsters with Angus Reid, concluded that 'Experience, rather than other sources of authority, is central to Canadian evangelical faith. The assertion is based on surveys and focus groups... Canadian evangelicals are rudderless.'[17]

In her news report on the conference, Krysia Lear writes, 'Emphasis on experience over doctrine to define an individual's position in the religious world "brings up a lot of questions," said Phyllis Airhart, an associate professor at Emmanuel College at University of Toronto. By those definitions, for example, Catholics could be considered evangelicals, a highly debatable idea in some evangelical circles.'[18] No wonder we see many in the Vineyard amenable to cultivating relationships with Roman Catholics who experience the Toronto Blessing. When experience, not truth, determines who my brothers and sisters are, anyone can be considered part of the 'family'.

Andrew Grenville, senior vice-president of Angus Reid Surveys, notes that 'Making doctrine the dividing line between faith groups would exclude many people who, in fact, put experience ahead of the Bible.'[19] But isn't that exactly why God gave us doctrine

— to discern, to define and to exclude those whose faith does not rest
upon eternal verities? You cannot have biblical experience without
biblical doctrine!

The conclusions of the conference concerning Canadian evangelicalism could just as surely be extended throughout much of the
evangelical world. Iain Murray writes that as an Arminian approach
to programming revivals took over in the last century, 'Religion
increasingly became a matter of mystic imagination ... experience,
rather than truth became the centre of American Christianity.'[20]

We are reaping an Arminian whirlwind that has blown off the
doctrinal roof sheltering us from the acid rain of error. With revealed
doctrinal distinctives blurred, shared experiences come to the fore
to promote 'tolerance' and 'acceptance'. In Britain, ordained Anglican priests leave their own church to join the Roman Catholic
Church. In America twenty Roman Catholics and twenty
evangelicals, including Chuck Colson, Bill Bright and J. I. Packer,
put out a joint statement, *Evangelicals and Catholics Together*, and
stir up a storm of controversy. In a response moderated by Dr John
Ankerberg and involving John MacArthur, James Kennedy and R.
C. Sproul, it is pointed out that what is at stake here is the very
definition of salvation itself![21]

When experience supplants the Bible, anything can happen. The
issues are not insignificant. They affect eternity. And without
doctrine to guide us, how can we distinguish biblically normative
experience from pagan or worldly experience?

Experience is universal

As I write this chapter a wave of devotion to the Hindu god Gannesh
is sweeping India. Idols of this god drink milk that is offered.
Devotees and other eyewitnesses actually see milk disappearing
from spoons put to the lips of images. The phenomenon has
galvanized Hindu devotion until demand for milk has created a
scarcity. What is happening? How do we interpret it?

When I served in Pakistan my Muslim calligrapher recounted a
dream he attributed to Mohammed. After taking an exam he came
home to bed. That night he dreamed that he saw the professor
showing him his paper with the mark he had received. When he met
the professor later, that was exactly the mark on his paper. How did
he know the mark before the professor had even marked the paper?

This Muslim tried to use his dream to authenticate Islam and counter my witness to Christ.

An early missionary to New York recounts an amazing story of 'miracles': 'One crippled woman arose and walked, instantly healed. Another who had been in bed for four years with palsy was restored to health. This second woman had complete paralysis of her right side. She was restored to perfect health. A child, who was suffering from brain fever and was given up to die by physicians, was healed and after a few hours was playing about the floor. A woman [who] had been ill in bed for six months, and her child also, suffering from the same disease,' were healed. And so began a ministry that attracted thousands. Baptismal services were held almost every day. Who was the missionary? One of the early pioneers of Mormonism![22]

Consider the sentiments of the three following quotations from the Middle Ages. The first was written by a woman who died in A.D. 802:

O my Lord, if I worship Thee from fear of Hell, burn me in Hell, and if I worship Thee from hope of Paradise, exclude me thence, but if I worship Thee for Thine own sake then withhold not from me Thine Eternal Beauty.[23]

Drunk is the Man of God, drunk without wine;
Sated the Man of God, full without meat.
Aghast is the Man of God in utter bewilderment
Knows not the Man of God slumber nor sustenance...
Taught by Creative Truth God's Man is learned;
Not wise in legal lore culled from a book.[24]

We have lost our heart in the way of the Beloved:
We have sown dissension in the world.
We have struck fire within the hearts of the people:
And have thrown lovers into confusion.
I have washed my hands of all my belongings:
We have set fire to house and home.
I had a heavy load on my back
But thanks be to God we have thrown aside that heavy load.
What is the wealth of the world but carrion?
We have cast the carcass to the dogs.[25]

Drunk with God; deep emotions; powerful experiences! Do the three preceding quotes come from disciples whose passion for Christ overwhelmed all else? No, all three were written by Muslim mystics to describe their devotion to Allah. They believed in pantheism and a view of absorption into Allah that reflects Hindu belief.

A host of other examples could be summoned: Hindu fire-walkers; whirling dervishes; Buddhist mystics; New Age visualizations; out-of-body experiences; people who claim to have been able to watch doctors labour over their bodies from a position high above; experiences of tunnels of light and returning from the dead; clairvoyants; savants; a hypnotist friend who regresses people to childhood to heal inner pain without reference to Christ and who delivers people from addictions under hypnosis.

A Scottish lady who attended spiritist services and séances regularly explained why: 'I have received so much benefit from them; I have found God in a much closer way and He has helped me so much.'[26]

All over the world in all cultures and in all ages people have had unusual experiences. Are they the result of demonic activity? Do they come from the dimly understood unconscious mind? Are they due to quackery, trickery, magic, or mass hypnosis? Unless you are willing to grant that Buddhism, Mormonism, Hinduism, Islam, New Age mysticism, witchcraft, etc. are of God, you must not start from experience to judge truth. Experiences shared by people from diametrically opposing faiths prove nothing. Truth alone must judge experience.

Feelings are universal

The emotions felt by the Muslim mystics I quoted above cannot be denied. The feelings of exhilaration felt by those healed through the Mormon pioneer were real emotions. We are all prone to be affected emotionally in a vast variety of ways. Some of us are much more emotional than others. That is often hard to tell from appearances. Looking at me, many might consider me an unemotional man who likes to read a lot. But to be honest, I can look at cows grazing in a field and find my eyes misting up. I can get emotional about horses frolicking in the meadow, or a blue jay scolding me from a pine tree, the sight of the autumn colours, the first taste of outdoor tomatoes in the summer, or Labrador dogs that look like our family's lost 'Skippy'. I can find tears spilling down my cheeks as I listen to a sad story — or a happy one. My throat can choke up when I see the Canadian flag or hear the national anthem.While I am off on a long trip the thought of my wife Mary Helen can trigger a paralysing longing for home. And to see the antics or hear the voices of our grandchildren — I'm just an old softy underneath. So far, I have not even mentioned the 'goose bumps' I get singing 'A Mighty Fortress is Our God,' reading a good Christian book, hearing a good sermon, or bowing in prayer.

What does all of this prove? Well, frankly, nothing except that I have a fairly active emotional life. It is wonderful to feel all these things. I would hate to be a dead stick. We must not be afraid of warm and lively emotions.

But having emotions and interpreting them are two different things. We don't have the moral or intellectual equipment to accurately test our own emotions. Warm feelings might cover pride, or laziness, or a sense of superiority. Not only are we sinfully ill-equipped to discern our own hearts, we are fallible. We lack understanding of spiritual things. 'There is no one who understands' (Rom. 3:11). We are also biased by our training, beliefs, environment, expectations and a hundred other variables. The peace we feel, or the joy we experience, may be due to a rosy sense of being in a happy group, or to having a good bank account, or to a sunny day, or to not having a headache, or to other causes.

Many of the reactions we have may, or may not, be driven by the Holy Spirit — they may be just the overflow of our humanity. I have heard Muslims and Mormons claiming peace with God. But neither has real peace with God, no matter what they feel deep down inside — because they do not have a saving relationship with Jesus Christ!

To discern feelings and experiences, we need a set of changeless standards completely objective to ourselves. We need the Bible, that inspired record of the experiences of biblical disciples. We need to understand biblical truth. We need to be able to use biblical doctrine to discern what is of God and what of man.

Dr Robert K. Rudolph[27] used to illustrate our human propensity to attribute our feelings and experiences to God, by describing a cruise ship. He would ask students to imagine the twilight falling in the tropics as a cruise ship plied its way through the islands. The passengers would be seated on deck chairs in the stern. Suddenly, a pyrotechnic display would light up the sky in front of the ship.

Passengers would 'ooh' and 'ah' over the sound and light. Imagine
their commenting, 'Look what heaven hath wrought,' attributing
the fireworks display to God when all the while it was sent up by the
ship's crew from the bow. He used to explain that this is what many
people say about the experiences and feelings that they themselves
generate. They claim that the feelings or phenomena come from
God, when they really come from within. In my opinion, this is what
many people who exult in the Toronto Blessing are doing.

Scripture is to produce, interpret and control experience. When
we are told to 'Test everything. Hold onto the good,' we are
commanded to use the Bible as the objective measure of all experience and doctrine. Unfortunately, the Vineyard movement and its
proponents allow experience and phenomena to usurp the role of
Scripture.

All experiences of genuine disciples draw them closer to Christ

Someone may protest at this point, 'But wait, these people have truly
drawn closer to Christ because they demonstrate changed lives.
They love the Bible more. They pray more. They have more of a
passion to witness.' I would agree that some of those who have had
Vineyard-type experiences have been genuinely drawn closer to
Christ. When we apply scriptural rules of evaluation to those who
have received the Toronto Blessing we find that some do seem to
show evidence of a work of God. I do not deny this. However, the
good fruit is not *because* of the experience, but *in spite of it*. Let me
explain.

The Bible records a whole gamut of experiences that God used
to draw people closer to himself and his will. Job suffered terrible
losses and horrendous personal pain. At the end he said,

> Surely I spoke of things I did not understand,
>   things too wonderful for me to know ...
> My ears had heard of you
>   but now my eyes have seen you.
> Therefore I despise myself
>   and repent in dust and ashes

                                                        (Job 42:3,5-6).

Job knew God in an enviable way before catastrophe struck. He was a man 'blameless and upright; he feared God and shunned evil' (Job 1:1). Nevertheless after his pain and loss he had a deeper relationship with God. God overruled Satan's intentions and used terrible loss and extreme pain to draw Job closer to himself.

David learned of God through victory over Goliath, through fleeing the jealousy of Saul, through the betrayal of his own son and even through his terrible sin with Bathsheba. Psalm 51, written after his adultery, is full of longing for God and a new awareness of his need of mercy:

> Have mercy on me...
> Wash away all my iniquity...
> Against you, you only, have I sinned...
> Cleanse me...
> Let me hear joy and gladness...
> Do not cast me from your presence...
>> a broken and a contrite heart,
>> O God, you will not despise.

Mysteriously, God overruled evil to draw David closer to himself. Think of the emotional experiences represented here!

Paul implored God to take away the thorn in his flesh, only to have God reply that his grace was sufficient for the trial. Evidently, the thorn was necessary to deepen Paul's experience of God. Many other unpleasant things happened to the apostle: '... troubles, hardships and distresses; in beatings, imprisonments and riots; in hard work, sleepless nights and hunger ... through glory and dishonour, bad report and good report; genuine, yet regarded as impostors' (2 Cor. 6:4-5,8). In spite of all these seemingly adverse circumstances, Paul grew in 'purity, understanding, patience and kindness; in the Holy Spirit and in sincere love; in truthful speech and in the power of God; with weapons of righteousness in the right hand and in the left' (2 Cor. 6:6-7).

Mature disciples experience that 'In all things God works for the good of those who love him, who have been called according to his purpose' (Rom. 8:28).

In my life the Holy Spirit has mediated the presence of Christ, not only in meetings but in accidents and in the midst of Muslim riots, in stringency, in malaria, in weighty responsibilities that seemed beyond me, in troubles and lightning strikes, in moving worship services and even in indifferent meetings.

Growing Christians realize how God works in our lives to draw us closer to himself and make us more like Christ. Like Paul we learn to 'rejoice in our sufferings, because we know that suffering produces perseverance; perseverance, character; and character, hope. And hope does not disappoint us, because God has poured out his love into our hearts by the Holy Spirit, whom he has given us' (Rom. 5:3-5; see also James 1:2-4).

Wherever we turn, we find this process described. True followers of Christ look upon anything that comes into their lives as an agent of spiritual growth, as a helper towards maturity and as a step towards intimacy with God. For this reason, I say unequivocally that some followers of Christ who attend Vineyard meetings may indeed have been drawn closer to God. If a believer comes to such a meeting with a hunger and thirst after more of God, God may honour that desire. That doesn't mean we honour the method or medium through which this happened any more than we honour the things that happened to Job. God may bless some in spite of unbiblical methods used by the Vineyard.

This happens to all of us. God overlooks many of the weaknesses in all of our churches in order to bless his people. None of us can claim that we have discovered an infallible way to 'call down the blessing of God'. God blesses many of us, not because of the way we organize meetings but in spite of our procedures. God's love for his children leads him to overlook their foibles. This does not mean that he condones a lack of preaching nor the experiences of uncontrollable laughter, shaking and disorder. God does urge us to develop a biblically balanced way of worship.

Several further questions arise. Why did those who have felt closer to Jesus as a result of a Vineyard meeting need such a meeting? Why did they not draw closer to Jesus through his prescribed means? What was there about their personal discipline and devotion to Christ that made their Bible study, their prayer life, their ministry and witness, their fellowship with other believers, their meditation on the cross and attendance at the Lord's Table, or their readings in Christian books ineffective in drawing them closer to Christ? Before they came to the exciting, music-filled Vineyard meetings, did they never feel the presence of the risen Christ as they read the living Word, listened to a sermon or walked in communion with Christ along a country road?

We might also ask, 'How long will the ecstasy last?' Are proponents of the Vineyard-style meetings not creating a false expectation of what Christian living is all about? How long will God warm the hearts of disciples who fail to seek him with all their hearts? The principle is clear: 'You will seek me and find me when you seek me with all your heart' (Jer. 29:13). Such seeking involves intense and disciplined Bible study, corporate prayer with God's people as well as private prayer in solitude, meditation on the cross, learning through all the circumstances of life and using one's spiritual gifts in ministry. These are the means of grace God's people have used for two millennia. It may also involve joining oneself to the people of God in a small and struggling church, pouring one's life out on some mission-field, enduring cancer or pain. It is one thing to be euphoric in a crowd of excited people; it is another to seek Christ in the hard places, year after year — and find him gracious and sufficient. One worries that many who are euphoric now will be disillusioned in the long run. The long-term effects of Vineyardism cannot help but be disastrous.

The danger involved in putting experiences first

Although God uses a variety of experiences in the lives of Christians, we must realize that many are one-off events. We should be foolish if we were to wander around the Sinai Desert in the hope of God speaking to us through a burning bush. No one would buy a donkey in the hope that God would speak through it as he did to Balaam. Nor would we try to handle poisonous snakes in an attempt to reproduce the apostle Paul's esperience on Malta! Surely, no one would be so foolish, or indeed sinful, as to think that by commiting adultery as David did, he would come to enjoy a closer walk with God after his repentance!

This whole attempt to create a climate in a meeting in which certain experiences can be reproduced is spurious. I find nothing about those who meet to seek the Toronto Blessing and cry, 'Do it again, Lord!' that echoes Scripture. Even if the initial experiences were genuine — and I have serious doubts — the passion to reproduce the phenomena over and over again is unhealthy and unbiblical. Unusual scriptural experiences are just that — unusual. Israel crossed the Red Sea once. The building in Jerusalem where they met to pray shook once. Paul was bitten by a snake once.

Pentecost occurred once. The Second Evangelical Awakening was different from the First Awakening. We have no warrant to try to reproduce even genuine experiences — apart, that is, from those mandated as part of normal Christian living or church life, such as baptism, the Lord's Supper, worship services, prayer times, study times, preaching, fellowship, etc.

Several times when I have seen the full moon rising over the countryside my eyes have filled with tears as I contemplated the creative majesty of God. How marvellous that God would create something so beautiful! He is infinitely glorious. But suppose I should try to reproduce that experience every month. Suppose I should say to my congregation, 'On the Sunday evening closest to the full moon I want us to meet outside on a hilltop to contemplate the creative glory of God so we can all feel as I felt.' Would that make sense? No, of course not. Experiences are individual and vary greatly.

A friend recently told me about how she got on a plane for her first flight with a considerable fear of flying. During the flight, however, God gave her an incredible sense of his nearness. She just felt nearer to heaven being airborne! Should we then try to reproduce this experience by saying we should all take a meditative flight once a year as a way of recovering intimacy with God? That would be not only preposterous but unnecessary.

From time to time someone suffering from cancer, or some other serious disease, has confided in me that the experience resulted in a new intimacy with God. Many find this to be the case. But we do not try to reproduce the experience of sickness and pain that Job, and others in our own day, went through, just to get nearer to God!

As soon as we start running after experiences we are in trouble. People who are high on experience inevitably crash or live in a self-created fantasy world. Thomas Morton wrote several years ago about why so many charismatics left the movement. He points out that for some the 'initial wondrous experience' is 'enough to sustain them... A number of charismatics, however, find that the initial experience was not as powerful as they would have liked. This can lead to dabbling in gifts, which shows a desire to maintain the initial emotional thrust. Yet it cannot remain this way for long. Our role as disciples is not to be centred on feelings. When charismatics, or Christians in general, constantly seek after an emotional high, no matter how firmly rooted it seems to be in the Spirit, disaffection results.'[28] Some inevitably end up in a spiritual nose-dive that further damages their walk with Christ and causes confusion among immature Christians or seekers.

The initial experience often creates a desire for renewed highs. Morton points out, from his own experience and observation, that this leads to 'contrived prophecies, false interpretations of tongues, and exaggerated stories of miracles', and all this 'further erodes confidence in such experiences' among those already disappointed.[29] The statements and prophecies coming out of the Toronto Blessing and those swept away in the Third Wave promise still greater signs and wonders — a promise that cannot be fulfilled. Once one becomes addicted to external phenomena, one's desire for ever more spectacular 'signs of the Spirit' increases exponentially. Disillusionment waits for many. As Morton explains, 'If "experience" is the reason to involve oneself in a belief, certainly experience can be the reason to abandon it.'[30]

He then makes an important point — one I have sought to affirm throughout this book: 'The most important cause for changing one's views about being a charismatic, of course, is a revaluation of Scripture. And many have left for this reason... Most of us were not trained to perceive the error of taking narrative accounts in Acts and making that normative for all Christians at all times... It was after the ecstasy wore off, that we could reasonably examine the Bible. The lack of didactic teaching from the epistles and Gospels disturbed us.'[31]

An emphasis on outward experience inevitably leads to distortions of Scripture and short-circuits genuine experience. Biblical experience is born through faith in revealed truth, truth that paints great and glorious pictures of our triune God. The next question we must ask, then, concerns whether or not this movement was really initiated by the Holy Spirit and whether it truly exalts Jesus Christ.

14.
Is Christ front and centre?

Jonathan Edwards believed that the primary mark of a genuine work of the Spirit is its Christo-centric nature. He comments that it raises people's esteem for 'Jesus who was born of a Virgin, and was crucified without the gates of Jerusalem; and seems more to confirm and establish their minds in the truth of what the gospel declares to us of his being the Son of God, and the Saviour of men... The person to whom the Spirit gives testimony, and for whom he raises their esteem must be that Jesus who appeared in the flesh, and not another Christ in his stead; nor any mystical, fantastical Christ; such as the light within. This the spirit of Quakers extols, while it diminishes their esteem of and dependence upon an outward Christ — or Jesus as he came in the flesh — and leads them off from him.'[1]

No one can seriously dispute Edwards' analysis. As Colossians reminds us, Christ must have pre-eminence (Col. 1:18). Edwards makes a very perceptive distinction, however. He separates those, such as the Quakers, who claim to exalt Christ while really exalting their own inner impressions, and those who exalt the real Christ in his objective and historic reality. The question I raise in this chapter concerns whether the proponents of the Toronto Blessing, and the Vineyard movement in general, fulfil Edwards' criterion or that of the Quakers. If they are closer to the Quakers' emphasis on inner impressions, their claims about the Holy Spirit will also be flawed. Edwards points out: 'If the spirit that is at work among a people is plainly observed to work so as to convince them of Christ, and lead them to him ... it is the true and right Spirit.'[2] In the previous chapter, we have already noted the danger of using feelings, perceptions or experiences, unsubstantiated by Scripture, to 'prove' claims about the spiritual nature of a movement. At this point we need to look more closely at the place given to Jesus Christ in Vineyardism.

Vineyard statements

Vineyard representatives claim to exalt Jesus Christ. John Arnott asserts, 'Almost everyone who has been touched by this thing is saying, "I didn't know God loved me so much and I'm more in love with Jesus than before."'[3] Larry Randolph at theToronto Airport Fellowship said, 'He is our focus. He is the centrality of everything we do and everything that we say and all that we are. It is Jesus! ... We love You, Jesus!'[4] Guy Chevreau claims, 'When interviewed, people declare time and again that there is a deeper love for Jesus, a greater sense of the power of the gospel ...'[5] Jim Paul from the Toronto Airport Christian Fellowship, while speaking at a meeting in Edinburgh, exhorted people not to focus on the manifestations but on Christ. He insisted that the movement should not be called the 'Toronto Blessing' but the 'Jesus Blessing'.

Jesus is mentioned in some songs of the movement, such as those about the coming of the Bridegroom, 'Be glorified', and the 'Song of the Lamb'. At Holy Trinity, Brompton in London, one of the main centres of 'renewal' enthusiasm in Britain, Eleanor Mumford said, 'There is no time to give any attention to the enemy or to all his works. Because the power of Jesus is great and the Person of Jesus is so preoccupying, and our passion for Jesus is on the increase to such a degree that it is a wonderful thing.'[6]

Some who give testimonies recount Jesus talking to them or mention a vision of Jesus: 'The Lord clearly spoke to me and I experienced His presence in a new way... I also saw Jesus dimly in His throne room.' 'Several times Lilo sensed Jesus before her, asking her questions: for instance, He stood before her with His crown of thorns in His hands and asked, "Can you wear this crown?"'[7]

A multiplicity of statements of this nature could be quoted from John Wimber and others in the movement. In *Catch the Fire* Guy Chevreau asserts that the purpose of the experiences coincides with a basic fact of Christianity: 'If we understand that fundamental to Christian faith is a call to intimate relationship with God in Christ, then an essential dynamic of the maturing of our relationship with God is an ever-deepening intimacy with the Lord.'[8]

I have no reason to question the sincerity of those who feel they are exalting Christ, or have met Christ in the movement. There is a naïve, uncritical aspect to these claims, however. Ron Allen expresses their approach well: 'I'm reminded of what my old Quaker uncle used to say: "Well, Ron, it's the duck test." Have you heard that? If it walks like a duck and quacks like a duck, it's a duck! If it looks like Jesus and sounds like Jesus, it's probably Jesus!'[9]

Does that mean the Roman Catholic experience of Christ in the Eucharist is the real Christ? And what of the Jesus of the modernist, or spiritist or New Age movement? Hindus, who would love to include Jesus among their pantheon of gods, could by this definition be genuine in their profession of faith in Christ! As Bob Hunter notes, Ron Allen fails to heed 'Jesus' warnings about wolves in sheep's clothing or Paul's statement in 2 Corinthians 11 about there being *another* Jesus, *another* Gospel and *another Spirit*'.[10]

The place of the gospel in the Vineyard equation

Although all involved in the movement unequivocally state their commitment to exalt Christ, their actions belie their profession. In *Catch the Fire* Chevreau places an overwhelming emphasis on external phenomena. Meetings where the Toronto Blessing is passed on send the same signal. They conclude with 'ministry time' when the phenomena are sought. Testimonies centre on the manifestations. Messages and 'prophecies' focus on signs and wonders.

Meetings I have attended and material I have read all fail to live up to their claim of being Christ-centred. In one meeting the whole message was an apologetic designed to explain and bolster faith in the phenomena. In another, a message on the importance of having the 'spirit of adoption', the preacher failed to turn people to Christ's atoning death as the basis of the believer's adoption. Indeed, at the end of the message unsaved people were called forward to receive this spirit of adoption through prayer and laying on of hands *without any explanation of the gospel* — which must precede adoption into God's family. This kind of vague talk about salvation erodes the Christ-centred content of the gospel. It betrays a naïve and inaccurate perception that Christ is being glorified even when he is not mentioned or described — and this at a crucial juncture!

Enthusiasm for the phenomena and the Spirit detracts from a focus on the essential elements of the gospel of Jesus Christ — his person, teaching, life, death, burial, resurrection and present session at the Father's right hand. Paul, on the other hand, used his whole energy to declare the gospel: 'God, whom I serve with my whole heart in preaching the gospel of his Son'. He gloried in the power of the gospel, 'for the salvation of everyone who believes' (Rom. 1:9,16). Paul repeatedly warned about counterfeit gospels, other gospels, or adding to the gospel.

Yet in John Wimber's book about evangelism, a subject concerning which the Bible tells us the gospel is central, the author fails to give 'any definition of the gospel message. Centre stage are healings, words of knowledge, phenomena of the Spirit's presence — all things Wimber believes will bring people to faith. One searches in vain for exposition of the content of the gospel itself.'[11] Evidently John Wimber regrets the fact that there was no definition of the gospel in the first edition of *Power Evangelism*. According to Wayne Grudem, 'That was simply an oversight: he assumed that his readers were Christians and knew the content of the gospel ... the oversight has been corrected in the revised edition of *Power Evangelism* [1992].'[12] Admittedly, Wimber himself says, 'If people are going to be converted, they need to know the essentials of the gospel, that they are sinners in need of God's grace and that grace is experienced through faith in Christ.'[13]

However, this shift from a focus on the content of the gospel to lengthy and detailed descriptions of healings and other signs has had a very dangerous result over time. As the movement has progressed, Wimber's followers have either misconstrued his meaning or taken his emphasis to its logical conclusion. Jack Deere says, 'This world ... is going to come to Jesus Christ when there's a cataclysmic outpouring of the Holy Spirit in Signs and Wonders.'[14] In meeting after meeting and in conferences the emphasis is always power evangelism through signs and wonders. Obviously, the present emphasis of the Vineyard and that of Paul are radically diverse. For Paul the power resided in the proclamation of the person and work of Christ. No matter what its proponents may say, Christ is not glorified through this kind of methodology.

At one time John Arnott turned from giving salvation messages to speaking on the love, joy, peace and power of God and 'How to be Filled with the Spirit'. He said, 'I've found that when I preach salvation messages ... the ministry's time was hard.' (Did he feel this because there were not as many physical manifestations during the ministry time at the end of the meetings?) 'I asked the Lord', who, he says, told him 'that he just wanted to "love up on My church for a while".'[15] When Arnott gave the invitation people responded anyway and 'got saved'. Supposedly, God told Arnott not to bother with preaching the gospel but to concentrate on messages about the Holy Spirit and joy and peace! How could this god be the same God who prescribed, by the Holy Spirit, 'Believe in the Lord Jesus and you will be saved'? (Acts 16:31).

I can understand the need to vary messages so believers are taught — but I cannot understand an expectation of unsaved people coming forward to receive Christ without an explanation of who he is and what he has done. As mentioned earlier, this is exactly what I found the night I went on 14 July 1995. The gospel was not preached, but people came forward and were supposedly saved, without any explanation of the gospel, through laying on of hands and prayer for a spirit of adoption.

If we lived in an age when people widely understood the gospel, the need for its presentation might not be so acute. However, this is not the case. Gospel ignorance is even worse in Canada than in the US where a survey done in February 1994 by the Barna Research Group discovered that 'Half of all people who described themselves as "born-again" had no clue what John 3:16 refers to. Large percentages of professing Christians were also at a loss to explain terms such as "The Great Commission", or "the Gospel". Many defined "Gospel" simply as "a style of music".'[16]

Perhaps John Arnott has received different guidance from the Lord since that time. When I attended the Toronto Airport Vineyard on 4 October 1995, he gave a much more careful invitation with the focus on Christ and the need to confess one's sins to him for salvation. I do hope that this is a sign of progress away from their prevailing pattern of letting signs and wonders upstage the gospel.

The cross of Christ

The failure of Vineyard enthusiasts to emphasize the gospel is combined with a lack of emphasis on the cross and the atonement of Christ. Jesus taught his disciples that they must take up his cross daily if they would follow him (Luke 9:23). Paul 'resolved to know nothing while I was with you except Jesus Christ and him crucified' (1 Cor. 2:2). It is 'the precious blood of Christ, a lamb without blemish or defect', that God has chosen to redeem us, purify us, make us holy, give us hope and fill us with 'an inexpressible and glorious joy' (1 Peter 1:19-20,8). The devil is overcome 'by the blood of the Lamb and by the word of their testimony' (Rev. 12:11). Surely, I need go no further in laying out the centrality of the atoning sacrifice of Christ, both in the Bible as a whole and in the messages of the apostles. Any serious student of the Bible will grant this point.

When we turn to the Vineyard — and to the Toronto Blessing — we find a failure to emphasize the cross. Although Guy Chevreau, in *Catch the Fire*, described all the dramatic events in Toronto and listed numerous testimonies I only discovered one or two references to the cross in the whole book![17] But how can people be genuinely blessed without a focus on the cross? The same lack of emphasis on the cross is seen in messages given at the Toronto Airport.

Vineyard-watchers frequently note this imbalance. Pastor Daniel Lundy asks about the movement, 'What ever happened to the centrality of the cross in defining the love of God? Those who have gone to meetings at the Toronto Vineyard note a lack of emphasis on the cross.'[18]

Wayne Grudem refutes this analysis by pointing out that eight out of 125 songs in the 1989 Vineyard songbook deal with Christ's death for us. He claims that 'The Vineyard publishes four supplemental songbooks per year, along with worship tapes and CD's... We sing songs like this [about the cross] regularly in church, and so do the other Vineyards I have visited... Many of the songs on these [worship tapes] are praise to Jesus Christ for his work of redemption.'[19] Like many others who have attended, I did not find this when I attended current Vineyard meetings associated with the Toronto Blessing. While these informal observations are not scientific, one would expect to find a focus upon our sinfulness and our need of cleansing through the blood of Christ in any real renewal meetings.

Some have done more careful analyses that back up what many of us have informally observed about the role of Christ in the movement. Bob Hunter, of the Christian Research Institute, compared the transcripts of thirty messages given at the Toronto Airport Fellowship over a period of three months with the New Testament. In the New Testament he found 1230 references to the name of

Christ, 324 to the Holy Spirit and 203 references to prophecy or prophets. In the messages at the Toronto Airport Christian Fellowship, however, the Holy Spirit was mentioned 383 times, prophets or prophecy 372 times and Jesus only 143 times. Christ runs a distant third behind prophecy and the Holy Spirit! The Holy Spirit is almost upstaged by prophecy![20]

The biblical text focuses four to one on Christ, while this sampling of practice at the Toronto Airport Fellowship focuses almost three to one on the Spirit and three to one on prophecy. Is this emphasis scriptural? Of course not. It does not in any way reflect the scriptural focus on the centrality of Christ — a focus that the Holy Spirit inspired.

Christ defines the role of the Holy Spirit

During the week before his crucifixion, Christ gave instruction to his disciples on a number of issues. One of the most important of his teachings concerned the ministry of the Holy Spirit. 'I will ask the Father and he will give you another Counsellor to be with you for ever — the Spirit of truth' (John 14:16-17). The Holy Spirit was given to continue Christ's teaching ministry and to remind his disciples of what he had said while he was with them (John 14:26). 'When the Counsellor comes, whom I will send to you from the Father, the Spirit of truth who goes out from the Father, he will testify about me. And you also must testify...' (John 15:26-27). In chapter 16 he explains that it is expedient for him to go away so he can send the Comforter, who will convict the world of sin, righteousness and judgement, besides guiding the apostles into all truth. The role of the Holy Spirit throughout the church age was defined by Christ in the following way: 'He will not speak on his own, he will speak only what he hears... He will bring glory to me by taking from what is mine and making it known to you' (John 16:13-14). He is the Spirit of Christ.

The Holy Spirit deserves worship, attention and obedience but, if we understand the New Testament correctly, he does not draw attention to himself. He glorifies Christ. Any truly spiritual movement will have a biblical emphasis on the wonder and glory of Christ. His teachings and person, his creative and redemptive majesty, his atonement and the amazing peace we have with God through justification by his blood, his bride the church, his resurrection and ascension, his present session at the Father's right hand, the extension of his kingdom among all peoples and his return will captivate the attention of those moved by the Spirit.

Historically, this has not been the emphasis of the charismatic movement. Their most recent cousins, the Vineyard movement, along with those who promote the Toronto Blessing, focus on the Holy Spirit — his 'anointing', 'soaking in the Spirit', 'being slain in the Spirit', 'resting in the Spirit', 'laughing in the Spirit', even 'marinating in the Spirit'! We repeatedly hear, 'It's the anointing!' 'We're really going to soak you tonight!' 'After you've marinated in the Spirit ...' The facts suggest that no matter what proponents claim about the movement being initiated by the Holy Spirit, it does not meet the scriptural criteria about what Christ predicted that the Spirit would do.

In 1984 J. I. Packer published his book *Keep in Step With the Spirit.* He challenged all evangelicals, charismatic or not, to recover a biblical perspective on the Spirit and to pray for revival. In writing about the Holy Spirit in the Bible he pointed out that 'The Holy Spirit's distinctive new covenant role, then, is to fulfil what we may call a floodlight ministry in relation to the Lord Jesus Christ... Floodlights are so placed that you do not see them... It is as if the Spirit stands behind us, throwing light over our shoulder, on Jesus, who stands facing us. The Spirit's message is never, "Look at me; listen to me; come to me; get to know me," but always, "Look at *him,* and see his glory; listen to *him,* and hear his word; go to *him,* and have life; get to know *him,* and taste his gift of joy and peace." The Spirit, we might say, is the matchmaker, the celestial marriage broker, whose role it is to bring us and Christ together and ensure that we stay together.'[21]

The Vineyard movement professes to be in love with Christ, but the floodlight points elsewhere. Those who receive the Toronto Blessing claim that it makes them love Christ more. Why, then, do all the excitement and interest focus on prophecy, phenomena and the Holy Spirit? One is forced to the inevitable conclusion that in this movement Jesus Christ is an ethereal Christ — a Christ who is very, very far from centre stage.

Jonathan Edwards' first criterion of a genuine revival raises serious questions about the movement. As we saw at the beginning of the chapter, he pointed out that people's esteem must be raised to glorify 'that Jesus who appeared in the flesh, and not another Christ in his stead; nor any mystical, fantastical Christ; such as the light within. This the spirit of Quakers extols, while it diminishes their esteem of and dependence upon an outward Christ.'[22]

Obviously, Edwards had grave problems with the Quakers' perception that they glorified Christ. And the emphasis we find in the Toronto Blessing is not only dishonouring to Christ, but it also fails to glorify the Holy Spirit as revealed in Holy Scripture. Contrary to what Ron Allen's Quaker uncle claimed, the duck test does not work. Not everyone who claims to exalt Christ actually does!

15.
Is this really a movement of the Holy Spirit?

'We've seen thousands of visiting pastors come, be touched by the Holy Spirit's power and love and filled to take God's blessing home to their churches. The kindling fires of revival are indeed beginning to spread around the world.' 'The impact of the Spirit's power continues to grow exponentially... Everywhere we are seeing God pouring out His Spirit in ever-increasing waves.'[1] So writes John Arnott in the Toronto Airport magazine, *Spread the Fire*.

While John Wimber and author John White come short of calling the Toronto Blessing a revival, they do believe it is a renewal.[2] Guy Chevreau unequivocally states that it is 'an outpouring of the Holy Spirit'.[3]

Vineyard leaders are not the only ones who believe that what is happening is a mighty move of the Spirit. David Mainse, host of Canada's daily Christian television talk-show, *100 Huntley Street*, 'endorsed the Toronto Blessing on-air during a week of programming dedicated to examining historic renewals, revivals, and Airport Vineyard-related issues'.[4] Mainse was 'slain in the Spirit' at Holy Trinity Anglican Church in Brompton, in central London. Mainse states, 'I can't and don't endorse everything that happens ... there is the flesh ... but the basic fact is that God is mightily at work and certainly the majority of what's happening is of God.'[5] Concerning Holy Trinity Church, Brompton, Gary Pritchard reports, 'The outpouring of the Spirit began here in April 1994.'[6]

Gail Reid writes that in 1995 'During April, the Airport Vineyard sent seven ministry teams to various parts of Great Britain. All experienced the outpouring of God's Spirit.'[7] Toronto Fellowship Baptist pastor Richard Long, who was present on one of those

teams, reports of a meeting in Norwich, 'All the usual manifestations of the Spirit were present and 13 people came forward... The
Spirit of God touched those outside just as much as inside... The
square was filled with bodies doing — not carpet time, but cobble
time.'[8]

With so many voices describing the Toronto Blessing as an
outpouring of the Holy Spirit, it seems cavalier, even dangerous, to
enter a caveat. Could we be sinning against the Holy Spirit? John
Arnott 'believes that this is a heaven-sent renewal meant for the
local church, to build up the body of Christ so that eventually it will
overflow into the community and usher in revival'.[9] In a message
I heard in October 1995, he chided those who criticize and analyse.
We have already looked closely at this red herring in chapter 5.
Warnings about quenching the Spirit do the Spirit disservice. It
was he who commanded us to 'Test everything. Hold on to the
good.' And as my wife Mary Helen comments, 'There are an
enormous number of things people attribute to the Holy Spirit that
will have to be repented of when they get to heaven. The Holy Spirit
must be grieved by our propensity to blame him for everything we
do.'

What do we make of Vineyard claims that they are in the midst
of a 'movement of the Spirit'? If the Toronto Blessing has been
produced by God it will manifest certain biblical characteristics.
The Holy Spirit himself recorded these criteria in Scripture. In the
preceding chapters of this book, however, we have already un-
earthed a considerable number of unbiblical tendencies. These
troubling characteristics already place the whole movement in
doubt. Look at them again.

In this movement Christ is in the shadows, not in the
spotlight. Leaders draw attention to the Holy Spirit, whose
job, we know from Scripture, is to draw attention to Christ.

The cross is downplayed.

A host of physical manifestations, such as being 'slain in
the Spirit', shaking, roaring, etc., are attributed to the Holy
Spirit although no such warrant can be found in the Scriptures
— the casebook which the Holy Spirit wrote for the very
purpose of testing all things.

Experiences, phenomena, testimonies and personal perceptions are used to judge the reality of spiritual life instead
of allowing the inspired Scriptures to interpret these things.

The central means God uses to awaken sinners and instruct believers, preaching and teaching the Word of God, are shunted to the periphery of the movement.

The great doctrines that the Holy Spirit revealed for our growth, comfort and encouragement are devalued by a general aversion to theology.

Instead of sanctification through the illumination of the mind being emphasized, participants are urged, against the inspired scriptural pattern, to empty their minds. As a result the Holy Spirit appears, in their movement, in the guise of an anti-intellectual crusader.

Instead of being the author of self-control and order, the Holy Spirit is declared to be the author of the disorder, repetitive singing and animal noises.

Church history is treated selectively. The role of preaching, reformed Pauline doctrine and the cessationist views commonly held in genuine revivals under Calvin, the Puritans, Jonathan Edwards and George Whitefield, among others, are glossed over or distorted.

Conviction of sin, one of the chief effects of the work of the Holy Spirit on the soul of man, and a common element in all the great revivals, is almost completely lacking in this movement. In its place we have laughter and other phenomena. There is no historical or biblical precedent for laughter preceding conviction.

These facts about the movement present a troubling picture that fails to undergird their claims that it is a move of the Spirit. A number of other very serious discrepancies surface as we continue to probe the place of the Holy Spirit in the movement.

Spontaneity and the Spirit

As we saw in chapter 3, proponents of the Toronto Blessing claim that it was initiated by a sovereign and spontaneous outpouring of the Spirit at the conclusion of a meeting led by Randy Clark. Arnott speaks of 'an explosion, as the Spirit of God just sort of fell on people... suddenly "kaboom" and 80 per cent of the congregation was all over the floor, laughing and rolling and totally overtaken by the Spirit of God'.[10]

It sounds as if Randy Clark and his team were just asked to come and conduct a series of family meetings during a special weekend with no expectation of anything spectacular. When we probe deeper, however, we discover a different story. James Beverley comments about events on 20 January 1994: 'Recently I received a copy of Randy Clark's message that he delivered that first night. I had been told by various people that the outpouring of the Spirit was a complete surprise to Airport Vineyard people, an unexpected move of God. But Clark's message should have prepared anyone present for the arrival of the manifestations. He gave a dramatic account of his own experience of the manifestations under the ministry of Rodney Howard-Browne. Thus, when Randy extended an invitation that night for "ministry" the people knew what was involved.'[11]

Let's probe a little further into John Arnott's background. He does not come from a position of evangelical neutrality on these issues. His whole ministry has been influenced by a Pentecostal outlook through people such as Kathryn Kuhlman and Benny Hinn. Inevitably his exposure to a charismatic world-view would have created an expectation that the Holy Spirit would manifest his presence by visible phenomena.

Rodney Howard-Browne came to the USA in 1987 from South Africa with the express purpose of spreading the 'laughing revival'. Randy Clark, like many of those involved, had heard of Howard-Browne's impact on some of his friends. He went to Tulsa, Oklahoma and received 'holy laughter' through the laying on of Howard-Browne's hands. In Vineyard conferences, John Arnott heard people, including Randy Clark, talk about these things and was deeply impressed. Arnott had already been in Argentina where he had been anointed by the Pentecostal Claudio Freidzon. Inevitably, he invited Randy Clark to come to preach at the Airport Vineyard on 20 January 1994, no doubt with the hope that physical manifestations would break out. They did![12]

But let's go even further back into the story of John Wimber himself. Carol Wimber describes what they believe launched them into power evangelism through signs and wonders: 'It was Sunday evening, Mother's Day 1981, and a young man whom John had invited to preach, gave his testimony. At the end of his message, the guest speaker invited all those under the age of 25 to come forward. None of us had a clue as to what was going to happen next. When we got to the front the speaker said, "For years now the Holy Spirit has been grieved by the Church, but He is getting over it. Come Holy Spirit!" And He came. Most of these young people had grown up around our home and we knew them well... One fellow, Tim, started bouncing! His arms flung out and he fell over, but one of his hands accidentally hit a mike stand and he took it down with him. He was tangled up in the cord with the mike next to his mouth. Then he began speaking in tongues, so the sound went throughout the gymnasium. We had never considered ourselves Charismatics and certainly never placed any emphasis on the gift of tongues. We had seen a few people tremble and fall over before and we had seen many healings, but this was different. The majority of the young people were shaking and falling over. At one point it looked like a battlefield; bodies everywhere, people weeping, wailing, speaking in tongues, much shouting and loud behavior. And there was Tim in the middle of it all — babbling into the microphone!'[13]

Carol Wimber comments that they did not consider themselves charismatics. However, they had experienced shaking, trembling and many healings before. John Wimber's first church was Quaker, with its emphasis on 'inner light'. John had received the gift of tongues as a young Christian. Carol Wimber had received a dramatic experience of tongues in 1976. During 1977 and 1978 Carol led a growing home prayer group with an openness to charismatic manifestations. John became its pastor and began his healing ministry in 1978. Surely all these events and ideas must have provided fertile ground for what the Wimbers say happened spontaneously on Mother's Day in 1981? They display a massive propensity to encourage charismatic phenomena. What else could be asked of a person to become a card-carrying charismatic?

Wimber went on to develop his theories on power evangelism through signs and wonders as he taught his controversial course at Fuller Seminary from 1982 to 1985. To an outside observer, events in Toronto seem to be the inevitable result of the long series of steps John and Carol Wimber took, that go back at least to the early 1970s. The churches they planted and the conferences they led encouraged a massive outbreak of physical manifestations. Toronto became the place where it happened.

Far from being spontaneous, the approach to the phenomena, particularly 'doing carpet time', has gradually become regimented, organized and manipulative. As time passes, the energy required to produce the phenomena seems to be greater. Like many charismatic groups, the initial excitement becomes tamed, codified, organized. In my last visits I saw nothing even remotely spontaneous. Apart from an occasional outburst of laughter, the whole meeting moved towards 'ministry time', where candidates for 'the anointing' were asked to line up along taped lines on the carpet at the back of the hall. There they waited until someone with a badge, indicating a member of the 'ministry team', prayed for them — often gently putting their hands close to their head, so they could fall to the carpet 'slain in the Spirit'. 'Catchers' waited behind those prayed for to help them to the carpet without injury.

It is one thing to admit that there are evidences of the flesh in much of what we as Christians do. It is quite another to specifically programme a meeting to produce opportunities for the flesh to flourish, as I believe is occurring in these 'renewal' meetings. In my opinion, the very *lack* of spontaneity in the movement throws doubt on their claim that it is all 'of the Spirit'. It smacks too much of a carefully choreographed mass event with dangerous overtones of conscious — or as I hope, unconscious — manipulation. But do these phenomena sometimes overcome those who do not want or expect them?

Hypnotism and the phenomena

Nader Mikhaiel has discovered scores of parallels between charismatic phenomena and what happens to subjects under hypnosis.[14] He examined descriptions from Pentecostal writer, Francis MacNutt,[15] testimonies from meetings led by John Wimber and, more recently, phenomena associated with the Toronto Blessing. He compared these descriptions with those of eminent writers on the subject of hypnosis such as Franz Anton Mesmer, who gave to the age-old practice of hypnotism used, for example, in ancient Egypt, almost the status of a science.[16]

As mentioned earlier, Mikhaiel discovered, for instance that 11% of a sample taken at a Wimber conference experienced catalepsy (immobility) while 45% shook.[17] 52% experienced tingling.[18] One who experienced phenomena associated with the Toronto Blessing said, 'I fell over and the Holy Spirit came through my feet like a tingling electric current and up my body to my chest where I felt resistance.'[19]

Table I		
Similarities between hypnosis and charismatic experience		
Feelings of weight-lessness	Feelings of heaviness	Feeling of being stretched
Catalepsy (being un-able to move)	Feeling that body parts are changing size	Repetitive movement of body parts
Rapid eye movement	Changes in breathing	Tinglings
Alleviation of pain and disease	Shaking	Feeling drunk
Hearing a buzzing noise	Changes in hearing	Smelling aroma of flowers
Seeing a bright light	Being aware of hot and cold areas on body	Feeling of detach-ment from body
Feeling washed clean	Time distortion	Age regression (e.g. to childhood)
Uncontrollable laughter	Imitation	Post-hypnotic suggestion

Table II	
Actual statements of participants	
'Slain in Spirit' experience	*Experience of hypnotism*
I felt like I'd been rolled over by a steam roller! God had sat on me.'	'My arm feels like a bag of cement or like a ton of lead.'
'She knew the meeting was going on … but she felt totally detached.'	'I feel like I am just detached in some way.'
'As she lay there she was aware continuously of energy passing through her body.'	'I feel as if current is passing through my body.'
'I felt totally clean.'	'Feeling very relaxed and clean.'

Every one of the phenomena I have listed in chapter 8, including healing, have routinely taken place where hypnosis has been practised. Many other effects, identical with those of hypnosis, are documented by perusing the testimonies of people who have charismatic experiences. Table I tabulates some of the similarities as shown by Mikhaiel.[20]

The general parallels noticeable in Table I are further enforced by comparing the actual statements of people under hypnosis and those who have been 'slain in the Spirit'. Table II gives several examples of this amazing similarity. What are described are sensations experienced by people under hypnosis and those who were 'being slain in the Spirit'.[21] Many more could be cited.

Proponents of the 'blessing' often refer to God doing a work of inner healing while people are doing 'carpet time'. The last couplet in the Table II has a direct bearing on this whole subject of 'inner healing'. Pentecostal writers Francis MacNutt and Charles and Frances Hunter describe a similar effect. MacNutt writes that 'Healing seemed more likely to occur when people were resting in this way [i.e. lying down].'[22] The Hunters state, 'We discovered an interesting fact. God often does a supernatural work in healing, deliverance or cleansing while a person is under the power.'[23] I shall not be able to follow up on this issue in this book, but it does raise serious concerns. How can people know real inner healing without scriptural truths leading to conviction of personal sin and trust in the atoning work of Christ?

Healing also occurs under hypnosis, and with similar, often short-term results. Anatol Milechnin notes, 'In some theatrical demonstrations of hypnosis a simple suggestion may be sufficient... Thus paralytics may be found to abandon their crutches, deaf people to hear, psychosomatic cases to lose their disorders, etc., even though this recovery may only be temporary.'[24] A famous hypnotist named Bernheim 'confessed to Freud that his own therapeutic successes were only found in his hospital wards where collective hysteria was in operation, and not in his own private practice'.[25]

Mikhaiel points out that as early as 1784 'Hypnotists claimed to cure head pain, sciatica, skin disease, congested spleen, convulsive asthma, tumours, body burns, putrid fever, catarrh, and after-effects of stroke, various diseases of the abdominal viscera and various eye diseases.' To this list modern hypnotists add 'healing of acne, warts, stuttering, bad habits, insomnia, smoking, loss of sexual power, habitual miscarriages, bursitis, back pains, paralysis and even blindness'.[26]

I have already mentioned in chapter 8 James Beverley's research into the healings that have been claimed at the Toronto Airport Vineyard. He picked three of the most dramatic cases and with the help of two doctors he sought to assess their credibility. He found false impressions, mistaken facts and exaggerations. In one case he found a recurrence of cancer; in a second he found improvement consistent with a change of psychological attitude and in a third he found 'Sarah's recovery as a dramatic psychological and physical response to prayer, friendship, and love'.[27]

Anecdotes such as the above are much more consistent with hypnosis than biblical healing. On 4 October John Arnott called to the platform Sarah Lilliman, one of the cases Beverley investigated, and her mother to show that healing had actually taken place. No doubt there had been a real improvement in her health, but even that night, Arnott pointed out that healing is seldom 100% and so he prayed for her and her mother. 'We will keep soaking them in the Spirit,' he said. The speaker on 11 October mentioned that healing can be progressive over a period of time. In many cases those healed retrogress back into their illnesses. Indeed, in a television broadcast Benny Hinn talked about the importance of learning how to keep one's healing by developing faith. He pointed out that some are healed in the meeting by being in a faith atmosphere but lose it when they leave! I am not saying that the Vineyard agrees with everything Benny Hinn does, but I do have the impression that similar ideas about healing prevail in Vineyard circles. This kind of incomplete, progressive, or retrogressive healing corresponds to what happens under hypnosis but is unknown in Scripture. (The case of the blind man seeing by stages took place in front of Jesus in the course of a few moments.)

We can also compare those who are susceptible to hypnosis with those who are more open to 'being slain in the Spirit'. Francis MacNutt believes that 'People who are more open (as opposed to closed personalities) are more likely to rest [in the Spirit]. Persons determinedly self-controlled are not nearly so likely to be overcome by the Spirit... I have also noticed that artistic, creative, intuitive people seem more likely to fall than rational, intellectual types... In general more women than men... If I could characterize the kind of person least likely to fall ... he would be an elderly man of Anglo-Saxon or Germanic ancestry who ... grew up in a church that emphasized discipline and self-denial.'[28] This corresponds closely with the findings of Hall and Grant about hypnosis.[29] It is interesting to note that those least susceptible to hypnosis and being slain in the Spirit manifest two characteristics of a mature Christian — self-control and self-denial! (See Luke 9:23; Gal. 5:22-23).

The similarities are too many to ignore. Suggestibility plays a crucial role in hypnosis and, I believe, in the Toronto Blessing. Five English doctors who attended meetings conducted by John Wimber in England in the late 1980s were of the opinion that the events at Toronto, like these earlier meetings, are examples of mass hypnosis. 'According to one of the five, a leading English psychiatrist, "It was a very expert performance, containing all the textbook characteristics of the induction of hypnosis."'[30]

Even those sympathetic with charismatic phenomena talk about 'altered states of consciousness' (ASCs). The March/April 1995 issue of the Toronto Airport Christian Fellowship magazine *Spread the Fire* featured a generally favourable review of Dr Patrick Dixon's book, *Signs of Revival*. In this work, Dixon writes, 'I believe it [ASC] is the key to making sense of Christian experience, particularly what is happening in many churches today... In our day-to-day vocabulary we may refer to ASCs as trance, hypnosis, dream or ecstasy... One could argue that ASCs in the context of faith in Christ and prayerful obedience, are the basis of dynamic, personal, relevant, living faith.'[31]

Evidently Dr Dixon finds nothing troubling about comparing present happenings with hypnosis, among other things. In explaining what triggers this altered state of consciousness (ASC), he states, 'Here attention is intensely focused on one thing, one thought or a task, literally blocking out almost everything else.'[32]

Dr Dixon's views, although suggestive of what is actually happening in many charismatic meetings, are diametrically opposed to what we find in Scripture about having a clear mind and exercising control over the emotions and will. We discussed this in chapter 11, where we noted the tendency proponents of the Toronto Blessing have of asking people to empty their minds and surrender their wills to an atmosphere and a spirit they claim to be the Holy Spirit. This attack on the mind and the will is consistent with hypnosis, but not with the illumination of the mind and 'the fruit of the Spirit [which] is ... self-control'.

Dixon's open admission that religious ecstasy as experienced in charismatic circles is due to an altered state of consciousness raises

serious questions. What is being experienced in the Toronto Blessing and described by Dixon has an uncanny affinity with Eastern
mysticism and New Age practice. This is reflected in the contempla-
tive prayer movement, with its emphasis on emptying to achieve
intimacy with God. Further study and exposure of this danger is
urgently needed.[33] No wonder many close to the movement have
expressed concern about alien spirts.

Is it unconscious hypnosis or demonic influence?

Vineyard leaders admit that early in the history of their movement
many of the present phenomena were attributed to demonic activity,
and exorcism was employed. John Wimber said, 'I recognize that
there are certain manifestations of the Spirit that have gone on in our
meetings for fifteen years that we supposed were demonic in
origin.'[34]

John Arnott has said, 'We used to think if people shook, shouted,
flopped, rolled, etc., that it was a demonic thing manifesting and we
needed to take them out of the room. That was our grid, that's what
our experience had taught us, that demons could be powerful ... [but
now we know] that the Holy Spirit was, you know, a million times
more powerful than all the demons in hell put together.'[35] Bill
Jackson, in his paper on the phenomena, admits that even now,
'Certain body movements [are] indicative of demonic presence.'[36]
He fails to identify these demonic marks.

If, as some claim, both the Spirit and Satan produce similar
phenomena, how can we distinguish the divine from the demonic?
Vineyard leaders give us no guidance here except to urge us to trust
God's power over demons.

Arnott is now so positive that the phenomena are produced by the
Holy Spirit that he travels all over the world to pass on the 'blessing'.
Surely, wisdom should make one much more sceptical of manifestations that the Vineyard admit that they earlier considered demonic, and which have no scriptural basis! Similar manifestations
were interpreted by Whitefield, Edwards, Charles and John Wesley
as demonic.[37]

Many Pentecostals today have serious doubts about the source of
the phenomena. Gordon Williams, who ministers across Canada,
claims he has exorcised demons twice from a woman about whom
he writes, 'Every time she went to a Vineyard meeting she came

away with an evil spirit.' He goes on to claim, 'There is a "transfer-ence of spirits" occurring at the Vineyard meetings. They are obviously unaware of the wiles of the devil... At Vineyard, the leadership is looking at these manifestations ... and misidentifying them as the Holy Spirit when they are either the work of an evil spirit or the flesh... Because of the Vineyard approach to ministry, their worship services expose people to the demonic more than many of the alternatives from which they have come.'[38]

Cheryl Thomson and her husband were married by John Arnott and participated in Toronto-area Vineyard meetings for some time. However, practices there led them to leave several years ago. Noting John Arnott's admission that for fifteen years certain manifestations were viewed as demonic, she comments in a letter to the editor of the Canadian magazine, *Faith Today*, 'It is our belief that significant doorways to demonic activity have been present in the Vineyard for all that time, and they still have not been closed.'[39] Significantly, the editor chose to cut out this section of her letter. In a much longer statement outlining a series of concerns, Cheryl Thomson expresses what is probably an extreme view: 'Demonic powers, I believe, have gained control over the Vineyard Movement and The Kansas City Fellowship "Prophetic Movement".'[40]

John Arnott's statement that 'God's desire to bless us is far greater than Satan's ability to deceive us,' may be true, but it does not take into account the third factor in the God-Satan-man equation. He naïvely overlooks the human propensity to self-deception that often blinds us to God's will or cuts us off from the means God uses to bless us. The failure in Toronto Blessing circles to give due place to preaching and teaching casts a pall of fuzziness over everything. Incisive biblical thinking is short-circuited. This rosy view of what is happening fails to take into account the human gullibility and suggestibility so repeatedly demonstrated by hypno-tists, the rise of the cults and history itself. Even more seriously, it fails to lend due credence to Satan's ability to go about 'as an angel of light'.

In spite of the dangers, Guy Chevreau adds: 'It is far healthier to focus attention on the wheat, and not the chaff, nor on the enemy sowing weeds.'[41] Why then did Paul's last words to the Ephesians not only include his commitment of them to God but his warning: 'Keep watch over the flock ... after I leave, savage wolves will come in among you and will not spare the flock. Even from your own number men will arise and distort the truth... So be on your guard!'? (Acts 20:28-31).

By contrast, Mikhaiel feels strongly that there is more in the Toronto Blessing than a little bit of the flesh. He believes, from his research, that the movement cannot be explained just in terms of the power of suggestion. Instead, he finds parallels between hypnosis and witchcraft, clairvoyance, shamanism and divination. He notes that hypnotists are often surprised by unpredictable reactions in their subjects. He feels that hypnosis, by bypassing the will, leaves the human being open to dangerous supernatural forces.[42]

While I would hesitate to label the Toronto Blessing demonic, I have no doubt that those involved with it are opening a dangerous doorway to satanic influence and distortion. I feel that the vast majority who participate and lead the 'renewal' sincerely want to glorify Christ — and this desire, at least for the present — rescues the movement from going further down the slippery slope that plunges into the cultic swamp. To further understand what is happening we need to explore the power of suggestion.

Suggestibility and expectation — unconscious forces behind the movement

What happens in a Vineyard meeting, it seems to me, can be traced to at least three factors: the expectations of those who attend; the suggestions of others; and the powerful atmosphere of the meeting itself. Let me consider these in turn.

1. The role of expectation

I have already established at considerable length my belief that the phenomena which occurred in January 1994 were not spontaneous. They were the inevitable result of a progression in John Wimber's life, theology and ministry, in the experience of Randy Clark and John Arnott, and indeed, of all the known principals involved in the Toronto Blessing.

Consider John Wimber's expectations in 1977 concerning healing. He already believed that healing should be a normal part of church life. During a series of messages from Luke's Gospel he noted the prevalence of healing and exorcism. He began to ask people to come forward for healing. For months nothing happened. 'It was a humiliating, gut-wrenching time when many people left the church in disgust. Yet Wimber would not give up. He *believed* that God would not let him. He was *determined* to see God heal people, and eventually — after ten months — he did. One young woman was healed in her home of a fever, and Wimber's exultation knew no bounds. "We got one!" he yelled at the top of his lungs on the way to his car.'[43] Obviously, Wimber's dogged determination to see what he expected to happen actually take place has played a large part in Vineyardism ever since.

The same can be said of John Arnott. In October 1994 he said, 'What we learned from Wimber and the Vineyard was, all of us could flow in the gifts of the Spirit. The Bible encourages us to desire to prophesy, you know, to desire spiritual gifts, desire the best gifts. What does that mean? *Earnestly desire them. And that's what we began to do,* and so when I went to Argentina last November [1993], … Carol and I both got powerfully touched in meetings led by Klaudio Freidzon, who's a Pentecostal leader in Argentina and a wonderful man of God. He prayed for us, but as he did he asked a question. He said, *"Do you want it?"* And I said, "Oh, yeah, *I want it all right!"* He said, "Then take it." Boom, he hits my hands and something clicked in my heart. I said, *"Yeah, I will, too, I'll take it,"* and it was just a click of faith.'[44]

Again, nothing could be clearer than the fact that John and Carol Arnott had been operating for some time with a desire burning within. They interpreted it as a simple desire for spiritual gifts. Their explanation, however, reflects a desire for some external manifestation that would fulfil their longing. This expectation had been fed for years by an admiration for Kathryn Kuhlman, Benny Hinn and others. The expectation was heightened by the visit to Argentina and the stories of Randy Clark's encounter with Howard-Browne.

Expectations of physical phenomena, including healing and words of knowledge, are common in those who attend a meeting where the Toronto Blessing is 'passed on'. In each of the meetings I attended a cursory glance around at the very beginning of the meeting — although filled with visitors from the US, Britain and all over the world — demonstrated that the vast majority were in sympathy with what was going on. One could tell by both sight and sound.

Such a rough estimation is confirmed by those in the movement. Todd Hunter pressed both Randy Clark and John Arnott for their opinion on whether it was 'God refreshing the refreshed', that is, giving more to those who already had charismatic experiences. Randy Clark estimated that 'About 80 per cent of the people who are being touched are people just like you, who have been touched once before.'[45]

The vast majority of those on whom the Toronto Blessing has made an impact are those who have already accepted the charismatic viewpoint. A decline in biblical literacy combined with an aversion to doctrine have produced a radical erosion of belief in the cessation of the miraculous gifts. Out of this fertile ground Pentecostalism mushroomed, the charismatic movement exploded and now the Third Wave is skyrocketing into the stratosphere. People have been taught to expect all the manifestations present in the early church, and 'greater works than these'. News from Toronto feeds a world-wide anticipation of something spectacular. It fits in with the expectations they already have.

Albert Dager writes, 'Most people who attend the hyper-charismatic meetings that result in pandemonium ... are normal, everyday folks ... may be professional people, hold responsible jobs and have a genuine love for God... But they come with a sense of expectancy to receive something from the touch of the preacher [or the atmosphere of the meeting] — something they are inclined to believe they can't receive from God on their own. They believe that God has placed a special anointing on the preacher.'[46]

Many of the testimonies Guy Chevreau uses in *Catch The Fire* illustrate this preparatory expectation in people who attend the meetings. Ron Allen, a Regional Overseer for the Association of Vineyard Churches who has participated in over 100 church-plants, came to Toronto and was 'slain in the Spirit'. Among his observations he writes, 'If we come to observe we'll just have opinions, but if we come to participate, we'll receive a fresh anointing of the Holy Spirit and have Him to impart [to others].'[47] Clearly, Vineyard leaders themselves realize that in order to experience the phenomena, one needs to anticipate an anointing of the Spirit. The expectant attitude of the participant is an important part of the whole scenario.

2. The role of suggestion

Some, however, come without expecting to be 'slain in the Spirit', only to find themselves on the floor. How does this happen?

The power of suggestion has been operating in the movement from the beginning. The expectant atmosphere generated in meetings is part of the Vineyard mystique. Meetings that pass on the Toronto Blessing duplicate, albeit on a larger scale, what has been happening in Vineyard circles since at least 1981. Cheryl Thomson left the Vineyard movement in the Toronto area a few years ago. She describes how what happened at the Toronto Airport Vineyard in January 1994 was part of Vineyard programming in 1987: 'Every meeting ended with "ministry time". The scene would be familiar now to many. It's the usual "Vineyard" technique. Local "Vineyard Fellowships" had sent teams of workers to the conference. When Wimber announced from the platform, "The Holy Spirit is here. He's moving across the room..." these people wearing identification badges, approached anyone who seemed to be manifesting a supernatural touch from God, or anyone who asked them for prayer. They held out their hands a few inches away from the person's head, or the location on the body where physical healing was asked for and prayed. Many times, people were "slain in the Spirit". They lay on the floor in what I perceived was truly another state of consciousness.'[48]

What Cheryl Thomson describes in 1987 is very close to what I saw when I attended Vineyard meetings in Toronto in 1994. Steve Long admits, 'Outward manifestations are not new at the Vineyard ... however, the number of people experiencing them was unique.'[49] James Beverley asked John Arnott if the phenomena taking place in Toronto were new to him. He answered, 'Not at all, I have seen everything before in Vineyard services around the world.'[50] Without any doubt Vineyard leadership had for many years encouraged physical phenomena. The 'Vineyard-style meeting' is almost like a franchise that over the years has become more and more specialized and refined — so that phenomena almost always now occur.

Certainly, there is little that can be viewed as spontaneous today. While people are told not to seek the manifestations but to seek Christ, everything in the meeting signals how important the phenomena are. Counsellors are trained to minister to people who have a temperament or approach that makes them 'hard to receive' the manifestations. As Gail Reid points out, 'Some people do not experience manifestations without inner changes [until their inner prejudices are broken down?], but Vineyard leaders then recommend continual prayer ministry until the "cumulative effect" is evident in their lives. John Arnott emphasizes the need to "soak in

God's presence for at least three days". There is a definite suggestion that one must be actively seeking God's blessing through prayer
and that the manifestations are a sign of his work.'[51]

Leaders promote an expectation of experiencing the phenomena
by songs, testimonies, demonstrations on the platform, in their
messages and in their instructions before 'ministry time'. A powerful perception is created that God the Holy Spirit is going to come
down at 'ministry time' and manifest his presence by creating
physical manifestations. They repeatedly sing, 'Do it again, Lord.'
This repetitious focus on the phenomena, this 'soaking', produces
a 'cumulative effect' that many would label brainwashing.

Dick Sutphen, a professional hypnotist, conducts seminars designed to educate people about how governments, the military, cults
and religious groups use persuasion and brainwashing techniques.
'He points out that many who use these techniques are not necessarily aware that they are using them.'[52] In other words, leaders in the
Vineyard may have witnessed the success of others and copied their
techniques in the belief that the Holy Spirit is the source.

While Sutphen is not a real believer in Christ, he nevertheless
believes that religion is valid as long as manipulation is not used.
Surely we should react with as much horror as he to any hint of
manipulation in a ministry in which leaders are to take a back seat
to Christ as he leads his church through the Word of God by the Holy
Spirit. I have already noted the alarming propensity in the movement to ask people to empty their minds and cut themselves loose
from their doctrinal moorings to become open to 'whatever the
Spirit wants to do'.[53] This kind of instruction certainly appears to me
like manipulation through the power of suggestion.

Sutphen explains how manipulation occurs. First people are set
up as 'marks' by giving them information they can agree on with the
goal of establishing trust in the speaker. ('God loves us. God wants
to bless us. God is greater than demons. The Holy Spirit is here
tonight in power.') Next the manipulator comes across with 'truisms
— facts that could be debated' but are usually accepted quickly as
true. ('Surely you're not satisfied with your Christian life. Don't you
want more of the Spirit? Don't you want whatever he has for you?
God wants to come in tonight and change your whole life. God
wants to heal you.') The listener increases in trust through this
second stage. Then the speaker makes a *suggestion* about what he
wants you to do, generally near the end of a long two- or three-hour
evening. Since agreement and trust have been developing people

often accept the suggestion ('Come forward if you want the blessing. Line up along the lines on the carpet. Ask for prayer. God is
going to do again tonight what he has been doing.')[54]

Sutphen writes that 'The progressive result of this mental condition is to impair judgment and increase suggestibility. The more this
condition can be maintained or intensified, the more it compounds.
Once catharsis, or the first brain phase, is reached, the complete
mental takeover becomes easier. Existing mental programming can
be replaced with new patterns of thinking and behavior.'[55]

Pentecostal writer Gordon Williams comments, 'People who
attend services at the Vineyard are having a religious experience.
Religious experiences are addictive. Christian services are not
usually very attractive because they call us to repentance, to self-
denial, to spiritual warfare from which we will often grow weary.'[56]

Vineyard leaders are not alone in consciously or unconsciously
using manipulative techniques. Too many supposedly 'successful'
Christian ministries rely on an unhealthy use of psychological
methods. During the same week that I attended my first meeting at
the Toronto Vineyard, I also went to a meeting in which an
internationally known preacher spoke. His message was long. He
led up to his invitation with a series of emotionally charged deathbed
stories. The invitation seemed interminable and manipulative. Later
in that same week I had contact with those in a business using highly
charged psychological methods to sell products. This pandering to
psychological manipulation is wrong wherever it is found.

Personally, at this point at least, I have not read or seen anything
that makes me believe that the leaders in the movement consciously
set out to manipulate people. However, they ought to be much more
conscious of psychological factors than they seem to be. But they
have found something that 'works' and instead of probing the
relationship between their powerful use of suggestion and the
susceptibility of human beings to psychological influence they
attribute whatever happens to the Holy Spirit.

3. The emotionally charged nature of the meetings

Early Pentecostals, in common with modern proponents of mass
meetings such as Oral Roberts, Benny Hinn, Howard-Browne, John
Wimber and now John Arnott, have discovered a potent way to run
meetings that almost inevitably results in strange things happening.

Meetings at the Toronto Airport Vineyard invariably have five parts, that correspond closely with what I have heard and read about other Vineyard style meetings:

1. Singing (forty-five minutes to an hour in one block);
2. Recognition of visitors and announcements;
3. Testimony time (thirty to forty-five minutes) in which the leader interviews people who have had experiences, healings, etc.;
4. Message (thirty to eighty minutes of anecdotes and apologetics on the movement with a widely varying degree of biblical content). Often messages are changed at the last minute;
5. Ministry time (from forty-five minutes to several hours), during which chairs are stacked, or in the new building, people move back to the open space and stand along taped lines on the carpet while 'prayers' and 'catchers' move from person to person with the result that many are 'slain in the Spirit' or show other manifestations.

Meetings last over three hours. 'Ministry time' can go on into the early hours of the morning. During 'testimony time', before the message, the leader calls for some 'catchers' and prays over the person or couple being interviewed. They fall backwards with the 'catchers' helping them avoid injury. The stage is often strewn with prone figures, some shaking, some laughing uproariously, some making other strange noises as they are 'soaked in the Spirit' throughout the rest of the meeting. On 4 October 1995, John Arnott preached with bodies strewn all over the platform. Sometimes, as on this occasion, student helpers or team members are called forward to pray over them, gently touch them or comfort them throughout the ensuing part of the meeting.

They have discovered that repetitive, emotional and lengthy singing, testimonies of phenomena and healings, exhortations to be open to whatever the Spirit has for them, combined with a meeting lasting three hours or longer, creates a charged atmosphere. The meeting is full of expectation of the unusual. The focus of the meeting is not on the preaching of the Word, but on the 'ministry time' at the end. During preaching many of those present get restless. As with hypnosis, the 'reactions of subjects depend upon the intensity of the emotions of the hypnotist and the general atmosphere'.[57]

During 'ministry time' excitement mounts and many respond by shaking, falling, moaning, etc. Albert Dager comments that the people who react in these meetings are 'normal, everyday folks', who 'can't believe that they can be brainwashed or manipulated. But the manner in which excitement and fervor builds in some meetings catches them off guard. They are susceptible to suggestion — even the suggestion that they have been healed.'[58]

The power of highly charged meetings is widely recognized. 'Any hypnotherapist who has had the chance of inducing hypnosis in a collective environment will confirm the ease with which untrained people, taken at random, rapidly enter the hypnotic state and present by simple imitation, the hypnotic phenomena they have just observed in others.'[59]

Francis MacNutt attributes what happens to the Holy Spirit without professing to understand it: 'If we are praying for people in a line, it is usually, the third or fourth person who is the first to fall. Whatever this power is, it seems to increase after a period of prayer until it fills the entire room; at this point people sometimes begin to be overcome by the Spirit just as they stand there, without anyone touching them.'[60]

The phenomena do not seem to me to be supernatural at all but rather psychological — the product of intense desire, expectation, suggestibility and the atmosphere of a Vineyard meeting. James Beverley comes to this same conclusion for slightly different reasons. He writes, 'Consider again the issue of the "manifestations". Are they proof of the supernatural outpouring of the Holy Spirit? Not at all. None of the manifestations associated with The Toronto Blessing are inherently miraculous. Each one of them can be imitated by most people. An actor could be hired to attend an evening meeting and imitate all the manifestations, and no one would be able to distinguish that person from others under the "real" anointing. Too much about the manifestations can be explained psychologically.'[61]

While Vineyard leaders may not set out to deliberately manipulate people or engage in mass hypnosis they are very naïve in their understanding of human emotions and the dangers they are unleashing. With the increase of writings on the movement that express alarm, the time has arrived when its leaders ought to take steps to distance themselves from manipulative practices. If the movement is of God, why does the Spirit never lead them to encourage times of quiet meditation, or intense Bible study? Why is there always so much sound and emotion? But there is another problem — the way they treat the Holy Spirit.

The Holy Spirit treated as a commodity

While it may be legitimate to compare the Holy Spirit to fire or water, the repetitious imagery used to portray this blessed Person seems to detract from his glory and focus more on what he can do for us. In one meeting I went to, he was referred as water, wind, sweet fire, a river, a well, spring rain, gushers, the heavenly water cycle, showers, fountains and some other images that I can't recall. The group sang, 'Light the fire again,' 'There's a wind blowing — sweet wind, water flowing, fire burning — oh sweet fire,' 'The river is here,' and 'Mercy is falling'.[62]

The imagery may be valid, but why is there so little personal address to the Holy Spirit, or to Christ for that matter? The imagery portrays something, almost like a commodity, flowing in, or falling on, the recipient. The focus is on what people receive, not the glory of who he is. Coupled with this concern is the whole matter of laying on of hands. It is as if those in the movement have a store of some powerful force or commodity that they dispense at will. Leaders and trained team members put their hands lightly on, or close to, people receiving. Often the movement of the hand towards the person is enough for them to be 'slain in the Spirit'. Sometimes people 'blow the Spirit' or wave their hands. Jewel van der Meere tells of being in a meeting in which people gathered in a circle and 'tossed the Holy Spirit like a ball' around the circle.

Admittedly, we have several examples in which the apostles laid hands on people in the New Testament. But we have no examples of this kind of wholesale process in which 'anointed people' are able to pass on the Holy Spirit at will. It is so foreign to the New Testament that I shudder.

James Beverley asks, 'What is one to make of two men who "shoot the Spirit" at one another, one using his right hand as a pistol while the other uses both hands in mimic of a machine gun? What about group encounters where every touch and wave of the hand produces fresh Spirit jolts? Is this really from the Holy Spirit?'[63]

No, it is not from the Holy Spirit! The blessed Comforter is not a commodity to be dispensed, a fire to be passed on, a burst of energy to be used to 'zap' others — as if the Holy Spirit were at the beck and call of men and women. Instead of a sovereign, he is treated as a servant who is expected to bless every meeting the Vineyard leaders choreograph.

This supposed intimacy with the Holy Spirit is not new. The 'laughing revival' was passed on by Rodney Howard-Browne, who calls himself 'the Holy Ghost bartender'. His emphasis on dispensing the Spirit, almost as if he is some magic elixir or heavenly cocktail, is profoundly disturbing. The imagery suggests that the blessed Spirit is some kind of liquid that can be poured out or passed around.

Tim Thornborough writes, 'This approach is reminiscent of the attitude of Simon Magus in Acts 8, who wants to buy from Peter the ability to dispense the Spirit. Peter, of course, roundly condemns him, for the Spirit of God is not a device or a tool to manipulate and dispose of as we will, but is rather a *Person* who disposes of us as He wills. If the Toronto Blessing is the work of the Spirit, then it seems strange that he only does His work at the appointed time in the meeting, on set days and at certain times.'[64]

Summing up

In conclusion, I am led inevitably to ask how the Toronto Blessing can be termed an 'outpouring' or 'renewal' of the Holy Spirit when it manifests the characteristics I have outlined. At the beginning of this chapter I summarized ten characteristics of the movement, noted in earlier chapters, which could not have been produced by the Holy Spirit. In this chapter I have described seven further features of a negative nature:

1. Lack of spontaneity;
2. Physical phenomena that correspond almost exactly with the results of hypnotism;
3. Dependence on people coming to the meetings with an expectation of what will happen;
4. Dependence upon suggestive techniques to generate openness to what happens;
5. Dependence upon a powerfully charged atmosphere produced in a carefully choreographed and lengthy meeting;
6. Similarities to what takes place in brainwashing;

7. Treatment of the Holy Spirit as a commodity to be dispensed by supposedly 'anointed' men and women.

In my opinion, the movement does not manifest the marks of 'a Holy Spirit revival'. It reflects more a powerful appeal to the psychological urges of mankind dressed in a communication package that speaks to the desires and needs of modern man. It speaks to mankind's deep longing for community and desire to escape from the drudgery and troubles of life. It engages the emotions rather than the intellect. It uses upbeat music, stories that entertain and a relaxed atmosphere, all wrapped up in a very exciting programme. The present movement also reflects the development in the Vineyard of a theology of signs and wonders that generates intense expectation and excitement.

16.
Power in the Vineyard

The Vineyard rides the crest of a wave of interest in the miraculous. Much of this interest can be traced to the promotion of John Wimber's vision of a great wave of revival through signs and wonders. The Toronto Blessing cannot be understood except against the backdrop of this current passion for 'power evangelism'.

The Vineyard movement has a laudable desire to evangelize this pagan generation. Every sincere disciple of Christ shares their burden to bring lost men and women to the feet of the risen Christ by a demonstration of supernatural living and powerful witness. John Wimber, however, asserts the necessity of adding to life and verbal witness a restoration of the miraculous. He claims that miracles, healings, words of knowledge, prophecy, exorcism, and to some extent tongues, are meant to buttress evangelism and demonstrate the realities of the kingdom of God.

This added dimension lies behind everything the Vineyard does. To a generation obsessed with power John Wimber has added an evangelistic power dimension. It is no accident that he has called his books *Power Evangelism, Power Healing* and *Power Points*. To what Vineyard proponents often call 'programmatic evangelism' — traditional evangelical methods of evangelizing through planned programmes — Wimber has added 'power evangelism'. While the Vineyard is not seeking to supplant traditional methods, such as personal evangelism, they do feel that current evangelistic methods are anaemic. They claim that traditional methods discount the power of the kingdom by failing to engage our generation in a 'power encounter'. The term 'power encounter' is used in a missionary context to describe the clash often produced when Christian missionaries confront anti-Christian beliefs and practices in a non-

Christian culture.[1] Proponents of power evangelism assert the need for this added dimension in the light of the secularization and materialism of our present pagan culture.

Historically, most evangelicals have believed in the *possibility* of miracles, but have denied that they are a *necessity* in normal church life and evangelism. On this point a considerable controversy rages. Classic cessationists, such as John MacArthur and James Montgomery Boice, have joined forces with John Armstrong, D. A. Carson and many others to criticize the signs and wonders movement with its rising crop of Vineyard theologians and leaders.

Power Religion,[2] a book critical of modern evangelicalism's obsession with power, included a number of chapters on the Vineyard movement. This led to a response by Wayne Grudem[3] charging Boice, Carson and Armstrong with serious inaccuracies and sloppy exegesis. Rich Nathan, in turn, responded to John MacArthur's *Charismatic Chaos* with *Vineyard Position Paper No. 5*, in which he states that 'Eliminating signs and wonders as a "door-opener" is "patently unbiblical (to use MacArthur's phrase in *Charismatic Chaos*).'[4]

John MacArthur has extended the debate by including a chapter in his book *Reckless Faith* asserting that the Vineyard, especially as manifest in the Toronto Blessing, lacks discernment. The debate will no doubt deepen. The issues raised are of profound concern for anyone interested in evangelism and missions — which should include all of us.

It is extremely important that I lay out carefully the basic beliefs of the Vineyard movement on this issue before seeking to refute their position. For this reason, I am going to spend this chapter to explain 'power evangelism'. We shall see, firstly, what the Vineyard believes about signs and wonders; secondly, list some texts that seem to support their view; and then, thirdly, clarify the basic issues at stake. In the next chapter I shall explain why 'power evangelism' should be rejected.

The Vineyard position on signs and wonders

John Wimber writes, 'By power evangelism I mean a presentation of the gospel that is rational, but that also transcends the rational (though it is in no way "irrational" or anti-rational). The explanation of the gospel — the clear proclamation of the finished work of Christ on the cross — comes with a demonstration of God's power through signs and wonders. Power evangelism is a spontaneous, Spirit-inspired, empowered presentation of the gospel. Power evangelism is preceded and undergirded by demonstrations of God's presence, and frequently results in groups of people being saved. Signs and wonders do not save; only Jesus and his substitutionary work on the cross saves... Through these supernatural encounters people experience the presence and power of God. Usually this takes the form of words of knowledge ... healing, prophecy, and deliverance from evil spirits.'[5] Wimber's views can be summarized under the following six headings (please note that I am expressing Vineyard views, not my own, in the six points that follow).

1. The kingdom

Proponents of power evangelism emphasize that Christ came to establish his kingdom. From the outset he clashed with rival religious and supernatural powers. We are called to continue to assail the kingdom of darkness. That kind of 'power encounter' calls for a demonstration of the power of God in signs and wonders to overwhelm opposition and extend God's kingdom. 'The kingdom of God suffereth violence' (Matt. 11:12, AV).

2. Signs and wonders in the ministry of Jesus and his disciples

They also emphasize that miraculous signs attended the ministry of Christ and his disciples throughout the New Testament era. The Gospels repeatedly portray Christ and his disciples, not only preaching the gospel, but casting out demons, healing diseases and even raising the dead. The book of Acts shows that this pattern continued in the ministry of Christ's disciples following his resurrection and ascension. The explosive growth of the early church can be traced to the fact that they knew the secret of power evangelism. They combined an explanation of the gospel with 'a demonstration of God's power through signs and wonders'.[6]

3. Signs and wonders in history

Supporters of the Vineyard position claim that wherever God has worked in revival power in history, signs and wonders have been in evidence. John Wimber gives a list of historical occurrences of signs and wonders in history at the end of his book, *Power Evangelism*. I have already dealt exhaustively with this part of his thesis in chapters 9 and 10.

4. Every Christian and power evangelism

They also draw attention to the fact that before his crucifixion Jesus promised his disciples, as declared in John 14:12, that those who believe in him will do the same works as he did. Indeed, 'He will do even greater things than these.' When the Holy Spirit anoints believers to extend the kingdom, he empowers them to do signs and wonders[7] (see Matt. 12:28; Acts 1:8). Wimber even gives the title, 'The Works of Jesus' to a chapter on this issue.[8] Every Christian should be engaged in power evangelism by helping to demonstrate 'the presence and power of God ... [through] words of knowledge ... healing, prophecy, and deliverance from evil spirits'.[9] Proponents of this view assume, then, that miraculous signs ought to be present wherever the gospel is preached in power. Indeed, as John Armstrong comments, the Vineyard teaches that 'Signs and wonders are the calling cards of the kingdom.'[10]

5. Preaching without signs and wonders

John Wimber is careful to assert the importance of 'the explanation of the gospel — clear proclamation of the finished work of Christ on the cross'.[11] Indeed in his revised edition of *Power Evangelism* he states that 'The Bible does not teach that evangelism apart from signs and wonders is invalid, or that the addition of signs and wonders somehow changes the gospel message. The heart and soul of evangelism is proclamation of the gospel.'[12]

However, Wimber and the Vineyard movement repeatedly emphasize that signs and wonders are powerful pre-evangelistic 'door openers'.[13] They imply that failing to use this means of evangelism is a tragic waste of God-given evangelistic power. Indeed Wimber contrasts 'programmatic evangelism', which contains the message alone, with 'power evangelism' that has both the message and signs and wonders. The thrust is that the first is good, but that the accompaniment of signs and wonders 'adds much more'. To use John Armstrong's terminology, 'power evangelism' is a passion to both 'show and tell'. It is adding to the gospel 'the snap, crackle and pop of the miraculous'.[14]

Stan Fowler summarizes Vineyard belief on this point by saying, 'Powerful signs done in connection with proclamation lead to more genuine disciples, as opposed to mere "decisions" which tend to result from simple proclamation.'[15]

In spite of his protestations to the contrary, John Wimber himself has demonstrated this tendency to exalt external demonstrations of power over proclamation. John Armstrong described what he saw in a meeting led by Wimber. After Wimber concluded his message, he moved the pulpit to one side to introduce 'ministry time'. He said, 'Now the Spirit of God is going to come and do his work.'[16] Did he not sense the Spirit working through the message? Does the Spirit work more through manifestations than through the Word he inspired? The perception is inevitable that the really powerful time in any meeting is the concluding 'ministry time' when the phenomena occur. This impression was buttressed and promoted in every Vineyard meeting I attended.

6. A revival of signs and wonders

Wimber has indicated that many churches today are powerless because they have been influenced by a Western world-view that is anti-theistic and anti-supernatural. This world-view has weaned multitudes of Christians away from living a supernatural Christian life. As a result they have lost touch with the power of the kingdom and its manifestation through signs and wonders. A revival of signs and wonders will rejuvenate the church, evangelize the world and prepare the way for the return of Christ.

In November 1994, Marc Dupont prophesied that radical evangelism will explode in cities in 2005. Churches 'that are responding to the Spirit, they're going to begin to experience the first-fruits … going to begin to see more and more radical evangelism, they're going to begin to see more and more miracles and signs and wonders'.[17] The Vineyard vision of evangelism in the end times is inextricably bound up with the spectacle of the church militant triumphing over darkness through powerful demonstrations of signs and wonders.

Some texts that seem to support the Vineyard position

Joel 2:28-32

Joel predicted a time when the Spirit would be poured out, sons and daughters would prophesy, old men would dream dreams and young men would see visions. The Spirit would be poured out indiscriminately on people from all nations and of both sexes. This outpouring would be accompanied by

> ... wonders in the heavens
> and on the earth,
> blood and fire and billows of smoke.
> The sun will be turned to darkness
> and the moon to blood
> before the coming of the great and dreadful day of the Lord
> (Joel 2:30-31).

At first glance, this appears to be a prophecy of what will happen at the very end of the age, just before the Lord's glorious appearing and the ensuing judgement.

Peter stood up after the outpouring of the Spirit at Pentecost and explained: 'This is what was spoken by the prophet Joel,' and then he quoted the verses in question including the portion describing fire and smoke and sun and moon. Peter seems to mean that Joel's prophecy is fulfilled in the outpouring of the Spirit and its effect on men and women of all ages — some will prophesy, some will see visions and dreams. He goes on to talk of Christ as 'a man accredited by God to you by miracles, wonders and signs, which God did among you through him' (Acts 2:22). Does Peter also mean that the prophecy of wonders on earth and in the heavens was fulfilled at the time of Christ? The sun was darkened as Christ died. The graves were opened and some resurrected saints walked the earth. But what of the prediction about the moon? Peter gives no indication of whether he believes that the prophecy of Joel, like many, is a compressed prophecy that covers the whole period of the end times. If that were true, part of it would be fulfilled at the beginning and part at the end — the glorious day of the Lord. Perhaps, like other New Testament authors, he viewed the time interval between the ascension of Christ and his return as a very small increment that would encompass easily the whole prophecy.

It seems best to interpret the prophecy as having a double fulfilment — in Pentecost and in the end of the age. One can understand why some in the Vineyard might believe that there will be a second period of Pentecost-like renewal before the Second Coming of Christ. Revelation 11:3-6 talks of the two witnesses demonstrating miraculous signs before the return of Christ. The signs, however, are performed by these two only and not by the whole church present at that time. It seems to me that the first group of signs mentioned in Joel were fulfilled in the descent of the Spirit and his effect on men and women. The second group of signs about darkness and fire in the heavens and on the earth await the Second Coming. I might add that I find it hard to square a post-millennial optimism of great revivals and great movements of the Spirit near the end of time with the New Testament. The Vineyard seems to have adopted a post-millennial interpretation of prophecy — a view I don't intend to debate in this book.

Mark 16:15-20

In Mark 16 we read that the preaching of the good news to all creation is to be associated with signs: '"And these signs will accompany those who believe: In my name they will drive out demons; they will speak in new tongues; they will pick up snakes with their hands; and when they drink deadly poison, it will not hurt them at all; they will place their hands on sick people, and they will get well.".... And the Lord worked with them and confirmed his word by the signs that accompanied it' (16:17-18,20). The NIV points out in a note that this passage is not in 'the most reliable early manuscripts and other ancient witnesses'. The emphasis on signs is unique to this Gospel and different from the other four places where the Great Commission is summarized (Matt. 28:16-20; Luke 24:45-49; John 20:21; Acts 1:8). The mention of poison and snakes finds no echo in other Gospel writings.

However, since this ending to Mark's Gospel may be genuine we need to consider its import. All of these predictions were fulfilled (with the possible exception of drinking poison) as the apostles took the gospel to the Roman and Greek world. It is not necessary, then, to say that it still awaits fulfilment. On the other hand, those who hold the Vineyard view could say that since the command to preach the gospel to the whole world continues, the need to confirm that word by signs continues. They could claim that this statement is a prediction of what will happen throughout church history — the gospel will be confirmed by signs that accompany its spread. It is highly unlikely, however, that this is the meaning, as we have noted in our survey of church history in chapters 9 and 10.

1 Corinthians 13:8

A passage sandwiched in the middle of the chapter on love has engaged the attention of interpreters on both sides of this issue. Paul declares that 'Love never fails. But where there are prophecies, they will cease; where there are tongues, they will be stilled; where there is knowledge, it will pass away' (1 Cor. 13:8). Cessationists claim that this passage teaches that prophecy and tongues cease when the canon of Scripture is complete, 'when perfection comes' (13:10). Non-cessationists seize on the apparent reference to the Second Coming, a time when we shall 'see face to face'. They assert that this proves that prophecy and tongues will continue until Christ returns. The interpretation from both sides is questionable given the main thrust of the passage. Neither argument seems conclusive to me.

Hebrews 2:1-4

In the opening verses of Hebrews 2 the writer speaks of the great salvation we have in Christ: 'God also testified to it by signs, wonders and various miracles, and gifts of the Holy Spirit distributed according to his will' (Heb. 2:4). Cessationists build on this verse by pointing out that the apostles are mentioned, and that it is in the past tense. Proponents of power evangelism reply that, since gifts of the Spirit are mentioned and since they must continue (e.g. the gifts of teaching and evangelism), so must signs and wonders. However, the author of Hebrews might be just expanding the phrase to clarify what he meant by extraordinary wonders through piling one word upon another — signs, wonders, miracles, gifts. The word 'gifts' might just refer to the sign gifts — healing, miracles, tongues and interpretation. Neither argument is very conclusive on this verse.

Other verses used by both sides will be dealt with in the material to follow. When we face inconclusive verses, such as those we have considered, we must search for other ways to clarify an issue of concern. Christians from both sides of the charismatic divide have sincere differences of opinion on Bible interpretation. These areas of disagreement occur because some evidence can be marshalled for either position. Understanding will not be served by exaggerated or emotional claims from either the Vineyard side or that of non-charismatics such as myself. For this reason, I want, first of all, to clarify some of the basic issues involved before I go on to give reasons why I reject power evangelism through signs and wonders.

Clarifying basic issues about signs and wonders

1. Signs and wonders attended the ministry of Christ and his apostles

First of all, we must grant that miraculous signs and wonders did cluster around the ministry of Christ and that of his apostles. Isaiah predicted that this would be part of the ministry of the Messiah:

> The Lord has anointed me
>   to preach good news to the poor.
> He has sent me to bind up the brokenhearted,
>   to proclaim freedom for the captives
>   and release from darkness for the prisoners
>
> (Isa. 61:1-2).

The last phrase was interpreted by Christ to mean 'recovery of sight for the blind' (Luke 4:18). Early in his public ministry we read, 'Jesus went throughout Galilee, teaching in their synagogues, preaching the good news of the kingdom, and healing every disease and sickness among the people' (Matt. 4:23). This same statement is repeated almost word for word slightly later in his ministry (see Matt. 9:35) We also find similar descriptions in Mark: 'So he travelled throughout Galilee, preaching in their synagogues and driving out demons' (Mark 1:39).

Signs and wonders were also to attend the ministry of the twelve apostles. 'When Jesus had called the Twelve together, he gave them power and authority to drive out all demons and to cure diseases, and he sent them out to proclaim the kingdom of God and to heal the sick' (Luke 9:1-2; see also Matt. 10:1; Mark 6:7). He also appointed seventy-two (Luke 10:1, NIV) to 'Heal the sick who are there and tell them, "The kingdom of God is near you"' (Luke 10:9). Paul describes his ministry as 'leading the Gentiles to obey God by what I have said and done — by the power of signs and miracles, through the power of the Spirit' (Rom. 15:18). He reminds the Corinthians that 'The things that mark an apostle — signs, wonders and miracles — were done among you with great perseverance' (2 Cor. 12:12).

Signs and wonders attended the ministries of the early church. 'Many wonders and miraculous signs were done by the apostles' (Acts 2:43). In the midst of persecution the Jerusalem church prayed, 'Stretch out your hand to heal and perform miraculous signs and wonders' (Acts 4:30). 'The apostles performed many miraculous signs and wonders' (Acts 5:12). 'Stephen ... did great wonders and miraculous signs' (Acts 6:8). The ministry of Philip in Samaria was attended by 'great signs and miracles' (Acts 8:13). In Iconium Paul and Barnabas '[spoke] boldly for the Lord, who confirmed the message of his grace by enabling them to do miraculous signs and wonders' (Acts 14:3).

2. In the time of Christ God did use signs and wonders to encourage belief

During the period of Christ's ministry, and in the apostolic period that followed, signs and wonders had a crucial role. In many cases they influenced people to believe in Christ and the message of the kingdom. The whole format of John's Gospel is laid out around certain carefully chosen miracles. John wrote, 'Jesus did many other miraculous signs in the presence of his disciples, which are not recorded in this book. But these are written that you may believe that Jesus is the Christ, the Son of God, and that by believing you may have life in his name' (John 20:30-31). 'Many people saw the miraculous signs he was doing and believed in his name' (John 2:23). When Jesus healed the official's son from Capernaum, 'He and all his household believed. This was the second miraculous sign that Jesus performed' (John 4:53-54). When Jesus raised Lazarus from the dead, 'Many of the Jews were going over to Jesus and putting their faith in him' (John 12:11). Jesus challenged unbelieving Jews: 'Do not believe me unless I do what my Father does. But if I do it, even though you do not believe me, believe the miracles, that you may know and understand that the Father is in me, and I in the Father' (John 10:37-38).

This pattern continued into the period of the early church. God used Peter to heal Aeneas, who had been a paralytic for eight years, and 'All those who lived in Lydda and Sharon saw him and turned to the Lord' (Acts 9:35). The raising of Dorcas 'became known all over Joppa, and many people believed in the Lord' (Acts 9:42). Paul's miracle of judgement, in which Elymas the sorcerer of Cyrus became blind, led to the conversion of the proconsul of the island (Acts 13:12).

3. Distinguishing the various signs and wonders

John Wimber lists words of knowledge and prophecy, healing and miracles, and deliverance from evil spirits as the main signs and wonders that are 'door-openers'. Some would also include speaking in tongues and their interpretation, although this is not a main part of Vineyard theology. In the current movement emanating from Toronto, and in the movement as earlier expressed in Vineyard circles, a whole gamut of external physical phenomena are considered to be among the wonders produced by the Spirit.

Physical manifestations/phenomena. I have already shown in chapter 8 that there is no biblical precedent for being 'slain in the Spirit', shaking, laughing, etc. These cannot be classed as signs and wonders in any biblical sense.

Tongues and interpretation. Since an emphasis on tongues is not central to the Vineyard movement I will not treat this at any length. What I say about the subject of healing and miracles, later in this chapter, can be taken to apply to tongues and their interpretation as well. They all stand or fall together.

Prophecy, words of knowledge, immediate illumination of the Holy Spirit, dreams, visions. I will deal with this important subject in chapters 18 and 19, but what I say in the pages to follow about miraculous signs in general will also apply to inerrant prophecy as well.

Healing and miracles. These are the two main miraculous signs that are being emphasized. I assert, with all evangelicals, that prayer for the sick is to be carried on as prescribed by James and in other passages. James lays down the importance of sick persons initiating a request for prayer by asking church elders to come and pray (see James 5:14-16). I believe that God can, and does — from time to time — heal the sick in answer to prayer. I believe that God can, and does — occasionally — perform miracles. Nothing that I say in the pages to follow should be taken to mean that I deny this.

We are distinguishing here between the *possibility* and the *frequency* — how often they occur. Vineyard leaders claim that healing and miracles should *often* occur in the course of normal church life. Some even claim that they should be part of normal Christian living. I believe that they are rare. I believe that God has not chosen to regularly perform miracles in this age — they are not a necessary or normal part of evangelism or church life.

Exorcism, deliverance from evil spirits. The power to cast out demons, as conferred by Jesus on his disciples, is one of the signs and wonders. But just as I believe that the elders of the church should pray for the sick, so I believe that as demonized people are discovered it is the responsibility of the elders to seek their deliverance. However, the statements of Jesus about binding the strong man indicate that his victory on the cross moderated the power and presence of demons. The present resurgence of interest in demonology and claims that people, even Christians, need deliverance from demon possession, betray a misunderstanding of human nature, human depravity, personal accountability, temptation and the role of the cross in Christian living. (This subject is too important to treat lightly but too vast to deal with adequately in this book.)

4. God's providence and the supernatural

The signs-and-wonders movement is in part a reaction against what its proponents perceive as the prevalent world-view of professing Christians. There is no doubt that many have been adversely affected by an Enlightenment world-view, a pseudo-scientific approach that explains everything in terms of natural forces. John Wimber claims that the relative lack of miracles in the evangelical church can be traced to this retreat from a belief in the supernatural power of God.[18] I join him in lamenting a lack of spiritual reality in the lives of many Christians that manifests itself in a failure to live a supernatural life in Christ. But I blame this on an erosion of faith in the providence of God.

Every genuine disciple must come to grips with the way God impinges on everything in and around him or her. He or she must come to realize that life is supernatural, that God is intimately involved in all the affairs of life. King Nebuchnezzar had to experience insanity among the beasts of the field before he came to acknowledge the sovereignty and providence of God in all of life. The king confessed:

> My sanity was restored. Then I praised the Most High; I honoured and glorified him who lives for ever.
>
> His dominion is an eternal dominion;
>   his kingdom endures from generation to generation...
> He does as he pleases
>   with the powers of heaven
>   and the people of the earth.
> No one can hold back his hand
>   (Dan. 4:34,35).

What God forced Nebuchadnezzar to learn, believers discover when they are saved by the transforming power of Christ. And they keep learning more of the breadth of God's providential care and involvement in life as they peruse the Scriptures. They rediscover it every time they sincerely pray, 'Thy will be done.' They keep on experiencing the supernatural presence of God as they interact with him in every facet of their lives.

As the gathering of eminent Christians at Westminster wrote, 'God, the great Creator of all things, doth uphold, direct, dispose, and govern all creatures, actions, and things, from the greatest even to the least, by his most wise and holy providence, according to his infallible foreknowledge, and the free and immutable counsel of his own will, to the praise of the glory of his wisdom, power, justice, goodness and mercy... As the providence of God doth, in general, reach to all creatures; so, after a most special manner, it taketh care of his church, and disposeth all things to the good thereof.'[19]

A belief in the fact of providence leads genuine disciples to live supernatural lives of prayerful dependence upon God. They trust him to overturn the seeming accidents of life so that all things might work out for good (Rom. 8:28). Followers of Christ repeatedly petition the courts of heaven to intervene supernaturally in human affairs. They face disappointments and suffering with perseverance and a supernatural trust in God. And they regularly see God answering their prayers through his providence.

Those who advocate power evangelism apparently fail to appreciate the difference between the miraculous and the providential. God rules the universe through providence. He may or may not work miracles — but he is always supernaturally involved in the lives of his children and the affairs of his church. We need a recovery, not of miracles, but of faith in the immanence, the nearness, of God as manifest in his providence and sovereignty.

5. Distinguishing providential answers to prayer from miracles

Both providence and miracles are supernatural — because both issue from the hand of our supernatural God. In providence God superintends the universe by dealing with all that happens according to his will, without working outside the natural laws he himself has established. As mentioned in chapter 9, a miracle, on the other hand, is an extraordinary work of God's power, in which God intervenes in a way that cannot be explained by the natural laws of the universe. It is a sovereign, inexplicable act of God.

A miracle occurs when something happens that is contrary to natural law. The Nile River turning to blood, the feeding of Elijah by a raven, the sudden stilling of the storm on Galilee, Naaman's sudden healing from leprosy, the resurrection of Lazarus — these are all miracles.

When I claim that the *gift* of miracles has ceased, I am not saying that God cannot still work miracles. God works a miracle whenever he overrules the fallen will of a sinful person in regeneration. He can miraculously heal. The question is: has God revealed that it is his will to do miraculous works in the normal course of our Christian living and evangelism? Has he anointed certain people to perform miracles? I believe the answer to both questions is, 'No!' I claim that God does not now endue men with special power to effect miracles as he did to Moses, Elijah, Peter, Philip and Paul. The gift of miracles has ceased. Miracles are now exceedingly rare.

Providential interventions of God, however, occur constantly in the lives of his children. Christians pray, and a person comes out of a coma, or the weather is fair for a significant Christian outreach event, or a person with severe headaches finds a specialist who

promotes relief, or a Christian escapes serious injury on the highway, or a man finds a good job, or when the money is gone a cheque
mysteriously comes in the mail from an unknown aunt — the list is
endless.

Another point needs to be made. The signs and wonders claimed
by those in Vineyard circles do not fulfil the criteria for biblical
miracles. As Stan Fowler says, 'If the miraculous gifts described in
the New Testament really do occur today, then one would expect
modern manifestations to genuinely duplicate the scriptural
examples, but it is not at all clear that this is happening. For example,
the apostles displayed the ability to simply *declare* a miracle, and it
was done (Acts 3 — the lame man; Acts 9 — Dorcas raised to life;
Acts 13 — Elymas declared blind). But when I read the accounts of
healings in the Vineyard movement, the claims are much more
modest, often involving partial or protracted healings, if there is
healing at all.'[20]

My own findings have been similar and I have already quoted
Beverley's researches of healings at the Toronto Vineyard to the
same effect.[21] Part of the problem can be traced to their confusion of
psychological 'so-called healings' with miracles.

6. Distinguishing psychosomatic healings from miraculous healings

There is a qualitative difference between healing as performed by
Christ and his apostles and that performed by hypnotists or followers of alien religions. In the previous chapter I drew attention to
the similarities between what happens through hypnosis and what
happens in gatherings such as those associated with the Toronto
Blessing. A combination of expectation and suggestion is created in
the context of a powerful meeting. This results in many strange
effects. I have not come across any charismatic or Vineyard paper
making the distinction between genuine biblical healings and psychosomatic or hypnotic healings. It may be an oversight on my part,
but I don't think so. Apparently, those in the movement just assume
that events that others would class as psychosomatic are in fact
miraculous.

John MacArthur points out that the healing ministry of Christ
and his apostles was characterized by six distinctives:

1. Healing occurred by word or touch without any theatrics, programmes or specially prepared environment. Publicity was avoided (see Matt. 8:3-4,6-8,13). Why do modern healing ministries focus on large meetings and wide publicity?

2. Healing occurred instantaneously (Matt. 8:13; Mark 5:29; Luke 4:39; 5:13; 17:14; John 5:9). Why is so much modern healing progressive instead of sudden?

3. Healing was complete — total — without any period of recuperation (Luke 4:39). Why is so much modern healing incomplete and even retrogressive (that is, problems recur)?

4. Healing was indiscriminate, not limited by a schedule or screening process. If God was willing, anybody could be healed. Why do many modern healers blame lack of success on lack of faith in the person not healed? Faith did have a role to play in many biblical cases, but at other times Christ healed everyone around. 'The people brought to Jesus all who had various kinds of sickness, and laying his hands on each one, he healed them' (Luke 4:40; see also 9:11).

5. Healing dealt with organic diseases and conditions — crippled legs, withered hands, blind eyes, paralysis, leprosy; not functional diseases — headaches, heart palpitation, lower back pain, etc., all of which can be profoundly affected by mental attitudes and emotions.

6. They raised the dead (Luke 7:11-16).[22]

In *Vineyard Position Paper No. 5,* Rich Nathan responds to these points made by MacArthur: 'As MacArthur applies his supposedly biblically derived model he finds (not surprisingly) that modern healers do not meet the Biblical tests as outlined above. Many modern healings are delayed or are partial. Beyond that, no one heals everyone and there are few verified reports of raisings from the dead.' Nathan accuses MacArthur of trying to prove that the modern gift of healing cannot be of God on the basis of a self-constructed model. He suggests that 'Model construction is a game anyone can play. There is no necessary (or Biblical) requirement to use the criteria for healing that MacArthur supposedly distilled from the scriptures.' He goes on to suggest that another model could be constructed according to which the healing gift could be distinguished:

1. Jesus (and the apostles) gave glory to God whenever a person was healed;
2. [They] healed ... out of a motive of compassion;
3. In every healing faith is required ... ;
4. [They] ... were selective in their choice of whom to heal.[23]

Nathan's reasoning takes my breath away and leaves me shaking my head! Instead of admitting that the six things MacArthur mentions are true of scriptural healing and that the four points he mentions can be added to MacArthur's list, he presents them as an example of an alternative model! He fails to admit that the six criteria chosen by MacArthur are objective, verifiable criteria that can be applied to all healings wherever they occur, while the four criteria he chooses are subjective and cannot be used in any form of verification procedure.

The fact is — and must be acknowledged — that there is a qualitative difference between healings performed by Christ and his apostles and healings today. In this Vineyard paper Nathan admits as much. How can he fail to see that hypnotists and practitioners of alien religions routinely perform healings similar to those performed in Vineyard circles?

To MacArthur's six distinguishing criteria, I would add a seventh. Healing as practised in the New Testament was not a learned skill that depended upon the dexterity of the practitioner. People were healed by the miraculous intervention of God! In Vineyard circles, however, healing is learned. John Wimber's book *Power Healing* presents a 'healing model' and proceeds to describe procedures to use in healing. I have nothing but admiration for a desire to contribute to the healing of the sick through words of encouragement and directed prayer. There is, however, a qualitative difference between learning to use the healing arts, as practised by pastors, counsellors, doctors, nurses, etc., and giving the impression that this learned procedure is one of the signs and wonders, the gift of healing that effects miracles!

John Wimber writes, 'So, shortly after I saw my first healing, I asked myself, "Is it possible to develop a model for healing from which large numbers of Christians may be trained to heal the sick?" I thought the answer was yes and became committed to developing that model... After testing and adapting this model for several years ..., I developed a healing seminar in which people are trained to pray for the sick.'[24]

The Toronto Airport Christian Fellowship carries on this practice of conducting seminars to train people to heal the sick. A school scheduled for November 1995 was billed as 'a four day conference to train, inspire and develop gifts of healing among the church... Part of the renewing work God has been doing is in the area of healing. People worldwide are testifying to the miraculous work God has done in many areas of their lives. This school will focus on how we as the church can minister the healing power of God...'[25]

Concerning this emphasis in the Vineyard movement, John Armstrong comments, 'Where are the courses the disciples took in order to learn to fill teeth, lengthen legs, smell God...? One wonders how far these practices are from the medieval superstition against which the Reformation was launched.'[26]

New Testament healing was qualitatively distinct from healing as practised by many in the Vineyard and in the charismatic movement at large. Their healings are not indiscriminate, instantaneous, complete, etc. If we do not make clear distinctions in this area, we shall have no way to distinguish God's work from healing that is psychosomatic or due to alien, even demonic forces.

7. Interpreting narrative portions of Scripture

Scriptural interpretation requires a close adherence to hermeneutical principles, one of which is that the narrative portions of Scripture must be interpreted by the didactic portions. For example, the Gospel narratives of the crucifixion are interpreted by teaching about the cross in the epistles. A serious interpretive problem arises when apologists for the Toronto Blessing find precedent for being 'slain in the Spirit' in the narrative example of King Saul lying on the ground prophesying in 1 Samuel. This historical happening, however, tells us little about the meaning of his actions. A search in the didactic portions of the Pentateuch, the prophets and the epistles turns up no teaching encouraging us to act like Saul. The context shows Saul as a vengeful man. It is perilous to use a narrative such as this to formulate a universal principle.

The experiences and happenings described in the Gospels and in the book of Acts must be interpreted by didactic portions of the Gospels and Acts (e.g. the Sermon on the Mount and Paul's instructions to the Ephesian elders in Acts 20). Since we are extremely fallible human interpreters, we must depend, not on our feelings about a passage, but on what the inspired writers of the teaching portions of Scripture wrote. The Holy Spirit interpreted for them events which are far beyond our understanding. The interpretations made by the writers of the epistles concerning the cross, the resurrection, Pentecost, Christian living, church order, spiritual gifts, etc. must be accepted as final and accurate. The epistles are manuals on Christian living, church order and church growth.

Thomas Morton, in explaining why many charismatics left the movement, notes that 'Most of us were not trained to perceive the error of taking narrative accounts in Acts and making that normative for all Christians for all times... It was after the ecstasy wore off, that we could reasonably examine the Bible. The lack of didactic teaching from the epistles and Gospels disturbed us.'[27]

Charismatics, including those in the Vineyard movement, largely ignore this principle. They derive their *modus operandi* from personal experience bolstered by their interpretations of narrative portions of Scripture. True, on the issue in question, Vineyard leaders do turn as well to 1 Corinthians. And what is in that epistle must be carefully considered. It would seem to me, however, that we are on perilous ground if we construct a vision of ministry based on Corinthian church practice when it finds no echo in Ephesians, the epistle that has the most general help about defining the church, and no corroboration in the Pastoral Epistles, which define church order and pastoral ministry. Neither of these contains the faintest hint of teaching about church growth through signs and wonders, or guidelines about a healing ministry in the local church. The silence is deafening.

Summary of basic issues

Most evangelicals agree with the Vineyard, and with charismatics in general, about the presence of signs and wonders in the ministry of Christ.

Most would grant that miraculous signs had a positive effect on many who witnessed them.

All would grant that normal Christian living is supernatural and that God gives providential answers to prayer.

Most would agree that we have authority in this age over demons.

Most would agree that God can, and does, effect miracles in this age although on a greatly reduced scale.

However, most non-charismatic evangelicals would deny that non-biblical phenomena, such those present in the Toronto Blessing, are signs and wonders.

Most non-charismatics would distinguish providential answers to prayer from miracles.

They would also distinguish psychological healings from miraculous healings. All would agree that we should pray for the sick.

Most would fault the charismatic movement's failure to abide by the interpretive principle concerning narrative portions of Scripture.

Historically, evangelicals have believed in the *possibility* of miracles but have denied that they are a *necessity* in normal church life and evangelism. Healings, miracles, exorcisms, etc. will *not* occur regularly in this age but intermittently and erratically as sovereignly determined by God.

I grant that in certain situations in alien or primitive cultures, God may choose to demonstrate his power more often than in places where the gospel is more commonly known. While I concede the possibility, my own missionary experience has not confirmed this to any great extent. I am inevitably compelled by biblical evidence to reject power evangelism as a theological system. Let me hasten to list my reasons.

17.
Why I reject the Vineyard power trip

I served for sixteen years in a tough Muslim land. When John Wimber and his friends postulated 'power evangelism', with its appeal for a renewal of gifts such as healing and miracles, many missionaries wondered whether this could be the edge we needed to reach Islam. As Vineyard churches, affiliated with John Wimber, began to spread in North America and around the world, missionaries pondered his ideas. Very few chose to go along with everything he taught. Yet many did begin to feel that miraculous healing and exorcism could be the missing secret of Muslim evangelism. We had often prayed for extra dynamism and effect to attend our efforts. Unfortunately, very little has been accomplished. The great promise of signs and wonders has not reaped a harvest of Muslim souls but has served more to encourage divisive charismatic elements. Ever more bizarre groups claim power to heal and do miracles, attracting segments of the Christian community, but failing to engage in, or inspire evangelism among Muslims.

However, I do not base my objections to the Vineyard scenario of signs and wonders on my own experiences. I have already pointed out in the previous chapter how the failure to make clear distinctions — the confusion of unbiblical physical phenomena with signs and wonders; the failure to distinguish providential answers to prayer from miracles and psychosomatic healings from miraculous healings — raises serious questions.

Let me give several further reasons why I reject power evangelism through signs and wonders. Much of the material that follows is adapted from chapter 4 of my book on spiritual gifts *Church — No Spectator Sport.*

1. God's design to use natural means

We desperately need a perspective on the world God created and our place in it. We tend to focus on spectacular events in history. But supernatural interventions of God, in which he sets aside the laws of nature that he created, are actually very rare. For every crossing of the Red Sea on dry land, millions of other people got their feet wet while crossing streams. For every rock smitten in the wilderness to miraculously provide water, thousands of wells were dug by the sweat of human effort. For every time Jesus miraculously fed thousands, ordinary people cooked millions of meals with a pot and a fire.

God normally provides food through means he has ordained — the ploughing and planting of the farmer, the grinding of the wheat, the distribution of food through merchants, the baking of bread. From creation God designed that we provide for ourselves using common, everyday means. Medicine, agriculture, technology, etc. all draw their 'magic' from principles and processes that God has enshrined in creation. All wisdom comes from him 'in whom are hid all the treasures of wisdom and knowledge'.

If, like Israel in the wilderness, we yearn for the spectacular, we shall tend to adjust badly to ordinary life. Indeed, a longing for the miraculous devalues the glory of life as God has created it. In past ages this mystic vision led multitudes to decry anything visible or real as carnal. It spawned the desert fathers. It created monasticism. Misdirected concern about worldliness led to a disdain of creation as God's handiwork. This failure plunged the church in the dark ages into a frantic pursuit of the supra-natural through attaching mystical value to relics, shrines, ceremonies, magic formulae. Magic overwhelmed rational science. In this blind pursuit, people failed to recognize the sovereign glory of God working through the common-grace aspect of his general providence.

God is not only Lord of the miraculous, he is also our Father who providentially cares for us through the seasons of life. And before one turns to a consideration of the miraculous one needs the perspective of thousands of years of providence in which God has provided and cared for uncounted millions of people through his common grace — farmers, families, merchants, explorers, judges, technicians, artists, thinkers. We do not find miraculous signs and wonders throughout history precisely because God created the world in which we live and superintends our lives through his providence without needing to continually overrule the very principles he created! Repeated dependence on miracles calls into question the infinite wisdom of God, and devalues his intimate involvement in all the affairs of life and history.

2. God's design in miraculous events

What was God's purpose, then, in miracles? Why did he part the Red Sea, rescue Jonah from the fish's belly, or call Jesus to heal the sick? Peter declares, 'Jesus of Nazareth was a man accredited by God to you by miracles, wonders and signs, which God did among you through him' (Acts 2:22). From the beginning God has communicated with mankind. The veracity of that communication, however, had to be established in the midst of the strident claims of a plethora of false prophets representing a host of false gods and goddesses, claims buttressed by false religious fervour and magic.

Firstly, miracles were the credentials God used *to confirm the authenticity of his messengers*. Moses' concern that his brethren would not believe him was allayed by signs and wonders. 'Then the Lord said, "If they do not believe you or pay attention to the first miraculous sign, they may believe the second"' (Exod. 4:8). God then went on to outline other signs to show to the elders of Israel and to Pharaoh. Moses 'performed the signs before the people, and they believed. And when they heard that the Lord was concerned about them and had seen their misery, they bowed down and worshipped' (Exod. 4:30-31). In similar vein, Paul could argue that he was an apostle because 'The things that mark an apostle — signs, wonders and miracles — were done among you' (2 Cor. 12:12).

Secondly, miraculous signs not only *confirmed* the messenger, but also *the message*. In Old Testament times, miraculous events confirmed the revelation given to Moses on the mount. In New Testament times the message of salvation 'which was first announced by the Lord, was confirmed to us by those who heard him. God also testified to it by signs, wonders and various miracles...' (Heb. 2:3-4).

The word 'sign' is used seventy times in the New Testament. Sixty of these refer to miracles (see John 2:11). Hence a miracle is a sign that something is genuine. Paul calls tongues a sign. For this reason I refer to the charismatic gifts as 'sign gifts'. The very purpose of signs is to point to something. Signs say, 'Look!' (see Mark 16:20; John 5:36; 10:37-38; 20:30-31; Acts 2:33; Rom. 15:19 for further passages on this point). Once confirmation has occurred, i.e. once the inspired writings of the New Testament have been attested, the need for confirming signs ceases.

Thirdly, miraculous signs also *pointed to great historical-redemptive acts of God*. The rescue of a whole people through the Exodus and the formation of that people into a nation with theistic laws was announced by dramatic signs and wonders. God performed these miraculous signs in Egypt, in the desert, at Sinai and in Canaan. Signs also accompanied the ministries of Elisha and Elijah, who ushered in the period of the prophets. Wonders attended the birth, ministry and death of Christ.

Pentecost was another of these great historical-redemptive acts of God. As predicted by Joel, the descent of the Holy Spirit at Pentecost initiated a new epoch. This climactic event shut the door on the old covenant and opened a new era centred on the church. Signs and wonders drew attention to the crucial nature of this transition.

The birth of the church marked a fundamental realignment in God's programme. In the Old Testament, the Jewish people constituted God's covenant nation. Under the New Testament, God welcomes people from every language and tribe and nation into the church. Such a revolutionary change flew in the face of centuries of Jewish tradition. It aroused massive prejudice. In other periods of transition, such as that between the patriarchal era and the Mosaic epoch, God attested his new approach by signs and wonders. We are not surprised then, when we find unusual events authenticating the birth of the church. God pours out the Spirit not only at Pentecost but on three other occasions: among the Samaritans (see Acts 8:14-17); in the Roman family of Cornelius (Acts 10:44); and upon Greeks in Ephesus (see Acts 19:1-7). Tongues occur on each of these occasions.

These three further Pentecosts mark particular steps God took to transform his mono-ethnic family into the multi-ethnic church. Their unusual nature served to convince reluctant Jewish Christians to accept a Gentile church. Far from promising a repetition of these spectacular phenomena, or encouraging us to 'tarry for the Spirit' (i.e. to seek some kind of pentecostal experience), Peter interpreted the event as a proof that the indwelling Spirit was now guaranteed to all repentant sinners at the time of their conversion (Acts 2:38-39; cf. Rom. 8:9). If we try to duplicate any of these pentecostal experiences, we deny their historic importance and contradict Peter's interpretation.

Fourthly, miraculous signs and wonders *signified judgement* as well as redemption. The Egyptian army and the city of Jericho were destroyed in miraculous ways. The sun stood still so Joshua could win a battle against the Canaanites. The Assyrians were destroyed by a miracle. The book of Revelation contains a wide array of judgemental signs and wonders. This facet of the subject seems to be seldom, if ever, acknowledged by the Vineyard movement.

Fifthly, *there is no evidence that signs and wonders were ever meant to be performed by all believers.* Among the catalogue of wonder-workers we find Moses and Joshua, Elijah and Elisha, Jesus and the apostles. With the exception of Philip, Stephen, and, possibly, some Corinthian and Galatian believers, New Testament miracles were performed only by New Testament apostles and prophets and those in their immediate circle. Their occurrence in the list of gifts in 1 Corinthians proves, at least, that they could only have been given to some, not to all: 'Do all work miracles? Do all have gifts of healing? Do all speak in tongues? Do all interpret?' (1 Cor. 12:29-30). The answer to these rhetorical questions is: 'Of course not'.

Signs and wonders could not serve *both* as unique apostolic calling cards and as the indiscriminate evidences that all believers can do power evangelism. Either they were 'the things that mark an apostle', or they were common occurrences in the early church. They could not be both. That they were restricted to certain believers is clear even from 1 Corinthians, one of the most charismatic passages of the New Testament.

This also helps us to understand John 14:11-12, verses often referred to in the movement. Vineyard representatives, in common with charismatics, assert that when Jesus said, 'Anyone who has faith in me will do what I have been doing. He will do even greater things than these,' this is a promise that all his followers will be able to do signs and wonders rivalling even his own. The main question that arises is: 'Does Jesus mean believers will do greater objective miracles — or greater evangelistic works?' Is not the conversion of 3,000 people at Pentecost a direct result of this promise? In his lifetime Jesus ended up with few real disciples. But in one day Peter saw 3,000 come to faith! Why? Because of Pentecost. As Jesus said, 'I am going to the Father... And I will ask the Father, and he will give you another Counsellor to be with you for ever — the Spirit of truth' (John 14:12,16). Even the raising of one dead person, as when God raised Dorcas through Peter, or shaking off a snake with no ill-effects, as happened to Paul, absolutely pale into insignificance when compared to the fantastic growth of the church. The Spirit descended at Pentecost from the presence of the risen Christ and thousands upon thousands of people were raised from spiritual death to life in the Saviour. To me the natural reading of John 14 is not that everyone will go around doing miracles but that every believer can be involved in a revolutionary work — the extension of the kingdom to the ends of the earth through evangelism!

However, even if John 14:11-12 includes doing miracles, Stan Fowler asks, 'Does this mean that *all* believers in *all* eras will do miraculous works? This hardly seems possible on the analogy of faith, since Paul explicitly declares that gifts of miracles belong only to *some* members of the body of Christ (1 Cor. 12).'[1]

3. The danger of the spectacular

We have already acknowledged that in the time of Christ and the apostles miraculous signs did lead many people to turn to Christ. Subtle dangers, however, have attended the demonstrations of the miraculous throughout history. Charismatics claim that signs and wonders always enhance church life and witness. Wayne Grudem rejects D. A. Carson's warning in his chapter in *Power Religion* about the dangers inherent in miracles. Grudem writes, 'In every instance the rebuke for seeking signs is addressed to hostile unbe-lievers... In no case are such rebukes addressed to genuine followers of Jesus who sought a miracle for physical healing or deliverance for themselves or others.'[2]

I find Grudem's comments inaccurate. Perhaps Christ did not rebuke people for seeking miracles. The word may be too strong, but the Bible clearly warns about the subtle dangers of becoming obsessed with the spectacular. If signs and wonders always have a positive effect, why was this not the case in Israel during their wilderness wanderings? The signs and wonders they saw were far

above anything we could expect today. Although they had witnessed the Red Sea opening before them, although they had seen
water gush from a rock, although they had daily feasted on God's
spectacular provision of their necessities, the Israelites were not
impressed. They lusted after the diet of Egypt. They grumbled. They
kept demanding greater miracles. Paul warns us about failing to
learn from their history (see 1 Cor. 10:1-13).

Jesus, too, talked about the subtle dangers inherent in the
miraculous. At the very beginning of his ministry, people began to
believe in him when they saw 'the miraculous signs he was doing'.
Jesus, however, responded without enthusiasm to their miracle-
driven faith. John records, 'But Jesus would not entrust himself to
them, for he knew all men' (John 2:23-24). Christ must have sensed
something lacking in the people who 'believed'. Wayne Grudem
claims that Christ never rebuked any but hostile unbelievers for
seeking miracles. But this text deals not with hostile unbelievers, but
with people in general who were attracted to Jesus. They responded
favourably to his message. In spite of this Jesus discerned something
defective in their allegiance, and the context seems to clearly link
this ambivalence with the miracles. John wrote his Gospel to
believers as well as unbelievers, and the inclusion of this comment
about Christ is meant to communicate a warning.

John chapter 6 records the dissipation of miracle-driven 'faith'
and the collapse of Christ's popularity. In verse 2 we read, 'A great
crowd of people followed him because they saw the miraculous
signs he had performed on the sick.' After the feeding of the five
thousand, his popularity soared. 'After the people saw the miraculous sign that Jesus did, they began to say, "Surely this is the Prophet
who is to come into the world"' (John 6:14). Their desire to make
him king, however, was misguided. Knowing this, Jesus slipped
away (v. 15). But an appetite for miracles had been aroused. They
came to him and asked, 'What must we do to do the works God
requires?' (v. 28). Jesus responded by telling them that 'The work
of God is this: to believe in the one he has sent' (v. 29). Faith in Christ
is the main thing. But no, this was not what they meant, so they
pursued the matter: 'What miraculous sign then will you give that
we may see it and believe you? What will you do?' They went on to
remind Jesus that their forefathers ate manna in the wilderness (vv.
30-31). They wanted Jesus to keep on caring for their physical needs
in miraculous ways as he had just done. Jesus responded by directing

their attention away from the physical realm to the spiritual. He entered into a lengthy description of himself as the bread of life 'who comes down from heaven' and an explanation of the implications of this metaphor (vv. 33-59).

He began to stress commitment and discipleship, concluding by saying, 'This bread is my flesh, which I will give for the life of the world... Whoever eats my flesh and drinks my blood remains in me' (vv. 51,56). In proportion as his instruction turned their attention from material bread and physical miracles to the necessity of discipleship, grumbling increased. Finally we read, 'On hearing it, many of his disciples said, "This is a hard teaching. Who can accept it?" ... From this time many of his disciples turned back and no longer followed him' (vv. 60,66). Jesus knew that many were attracted not from a concern for spirituality but out of a desire for miracles. This attraction reflected the shallowness of their faith. He said, 'The words I have spoken to you are spirit and they are life. Yet there are some of you who do not believe' (vv. 63-64). As the crowds of 'disciples' dissipated, Jesus turned to the Twelve and asked if they would also leave. Peter responded for them all, not out of a concern to be involved in a miracle-saturated environment, nor to eat bread, but by focusing on the most crucial issue: 'You have the words of eternal life' (v. 68).

I am not denying that the miracles Jesus performed had an important function. They helped to affirm his identity but, as this chapter shows, if they are pursued with too much vigour they arouse the baser instincts. They derail genuine discipleship. In this chapter, John takes us behind the scenes to unravel the mixed motives aroused by Jesus' miraculous ministry. Signs and wonders can produce good results in a few people. They seem to affect the majority adversely.

At first, the miracles of Christ advanced his popularity. Crowds thronged him. Then, at the beginning of his second year of ministry, he began to talk about the cross. The crowds dissipated quickly. John comments that, although he had performed many 'miraculous signs in their presence, they still would not believe in him' (John 12:37). Jesus himself warns us, 'A wicked and adulterous generation aks for a miraculous sign! But none will be given it except the sign of the prophet Jonah [i.e. death and resurrection]' (Matt. 12:39). In this passage Christ calls up the witness of the Ninevites, who repented without any signs and wonders. He points to the

Queen of the South, who came to Solomon in search of wisdom, not signs and wonders (Matt. 12:40-42). He knew that no necessary connection exists between seeing a wonder and becoming a believer, or even a better disciple. Power evangelism through signs and wonders is clearly misguided.

I have already quoted how Wayne Grudem faults James Boice in *Power Religion*[3] for quoting these verses to warn believers against seeking miracles. Grudem says, 'All these warnings about miracles are addressed to hostile unbelievers.'[4] But I thought that was the very point the Vineyard was making, that power evangelism through signs and wonders is needed to impress a hostile, antitheistic generation! The point John makes affirms Boice's contention. Signs and wonders affirm Christ's identify, but often fuel a never-ending pursuit for the spectacular. What is needed is the preaching of the sign of Jonah — the resurrection of Christ and all that is involved in the gospel.

Stan Fowler comments, 'Signs have no inherent power to convert sinners to faith. This ought to be evident from the effects of Jesus' ministry, in which the powers of the age to come were regularly displayed in connection with a perfect life and an infallible declaration of the truth, and still his own people rejected him.'[5]

Paul refused to succumb, either to the Greek passion for philosophic knowledge, or the Hebrew passion for miraculous signs: 'Jews demand miraculous signs and Greeks look for wisdom, but we preach Christ crucified' (1 Cor. 1:22-23). While Paul did perform miracles, and these miracles affirmed his apostleship, his emphasis was not on the miraculous but the cross and resurrection of Christ. 'I resolved to know nothing while I was with you except Jesus Christ and him crucified' (1 Cor. 2:2). I am not denying the presence of the miraculous in apostolic ministry but I am affirming that it was peripheral. The main emphasis was on a message, the gospel. The Vineyard has chosen to emphasize signs and wonders and inevitably their message has suffered. No matter what they say, Christ is not central. The cross is not centre-stage. Preaching and teaching are far down their list of priorities.

Our Lord speaks of a future generation in which 'False Christs and false prophets will appear and perform great signs and miracles to deceive even the elect — if that were possible' (Matt. 24:24). Could he be speaking of our day? While I do not believe the Vineyard is promoting a false Christ, nevertheless they are laying themselves open to deception!

A further danger concerns the effect a focus on signs and wonders has on faith and Christian maturity. As I have already shown earlier in this book, while referring to the catalogue of the faithful in Hebrews 11, God calls us to walk by faith and not by sight. A penchant for spectacular objective phenomena blunts the growth of faith. Signs and wonders can be very dangerous. Far from encouraging faith, they often arouse the baser instincts, create unrealistic expectations and derail real discipleship. For this very reason, once their function was fulfilled, God providentially arranged for their decline.

4. The decline of the miraculous

Signs and wonders occurred during three main periods: the Mosaic age, the prophetic era which followed Samuel and the time of Christ. Miracles did not occur in all epochs. Five hundred years passed without miracles before Moses arose to lead Israel. Following Joshua we look in vain for signs and wonders for a full 600 years until the rise of the prophets. Miracles also ceased during the 400 silent years leading up to Jesus' birth.

Miracles occurred periodically, because they fulfilled a limited role in God's economy. God used them to authenticate crucial revelations of truth, not to satisfy some ongoing supernatural need in mankind.

In the New Testament era itself, we discover a decline in emphasis on miraculous signs and wonders. Even during the life of Christ we find miracles clustered around the time of his birth and during his first year of popular ministry. The last two years leading up to the cross showed a decline in their occurrence. A similar decline can be charted in the book of Acts. The book begins and ends with an emphasis on preaching and witness (see Acts 1:8; 28:30-31). In the epistles, if we arrange the passages that refer to spiritual gifts or to signs and wonders according to when they were written, we find the same pattern. Paul wrote 1 Corinthians, with its mention of the sign gifts, around A.D. 55. Next comes Romans and then Ephesians, both with no reference to these gifts. Peter, who wrote his first epistle in about A.D. 66, ignores charismatic gifts. The silence concerning the use of signs and wonders in the Pastoral Epistles is no less than an astounding omission if, as our Vineyard friends assert, power evangelism through signs and wonders is to be

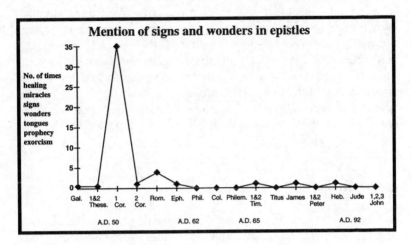

Figure 1

normative in church life and outreach. Figure 1 charts the occurrence of references to the miraculous in any form whatever, including healing, miracles, signs and wonders, tongues and their interpretation, prophecy and exorcism, in the New Testament epistles.[6]

We could chart the references to preaching, teaching and other ministries related to the Word and we would find the opposite results. We must conclude that the supernatural gifts occurred periodically in biblical history and declined in usefulness as their purpose ceased.

When we compare the epistles that make no mention of signs and wonders with those that do, we find that a larger proportion do not mention them, as shown in Figure 2.[7]

Comparing the proportion of epistles that mention signs

Figure 2

5. The development of Scripture

God used signs and wonders to authenticate each significant addition to his developing corpus of truth. Signs and wonders authenticated the ministry of Moses. This in turn affirmed what God revealed in the Pentateuch. Miracles also attended the ministries of Elijah and Elisha, who introduced the prophetic period of revelatory activity. Wonders also introduced the Messiah and affirmed the divine origin of the New Testament documents.

The early church did not have a complete Bible as we have today. For several centuries the church endured intense persecution. They had to rely on scattered Gospels and epistles. Until that body of new revelation was incorporated into the canon of Scripture and became readily available to all, individual books were open to question. We can readily appreciate that God, in tune with the way he authenticated other revelations, arranged for signs and wonders to attest the character of those who wrote the New Testament books. For this reason we see some miraculous activity among early churches such as those mentioned in Corinthians and Galatians. But signs and wonders decline sharply as the apostolic era passes.

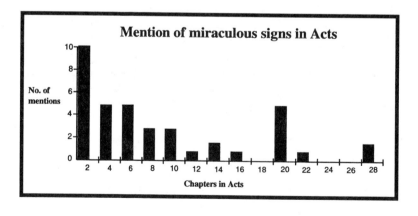

Figure 3

As Figure 3 demonstrates, we can note their decline even during the lifetime of the apostles, as recorded in the book of Acts. If signs and wonders were such an important part of apostolic evangelism, why did Paul not use their occurrence as an evidence in his defence of his ministry before the crowds in Jerusalem, the Sanhedrin, Felix, Festus or Agrippa? Instead his focus is on one wonder — the resurrection of Christ (see Acts 21-26).[8]

With the Bible complete, the need for God to authenticate what he had revealed ceased. The Bible now contains all that any man or woman needs to become holy or to be equipped for every kind of compassionate ministry. 'All Scripture is God-breathed and is useful for teaching, rebuking, correcting and training in righteousness, so that the man of God may be thoroughly equipped for every good work' (2 Tim. 3:16-17). The very sufficiency of Scripture affirms that the need for authenticating signs has ceased. (The role they played in authenticating the ministry of apostles and prophets has also ceased since the Twelve died and the office of the inspired prophets has closed. We shall look into this matter further in the next chapter.)

The Bible is self-authenticating and its message is the power that we need to unleash. Great preachers such as Whitefield and Edwards knew this. And this is why Paul immediately follows up his great affirmation on the sufficiency of Scripture by urging Timothy to 'Preach the Word' (2 Tim. 4:2). There is no hint that signs and wonders are needed to undergird preaching or evangelism. 'For the Word of God is living and active. Sharper than any double-edged sword, it penetrates even to dividing soul and spirit, joints and marrow; it judges the thoughts and attitudes of the heart' (Heb. 4:12).

I have put forward six evidences from the inspired record of over 2,000 years of history to disprove power evangelism through signs and wonders. Another evidence is more subtle.

7. The danger of distraction

Signs and wonders, by their very nature, attract attention. Modern TV producers understand how an emphasis on the spectacular generates an ever-increasing pressure to raise the stakes. Viewers' appetites become jaded. Writers vie for ratings by throwing in more murders, more adultery and more stunts.

The Toronto Blessing has attracted media attention from around the world. It has been documented by the BBC and by the Canadian Broadcasting Corporation. A talk-show in the USA has featured Toronto Airport Fellowship leaders. A multitude of magazines and newspapers have followed the story. Has all this attention helped to further the kingdom? Those involved answer with a resounding 'Yes!' The answer of other evangelicals is very different.

The image of Christian faith and living portrayed by the Toronto Blessing, and the Vineyard movement in general, attracts media attention because it provides a gaggle of sensational sound-bytes that satisfy the media's search for the spectacular. Instead of portraying the salt and light of the gospel and the message of the cross, a fascination with signs and wonders reflects the mood of the culture in which we live. Loud and fast music, an upbeat message and testimonials about mystical experiences play to the same urges that electrify sports fans in a great stadium, or rock fans at a concert, or New-Agers in their frenetic search for mystery.

If we are to seek first the kingdom of God and his righteousness, however, we must tear ourselves away from a fascination with the spectacular. We must focus on the real issues. Christ describes some of the basic issues in the Sermon on the Mount — adopting the beatitudes, being salt and light, overcoming anger and lust, being truthful, demonstrating forgiveness and love, generosity, compassion, prayer, contentment, and much more. He left us with the Great Commission. Paul wrote of the fruit of the Spirit — love, joy, peace, etc. Most of the biblical authors talk about harmonious relationships in the family and society. James writes about facing the trials of life with faith, perseverance and joy.

An emphasis on healing, miracles, tongues and prophecy tends to distract believers from the real focus of God's work in this age. At least five things become devalued where signs and wonders are given star billing.

The wonder of conversion

Attracted by the miracles Christ had performed, Nicodemus sought out the Master. Instead of encouraging his interest in signs and wonders, Christ quickly turned Nicodemus' attention to his need to be born again. We must allow nothing to upstage the wonder that we feel when someone like Watergate conspirator Chuck Colson bows to Christ. The conversion of head-hunters in Papua, the transformation of Quichua Indians in Ecuador, the salvation of Iranians, the regeneration of a materialistic Wall Street broker — nothing can compare with these signs and wonders!

The witness of holiness

Even though they fulfilled a necessary role in redemptive history, the excitement that signs and wonders generated was extremely superficial. Disdaining the hollow plaudits of the crowd, Jesus said to his followers, 'If any one would come after me he must deny himself and take up his cross daily.' He demanded exacting discipleship demonstrated by spiritual fruitfulness. The real confirming signs of genuine faith are manifested love, integrity, purity, good works and holiness.

The warfare of Christian living

An emphasis on external signs and wonders distracts us from preparing for spiritual warfare. We are in a cosmic conflict, 'fighting against principalities and powers, the rulers of the darkness of this world'. If we keep emphasizing external manifestations of God's power, we may fail to develop the invisible weapons we need to overcome evil in all its subtleties. We shall tend to think in terms of simplistic formulae. We may even come to believe that Satan can be defeated by emptying our minds and hearts, 'soaking in the Spirit', 'being slain in the Spirit', speaking in tongues, giving words of prophecy, or by the laying on hands. Rather, we must put on the armour of God. That armour consists of: the belt of truth — a thorough understanding of biblical truth that dispels our ignorance and shame; the breastplate of peace — a consciousness of our standing with God that covers all our emotional life; the helmet of assurance of salvation; the shield of faith; shoes that indicate our readiness to go forth and witness to the lost; and the main aggressive weapon, the 'sword of the Spirit, which is the Word of God' (Eph. 6:14 -17).

In this age of instant rice and frozen meals we look for short-cuts to spiritual power by toying with the spectacular gifts. We long for power and yet we have the source of spiritual power living within us. There are no short-cuts to spiritual effectiveness through some mystical experience of felt power. Jesus' way is the way of the cross. There will be suffering. There will be trials. Those who persevere in holiness, in spite of sickness and weakness — these know real spiritual power.

Too many blame their temperamental sins on the influence of demons. They fail to accept responsibility, confess their sins and apply the discipline necessary to overcome. They beat about for some instant road to sanctification. Sometimes they resort to calling for an exorcist. How sad to trivialize the very serious challenge of demonic activity by seeing a demon under every bush! There is no substitute for the disciplined exercise of the means of grace as we trust in the Spirit (see Eph. 6:10-20; Rom. 5:3-5; Phil. 1:29-30).

Signs and wonders, as proposed by the Vineyard, have no power against 'the devil's schemes'. Indeed Satan uses them himself to multiply deceit in the form of false cults and religions. The seventh article of the Mormon religion reads: 'We believe in the gifts of tongues, prophecy, revelations, visions, healing, interpretation of tongues.' Mormon belief in these so-called sign gifts stems from their experiences, yet the Bible shows their experiences to be false.

The work of prayer

While we all realize the crucial importance of prayer, we tend to shrink from its discipline. Prayer is hard work. Answers may be long delayed. Again we look for short-cuts. We seek external manifestations to bolster our invisible faith. Jesus, however, rebuked doubting Thomas by commending those who believe even though they do not see.

Rather than expending our energies in the development of the very questionable charismatic gifts, why not give ourselves to developing the supernatural work of prayer? Jesus said, 'I tell you the truth, my Father will give you whatever you ask in my name... Ask and you will receive, and your joy will be complete' (John 16:23,24). Of course, our requests must be consistent with the will of God and promote the glory of Christ in order to be answered. It is when we are on our knees that the real supernatural events of this kingdom era take place.

Distraction is one of Satan's main weapons. When he woos believers from concentrating on evangelism, seeking holiness, putting on the Christian armour and praying to the triune God, he blunts the cutting edge of the kingdom. We shall return to these crucial issues in chapter 20.

8. The testimony of church history

We saw in chapters 9 and 10 that verifiable signs and wonders were not present in church history, although there were many counterfeit miracles. These questionable miracles increased in number as the Dark Ages advanced. This increase in claims about miracles corresponds to a decrease in adherence to biblical doctrine and reflects a growing mysticism in which magic, relics and the tombs of saints played the major role.

Let me quote Warfield again in this regard: 'There is little or no evidence at all for miracle-working during the first fifty years of the post-Apostolic church; it is slight and unimportant for the next fifty years; it grows more abundant during the next century (the third); and it becomes abundant and precise only in the fourth century, to increase further in the fifth and beyond ... the greater proportion of the miracles ... wrought in support of distinctively Romish teaching, which it would seem, must be accepted, if their attesting miracles are allowed.'[9] We must reject spurious miracles along with false doctrine.

The great reformers and preachers of the sixteenth, seventeenth and eighteenth centuries were almost universally cessationist in view. Any claim that power evangelism through signs and wonders was God's main method through history must grapple with the fact that the men God used in the main evangelical movements of history totally repudiated signs and wonders. How could God bless them so obviously if they denied what the Vineyard claims is essential?

An emphasis on miraculous signs and wonders is misplaced. Indeed, I believe they have ceased. I have sought to establish this conclusion from both church history and biblical history and by reference to supernatural Christian experience. What we need is a return to the cultivation of the normal gifts, the non-spectacular but God-ordained gifts of the Spirit. While conjecture and debate about signs and miracles may be fascinating, what we really need is a revival of discipleship and ministry in all its variety.

God's people need the more immediate comfort to be found when the love of Christ is applied through the exercise of the non-controversial gifts. The lonely need hospitality. The hurting need mercy. The puzzled need wisdom. The lost need evangelism. The troubled need shepherding. The unorganized need leadership. But do we need prophecy, as the Vineyard claims?

18.
Navigating the prophetic wave

At the October 1995 Catch the Fire Again Conference held by the Toronto Airport Vineyard, dynamic preacher Wes Campbell 're-leased a prophetic anointing on the crowd. This led to a wild round of shaking, screaming, and body contortions among hundreds who may now believe they have received gifting in prophecy.'[1]

Cindy Witt, wife of the pastor of Rothesay Vineyard in New Brunswick, shakes as she 'prophesies'. 'Periodically the Holy Spirit comes on her and she prophesies with great power. Sometimes we have had to hold her up because her head shakes with such intensity it becomes a blur.'[2]

Marc Dupont, associate pastor at the Toronto Airport Christian Fellowship, wrote that 'Almost anybody can walk into a meeting, and if there's a certain amount of revelation flowing, can pick people out that have adultery in their lives, and maybe hidden homo-sexuality, have drug problems. You know, when you really start cranking in this stuff, you know, it comes when you're not even asking for it. You can walk into the malls and you can begin to pick people out if they're in adultery or, you know, have gone through divorces, or sexual abuse, all sorts of things.'[3]

From rather bizarre incidents such as these to more moderate 'words of knowledge' shared over cups of coffee, an emphasis on prophetic revelation is increasingly captivating people wherever the Toronto Blessing is passed on. Supposed words of knowledge were given in every meeting I have attended. A pamphlet *What to do when you Receive Prophetic Words* is available, along with announce-ments of coming meetings, as you enter the foyer of the Toronto Airport Fellowship. The October 1995 issue of their magazine

Spread the Fire was given over almost exclusively to articles on prophecy. It included an article by Mike Bickle and an interview with Paul Cain, both famed 'Kansas City Prophets'. Most of the issues of this magazine include a section called 'News Before it Happens', to document prophetic predictions. The fact that 'prophets' and 'prophecy' are mentioned over two and half times more often than Jesus Christ in an analysis of three months of sermons at the Toronto Airport Christian Fellowship is no accident.[4]

I want to make clear that I completely disagree with this emphasis. In the next chapter, I will show from the Scriptures why I am so appalled by this elevation of human impressions to the status of revelation. But first, let us wade through the waves of prophetic excitement that engulf the movement. Before we seek to answer their claims we must understand what they are. One of the first questions we must ask is, how prophecy became so important in the Vineyard?

1. Prophecy and the Kansas City connection

True to its designation as the Third Wave, there is a tendency in Vineyard circles for certain emphases to rise and fall. Early on, healing came to the fore, then a full-blown emphasis on signs and wonders. This led inevitably to a revival of interest in the prophetic. From 1988 to 1991 the Vineyard embraced the prophetic with verve as members of the prophetic movement out of Kansas City began to influence John Wimber. In 1991 that interest seemed to wane when John Wimber recognized negative aspects of the emphasis. But now it is on the increase again with the rise of the Toronto Blessing.

The Vineyard first became interested in the prophetic through the 'supernatural rescue' of the Vineyard organization from deep internal problems by a 'prophetic word' given in the summer of 1988. Evidently, Paul Cain received 'revelations from the Lord which were forwarded by telephone to John Wimber by a third party'.[5] According to David Pytches, John Wimber was 'astounded at the insight of Paul Cain who had provided him with such very perceptive information, which Paul could not possibly have gained from any human source'.[6]

Beverley comments, 'The situation addressed by Cain involved a political crisis, but the sad story is not helped by allusions of prophetic rescue. It is, rather, a tragic case of bungled church politics. The idea that Cain could not have had human sources for his information is nonsense. There are several people who could have been in regular contact with Cain about the very matters he raised.'[7] Even Vineyard insiders, including John Wimber, now discount the dramatic aspects of the accounts given.

Nevertheless, in 1988 Wimber led the Vineyard into a close relationship with the Kansas City Fellowship (KCF) and pastor Mike Bickle, including associated prophets, Bob Jones, John Paul Jackson and Paul Cain. In mid-1990 this church became linked to the Vineyard group of churches and changed its name to Metro Vineyard.

In May 1990, Ernie Gruen, pastor of a large Pentecostal church in Kansas, issued a 200-page bombshell. His report documented a series of charges against the teachings and practices of the KCF. Gruen had become alarmed by their élitism, certain theological aberrations rooted in mystical experiences of Bob Jones, teaching about 'Joel's Army' — a new breed of humans supposedly created by God in 1973 to form a super-church — as well as false and foolish prophecies of Jones, Jackson and, to a lesser extent, Mike Bickle.

John Wimber sought to mediate in the dispute between Mike Bickle, the pastor of KCF, and Ernie Gruen. Unfortunately, he prematurely released 'an unbalanced and faulty reply to Gruen' that had been prepared by Jack Deere. This report was published in the Vineyard magazine, *Equipping The Saints*.[8] Others such as David Pytches sprang to the defence of KCF in a best seller, *Some Said It Thundered*. John White wrote a foreword to the second edition of this work, adding his name to the fray. James Beverley finds Pytches' work seriously flawed.[9] Although Gruen admitted some errors in his original document and sermons, his basic objections stood up to scrutiny. In a conversation in 1993, Mike Bickle admitted to James Beverley that 'God used the critique of Ernie Gruen to bring a deeper level of legitimate caution about prophecy to Kansas City. Later that same year Gruen and Bickle signed a declaration of peace between their two churches.'[10]

Since that fray, Mike Bickle has survived unscathed as pastor and Paul Cain has emerged as 'a biblical seer' of great reputation. But John Wimber's interest and connection with KCF dwindled after 1991. Beverley comments, 'While he did not abandon belief in the exercise of this gift [prophecy], he gradually returned to the original emphases in the Vineyard. This meant, in part, some separation and distance from Bob Jones, Paul Cain and Jack Deere. By 1992 Jones was associated with another group, Paul Cain became affiliated with other prophetic leaders, and Jack Deere returned to Texas as a base for a worldwide teaching ministry.'[11]

2. Prophecy in the Vineyard

In the light of fall-out from the Kansas City showdown, Vineyard leaders have sought to moderate prophetic extremes and drawn up a list of guidelines to discourage abuse. The storm of criticism they received between 1989 and the present from John H. Armstrong, D. A. Carson, James Boice, John MacArthur and others probably influenced this. (This trend is now being reversed in meetings associated with the Toronto Blessing.) Nevertheless, confusion has reigned over just what the Vineyard believes about prophecy.

One of their key apologists has been Dr Wayne Grudem. He defines prophecy and gives an example as follows: 'The gift of prophecy in the New Testament consists of, "Reporting something God spontaneously brings to mind". Someone giving a prophecy may say something like, "I think the Lord is putting on my mind a need for us to pray for Tom right now" (and later you discover that Tom was in an auto accident just at that time and needed prayer).'[12]

Grudem continues, 'So prophecy has the same kind of authority as spiritual counsel or advice from a friend: it can be very helpful, but we are to test it for conformity to Scripture and to the rest of what we know to be true.' He claims that 'This kind of thing does not challenge the sufficiency of Scripture, or lead to mysticism... It is a "sign" for believers... It simply gives powerful evidence of God's continuing love and presence.'[13]

But this definition reduces the stakes considerably! What Grudem calls 'prophecy', evangelical Christians have tradition-ally called a providential leading of God — without investing it with the aura of mystery and authority that surrounds prophecy. For example, Hudson Taylor's mother, while away from the family on a visit, 'suddenly felt the urge to pray for his [Hudson Taylor's] salvation, so she went to her room and prayed until she was certain God had answered her'. While she was praying Hudson carelessly picked up a religious tract and came under conviction as he read. He fell to his knees in submission to the saving call of Christ.[14]

John Armstrong asks why we need prophecy when we have the Scriptures and Vineyard prophecy is like a 'fallible hunch at best'.[15] Grudem replies, 'Why do we need it? Because it can bring to mind more facts about a situation, facts we had forgotten or were not aware of.' Grudem illustrates this by referring to an occasion when Paul Cain urged him to telephone a friend, named Robert, who had moved away and with whom he had no contact for some time. When Grudem rang, he was astounded to find that Robert had harboured some anger towards him, but had, that very week, been considering re-establishing contact.[16]

True, such advice may not be a hunch, but in the light of biblical data it can hardly be called prophecy. Historically, evangelicals have called incidents such as these 'providential leadings of God'.

However much Wayne Grudem might seek to moderate Vineyard language about prophecy, the fact remains that the Vineyard movement believes God gives revelation today. Why is this point so important to them? Jack Deere, a former Dallas Seminary professor and sometime staff member at the parent church in Anaheim wrote, 'In order to fulfill God's highest purpose for our lives we must be able to hear His voice both in the written word and in the Word freshly spoken from heaven... Satan understands the strategic importance of Christians hearing God's voice so he has launched various attacks against us in this area. One of his most successful attacks has been to develop a doctrine that teaches God no longer speaks to us except through the written word. Ultimately, this doctrine is demonic even [though] Christian theologians have been used to perfect it.'[17]

When circulated, Deere's statement set off a fire-storm of incredulity among non-charismatics. Deere unequivocally charges that to deny that God gives fresh revelation today is demonic. These are harsh words! John Armstrong, among others, questioned how Deere could make statements such as these and still claim to believe in the sufficiency of Scripture. Since that time both Jack Deere and Wayne Grudem have repeatedly asserted that they do not question the central role of Scripture, nor its sufficiency. Grudem says, 'I have taught and written at length in defence of both the gift of prophecy today and the doctrine of the sufficiency of Scripture for doctrinal and moral guidance for Christians.'[18] Nevertheless, the implication from their side is clear: either one believes in, and pays attention to, continuing prophetic revelation, or the flow of one's Christian experience will be flawed. For non-charismatics the implication is equally clear — to demand continuing revelation is to detract from the role of Scripture.

Keeping in mind the chequered history of prophecy in the Vineyard, and the moderation of their claims about prophecy, let us move on to consider its role today. Prophecy is increasingly coming to the fore among proponents of the Toronto Blessing.

Prophecy as practised in the Vineyard Movement

To gain an accurate view of what those involved in the movement believe and practise, I will summarize their views as found in the October 1995 issue of *Spread the Fire,* an issue dedicated to the subject. This issue seems to represent the whole movement fairly.

1. All believers can prophesy. Paul Cain claims, 'Everybody is going to prophesy, but not everybody is going to be a prophet. Everybody is going to have revelatory giftings, and if you're not experiencing revelatory giftings and really want to, then I would say you have not because you ask not. So labour in prayer for words of knowledge. Labour in prayer for revelatory ministry. It'll come to you because all Christians can hear God's voice.'[19]

2. Believers can learn to prophesy. Toronto Airport Vineyard associate pastor Mary Audrey Raycroft writes, 'It takes our teaching team about four, two-hour sessions to train people in a workshop setting to understand and release prophecy.'[20]

3. Prophecy is fallible. John Arnott writes, 'They do make mistakes... The people of the congregation must be aware that no prophecy or prophet is infallible or equal in authority to the Bible.'[21]

4. Prophecy should be tested. Prophecy has 'potential to be the greatest blessing or the greatest problem... Prophetic and inter-cessory people ... often need help in bringing "feelings" into balance with certain realities ... that the "prophets" don't run the church, but that church government does.' Since they believe that modern prophecy is fallible, most Vineyard churches have guide-lines on how to test prophecies. The most common tests are waiting for a while, accuracy of prediction, conformity to Scripture, good effect in people's lives and confirmation from other sources.[22]

5. Prophecy should be administered under the direction of church leaders. In the movement, new prophets, or visiting prophets, are urged to submit their revelations to the leadership team and not share them privately or indiscriminately. 'Those who are budding prophets but are still unrecognized, unknown, and untried, are asked to submit any strong, specific words to their team leaders or pastoral staff for weighing and wisdom.'[23]

6. *A few have the office of prophet.* In the movement, the office of the prophet is distinct from the general prophetic gift and has a great aura of divine authority. 'Paul Cain functions in the office of a prophet. He not only receives prophetic revelation, but he has a divine level of authority that allows him to be a father to other prophetic people, to impart prophetic gifts, and to speak with authority into situations inside and outside the church.' Paul Cain himself said, 'I think it's wrong for anyone to seek the office of a prophet or the office of authority in any way. These offices are usually assigned in a sovereign way by the Lord.'[24] Paul Cain has been called 'a new breed of man'.[25]

Other personalities are coming to the fore as recognized prophets, and as such they seem to be increasingly regarded as occupying a prophetic office. I have already mentioned Wes Campbell who 'released a prophetic anointing on the crowd' at the conference held in October 1995 by the Toronto Airport Vineyard.[26] Marc Dupont is often featured in *Spread The Fire* in the role of prophet. In the March/April 1995 issue he gave a major prophecy about what was to happen in 1995 in England, Japan, Germany, etc.[27]

7. *How prophecy is expressed.* In the movement prophecy can vary from 'simple prophecy often spoken to another as an anointed word of life over a cup of coffee, while driving in the car, or sitting sharing heart to heart after a service,' to 'vivid dreams, quite explicit words of knowledge'.[28] Prophecy may also be expressed in the form of words of exhortation. The October 1995 issue of *Spread the Fire* gives two examples of this style.

8. *How prophecy comes.* As to origin, Vineyard supporters adamantly claim that much prophecy is 'revelation for the need of the moment' direct from God. But they also admit that often it is 'the release of His word deposited within the storehouse of the one praying'.[29] In distinguishing 'inspirational prophecy' from 'revelational prophecy', Mike Bickle says, 'Almost every Spirit-filled believer is able to prophesy on an inspirational level. These prophecies are general in nature and frequently based on a passage of Scripture... Revelational prophecy may include new direction, correction and different doctrinal emphases or practices than those officially held in our fellowship.'[30]

9. The uses of prophecy. As to purpose, those in the movement believe that prophecy is given to strengthen, encourage and comfort believers. The Toronto leadership reaffirmed Mike Bickle's statements from 1989 that prophecy sustains hope and faith, helps to discern and specify key leaders by name, aids in decision-making and provides warning of satanic attack.[31]

As an example of a prophetic word of comfort, Jim Paul described a private revelation he claimed to have received from God in which the Lord kept saying to him, 'My arms ache.' When he enquired of God why, the reply came: 'Because I want to hug my people.'[32]

Mary Raycroft states that at the Toronto Airport Fellowship, 'We are adamantly against words of "direction, correction, dates or mates,"' — that is, prophecies that deal with dating, that profess to give others direction about marriage partners, or that specify correction, because there 'has not been a proven track record of accuracy'.[33]

Marc Dupont, however, claims that 'Many times in my ministry, the Lord has pointed out sins and hypocrisy to me about people, but there are ways of dealing rebukes and warnings without destroying the person.' He does urge caution and compassion in handling 'prophetic insight into hidden sins'.[34]

Considerable confusion reigns in this area, however. Dupont's view that almost anybody can prophesy in a powerful meeting[35] seems to contradict Raycroft's cautious approach.

10. Phenomena accompanying prophecy. In the Toronto Blessing, at least, visible manifestations often accompany prophetic episodes. Mary Raycroft writes, 'In these days we are aware of an increasing prophetic anointing being released in the church which, admittedly, we don't totally understand... [It comes with] strong physical manifestations of hand movements, body shaking and jerking, intercessory type travail, and acting out with body language the message to be declared.'[36]

Wesley Campbell describes an occurrence in his church when between forty and fifty individuals 'were anointed in such a way that they would be physically shaken while they spoke forth prophecy... Almost all testified to sensing a direct communication with God through the Spirit via revelation in the form of visions, pictures and words... Others could see angels who directed them in words of knowledge and healing.' When his wife Stacey delivers a prophecy her head often gyrates in a blur of motion.[37] As we saw earlier, Cindy Witt, wife of the pastor of Rothesay Vineyard in New Brunswick, has similar experiences.[38]

Steve Witt makes an astounding claim about nausea accompanying prophecy. He says, 'I had come to learn that nausea can occur during revelation from God. At my home church on many nights as many as ten to 20 people might come to me complaining of nausea.' Concerned lest it be demonic in origin, Witt prayed for clarity and while visiting a church in Florida he dealt with the pastor's wife who was on the floor, suffering from nausea. He writes, 'A picture came to my mind of her stomach full of words. Words that had grown stale and putrid needing to be released. She had been prophetically gagged!'[39]

I mentioned at the beginning of this chapter the 'wild round of shaking, screaming, and body contortions' let loose by Wes Campbell.[40] The Toronto Blessing seems to be riding the crest of a new wave of enthusiasm for prophecy. And one gains the distinct impression that however much Vineyard scholars such as Wayne Grudem tried to moderate the excesses, they have not been able to contain a tidal wave of unbiblical side-effects.

3. Prophecies about the Toronto Blessing itself

Those caught up today in the excitement of the Toronto Blessing draw considerable comfort from believing that it is a movement of historic proportions and that its origin was heralded by prophecy. In the May/June issue of *Spread the Fire*, James Watt claims that the Puritan Reformers issued a prophetic warning to zealous Americans not to persecute the British Empire loyalists who came to Canada to remain under British rule. Around 1776, 'The Spirit of the Lord spoke through their prophets saying: "Do not hinder these people... I am in the independence of America from Britain, and will mightily use this country. But Canada has been reserved by Me for the last days for a special work."'[41]

The editor then wonders whether this 200-year-old 'prophecy' could be a confirmation of 'a prophetic word concerning Canada delivered by Dr David Yonggi Cho of Seoul, Korea in 1975 and 1984'.[42] During his visit in 1984, Dr Cho explains that he was afraid to express a prophecy about Canada because of America's relatively

larger resources, but finally in Toronto, 'I prophesied as the Holy
Spirit anointed me... I really believe that God is going to bless
Canada and the Canadian church is going to rise up once again and
go to the four corners of the world and bring the gospel of Jesus
Christ to pave the way for His second coming.'[43]

Randy Clark, the 'fire-lighter, vision-caster and bridge-builder'
whose ministry in January 1994 initiated the Toronto Blessing,
claims that one of his church members in St Louis had a 'vision in
which she saw a map of Canada with fire breaking out in Ontario.
"Then little blades of fire ran out of the Toronto area in every
direction."'[44]

Marc Dupont often writes in the Toronto Airport Christian
Fellowship magazine about the prophetic. When interviewed by
Lynda Hurst in 1994 he explained about having a 'prophetic vision
two years ago that a wave of water "the size of Niagara Falls" would
wash over Toronto, refreshing and renewing its people. It would
happen in early 1994 and would be the beginning of a global
spiritual revival'.[45]

4. Vineyard prophecies of the triumph of signs and wonders

While Vineyard supporters claim that exhortation, encouragement
and comfort play a greater role than prediction, nevertheless 'prophetic words' about the future of the movement seem to come
frequently. This is to be expected, since they believe that 'Every new
step forward in the plan of God has been introduced by the prophetic
word. It is therefore not surprising that the Kansas City Fellowship,
which had become a focal point for prophetic ministry in the '80s,
also became a focal point for those who sought to understand the
strategy of God.'[46]

The pastor of Kansas City Fellowship, Mike Bickle, describes in
his book *Growing in the Prophetic* an 'encounter he had with the
Lord' in Cairo in 1982: 'The awe of God flooded my soul as I
experienced a little bit of the terror of the Lord. I literally trembled
and wept as God himself was communicating to me in a way I've
never known before or since. The Lord simply said, "I will change
the understanding and expression of Christianity in the earth in one
generation."'[47]

This messianic sense of mission pervades the movement. One
does not have to be long in their meetings before gaining the

impression that they feel that the Vineyard has been singled out by God to prepare the church — and the world — for a new type of ministry leading up to the return of Christ.

In the view of those in the movement, this new day of prophetic ministry may do a bit of damage in non-charismatic churches. The pastor of Boulder Colorado Vineyard, James Ryle says he received a revelation one night in the form of a dream in which God said, 'I am about to do a strange, new thing in My church. It will be like a man bringing a hippopotamus into his garden. Think about that.' Ryle concluded that the hippo was the restoration of 'the power of His prophetic word by His Holy Spirit into churches that (presumptuously) no longer have any place for it... Not only is the hippo in the garden the unusual thing God will do prophetically, *within* His church, but it also heralds His release of a prophetic voice into the world *through* His church, bringing in a great last-days harvest.'[48]

John Arnott links this messianic series of prophecies to what is happening in Toronto. He wrote, 'We are now in an introductory and preparatory phase of the Blessing. There is much greater power and anointing yet to come. [A prophecy given by Lois Gott] indicated that we are currently in a time similar to the ministry of John the Baptist, which is preparing the ways for a soon-coming time resembling the ministry of Jesus where powerful signs, wonders and miracles will take place.'[49]

In the view of many in the Vineyard, this will even involve a restoration of apostles. Back in 1989 John Wimber prophesied, 'The prophets God is giving to the church will build altars for the apostles to work from. God is also going to restore the apostolic office to the church. In this instance, I am speaking about the true apostolic office. They will be men who have seen the Lord Jesus Christ and who do the signs and wonders of an apostle. We have not had men like this since the first century.'[50]

Jack Deere expresses a triumphalism that is common in the movement: 'I believe that in my lifetime the majority of the church is going to believe in the practice of the gifts of the Spirit. All of the current statistical evidence from church growth studies indicates that the church is moving swiftly and inevitably to the miraculous gifts of the Spirit... One day the church will be unified over the issue of the miraculous gifts of the Spirit. That issue was settled when the Lord Jesus Christ uttered his high-priestly prayer.'[51]

Evidently, they believe that until all the churches become charismatic there will be conflict. I quoted earlier in the book the predictions by Wes and Stacey Campbell that there will be a war among Christians between those who accept the sign gifts and those that don't. This is a repeat of an earlier vision to the now disgraced Bob Jones,[52] of Kansas City fame, and James Ryle. The vision presents a civil war-like picture of grey-coated Christians, who supposedly emphasize the grey matter, 'man's wisdom', fighting with blue-coated Christians who represent all those who believe in ongoing revelation — the charismatic block.[53]

Triumphalistic predictions such as these cannot help but leave non-charismatics reeling. The impression given is clear: those in the movement view those outside as being forced to stumble along with an inferior kind of faith. This élitism is one of the least attractive fruits of the movement.

Words of knowledge, visions, dreams, predictions — the Vineyard movement claims them all! Strangely enough, Jonathan Edwards, whom they revere as a kind of patron saint, believed otherwise. At the height of the Great Awakening Edwards warned about the danger of claiming that God gives prophecy today. He said, '[An] erroneous principle, than which scarce any has proved more mischievous to the present glorious work of God, is a notion that it is God's manner in these days to guide His saints ... by inspiration, or immediate revelation.'[54] While proponents of the Toronto Blessing continue to appeal to Jonathan Edwards' writings to support the movement, in practice, they reject his wise advice. We would do well to follow Edwards into a renewed study of the biblical parameters of prophecy as we seek to respond to Vineyard claims.

19.
Vineyard prophecy in biblical perspective

Whether seeking to read tea-leaves or interpret the stars, mankind has always aspired to the prophetic gift. Many evangelical Christians are not content to wait until they gather around the banqueting table of the Lamb to hear the actual voice of God. They want to hear it now! Somehow the voice of the Holy Spirit breathing through the pages of the Bible seems too soft. 'There has got to be something more!' they cry. To these restless evangelicals the Vineyard claims about present-day revelation sound a siren song too irresistible to deny.

In the previous chapter we surveyed what the Vineyard movement and those involved in the Toronto Blessing believe and practise about prophecy. Serious differences on this subject exist between the Vineyard and the evangelical church at large. These differences are not minor peccadilloes on which good friends can happily differ. (I have summarized these differences in a chart to be found at the conclusion of this chapter.)

Discussions about prophecy raise a host of questions. What is it? Has God always spoken to his people through prophecy? Did prophecy cease or does it continue? Should every Christian expect to receive new revelations from God? Are there different kinds of biblical prophecy? Were any biblical prophets fallible in what they proclaimed? What was the purpose of prophecy? Was that purpose fulfilled? Is the Bible sufficient or do we look to prophecy for further guidance? How do we distinguish genuine prophecy from false prophecy? Do signs and wonders always accompany prophecy? Was prophecy always predictive? What has preaching got to do with prophecy?

As you can see, we have come to a perplexing but extremely important subject. Upon the answer to these questions swings the great gateway that separates charismatics from non-charismatics. I want to answer these questions under a number of headings. In this first section we will see that the Vineyard (and charismatic) cry for frequent revelation must be understood against the backdrop of its rarity in biblical history.[1]

1. The periodic nature of the prophetic office

Some may assume that prophets were present during the whole Old Testament period. Such is not the case. Certainly, all Old Testament Scripture is prophetic in nature. Christ declared, 'All the Prophets and the Law prophesied until John [the Baptist],' indicating that even the Law was prophetic (Matt. 11:13). Further, Peter writes, 'No prophecy of Scripture ... had its origin in the will of man, but men spoke from God as they were carried along by the Holy Spirit' (2 Peter 1:21).

If we conclude, however, that prophets were always part of the Old Testament scene, we shall err. God revealed Old Testament Scripture at widely spaced intervals, not in a continuous process. Periods of revelation were interspersed with long periods of prophetic silence.

Moses appears as the first major prophet of Old Testament history. Of him, God's mouthpiece during the Exodus, we read, 'Since then, no prophet has risen in Israel like Moses, whom the Lord knew face to face' (Deut. 34:10).

The period of the judges follows the victory years of Joshua. During this era, prophets disappeared. Vision was rare (1 Sam. 3:1). Finally, Samuel arose to take up the prophetic mantle last worn by Moses. From the days of Samuel on through the kingdom period, as priests became increasingly corrupt, prophets became more common. God raised up the schools of the prophets to compensate for priestly failure. Elijah and Elisha prepared the way for the great writing prophets to follow.

The golden period of prophetic greatness extended for about four hundred years, from approximately 800 B.C. to 400 B.C. During this era prophets such as Isaiah, Jeremiah, Ezekiel and Daniel produced major works. Others, such as Amos, Hosea and Malachi, contributed powerful, but short prophetic collections.

Malachi, the last of the Old Testament writing prophets, ushered in four hundred years of prophetic silence. This era extended until the coming of Christ. John the Baptist broke that silence to introduce the Messiah.

The magnitude of Christ's ministry as Prophet, Priest and King in turn eclipsed John. Jesus introduced a new prophetic era. This period produced the New Testament canon, written, as he predicted, by the inspiration of the Holy Spirit under the supervision of the apostles. The twelve apostles occupied a dual office. They were both apostles and prophets (Eph. 2:20). As apostles they founded churches, while as prophets they completed the canon of Holy Scripture.

Besides the Twelve, other prophets appeared during the New Testament era. Agabus, one of a group of prophets who came down to Jerusalem from Antioch, 'predicted that a severe famine would spread over the entire world. (This happened during the reign of Claudius)' (Acts 11:28). In Acts 21:11 Agabus predicted Paul's imprisonment. Besides Agabus, the text tells us that Philip's daughters 'prophesied' (Acts 21:9).While they evidently had the 'gift of prophecy', there is no indication, pro or con, whether, like Agabus, they had predictive powers.

This brief overview establishes that before Christ came, God activated the prophetic office intermittently. He raised up prophets as the bearers of his revealed Word during periods of great need.

Prophecy has ceased

The whole flow of biblical prophecy leads inevitably to the conclusion that this extraordinary ministry has ceased. Although the Bible nowhere explicitly states this, several different strands of evidence lead to this conclusion.

1. The intermittent nature of prophecy. God did not give prophecy continuously in biblical history. History is broken up by hundreds of years of prophetic silence. A belief in the cessation of prophecy after the establishment of the early church and the death of the apostles fits best with the way God worked in past redemptive history.

2. The completion of the canon of Scripture. The function of prophecy is inextricably linked to the development of the canon of Holy Scripture. Once the function was fulfilled, the necessity of prophecy ceased. Paul wrote to Timothy that Scripture contains all the truth necessary for any Christian to be mature and complete in Christ (2 Tim. 3:15-17). To seek to revive a prophetic gift through clamouring for a 'revelation', a 'word from God', or a 'prediction' calls into question the sufficiency of the Scriptures.

3. *The goal of revelation.* Moses predicted the rise of a prophet like himself (Deut. 18:15). Peter interpreted this passage as a reference to Jesus Christ the Lord (Acts 3:22-26). Hebrews connects prophecy with the arrival of Jesus Christ. 'In the past God spoke to our forefathers through the prophets at many times and in various ways, but in these last days he has spoken to us by his Son' (Heb. 1:1-2). A contrast is set up between the way God spoke in the past and the way he speaks now. Formerly it was intermittently through prophets, now it is permanently through Christ. This contrast leads ultimately to the conclusion, affirmed by the rest of Scripture, that Christ is the focus and fulfilment of this whole process of prophecy. He is the end in view. Leading lost men and women into a relationship with Christ through the gospel renders previous methods of communication from God obsolete. Our link with God is now much firmer, much more miraculous. With the purpose of prophetic revelation fulfilled in Christ, why now seek to resurrect it?

O. Palmer Robertson, in his tightly argued book, *The Final Word,* eloquently describes why we should celebrate the cessation of prophecy. I gratefully acknowledge the help his book has been in writing this chapter. He notes, 'The end-goal of "revelation" is *not the perpetual experience of revelation itself.* Revelation instead is a means to an end... The goal of revelation has been realized! In Jesus Christ revelation from God, in so far as the present era is concerned, has reached its climax.'[2] Rather than seeking more revelation, we should rejoice in its conclusion and revel in the knowledge of the glory of God in the face of Jesus Christ!

4. *Biblical injunctions not to add to revelation.* After the revelation of the Mosaic covenant, the people of Israel were enjoined: 'Do not add to what I command you and do not subtract from it, but keep the commands of the Lord your God that I give you' (Deut. 4:2; similar exhortations are also found in Deut. 12:32; 18:20). The Bible concludes with John's inspired warning about adding to the words contained in his book of Revelation. Although the primary application of this text is to Revelation itself, its providential positioning in the final chapter of the Bible cannot be accidental. As we have already noted, revelation came in unique and sovereign

circumstances. Surely we are warned by the very sacredness of the Word of God and the exhortations not to add to it that revelation is something to be cherished. We must not take it lightly — or seek to sanctify fallible human statements by putting them in the same category as God's final revelation, the Bible.

5. Decline of the miraculous gifts in the New Testament era. If we stand back and look at this whole era we find an explosion of miraculous signs and wonders, including prophecy, at the beginning and a decline after the establishment of the early church. As we saw in chapter 17, by the time the apostolic prophets were ready to pass from the scene, references to prophecy are almost non-existent in the New Testament documents.

Palmer Robertson adds to this analysis the point that: 'The manifestation of the gifts of prophecy and tongues in Acts coincides exactly with the stages and phases of the advance of the gospel.' As Christ predicted, the early disciples became his witnesses first in the mono-ethnic Jewish culture in Jerusalem and beyond in Judea proper; then they spread the Word to Samaria, before beginning to take it to the ends of the earth (Acts 1:8). This expansion of the gospel is marked exactly by a burst of signs and wonders at each point of crucial advance: first, at Pentecost among the Jews in Jerusalem (Acts 2); then in Samaria among half-Jewish Samaritans (Acts 8); then to the pure Roman family of Cornelius (Acts 10); until finally the church is established with power in Ephesus (Acts 19). 'The externalized display of the gifts of the Spirit indicated the sanction of the Lord on each of these new stages of advancement... Once the process of advancement has come to its final stage, no need exists for a continuation of the confirmatory gifts.'[3]

If we examine Paul's earlier and later epistles, we also detect a shift of emphasis from signs and wonders, including revelatory prophecy, to teaching the truth deposited already in the Scriptures (see Titus 1:9,13; 2:1; 2 Tim. 1:13-14; 2:2,15; 3:8; 4:7).

To claim that prophecy continues in the church today is to claim a historical continuity that never existed in history. It is tantamount to asserting that God continues to deliver infallible revelation. Such a claim is both inconsistent with Scripture and extremely dangerous. The canon of Holy Scripture is complete. Jesus predicted that the Spirit would lead the apostles into all truth. Did he do that, or not? Is the Bible complete or flawed? If the Lord's promise was fulfilled, we have no further need of new revelation.

The prophetic office does not now exist

Our survey of the biblical office of the prophet and its cessation
establishes that any claim to its reinstatement must be fallacious. In
this matter the Vineyard is riding a very dangerous and murky wave
indeed. As mentioned in the previous chapter, John Wimber predicted the restoration of the offices of the apostle and prophet.[4] He
made this prediction during the time of his fascination with the
Kansas City Prophets. Others in the movement seem to be reintro-
ducing this vision. As previously noted, the October 1995 issue of
Spread The Fire states that 'Paul Cain functions in the office of a
prophet. He not only receives prophetic revelation, but he has a
divine level of authority.'[5] The man who was billed in 1989 as 'a new
breed of man' is again commanding the attention of proponents of
the Toronto Blessing and said to be exercising divine authority.[6]

We have already noted in the previous chapter the Toronto
church's paradoxical approach to authoritative prophecy. The same
issue of *Spread the Fire* that confirms Paul Cain's prophetic office
warns that the Toronto Airport Fellowship is 'adamantly against
words of "direction, correction, dates or mates"' — the kind of
predictions someone who held a prophetic office could be expected
to make.[7] Then in another article, Toronto Airport Christian Fellowship prophet Marc Dupont claims to be able to spot sins and
hypocrisies in people that call for warnings and rebukes. Such a
ministry requires the exercise of authority dangerously close to the
apostolic authority that exposed Ananias and Sapphira. Prophetic
words of this type tend to promote the reputation of those making
them — and open the door to the restoration of the prophetic office.

So far Vineyard supporters have been careful to avoid claiming
that Paul Cain is inerrant. Mistakes he has made can be documented
— even about the apostolic office itself. James Beverley writes, 'I
believe that Paul Cain has made significant errors in both prophecy
and words of knowledge. For example, he has said that John
Wimber was to be "the End-Time Apostle" to lead Joel's Army and
that Wimber was "unique in all the earth". To his credit, John
Wimber has refused this kind of prophetic speculation.'[8] How then
can Cain operate in 'a divine level of authority' when he is so
fallible? And how does his supposed level of authority differ from
that of Peter and Paul?

Before long we shall no doubt read of more and more proponents of the 'blessing' saying 'Thus saith the Lord,' and thereby claiming prophetic prerogatives. History is littered with the shipwreck of those who have made such claims. The Latter Rain movement that spread from North Battleford, Saskatchewan, in 1948 proclaimed the restoration of the offices of apostles and prophets. They also promoted the guidance of individuals and congregations through 'directive prophecy'. This ultimately led into the heretical Manifest Sons of God movement. Their 'dominion theology' presented a vision of perfected saints under the guidance of latter-day apostles and prophets ruling over the earth.[9] Out of the Latter Rain also evolved another heretical movement, the Shepherding-Discipleship Movement. At the same time, the followers of William Branham proclaimed that he was the apostle of the final church age. In spite of his unbiblical teachings he exerted considerable influence. Ominously, Rodney Howard-Browne, the South African progenitor of the 'laughing revival', praised Branham, at least for his earlier ministry.[10]

Historically, there has been an inevitable connection between claiming prophetic gifts, divine anointing and divine authority, and claiming the revival of the apostolic or prophetic office and thus drifting into heresy. Realizing the danger, many traditional Pentecostals react with alarm to the claims of modern 'prophets'. Dr Carlson, the General Superintendent of the Assemblies of God writes, 'Arbitrary and absolute direction by a prophetic gift is not in accordance with New Testament teaching... A study of church history indicates that every group of people who have claimed to restore apostolic authority to the Church and its government have been arbitrary and demanding. Those who come under their leadership find themselves under bondage.'

Most of those who speak on behalf of the Vineyard movement grant that no prophet today has the authority, or infallibility, that characterized biblical prophets and apostles. However, they insist on a secondary kind of prophecy that is non-authoritative and fallible. But if it is fallible, why bother with it? Why not just promote biblical preaching and mutual encouragement? To discover whether the Bible lends credence to their view we must look a little closer at the prophetic function itself. How did revelation originate? How was it delivered? Was it fallible or infallible?

2. The inspired function of the prophets

The word 'prophesy' in Hebrew means 'to flow forth'. Andrews explains, 'These words convey the idea that in prophetic utterance the message of God was laid upon the heart of the prophet and flowed forth from his lips or from his pen.'[11]

God appointed prophets to be his spokesmen, to bring to men a revelation of his will. Repeated phrases such as, 'The Lord said to Moses,' demonstrate that Moses served as God's mouthpiece. In Exodus we read that Moses conveyed to the people the very words of God: 'Moses assembled the whole Israelite community and said to them, "These are the things the Lord has commanded you to do"' (Exod. 35:1). In similar vein the book of Jeremiah, while it contains what Jeremiah wrote, really records what God told the prophet to write (see Jer. 1:1,2,4, etc.) To take one more of thousands of examples, we read in Haggai, 'The word of the Lord came through the prophet Haggai' (Hag. 1:1). The office of the Old Testament prophet represented, in authority, the very voice of God.

Exodus 4:15-16 uses the relationship between Moses and Aaron to illustrate the prophetic process: 'Now you shall speak to [Aaron] and put the words in his mouth. And I will be with your mouth and with his mouth, and I will teach you what you shall do. So he shall be your spokesman to the people. And he himself shall be as a mouth for you, and you shall be to him as God' (NKJV). Palmer Robertson comments: '"Mouth to mouth": the descriptive phrase underscores the immediacy of the relationship that exists between God's Word and the prophetic word. The divine revelation goes directly from the mouth of God to the mouth of the prophet... The word of the prophet is the very Word of God. God does not communicate his revelation to the prophet "thought to thought" or "mind to mind," but "mouth to mouth". Prophetism, by definition, is concerned not merely with the reception of the Word of God, but with its communication as well... This... underscores the absolute perfections of the prophet's speech... God's Word is preserved in its integrity as it passes through the vehicle of the prophet.'[12]

God protects prophecy from errors both of reception and of transmission. This unique quality of prophecy is reinforced in the New Testament. 'For prophecy never had its origin in the will of man, but men spoke from God as they were carried along by the Holy Spirit' (2 Peter 1:20-21). This phrase 'carried along' means that 'They were "borne along" by the Holy Spirit as a ship is carried by the wind.'[13] According to B. B. Warfield, 'This language of Peter emphasizes ... the passivity of the prophets with respect to the revelation given to them... To be "borne" ... is not the same as to be led ... much less to be guided or directed... He that is "borne" contributes nothing to the movement induced, but is the object to be moved.'[14]

Peter states without equivocation that this quality applies to all prophecy. In verse 20 he explains, 'No prophecy of Scripture came about by the prophet's own interpretation.' By contrast Jeremiah accuses false prophets of speaking from their own hearts and impressions: 'They speak visions from their own minds, not from the mouth of the Lord' (Jer. 23:16).

From these contexts, we are forced to conclude that prophecy originates with God and is kept inerrant in its transmission by God. Prophecy is synonymous with revelation. Revelation contains what God chose to reveal. It owes its origin to the will and movement of God and is not due to impressions, reflections, ideas, meditations, or dreams originating in the mind and heart of the prophet.

This unbidden quality of prophecy is constantly reflected in the New Testament writings. New Testament prophets spoke and wrote, not what they themselves originated, but mysteries, as they were borne along by God. Paul describes 'the mystery made known to me by revelation ... the mystery of Christ, which was not made known to men in other generations as it has now been revealed by the Spirit to God's holy apostles and prophets' (Eph. 3:3-5). Palmer Robertson comments, 'The New Testament consistently represents a "mystery" as a truth about God's redemptive programme once concealed, *but now revealed.* This "mystery" now has been "re-vealed" by the Spirit to God's holy apostles and prophets. The two offices of apostle and prophet are joined together as the vehicles of divine revelation.'[15]

God specifically chose prophets (and apostles) to receive and transmit divine revelation, also called 'mystery'. The mystery mentioned by Paul in the Ephesian passage noted above was not about future things but about the multi-ethnic make-up of the church as the body of Christ. The revealing of this mystery has important implications in any claim made about further prophecy. Why would there be the need for prophecy when the apostles and prophets had already unveiled the mystery hidden from all ages? Are there mysteries yet to be unveiled? If so, why would the Holy Spirit proclaim the sufficiency of Scripture? (2 Tim. 3:16-17).

God inspired New Testament prophets, just as he had their Old Testament counterparts, to receive and transmit revelations from himself. He specifically arranged through the Holy Spirit that their teaching, preaching and writing be inspired. The completeness of the New Testament canon, coupled with the finality of its revelation, force us to conclude that New Testament prophecy was necessary only as long as God continued to reveal the Scriptures.

In his classic work *The Doctrine of the Holy Spirit* George Smeaton writes, 'The Holy Spirit supplied prophets and apostles, as chosen organs, with gifts which must be distinguished from ordinary grace, to give forth in human forms of speech a revelation which must be accepted as the Word of God in its whole contents, and as the authoritative guide for doctrine and duty.'[16]

God does not give new revelation to believers today

God never gave revelation indiscriminately to all believers. A sovereignly chosen few — men such as Moses and Samuel, Elijah and David, Isaiah and Peter — were its recipients. The process whereby God inspired prophets and apostles is without parallel in common Christian experience. It has never been duplicated since their time. To claim otherwise is to undermine the authority and inspiration of Scripture — which any serious evangelical Christian will avoid at all cost.

All believers could not have been chosen by God to receive revelation or Paul would not stress his own uniqueness in this regard. Note how emphatically Paul links his prophetic and apostolic credentials to his reception of revelation: 'I want you to know, brothers, that the gospel I preach is not something that man made up. I did not receive it from any man, nor was I taught it; rather, I received it by revelation from Jesus Christ' (Gal. 1:11-12). If revelation was common, Paul's appeal could not have been used to prove his uniqueness.

Our relationship with Christ is God's ultimate revelation to us. He is the 'Word of God'. Robertson makes the point that hankering after revelations, which have always been rare in history, would be like Israel lusting after the manna they ate in the desert after they had crossed into the promised land. Christ is our promised land! The cessation of the miraculous gifts is like the cessation of God's miraculous provision of daily manna to Israel when they conquered Canaan. How foolish it would have been for them to complain about this cessation when all the while they had been travelling towards a goal — Canaan — where they could enjoy milk and honey! And how foolish for us to lament the passing of revelation when God's eternal Word lives in our hearts![17]

Of course, the cessation of prophecy does not mean that God does not communicate with us in any way. 'It is not that God is dead and no longer communicates with people. The heavens still declare the glory of God, and the firmament displays his handiwork. The Holy Spirit who lives in every believer illumines the truth of God as found in Scripture, and applies it constantly to life and conscience. The Bible embodies God's personal selection of the special revelations he determined that the church would need through the ages. In this written revelation from God is contained all that is needed for life and godliness. No further words, ideas, or supposed visions and prophecies shall supplement the completed revelation of Scripture. It is not just that the written canon is closed, meaning that no more words are to be added to the Bible. The end of revelation means that all those former ways of God's making his will known to his church have now ceased.'[18]

The present fascination with prophecy is a blind alley. It leads away from the goal of prophecy, Jesus Christ. It leads away from the inspired record of prophecy, the Scriptures. I find it not only 'predictable', but alarming, that prophecy was mentioned 2.6 times more often than Christ in a three-month period at the Toronto Airport Vineyard. This imbalance is also reflected in the neglect of serious scriptural exegesis. Three times I scanned in vain this church's bustling bookshop for evidence of Bible study guides, commentaries, Bible dictionaries, works of general theology, etc. The results of this prophetic craze cannot but be disastrous in the long run — especially so when we measure Vineyard prophecy by biblical standards.

3. Testing prophetic validity

Around the world and down through history, people have claimed the ability to predict the future. With so much erroneous prophecy flying about, some method of distinguishing the true oracle of God from the false is essential. The Bible warns, 'Dear friends, do not believe every spirit, but test the spirits to see whether they are from God, because many false prophets have gone out into the world' (1 John 4:1).

What are the tests of a prophet? Scripture gives us four criteria. First of all, *prophecy must conform to the teaching of Scripture*. 'If a prophet ... appears among you and announces to you a miraculous sign or wonder, and if the sign or wonder ... takes place, and he says, "Let us worship other gods," you must not listen' (Deut. 13:1-3). Later on we read, 'But a prophet who presumes to speak in my name anything I have not commanded him to say, or a prophet who speaks in the name of other gods, must be put to death' (Deut. 18:20). Any divergence from the revealed biblical content called for the death penalty! (See also 1 John 4:2-3).

I have no doubt that the present fixation with signs and wonders is, unconsciously at least, an attempt to lend authenticity to prophetic ministry. No genuine miracles mean no genuine prophecy. But the warning in Deuteronomy reminds us that we must be very careful in the presence of supposedly miraculous signs. The magic of the Egyptian magicians initially mimicked the signs Moses performed. In India, Hindu, Sikh and Buddhist gurus echo Muslim 'holy men' in claiming power to effect miraculous cures. Some even demonstrate their power by walking on fire. Conformity to revealed truth takes precedence over startling manifestations of power.

Secondly, *prophetic prediction must be 100 per cent accurate.* Since God can infallibly predict the future, true prediction has no margin of error. God gave Moses a prophetic litmus test: 'You may say to yourselves, "How can we know when a message has not been spoken by the Lord?" If what a prophet proclaims in the name of the Lord does not take place or come true, that is a message the Lord has not spoken. That prophet has spoken presumptuously' (Deut. 18:21-22). Since less than perfect accuracy is a distinguishing mark of false prophecy, the perpetrator of a failed prophecy was to be put to death. Although proponents of modern prophecy deny it, all New Testament prophecy practised in the early church passed this litmus test. We shall consider their claims shortly.

Thirdly, *prophets of God exhibited godly character.* All the prophets, from Moses to Paul, were holy in life and witness. Although none was sinless, the revelation God inspired them to give was enhanced by their integrity and devotion to God, a fact that few will deny.

Fourthly, *genuine signs and wonders usually,* but not always, *attested the ministry of prophets.* As pointed out in chapter 17, each of the main revelatory epochs was introduced and attested by signs and wonders performed by, for example, Moses in the Exodus, Elijah in the prophetic period of the kings and Christ at the inauguration of the gospel age. We read that Moses was a prophet 'who did all those miraculous signs and wonders' (Deut. 34:11). Peter says that Jesus was 'a man accredited by God to you by miracles, wonders and signs' (Acts 2:22).

Scripture repeatedly reminds us of this principle. The crossing of the Red Sea and the gushing of water from a rock, among many other wonders, bore testimony to the authenticity of Moses' leadership. Likewise, an amazing cluster of marvels during the life of Christ and in the ministries of the apostles attested their veracity. The deaf heard, the lame walked, the dead were raised, snake-bite was neutralized and hearts were discerned. Some of the spiritual gifts themselves — notably tongues, healing and miracles — served to confirm revelation (Heb. 2:4).

No serious evangelical denies that God used signs, wonders and miracles to attest the ministries of the apostles and prophets. Although the wonders claimed by false prophets were bogus, the miracles of true prophets were genuine. Indeed it is precisely the biblical clarity on this point that compels those who believe in continuing revelation to manufacture miracles to demonstrate the authenticity of their claim. God has tied revelation and wonders together. If signs and miracles cannot be demonstrated, new revelations will be in serious doubt (see also Exod. 4:8,30-31; 2 Cor. 12:12). As demonstrated in chapters 16 and 17, Vineyard miracles do not meet biblical standards.

Error in modern prophecy proves its human origin

Traditionally, upon solid biblical grounds, prophecy has been considered inerrant. It is unthinkable to attribute error to a process that owes its origin to the superintendence of the perfect God! But this is exactly what proponents of modern prophecy do. They assert that God is behind both the process that resulted in the infallible Word of God and that which results in fallible prophecies today. In a conference in England several years ago, Bernard Thompson articulated this view. He said that we can 'claim *inspiration* but not *inerrance* for words of revelation which Spirit-baptized believers bring'![19] But how can we conceive of errant inspiration? It is a contradiction in terms.

Modern prophetic enthusiasts use three main texts to try to prove that some New Testament prophets were fallible. 1 Corinthians 14:29 states: 'Two or three prophets should speak, and the others should weigh carefully what is said.' Mike Bickle interprets this to mean: 'Paul instructs us to discern the words of genuine prophetic people because they are not infallible. Fortunately, the New Testament doesn't require such high standards as the Old Testament when 100 per cent accuracy was required on penalty of death.'[20] In other words, Bickle believes that the group of prophets present in Corinth were fallible and had to carefully evaluate each other to avoid error.

The context and the Greek, however, give a completely different picture. Paul writes in the context of conducting services in an orderly way: 'For God is not a God of disorder but of peace ... everything should be done in a fitting and orderly way' (1 Cor. 14:33,40). Paul assures the prophets that all will have an opportunity to speak (14:31). He reminds them that the prophets can control themselves (14: 32). In verse 29 the NIV adds words that are not in the Greek, 'what is said', to qualify the meaning of the words, 'weigh carefully'. However there is nothing else in the context to indicate a need to weigh the *content* of the prophets' messages. Palmer Robertson points out that the word translated 'weigh' is the Greek word *diakrino*, which most often is used of distinguishing *between people.*[21] What the prophets were asked to do was to *diakrino* who would speak first, and who later, so order might prevail. The inference that prophetic messages given in the Corinthian church had to be evaluated as to their correctness cannot be established from this text.

Another text used is 1 Thessalonians 5:19-21. In a string of general exhortations on working, revenge, joyfulness, prayer, thankfulness and not putting out the Spirit's fire, we read, 'Do not treat prophecies with contempt. Test everything. Hold on to the good. Avoid every kind of evil.'

Bickle interprets the exhortation, 'Test everything,' to mean that 'Some prophetic utterances will contain a measure of error...

Nowhere in the New Testament is there the suggestion that a Christian should be executed, excommunicated, or even branded a false prophet simply for relaying an inaccurate prophecy. False words are supposed to be weeded out as the church responds to prophecy.'[22] John Piper adds, 'This implies that there is genuine prophecy that is not perfect, so that the good needs to be sorted out from the bad.'[23]

Since 1 Thessalonians is one of the earliest epistles written by Paul and the canon of Scripture was not complete at the time he wrote it, we can assume that inspired prophecy was still being received from God. This was part of the unique nature of life in the early church. But with a period of 400 years void of prophecy preceding the gospel era, believers must have been sceptical of prophecy, even when genuine. In this context, Paul urged them not to despise prophecies. The question now arises: what were they to test — the true and the false in prophecies — or the man and his message *in toto*?

Proponents of modern-day prophecy assume this means that believers were asked to pick and choose from a prophet's message what was true and discard what was false. They try to prove this by assuming that Old Testament prophetic messages were not tested as to content. Rather, they claim that the person of the prophet was evaluated as to whether he represented God or Baal. If a prophet represented God he was to be accepted. This principle they would carry over into the New Testament to suggest that a prophet should be accepted if he was from God even if some of the content of his prophecy was defective.

In this they misread the Old Testament. The instructions given in Deuteronomy make it clear that believers were to test both the message of the prophet and his character and origin. The discovery of any discrepancy meant that both the person and his message were to be rejected. 'The total message is to be rejected, not merely the portion found to be in error, since any error in a prophecy indicates that the prophet has spoken presumptuously' (see Deut. 13:1-5; 18:21-22).

Numerous examples of exhortations about false prophets can be found in the New Testament. 'Keep watch... Even from your own number men will arise and distort the truth... So be on your guard! Remember that for three years I never stopped warning each of you night and day with tears' (Acts 20:28,30,31; see also 2 Cor. 11:2-6;

Gal. 2:4; 1 Tim. 6:3-4; 2 Peter 2:1). The discrimination believers are to make is not just between truth and falsehood in a prophecy, but between true and false prophets. Any error denoted a false prophet.

Acts 20 presents another line of Vineyard argument. In his book *The Gift of Prophecy in the New Testament and Today*, Wayne Grudem argues that Agabus' prophecy about Paul's coming imprisonment was inaccurate in two points: first, that the Jews did not bind Paul as Agabus said they would; and secondly, that they did not deliver him over to the Romans.[24] Robertson points out, however, that 'Twice it is reported that the Jews "seized" Paul (Acts 21:27,30). Is it so very clear that they did not "bind" him as they "dragged" him from the temple (vs. 30)? In a similar way, is it actually so clear that the Jews did not "deliver" Paul to the Romans as Agabus had predicted? The Jews seized Paul and were in the process of beating him when the Roman officials arrived at the scene (Acts 21:32). Is it to be insisted that there was no "delivering" of Paul by the Jews as the Roman commander came up and arrested him?'[25]

Obviously, the record of Paul's arrest does not contain every single particular — whether a rope or chain was used, what was said to the Roman commander, etc. Using this text to try to prove that Agabus made some errors in prediction and that therefore fallible prophets existed in the New Testament church is to seriously strain the text and its context. Grudem's arguments, although ingenious, are implausible, to say the least.

The presence of this kind of prophetic knowledge in the early church about Paul's coming imprisonment also explains an apparent contradiction a few verses earlier in Acts 21. When Paul arrived in Cyprus, 'Through the Spirit [the brethren] urged Paul not to go on to Jerusalem' (21:4). But Paul had already stated God's will in Acts 20:22: 'Compelled by the Spirit, I am going to Jerusalem.' It appears as if the leading of Paul contradicted the leading of the brethren in Cyprus. But how can the Spirit be the author of conflicting guidance? Advocates of modern prophecy use this apparent contradiction to assert that this is another example of fallible prophecy. A considerable number of commentators, however, interpret this to mean that 'The Spirit revealed to these disciples the sufferings Paul would undergo at Jerusalem [exactly the same as the revelation given to Agabus a few verses later]. To this perfected revelation the concerned disciples appended their own conclusion: that Paul should not proceed to Jerusalem. It was not that the Spirit or prophecy erred at this point. Instead, it was simply that the disciples' concern for the well-being of their mentor limited their apprehension of the good that might come from Paul's suffering for Christ's sake. As Calvin so aptly summarizes the matter: "It is no marvel if those who excel in the gift of prophecy be sometimes destitute of judgment or fortitude".'[26]

Use of the texts we have considered to try to prove that some New Testament prophecy was fallible falls far short of the Vineyard goal. They fail to show that the New Testament illustrates a second kind of prophecy akin to prophecy as practised in the Vineyard movement today. And since what is practised in Vineyard circles is admittedly subject to error, biblical criteria would term it false.

Let me give several examples. Although Bob Jones, of Kansas City fame, is not now associated closely with the movement, a Vineyard spokesman used his statement about prophecy to describe the Vineyard view: 'Bob [Jones] was told that the general level of prophetic revelation in the church was about 65% accurate at this time. Some are only about 10% accurate, a very few of the most mature prophets are approaching 85% to 95% accuracy. Prophecy is increasing in purity, but there is still a long way to go for those who walk in this ministry.'[27]

He is certainly correct about modern prophetic inaccuracy. Jack Deere warned people not to shy away from prophecy because of its messy nature. Then he went on to describe how a 'wonderfully effective prophetic minister' came before a group of 800 high school young people. He began to give prophetic words about youth in the audience. Then he called up a young eighteen-year-old man and said to him, '"You're into pornography. And the Lord says you have to repent." The young man begins to cry. Sits back down. The only problem was, the young man wasn't into pornography. He was publicly humiliated before 800 high school kids. We had to go back to his church, apologize to his whole church, apologize to the whole conference. It was a horrible mess.'[28]

Unbelievably, Jack Deere writes off this serious breach as a normal part of ministry! 'There's going to be stumbling blocks in every ministry that the Holy Spirit is really responsible for.'[29] How can Deere attribute such a terrible mistake to the Holy Spirit? Does he not worry about what Christ said about those who cause stumbling-blocks, especially to young ones?

Prophecies such as these cannot originate with God. God is not the originator of this kind of thing. Where do prophetic words such as these come from then? I shall consider that question at the end of this chapter.

God is not the author of two kinds of prophecy, one infallible and the other fallible

John Piper, in one of the most compelling arguments for a Vineyard style of continuing prophecy writes, 'We need another category of prophet besides the one of *true prophet*, on the one hand, who spoke with infallible, verbal inspiration (the prophetic Biblical authors and Jesus and the apostles), and *false prophet* ... We need a third category for the *"spiritual gift of prophecy"* — Spirit-prompted, Spirit-sustained, revelation-rooted, but mixed with human imperfection and fallibility and therefore in need of sifting.'[30]

Piper then seeks to show from the Old and New Testaments that such a group of fallible prophets existed. He refers to the seventy elders of Numbers 11:24-29; the band of prophets among whom Saul prophesied in 1 Samuel 10:5-6,9-12; the prophesying predicted by Joel that occurred at Pentecost; the prophesying of those in Cornelius' house in Acts 10:45-46 and of the Ephesians in Acts 19:6. This second kind of prophesying he calls a 'kind of "prophecy" that does not have apostolic authority but is a Spirit-prompted, spontaneous utterance about God's great character or his ways'.[31]

I don't dispute that biblical prophecy, as exemplified among the Old Testament bands of prophets, at Pentecost, in Cornelius' house and at Ephesus included a kind of 'Spirit-prompted, spontaneous utterance about God's character or his ways'. But this is consistent with *one* kind of prophecy — namely, inerrant, Spirit-prompted revelation. The fact that we have already shown that error cannot be attached to any class or kind of biblical prophecy already disproves this thesis. One of the main goals of the Vineyard search for fallible New Testament prophecy is to prove that revelation came to two kinds of prophets in biblical times: inspired and authoritative prophets such as Elijah and Peter and fallible prophets such as Agabus and the Corinthians. By showing that error cannot be laid at the feet of any prophet, we have effectively demonstrated that two classes of inspired prophets did not exist. Whenever God gave revelation, he preserved its inerrancy. And thus we can conclude that those who are called 'prophets' in the Vineyard movement are not prophets in the sense that they bring new revelations from God.

4. The preaching and predictive mix in biblical prophecy

On the whole, prophets were not predictors — *foretellers* — but rather *forthtellers,* preachers. Moses and John the Baptist, two of the greatest prophets of all time, recorded little in the way of prediction. With minor exceptions, the entire content of Moses' prophetic ministry was either history, ethical statements (law), or exhortations for Israel to heed God's directives. He did warn them about the consequences of disobeying the law and he did predict that there would be another prophet raised up like him.

John prepared people for the coming of Christ by preaching of sin and calling for repentance. With the exception of his prophecy that the Messiah would appear among them, he did not engage in prediction.

Prophets cannot be understood outside their historical context. God commanded Isaiah to 'Go and tell *this* people...' The message God gave him dealt with people in a specific historic setting (Isa. 6:9-13). Elijah spoke to the rise of Baal worship. Jeremiah preached under the shadow of the Babylonian crisis. The prophetic ministry of the apostles followed a similar pattern. Prediction was minimal. The major portion of their messages concerned God's will for his people in concrete situations. The Gospels and epistles each appeal to different audiences. Even the most predictive of books, Revelation, brought a message from God to the seven churches of Asia in specific historical situations.

I am not saying that the messages prophets brought cannot be applied in our situations. All Scripture is profitable wherever we are. The book of Psalms blesses people all over the world, as does Nehemiah — or any Old Testament book. What I am saying is that the primary focus of the prophet was not on the future but on the present. He declared God's will in a particular historic situation.

Christ prepared the apostles for a prophetic ministry. He described how the New Testament canon would be formed: 'The Holy Spirit ... will teach you all things and will remind you of everything I have said to you' (John 14:26). 'I have much more to say to you, more than you can now bear. But when he, the Spirit of truth, comes, he will guide you into all truth. He will not speak on his own; he will speak only what he hears, and he will tell you what is yet to come' (John 16:12-13).

These passages in John mention three categories of content: first, an accurate reminder of what Jesus taught which became recorded for us in Scripture as the four Gospels; second, a complete revelation of further truth which Jesus up to this time had withheld due to their immaturity, and which became inscripturated for us as the epistles; and, third, a revelation of things to come, the predictive element, which we find mainly in the book of Revelation.

A study of the New Testament shows that the vast majority of content can be categorized as gospel, early church history and teaching on a variety of subjects, especially Christian living. A few predictive elements, such as those found in Jesus' Olivet discourse, are included here and there. Revelation contains prophecy addressed as much to the specific situation in which God gave it as to future generations.

Prophecy, then, in both testaments consists of a maximum of forthtelling and a minimum of foretelling. To cry out for a return of the prophetic office out of a desire to listen to predictions is to demand something of the prophetic office that, even in its zenith, it rarely exhibited. Prophecy is much more akin to inspired preaching than ecstatic utterances. But more about that shortly.

Modern prophecy is an unbiblical mix high in prediction and low in preaching

When we compare the frequency of predictions made in the Vineyard movement to the rarity of prediction in biblical times, we immediately sense that something is wrong. Vineyard prophecy has a fairly high proportion of prediction that is inconsistent with New Testament prophecy. Among the New Testament prophets that they turn to for precedent, we only discover two predictions, both made by Agabus. One concerned a famine that was to spread throughout the Roman world and one concerned the imprisonment of Paul (Acts 11:27-28; 21:10-11). There is a possibility that the daughters of Philip also gave predictions. All the rest of the prophets that the Vineyard seeks to use in establishing their view — the Corinthian prophets, Barnabas, Silas, Judas, etc., — preached and taught. Yet preaching and instruction are hardly given lip-service in connection with prophecy in the Vineyard. Indeed, preaching is seriously undervalued. The mix is suspect, casting further doubt on Vineyard, and charismatic, prophetic practice.

Present-day predictions are not biblical prophecy

What do we make of the actual predictions associated with the movement? When we compare the accuracy of biblical prophecy with the inaccuracy of the Vineyard brand we become alarmed. Soothed by their strange view that present-day revelations are fallible, they encourage a hotchpotch of supposed revelations and predictions.

Many predictions in the past few years have proved wrong. Bob Jones predicted that 1,000 religious leaders would die in 1989 because of their abuse of spiritual gifts. John Paul Jackson wrongly predicted the collapse of the stock market. Paul Cain wrongly predicted the nature and length of the Gulf War. Both Paul Cain and John Wimber were wrong in their predictions about a revival in Britain in 1990.[32]

Furthermore, claims that Paul Cain could smell cancer, demons and different kinds of sin as a young man, that he heard the audible voice of Christ, that he had Jesus appear beside him in the passenger seat while driving in California are bizarre, to say the least.[33]

This kind of error does not need to be documented further, since those in the movement readily admit their fallibility. Perhaps the wild predictions and claims made earlier in the movement have moved many today to moderate their claims. Most predictions I heard in Toronto were very general: 'I see fountains bursting out all over the world.' 'I see fire spreading from Toronto around the world.'

The predictions of Marc Dupont in an issue of *Spread The Fire* in 1995 called *News Before It Happens* are so general that they cannot be called prediction because anyone with moderate insight could make similar statements. For example, he said of England, 'Many people in the church will start going out and ministering God's love to those outside, and begin bringing them into the Kingdom.' Of Japan he predicted, 'Japan will be shaken economically, politically, physically and spiritually for about 18 months.' Concerning Germany he said, 'There are tremendous fields of ripe wheat ready for the harvest.'[34] Jean Dixon, a popular psychic, makes this kind of general prediction all the time! These can hardly be classed with the prophecies of Agabus, let alone Isaiah or John.

Since Vineyard prophecy does not come anywhere close to the biblical criteria of absolute accuracy, it cannot be a viewed as of divine origin.

5. Preaching as the partial continuation of the prophetic gift

Do our studies thus far exhaust the New Testament teaching about prophecy? Classically, evangelicals have believed so. Palmer Robertson argues persuasively to this effect. Personally, I find another class of texts in the New Testament about prophecy that do not fit the pattern of revelational prophecy. It is this group of texts that has led to the Vineyard confusion on the subject. These texts seem to present some kind of ongoing prophetic gift. They give no reason to believe in the continuation of inspired, inerrant revelation. But they do suggest that one of the prophetic functions continues. Let me explain, very, very carefully what I mean.

It is at this point that Vineyard ideas about two kinds of prophecy have some validity. As we saw earlier, Mike Bickle writes, 'It is vital to distinguish between *inspirational* prophecy and *revelational* prophecy.'[35] He would no doubt claim that both kinds of prophecy involve divine revelation. We have already disproved this thesis, since the Bible asserts the infallibility of all revelation. But Bickle goes on to explain the purpose of 'inspirational prophecy' as 'general in nature and frequently based on a passage of Scripture. They refresh, encourage, exhort, motivate and comfort God's people.'[36]

Statements such as these come closest to my view that the ongoing gift of prophecy is preaching. Let us be clear, however, that claims to revelational prophecy as 'new direction, correction and different doctrinal emphases' must be rejected out of hand because, as we have already seen, Scripture has no category for fallible revelation. Revelational prophecy came to inspired prophets who occupied the prophetic office, an office that does not now exist. The Vineyard category of 'inspirational' prophecy, however, has a certain resonance with other Scriptures that have nothing to do with revelation.

Up to this point, I have argued for the absolute cessation of prophecy. As revelation, I believe it has ceased. But as a way of communicating truth many of its functions continue as prophetic preaching. Several categories of evidence lead me to this conclusion.

1. Prophets as preachers. As we have already seen, prophets fulfilled two functions, one of which was preaching. The Greek word for 'prophecy' means simply 'making public utterance' or 'speaking out'.

Moses spoke to Israelites groaning under Egyptian bondage. Isaiah preached to a nation in declension. Paul appealed to a Corinthian church in disarray due to scandals. The relevance of their messages to particular situations rendered their preaching memorable to their audiences.

They fulfilled two functions at the same time: transmitting divine revelation and preaching to concrete situations. God inspired them to perfectly transmit the revelation of his will which became incorporated in the Bible. Simultaneously, they preached to historical situations. They were both prophets and preachers.

There is considerable evidence that New Testament prophets functioned as preachers. Note first the abundance of prophets present in the early churches. There were both inspired prophets responsible for the recording of revelation in Scripture and more ordinary prophets who carried on a ministry of preaching and teaching. The five men, including Barnabas and Saul, who gathered to worship God in the church at Antioch in Acts 13 are called 'prophets and teachers' (Acts 13:1). The text denotes either that there were at least two prophets, or that all five had both the gift of teaching and that of prophecy. I prefer this latter view.

We also read of two prophets, Judas and Silas, going down to Antioch to 'encourage and strengthen the brothers' (Acts 15:32), and of Paul and Barnabas staying in Antioch 'where they and many others taught and preached the word of the Lord' (v. 35). It is not necessary to understand that they brought new revelations to Antioch. It seems more reasonable to suppose that they proclaimed God's Word with a view to encouraging believers. Prophetic ministry must involve preaching and teaching.

1 Corinthians contains an extended description of the gift and how it contrasts with tongues (1 Cor. 14). Evidently, a considerable number of men with the gift of prophecy took turns in speaking to the Corinthian church. 'You can all prophesy in turn so that everyone may be instructed and encouraged' (v. 31). Clearly, Paul is not suggesting that they give revelations of new truth. He is

suggesting that they take turns in bringing messages of instruction and encouragement — functions of preaching.

In 1 Corinthians 14, Paul establishes the superiority of prophecy over tongues. In verses 3-4 we read, 'Everyone who prophesies speaks to men for their strengthening, encouragement and comfort... He who prophesies edifies the church.' Obviously, God designed the gift so it could be used to build up the church. How? Prophets edified by applying God's Word, not necessarily by bringing new revelations, but by drawing from what God had already revealed. They strengthened those who were weak. They encouraged the discouraged. They comforted the sorrowing.

In the section beginning at verse 22 we read, 'Prophecy, however, is for believers.' In verse 31 prophecy is exercised so that 'everyone may be instructed and encouraged'. Note how important heart-warming instruction was in all the references we have used above.

2. Exhortations to seek the gift of prophecy. If God had reserved the gift of prophecy exclusively for those he chose to lay the foundation of the church, we would not find a general exhortation to seek the gift. We read, however, 'Eagerly desire the greater gifts.' One of the greatest is prophecy. Paul specifically states, 'Desire spiritual gifts, especially the gift of prophecy... I would rather have you prophesy... Be eager to prophesy' (1 Cor. 12:31; 14:1,5,39).

These exhortations would be problematic unless they were meant to encourage not only the Corinthians, but believers today, to seek the gift. To deny this is to empty the epistles of their relevance. You may ask, 'But isn't this exactly what the Vineyard is saying?' In a sense yes, but their pursuit of prophecy as *revelation* blinds them to prophecy as *preaching*. They do not view their prophetic practices as involving preaching, but Spirit-inspired revelation. Paul could not have been urging the Corinthians to uncover new mysteries through revelation. His role in bringing mysteries to light as an inspired prophet was unique (see Eph. 2:2-13) No, Paul urges many believers to seek to prophesy because preaching is an absolutely foundational ministry in the church. Through preaching God edifies the church by instructing and teaching and encouraging.

Each of the three main lists of gifts mentions the gift of prophecy. Only the gift of teaching is mentioned as consistently. The frequency with which it is mentioned, in epistles of both early and late origin, shows that its use is crucial. If we arbitrarily excise from our corpus of teaching about the church any role for prophecy at all, how can we confidently apply other apostolic directives? Such a procedure would call into question our whole system of interpretation.

Of particular note is the inclusion of prophecy in the list of the five key equipping gifts in Ephesians chapter 4. Prophets join apostles, evangelists, pastors and teachers as men given to 'prepare God's people for works of service so that the body of Christ may be built up' (v. 12). The mention of prophets and apostles in this passage makes no sense unless they have some continuing function. If three of the gifts — pastors, teachers and evangelists — continue, and the need for equipping the saints continues, then why are apostles and prophets included only to be withdrawn? (I explain in *Church — No Spectator Sport* that apostleship, like prophecy ceased as an office, but, like prophecy, one aspect of its function continued — church-planting. The gift of missionary church-planting is a fundamentally important gift that continues without the necessity of the authority and inspiration of the apostolic office continuing. The twelve apostles died and the office ceased with them. Prophecy should be understood in a similar way.)[37]

I would define the ongoing gift of prophecy, not as the ability to communicate new revelations, but that spiritual ability to communicate biblical truth in powerful and relevant ways so that people sense a word from God directed to them in their situation. It is Spirit-filled preaching that may include instruction, encouragement, exhortation or comfort.

Inspired prophecies have an unbidden, Spirit-produced element to them, as if the Spirit overrides the will of the prophet. Edifying prophecy, however, is a gift controlled by the person: 'The spirits of prophets are subject to the control of the prophets' (1 Cor. 14:32). Prophecy, in this form, involves orderly presentations of truth which flow from the speaker's mind and will.

A picture of two categories of prophecy emerges: inspired prophecy that produced the inerrant canon of Holy Scripture (and occasionally included prediction); and prophecy as convicting and edifying preaching. Prophetic preaching draws its power from a broadly based acquaintance with Scripture and ongoing dependence on the Spirit. It includes the ability to size up situations and needs and to bring a relevant message. Prophetic preaching leads to conviction, consolation, rebuke or encouragement. As a continuing gift, it requires the *illumination* of the Spirit but not his *inspiration*.

As the New Testament unfolds we read less about prophecy and more about preaching. Paul exhorts Timothy to 'Preach the Word;

be prepared in season and out of season; correct, rebuke and encourage — with great patience and careful instruction' (2 Tim. 4:2). This kind of preaching is indistinguishable from the prophecy described in 1 Corinthians 14! Both involve instruction based on a careful evaluation of people's needs. Being prepared 'in season and out of season' reflects the need for preaching to be relevant to specific times and situations. Paul writes to Titus of how God 'brought his word to light through ... preaching' (Titus 1:3). The gift of prophecy involves preaching Christ and him crucified in order to challenge people to submit to him. 'The testimony of Jesus is the spirit of prophecy' (Rev. 19:10).

This transition in terminology in the New Testament from the use of 'prophecy' to 'preaching' shows that God wanted to phase out the term 'prophecy' in order to safeguard the unique position of those few prophets who were the bearers of inerrant revelation. The ongoing gift of prophecy, then, is not the gift of bringing revelations but preaching.

Vineyard descriptions of two kinds of prophets are half right

As already noted, Wayne Grudem, John Piper, Mike Bickle and others at the Toronto Airport Christian Fellowship distinguish two or more kinds of prophecy. They admit that modern prophets are categorically distinct from the authoritative and inerrant prophets chosen by God to bring us the completed canon of Scripture. Then, in an attempt to harmonize biblical passages that describe New Testament prophets as speaking words of encouragement, comfort and edification, they conclude that there are two further categories; 'inspirational' and 'revelational'. They connect 'inspirational prophecy' with communication based on a passage or passages of Scripture. This is halfway to admitting that this is preaching and teaching. But unfortunately, they insist that inspirational prophecy, no less than 'revelational prophecy', is a form of revelation. Our studies in the infallibility of all revelation compel me to conclude that their interpretation is damaging, to say the least. Perhaps this is why preaching takes a back seat in meetings associated with the Toronto Blessing.

They are confusing their own interpretations of inner impressions with divine revelation. This, in turn, can be traced to a pervasive failure to distinguish illumination from revelation. In *illumination,* the Holy Spirit assists believers in interpreting the Scriptures. As sinners, albeit redeemed sinners, our minds are relatively darkened. We must depend upon the Spirit to grant us understanding of Scripture because 'These things are spiritually discerned.' As the Spirit helps us to understand and apply the Scriptures to our daily lives, our ability to interpret Scripture progressively increases. Our ability to interpret Scripture will never be absolutely perfect in this life. 'Now we see but a poor reflection as in a mirror; then we shall see face to face' (1 Cor. 13:12). The illumination of the Holy Spirit, then, unlike inspiration, is a relative grace because its pragmatic application depends so much on the exegetical skill and spiritual wisdom of the interpreter. While inspiration is inerrant, illumination is, of necessity, partial and its results therefore fallible.

No wonder Vineyard-type prophecies are fallible. They are not prophecies at all! They are attempts to interpret the will of God, attempts to apply the Scriptures to the issues they see around them! Why don't they admit that this is what they are doing instead of claiming that they receive revelation? This is the real mystery in modern so-called prophecy!

If prophecy continues in any sense, it continues as preaching

J. I. Packer sums it up: 'Rather than supposing prophecy to be a long-gone first-century charisma now revived and therefore to be dressed up in verbal clothes that will set it apart from all other forms of Christian communication over the past eighteen or nineteen centuries, we should realize that it has actually been exhibited in every sermon or informal "message" that has had a heart-searching, "home-coming" application in its hearers, ever since the church began. Prophecy has been and remains a reality whenever and wherever Bible truth is genuinely preached — that is, spelled out and applied, whether from a pulpit or more informally. Preaching is teaching God's revealed truth with application.'[38]

Calvin gives his view: 'By prophesying I do not understand the gift of foretelling the future, but the science of interpreting Scriptures, so a prophet is an interpreter of the will of God.'[39] Interpretation of the will of God underscores a preacher's need to size up a situation and then bring relevant Scripture to bear on the central issues involved.

The gift of prophecy, in its continuing form, is heart-searching, applicational preaching deeply rooted in biblical exposition. The kingdom needs preaching prophets today as never before!

6. What is it that the Vineyard identifies as prophetic revelation?

If it is not preaching, and not divine revelation, what is it that the Vineyard describes as prophecy? In describing how he received the Toronto Blessing, Jim Paul explained that 'God spoke to him privately and commanded him to go up to the front the following night and be prayed for three times.'[40] Presumably this 'communication' from God came to Mr Paul in the same way as proponents of modern prophecy believe revelations are given. What is going on here?

Mike Bickle explains the experience of the Kansas City Prophets: 'John Paul [Jackson] stands up here, he gets impressions. He gets distinctives. He'll see faith visions and everything is in a movie screen and it's accurate, but you've got to move by faith. It's like Paul Cain says, "You've got to give expression to your impressions or you'll never grow." And you have to grow by stepping out.'[41] Obviously, what charismatic believers call 'revelations' are what most of us call 'impressions'. Bickle seems to be saying that a modern prophet grows in his ability to prophesy as he steps out in 'faith', by believing that his impression is from God. As he does this more and more he grows as a prophet.

In a message at the 1994 Catch The Fire Conference in Toronto, Wes Campbell confirmed this practice. He described how many people in his church have 'prophetic stuff', presumably revelations. He encourages them to express this 'stuff' while others discern what they are saying. They learn to prophesy by expressing impressions. This learning process involves a lot of trial and error on the part of interpreting impressions. He says, 'Let them begin by blessing, and let them begin by affirming... I would say, you know, "Speak it" and I would then stop and say [to the person to whom the prophecy is coming] "Does this relate to you?" And if ... they've given ten or fifteen bogus impressions, you sit the person down and say, "I'm sorry. This one was not of God; this one wasn't God; this one wasn't God; this one wasn't true; this one wasn't accurate; this one wasn't right. You are not hearing." Now, tuck in behind three or four that are, and watch and affirm... Put them in the room, week after week, prophesy week after week, record it week after week, measure it week after week, affirm it week after week, prune it week after week, encourage it week after week and after a good while you'll have a mature plant. A mature plant with good, good fruit. And yet God wants all of you to hear from Him.'[42]

So, in the movement, prophecy is a learned skill that comes first of all from being bold about expressing one's impressions and then having those expressions corrected week after week. With such a process, anyone could learn after a while how to say what will sound like a genuine prophecy because the leaders keep directing neophytes towards what they consider real revelations! Can you imagine all the damage that must be done by this quantity of bogus prophecy flying around a local church? I have already mentioned the example Jack Deere gave of the young man falsely accused of reading pornography. Why any church leader would seriously encourage such a subjective and dangerous practice is beyond me!

Of course, many in the movement lay claim to revelations that seem much more dramatic than simple impressions. James Ryle, pastor of the Boulder Valley Vineyard Fellowship in Colorado, believes 'God is a supernatural being and surely speaks through supernatural means. I refer to the audible voice of God, divine manifestations of his presence, angelic encounters and similar phenomena.'[43]

But after the fall-out from Gruen's exposé of problems in Kansas City, most in the movement are content to tone down their rhetoric. Wayne Grudem defines prophecy simply as: 'reporting something God spontaneously brings to mind'.[44] In another place he has said, 'Remember that what is spoken in any prophecy today is not the word of God, but is simply a human being reporting in merely human words something which God has brought to mind.'[45] He has written to urge charismatics to 'Stop calling [prophecy] "a word from the Lord" — simply because that label makes it sound exactly like the Bible in authority.' Instead he urges people to preface words of prophecy with statements such as, 'I think the Lord is showing me that...', 'I think the Lord is indicating that...', 'It seems that the Lord is putting on my heart a concern that...'[46] Following a similar line, James Ryle counsels would-be prophets to say, 'It occurred to me...,'[47] even though, as John MacArthur points out, he does not preface his own prophecies this way in his book, *Hippo in the Garden*.[48] And as quoted above, some of the means Ryle claims that God uses to communicate revelation are much more bizarre than having a thought come to mind!

How can a person sort out the thousands of mundane, even satanic, impressions that come to mind, from the one put there, ostensibly, by God? How do we distinguish the human capacity for intuition from the Vineyard brand of prophecy? What about dreams, a frequently mentioned source of revelation in the movement? My wife Mary Helen has a very active dream life! When I bring her morning coffee, I am often fascinated by her accounts of dream activity. Should we be interpreting them as revelations? On what basis did Wes Campbell and those with him discard the hundreds of bogus impressions presented in his church as revelations? Is there an objective standard to apply to all these subjective impressions?

John Blattner, in the Vineyard magazine *Equipping the Saints,* gives a number of ways to test the authenticity of the prophecy and the person bringing it. Although Blattner wrote this in 1989, leaders in the Vineyard seem to promote the same tests today. He distinguishes between testing the prophetic message and testing the person who gives the prophecy. First he gives four ways to discern the quality of a prophecy:

1. Conformity to Scripture and established Christian teaching...
2. Test the spirit of a prophecy by observing its tone and effect. A message that is harsh and mean-spirited is seldom from the Spirit...
3. Do predicted occurrences actually take place? ...
4. Does it bear good fruit? [Since] our character always multiplies, for good or ill, the effects of our gifts.

Blattner adds to these four ways to test prophecy, five ways to test the person prophesying:

1. Is the person solid and stable in the Christian life? ...
2. Is the person free of serious wrongdoing? ...
3. Is he or she a person of basic emotional and psychological health? ...
4. Is his or her motivation pure? ...
5. Is the person submissive to proper authority?[49]

None of these criteria is objective or absolute, with the exception of conformity to the Bible and seeing whether a prediction actually takes place. Indeed, these tests seem more like criteria for evaluating a Christian for church office or Christian ministry.

What we have here is an attempt to bring into the arena of prophecy some of the spiritual gifts that have been displaced by their emphasis. These criteria underscore the need for biblical knowledge, wisdom, discernment and encouragement. In fact many of the attempts at giving a prophetic word strike me more as attempts at giving to an individual or congregation a word of biblical encouragement, comfort, wisdom or discernment. The whole Bible fosters the development of these gifts — without any reference to the need for receiving fresh revelations from God.

To associate divine authority with even the best human efforts to minister to people harms the church and misleads the individual trying to help others in this way. Blattner admits the problem. At the outset he asserts that 'Our prophesying is imperfect. It will always be imperfect. We can count on it.'[50] He explains that this is due to 'sinful aspects of our humanity ... our carnality. Prophecy can be a vehicle for spiritual ambition ... can be used as a weapon ... to silence opponents in a discussion ... to discredit others.'[51]

One wonders why the Vineyard insists on treading such a minefield of explosive problems when all we need is already in the Bible. The ascended Christ has already given to the church all the spiritual gifts it needs for its edification: preaching, teaching, evangelism, shepherding, leadership, encouragement, mercy, faith, etc.

This continual effort to invest something very subjective — human impressions — with an aura of objectivity is dangerous and bound to fail. Would that the incident related by Jack Deere, in which a teenager was falsely accused of pornography, was enough to scare would-be prophets back to the Bible!

In 1983 I was immensely helped by Garry Friesen's book, *Decision Making and the Will of God.* John MacArthur very wisely refers to this book in dealing with this whole issue of impressions in *Reckless Faith*. In a chapter entitled 'Impressions are Impressions', Friesen asks, 'How can one tell whether these impressions are from God or from some other source?'[52]

He writes, 'This is a critical question. For impressions could be produced by any number of sources: God, Satan, an angel, a demon, human emotions (such as fear or ecstasy), hormonal imbalance, insomnia, medication, or an upset stomach. Sinful impressions (temptations) may be exposed for what they are by the Spirit-sensitized conscience and the Word of God. But beyond that, one encounters a subjective quagmire of uncertainty. For in non-moral areas, Scripture gives no guidelines for distinguishing the voice of the Spirit from the voice of the self — or any other potential "voice".'[53]

Instead, Scripture urges us to develop wisdom and discernment through storing God's Word in our hearts and taking responsibility for decision-making ourselves. To be tossed to and fro by impressions is to stifle the development of wisdom, which is urged so strongly upon us in the book of Proverbs, in the Sermon on the Mount and in the epistles.

Friesen points out that 'Inner impressions are not a form of revelation. So the Bible does not invest inner impressions with authority to function as indicators of divine guidance. Impressions are real; believers experience them. But impressions are *not authoritative*. Impressions are impressions. Call them "spiritual", or attribute them to the Holy Spirit, and they are still the same — just impressions. Impressions by any other name confuse the issue and confound the believer...'[54]

Jonathan Edwards battled against the tendency to grant to impressions an aura of spirituality. As mentioned earlier, he viewed this as one of the most damaging emphases that hindered the Great Awakening. He condemned the notion as mischievous 'that it is God's manner in these days, to guide his saints, at least some that are more eminent, by inspiration, or immediate revelation. They suppose he makes known to them what shall come to pass hereafter, or what it is his will that they should do, by impressions made upon their minds, either with or without texts of Scripture: whereby something is made known to them that is not taught in the Scripture. By such a notion the devil has a great door opened for him; and if once this opinion should come to be fully yielded to, and established in the church of God, Satan would have opportunity thereby to set up himself as the guide and oracle of God's people...'[55]

This is the terrible danger the movement faces. Indeed this propensity to listen more to inner impressions than to the objective Word of God is a plague threatening the health of the whole evangelical church. Haddon Robinson says, 'If we lift our inner impressions to the level of divine revelation, we are flirting with divination.'[56]

This is exactly why God warned the people about 'the detestable ways of the nations... Let no one be found among you who ... practises divination or sorcery, interprets omens, engages in witchcraft, or casts spells, or who is a medium or spiritist or who consults the dead. Anyone who does these things is detestable to the Lord' (Deut. 18:9-12). All around us today we find the rise of these same occult practices. They exalt some supposed divine inner light. Impressions brought by a contemplation of the stars, or crystals, or regression therapy are given more credence than objective revelation. The Vineyard is in danger of falling into this quagmire.

Palmer Robertson makes a crucial point in this regard: 'In today's pluralist society, people find it almost impossible to express a categorical "no" to any form of speaking or experience promoted in a devotional atmosphere by Christians. But God's word says "no". An unyielding resistance is required of the people of God with respect to any proposed substitutions for the divinely inspired prophetic word.'[57]

Hymns composed during the remarkable days of the Great Awakening expressed clear sentiments on this subject. Unfortunately, these feelings fail to engage the minds and hearts of many evangelicals today.

> How firm a foundation, ye saints of the Lord,
> Is laid for your faith in his excellent Word!
> What more can he say than to you he hath said,
> To you who for refuge to Jesus have fled?

Remember that hymn? Many of us still love it — because we love the Book. A daily plodding perseverance through the pages of Holy Writ is not too mundane. We don't shy away from commentaries and study guides, concordances and dictionaries as too ponderous. Time spent reading, memorizing, mediating and studying the Bible doesn't seem dry and mechanical. Why? Because we have often felt the soul-searching awe that comes when Scripture speaks to the intimate and daily issues of life. We have met the Master.

We still believe that what the author of the book of Hebrews said is true: 'In the past God spoke to our forefathers through the prophets at many times and in various ways, but in these last days he has spoken to us by his Son, whom he appointed heir of all things' (Heb. 1:1-2). Thank God for the prophets and apostles through whose writings we have come into intimate fellowship with Jesus Christ, God's final Word.

Points of comparison	Prophecy as viewed by non-charismatics
Kinds of prophets	One kind only; inspired, inerrant authoritative vessels of revelation.
The prophetic office	Ceased with the last of the New Testament prophets and the completion of the canon.
Transmission	God kept both the reception and transmission of revelations free from error.
Result	Inerrant, authoritative words from God. All necessary revelation is contained in the Scriptures. All can be trusted.
Developing prophetic ability	The prophet was not required to learn how to prophesy, since revelation and perfect interpretation were under God's control. God spoke through the mouth of the prophet.
Frequency	Infrequent. Prophecy came in several main periods: the Exodus, the Jewish kingdom and the apostolic period.
Purpose	God chose prophets to be the bearers of a revelation of his will at key periods of time, until the canon of Scripture was complete.
The sufficiency of Scripture	The Bible contains the complete revelation of God's will for men and women. It is sufficient for every spiritual need.
The gift of prophecy today	God has ceased to give revelation today. God speaks to us through the Bible. Some, such as Calvin, believed that the gift continues as preaching.
Tests for prophecy	It must be free from any error in prediction or any divergence from biblical teaching. Failure here classes it as false teaching. In the Old Testament this called for the death penalty.
End or goal of prophecy	Prophecy culminated in the ultimate revelation of God in Christ. All biblical history moved towards this goal and towards completing the revelation of God's will in the full canon of Scripture. And thus prophecy ceased.
How the Spirit speaks to people today	Besides natural revelation, God speaks through *illumination* of the Scriptures and through the providential leading of the Spirit.

The Vineyard view of prophecy

Two kinds in the Bible: authoritative and inspired prophets such as Moses, and fallible, 'ecstatic prophets' such as Agabus who give spontaneous utterances.[58] In this latter, fallible category there are also 'inspirational' and 'revelational' prophets: those who bring general words of comfort based on Scripture, and those who bring words about people, dates, facts, etc.

From time to time God sovereignly chooses believers, such as Paul Cain, to occupy the prophetic office. They have special divine authority and are unusually reliable.

Prophecy of inspired and authoritative prophets was kept free from error in its reception and transmission. Those with the general gift of prophecy, such as Agabus and believers today, receive inerrant revelation but it is subject to error as it passes through the mind of the believer who presents it.

That prophecy which is incorporated in the Bible is inerrant and authoritative, but that given today is not authoritative in the same way. Since it is fallible, it must be tested.

People can be taught today how to exercise the ongoing prophetic gift. Its use takes time and maturity, trial and error.

Various views. Most stress that receiving revelation is part of normal Christian living. It was neglected in church history but is being revived in these last days.

Agreed about the role of the inspired prophets in delivering the complete canon of Scriptures. But the ongoing gift of prophecy provides encouragement, exhortation, comfort, guidance, warning, conviction and prediction necessary for modern believers to be assured of God's presence.

Scripture alone is authoritative and it is sufficient. But the gift of ongoing prophecy provides believers with the guidance and encouragement that comes from ongoing revelation about extra-biblical things.

Inerrant revelation comes to people today but their interpretation of what they have received from God is fallible.

Perfection was a test for inspired prophecy, but it is not a standard required of those with the modern gift of prophecy. However, the character and demeanour of the person bringing the prophecy, the conformity of what they say to Scripture and the accuracy of any prediction must be tested.

Although the incarnation of Christ and the completion of the canon of Scripture are climactic events in history, yet God continues to reveal himself to his people, as he has always done. Indeed, every step forward in the kingdom — including this current age — is heralded by fresh prophetic insights. God does nothing without revealing it to his prophets.

Through *illumination,* and *leading,* but also through *revelation* in which 'God spontaneously brings to mind' something he wants to communicate.[59]

20.
The indispensable signs of Pentecost

Thousands continue to come to Toronto seeking the Toronto Blessing. Now, don't get me wrong. I am happy that people come to Toronto. I grew up there and today live only an hour's drive away. It is a great city to visit! It can offer world-class museums, zoo, ballet and art galleries; the world's tallest free-standing structure; world-series baseball championships, basketball and ice hockey. Not far away in one direction are the Niagara Falls, and a couple of hours away in the opposite direction is an enormous wilderness area where wolves and moose roam free. But if you are coming to Toronto for a spiritual blessing and not as a tourist, stop before you buy your ticket. First revisit Pentecost.

After all, the pentecostal phenomenon that has now crested in the Third Wave, is supposed to find its genesis at Pentecost. As we travel in our imagination back to the birth of the church, we need to ask ourselves some serious questions. What were the indelible marks of the Holy Spirit's presence at Pentecost? What characteristics must always be present in any movement of the Spirit?

All genuine disciples of Jesus Christ, in some sense at least, long for a return to Pentecost because we thirst for times of refreshing. We are saddened by lack of enthusiasm for Bible study. We weary of trying to persuade professing Christians to storm the bastions of prayer. We grieve over the decline in interest in missions. We cringe every time we hear of another affair or another divorce. We labour to help troubled saints wash their guilt away in the ocean of grace and unconditional love that flows from Christ. We long to see unsaved neighbours and relatives embrace Jesus. Yes, we need *real* revival.

It is not as though the marks of evangelical success are missing. We have organizations galore. Presses hum with new titles. Videos and cassettes crowd the shelves of multiplying Christian book-shops. Evangelicals make inroads into radio and television. They even run for political office. Brochures about conferences and seminars clutter our letterboxes. But superficiality reigns and schol-arship declines. Serious disciples realize that Zechariah's procla-mation, '"Not by might, nor by power, but by my Spirit," says the Lord Almighty,' also means, '"Not by organization, nor marketing, nor musical packages, nor seminars, and not even by mobilization — but by my Spirit," says the Lord Almighty'!

There is a thirst in the land. I can understand why thousands of parched saints throng the Vineyard to sing, 'The River is Here!' 'There's a Wind Blowing', 'Mercy is Falling, Falling, Falling.' The energy and enthusiasm found on a typical night at the Toronto Airport Christian Fellowship mock the lethargy of many. Does not the phenomenal numerical success of the movement prove its spiritual validity? Can these thousands be wrong? Yes, I believe they can. Zeal and energy, while commendable, produce wildfire unless ignited within the confines delineated by Holy Scripture. And it is within the sixty-six books of the Bible, not within the arena of personal experience, that we find the marks of the Spirit's work recorded. There we read of spiritual saltiness, of the characteristics of holiness, the marks of discipleship, the attributes of love and the qualities of light. These are the real signs and wonders. The Holy Spirit has never stopped reproducing these wonders in the lives of those who hunger after God. Let us return to the birth of the church to get a closer look at these indispensable marks of spiritual vitality.

It is with some considerable relief that I leave off ploughing through Vineyard writings to roam through the Scriptures. Turn with me to Acts chapter 2. I want to list the spiritual attributes that characterized the early church from its very birth. Then, I will return briefly to compare these qualities with those manifest in the Vine-yard and those associated with the Toronto Blessing.

Spiritual attributes which characterized the early church

Amazing physical phenomena certainly marked Pentecost. We read, 'When the day of Pentecost came, they were all together in one place. Suddenly a sound like the blowing of a violent wind came from heaven and filled the whole house where they were sitting. They saw what seemed to be tongues of fire that separated and came to rest on each of them. All of them were filled with the Holy Spirit and began to speak in other tongues as the Spirit enabled them' (Acts 2:1-4).

The sound soon attracted a crowd made up of 'Jews from every nation under heaven' who had come to Jerusalem to celebrate the feast (v. 5). The people in the crowd were bewildered 'because each one heard them speaking in his own language. They asked: "Are not all these men who are speaking Galileans? Then how is it that each of us hears them in his own native language? Parthians, Medes, and Elamites..."' (vv. 6-9).

Some made fun of the apostles, accusing them of having drunk too much wine. Most were 'amazed and perplexed' (v. 12). Peter stood up and began to explain:

> These men are not drunk, as you suppose. It's only nine in the morning! No, this is what was spoken by the prophet Joel:

> 'In the last days, God says,
>   I will pour out my Spirit on all people.
> Your sons and daughters will prophesy,
>   your young men will see visions,
>   your old men will dream dreams.
> Even on your servants, both men and women
>   I will pour out my Spirit in those days,
>   and they will prophesy.
> I will show wonders in the heaven above
>   and signs on the earth below,
> blood and fire and billows of smoke...'

(Acts 2:15-19).

Palmer Robertson points out that in the reference Peter uses from Joel his 'terms for "dreaming dreams" and "seeing visions" are identical with the words used in Numbers 12 to describe the communication of revelation throughout the ages... Joel predicted a widespread manifestation of prophetic revelation in the future.'[1] Peter specifically applies Joel's prediction to Pentecost, 'This is what was spoken by the prophet Joel' (v. 16). In other words, the people who rushed together heard the disciples giving forth a prophetic word in their own language. Pentecost was a prophetic miracle. But wonderful as the physical phenomena were, Peter did not dwell on them. He immediately turned their attention from the wonder of tongues to the person of Christ.

1. Christ-centred preaching

Peter cried, 'Men of Israel, listen to this: Jesus of Nazareth was a man accredited by God to you by miracles, wonders and signs, which God did among you through him, as you yourselves know. This man was handed over to you by God's set purpose and foreknowledge; and you with the help of wicked men, put him to death by nailing him to the cross. But God raised him from the dead...' (vv. 22-24).

In the most 'charismatic' environment we can imagine, Peter preached a powerful message centred on the person of Christ. He concluded with the words: 'Therefore let all Israel be assured of this: God has made this Jesus, whom you crucified, both Lord and Christ' (v. 36). The sound of a violent wind and the appearance of tongues of fire never again characterized an outpouring of the Spirit. But throughout the rest of the New Testament era, indeed throughout history, whenever the Holy Spirit was poured out, preaching became the instrument he used with power. And the main subject was Christ and him crucified. Acts begins this way and closes with a description of Paul: 'Boldly and without hindrance he preached the kingdom of God and taught about the Lord Jesus Christ' (28:31). There they are, two indispensable signs of the Spirit's activity fused into one: preaching and preaching that centres on Christ and his kingdom.

What other characteristics do we find that must be present in any work of the Holy Spirit? Fortunately, that same Spirit guided Luke to summarize thirteen other characteristics before he led him to record the events of chapter 3. These indispensable signs are found in verses 37-47. Let me describe them in turn.

2. Faith

Notice that many in the crowd responded to Peter's message. We read, 'When the people heard this, they were cut to the heart and said to Peter and the other apostles, "Brothers, what shall we do?"' (v. 37). They came as sceptics. They left as believers because they received as true what Peter said about the death and resurrection of Christ. Their infant faith — a gift of God (Eph. 2:8-9) — swept away their doubts, leaving them convicted and fearful of judgement. Whenever the Spirit moves in power, people respond to preaching by reaching out in faith to accept what is said. Absolute trust in Christ is an ongoing sign of the Spirit in our life.

3. Repentance

The infant faith conceived in the hearts of Peter's hearers immediately produced conviction: 'They were cut to the heart.' With hearts lacerated by guilt, they cried out, 'Brothers, what shall we do?' (Acts 2:37). Peter responded by urging them to repent (v. 38). Their cry of distress poignantly captures the essence of repentance: conviction leading to confession, a desire for forgiveness and an openness to walk in a new direction.

Conviction matures into the sensitivity to sin and humility spoken of by Christ in the Beatitudes. Faith and sensitivity to sin are crucial and ongoing signs of the Spirit's presence and are stressed throughout the epistles.

4. Obedience

When Peter suggested that the enquirers should be baptized, 'Those who accepted his message were baptized' (2:41) — no waiting; no more questions. The next indispensable sign of the Spirit is obedience. Whenever a convicted sinner, or a new believer, asks a representative of God what to do, we know the Spirit is at work producing a desire to please God by doing what is right.

Jesus said, 'Whoever has my commands and obeys them, he is the one who loves me' (John 14:21). When the Sanhedrin rebuked Peter and the apostles for disobeying their orders to stop preaching about Christ they replied, 'We must obey God rather than men! The God of our fathers raised Jesus from the dead — whom you had killed... We are witnesses of these things, and so is the Holy Spirit, whom God has given to those who obey him' (Acts 5:29-30, 32).

5. Joining other believers

Returning to the account of Pentecost in Acts 2, we next read that 'Three thousand were added to their number that day.' Another sign of the Spirit's presence is a new desire to join other believers. Canada Geese seek each other out — they fly in flocks. Those interested in model trains or baseball or skiing or knitting do the same thing — they seek out those with similar interests. How natural that those born from above would immediately search for a local church fellowship to join!

In this case there was no formal procedure, no membership cards, no list, no vote in a church meeting. They lived during a time of clarity about membership when to join Peter and the apostolic band meant ostracism. Church discipline was strict (Ananias and Sapphira died; Simon, the sorcerer, was rebuked). A certain fear kept most of the insincere from joining. Even so, letters of introduction and commendation were sent from church to church to keep it clear who ought to be received and who rejected (see Rom. 16; 2 Tim. 4:14-15).

Today, we live in a period of confusion about membership when the word 'Christian' could be interpreted to mean Jehovah's Witness, Christian Scientist, liberal, evangelical, Roman Catholic or Mormon — to name a few. Even some political parties and nations are termed 'Christian'. For this reason, most evangelical churches take time to seek the Spirit's guidance in discerning the genuine nature of a person's profession. Church leaders evaluate a candidate by looking for signs of the Spirit's work — for example, genuine faith in Christ, sensitivity to sin, obedience as evidenced by baptism and an ongoing commitment to God's will as revealed in the Word.

In this day of great evangelical campaigns and parachurch organizations, local church membership has fallen on bad days. Vast numbers of professing Christians attend churches but refuse to join the membership. They are happy to remain as adherents. This commitment problem strains the resources of local churches as they struggle to raise the standard of Christ in a geographical area. Any great movement of the Spirit will correct this imbalance. Thousands will become members of solid churches and immediately volunteer their services.

Luke next describes some general characteristics of the church born at Pentecost (Acts 2:42-47).

6. Teaching of doctrine

The first thing we notice in this summary is that these infant believers 'devoted themselves to the apostles' teaching' (Acts

2:42). Apostolic doctrine occupied such a high place on the Spirit's agenda that he inspired four Gospels, a book of history, twenty-one doctrinal epistles and a book of prophecy!

It was Confucius — not Christ, the eternal Word — who said, 'A picture is worth a thousand words.' Faced with a generation mesmerized by the tube, Marshall McLuhan claimed that 'The medium is the message.' Swallowing Confucius' and McLuhan's strangely similar dictums, too many 'market-driven' church leaders want to cut back on preaching and doctrine. How can these enthusiasts say their choice comes from the Spirit when he is the very one who inspired Paul to write to Timothy, 'Let the elders that rule well be counted worthy of double honour, especially they who labour in the word and doctrine'? (1 Tim. 5:17, AV). No! An infallible sign of the Spirit's work is the pattern we see at Pentecost: 'They devoted themselves to the apostles' teaching.'

7. Fellowship

Next we notice that commitment to doctrine is balanced by an adherence to fellowship. Although they represented different classes, languages and cultures, They 'were together,' they 'continued to meet together ... and ate together,' and were 'one in heart and mind' (Acts 2:44,46; 4:32). *Koinonia* (fellowship) is the natural outgrowth of love. As MacArthur comments, love is not a squirt from a distance.[2] Love manifests itself in caring for one another, sharing what resources we have and moving towards other people — not keeping our distance. In the early church they kept meeting together in large groups 'in the temple' for praise and worship and to listen to teaching. They also gathered in small groups 'in their homes'. We need both public assembly and informal fellowship in small groups meeting in homes where we have the opportunity to really get to know and pray for one another.

8. Breaking of bread

Since fellowship can quickly become self-serving, the Spirit always produces, as well, a commitment to the breaking of bread (Acts 2:42). Christ had revealed himself to two disciples in Emmaus through the breaking of bread. Bread is the staff of life. Jesus chose this common symbol to remind us of our daily dependency upon him: 'I am the bread of life. He who comes to me will never go hungry, and he who believes in me will never be thirsty,' but 'Apart from me you can do nothing' (John 6:35; 15:5). Just as the manna in the wilderness had to be gathered each day or it would stink, so we must come to Christ each day to remind ourselves of the cross and our atonement, the forgiveness of sins through his blood, the grounds of our justification and eternal hope. Wherever the Spirit moves, God's people love to gather around the Table of the Lord!

9. Prayer and worship

That first congregation also 'devoted themselves ... to prayer'. Then 'Everyone was filled with awe' (Acts 2:42,43). When the Spirit reminds us of the glory of Christ as we break bread, he naturally produces within us a sense of reverential awe that moves us to praise. The early church was found 'praising God' (Acts 2:47). In Antioch, God chose a missionary team in the midst of a time of worship (Acts 13:2). Paul and Silas, though in jail in Philippi, could not help praising and worshipping God (Acts 16:25).

This profound sense of God's presence that produces awe creates a climate of prayerfulness. When Peter and John were arrested the congregation immediately went to prayer, interceding for their release — which happened quicker than they imagined! (Acts 4). The Holy Spirit loves it so much when believers pray that he shook the building that day.

10. Generosity

We also read that 'All the believers were together and had every-thing in common. Selling their possessions and goods, they gave to anyone as he had need' (Acts 2:44-45). Living as we do in a society driven by the engine of greed — whether we label that engine 'the free-market economy', 'capitalism' or 'materialism' — it may be impossible for us to even imagine the extent of their generosity.

Their new-found love for Christ opened their tight fists and moved them to sell land or possessions to care for those in need. Acts 4 records that 'No one claimed that any of his possessions was his own, but they shared everything they had.' The result? 'There were no needy persons among them' (vv. 32,34).

11. Harmony

The generosity of the early Christians contributed to harmony. Imagine the diversity of the Jerusalem church. Country folk from Galilee, sophisticates from the city, religious bigots from among the Pharisees and Sadducees, Zealots fresh from preaching revolution, Herodians (the political opportunists of the day) mingled with merchants and fishermen, farmers and artisans, men and women, and Jewish proselytes from diverse cultures. In spite of this, 'All the believers were together and had everything in common ... they continued to meet together ... and ate together,' and 'All the believers were one in heart and mind' (Acts 2:44,46; 4:32).

Paul points out in Ephesians that all the signs of the Spirit's activity are interconnected: 'Be completely humble and gentle... Make every effort to keep the unity of the Spirit ... one body and one Spirit ... one Lord, one faith, one baptism' (Eph. 4: 2,3-5). A common faith manifest around the Lord's Table, in fellowship and prayer, in the sharing of resources and in a commitment to apostolic doctrine, generates harmony.

Knowing just how precious harmony is, the early church dealt quickly with issues such as the deceit of Ananias and Sapphira in Acts 5, the neglect of the Grecian widows in Acts 6 and the legalism of Acts 15.

12. Gladness

With harmony unbroken by jealousy or suspicion, we find that 'They ate together with glad and sincere hearts' (Acts 2:46). Gladness is another key sign of the Spirit's work. Before the Spirit can produce a deep sense of well-being, he must make us miserable for our sins by producing clear-cut conviction. While the devil would deceive us into thinking God is a divine spoil-sport determined to keep us unhappy, Paul explained to the Lystrans that the true God shows 'kindness by giving you rain from heaven and crops in their seasons; he provides you with plenty of food and fills your hearts with joy' (Acts 14:17). God intends that people should know joy and gladness. Sin and selfishness, competition and greed — not God — produce misery.

The wicked are like the tossing sea,
    which cannot rest,
    whose waves cast up mire and mud.
'There is no peace,' says my God, 'for the wicked'
                                        (Isa. 57:20-21).

Knowing this, David cried for the Lord to wash him from his sins
that he might hear 'joy and gladness' (Ps. 51:7-8).

It is too bad that we so often limit joy to one day a week, or to
times when the sun is shining and things are going well. As Peterson
paraphrases Colossians 1:11, 'We pray that you'll have the strength
to stick it out over the long haul — not the grim strength of gritting
your teeth but the glory-strength God gives. It is strength that
endures the unendurable and spills over into joy, thanking the Father
who makes us strong enough to take part in everything bright and
beautiful that he has for us.'[3]

13. Sincerity

Gladness is not something worked up in an emotional meeting, but
something that goes hand in hand with sincerity. Acts 2:46 mentions
their 'sincere hearts'. Jesus reserved his sternest rebuke for hypocrisy (Matt. 23:1-3,27-28). Sincerity was so important in the early
church that Ananias and Sapphira fell down dead because they
pretended to be more generous than they were. Peter accused them
of lying to the Holy Spirit (Acts 5).

When the *Queen Mary* was converted into a floating hotel and
museum in Long Beach, three massive chimneys were taken off and
put on the dock. Before they could be scrapped down and repainted,
however, they crumbled into rusty junk. The 3/4 inch steel plate had
all rusted away. All that was left was more than thirty coats of paint!
They were not what they seemed to be!

Many stay away from our churches because they believe we are
all hypocrites. Do we give the wrong impression? Are we open and
honest with each other? True *koinonia* requires genuine openness in
prayer for each other. Everyone knows we are not perfect. It is better
to admit our spiritual warts than profess a lie. Some advise preachers
never to admit their weaknesses. But how then can preaching be
real, sincere?

14. Impact

Acts 2 concludes by recording that they were 'enjoying the favour of all the people. And the Lord added to their number daily those who were being saved' (2:47).

The life of changed sinners is winsome. A young couple I baptized testified at their baptism about the influence of another couple's life. Wherever the gospel has gone, society has been changed. Twins are no longer buried alive in Africa. Burning of widows is outlawed in India. Hospitals, schools and literacy programmes have sprung up.

Another sign, then, of the Spirit's work is impact on society and numerical growth in the church. After Pentecost, the Spirit began to save people and add them to the church daily. Where the Spirit convicts he also converts and he uses the signs of change in converts to gain the attention of others. Of course, he used means — the preaching of the gospel and the testimony of newly converted souls.

Signs and wonders

There is no doubt that another indication of the Spirit's work at Pentecost was the presence of signs and wonders. 'Many wonders and miraculous signs were done by the apostles' (Acts 2:43). We have the sign of Galileans speaking in almost a score of foreign languages as tongues of fire rest on them; we have the wonder of the sound of a violent wind. As the story develops in Acts we find the Holy Spirit doing many miracles. In Acts 4 he shakes the building where believers gather to pray. In Acts 8 he translates Philip through the air to meet the Ethiopian. In Acts 9 Paul is smitten by Christ speaking from a light that flashes from heaven. In Acts 10 Peter sees a vision and Cornelius' household speaks in tongues as the Spirit is poured out on them. In Acts 12 Peter is miraculously released from prison. Acts 14:3 records that in Iconium, 'The Lord ... confirmed the message of his grace by enabling them to do miraculous signs and wonders.'

This is exactly what I have stressed again and again in this book: miraculous signs and wonders were given to confirm 'the message of his grace'. With the canon complete these kind of signs and wonders slowly fell off and ceased. What are left are universal signs of the Spirit's activity present in all ages and among all converted peoples.

In Galatians Paul gives the fruit of the Spirit, another list of the indispensable marks of his presence in a believer: 'But the fruit of the Spirit is love, joy, peace, patience, kindness, goodness, faithfulness, gentleness and self-control' (Gal. 5:22-23). In the chart I have compared the fourteen indispensable signs of the Spirit with the nine fruits produced by the Holy Spirit. I then marked every characteristic of the infant church that corresponds to the fruit of the Spirit with a tick.

There is not exact correspondence, because some of the characteristics of the early church are organizational functions — a commitment to apostolic teaching, church membership and breaking of bread. Impact describes the effect of the early church on unbelievers. Even here, however, in the commitment the early Christians had to each other, and to the Lord over an extended period we discover long-suffering, a fruit of the Spirit.

Marks of the infant church	Fruits of the Spirit
1. Christ-centred preaching	Love
2. Faith✔	Joy
3. Repentance, humility✔	Peace
4. Obedience✔	Long-suffering, patience
5. Joining other believers	Gentleness
6. Apostolic teaching	Goodness
7. Fellowship✔	Faith
8. Breaking of bread	Meekness, humility
9. Prayer, worship	Self-control
10. Generosity✔	
11. Harmony✔	
12. Gladness, joy✔	
13. Sincerity✔	
14. Impact	

Many of the characteristics of the early church reflect closely the fruit of the Spirit mentioned in Galatians. Faith and joy are mentioned specifically. Harmony, generosity and fellowship are functions of the love believers bear for one another. Generosity is also a function of kindness. Obedience is related to faithfulness and self-control. Sincerity and the sensitivity to sin reflected in a repentant life are aspects of goodness. This sensitivity to sin also produces humility.

When we stand back and compare the Toronto Blessing with these characteristics of the early church certain glaring differences emerge. I am not saying that Vineyard leaders have no concern for the fourteen indispensable signs of the Spirit that I have uncovered. They do. They talk and sing about Christ. They emphasize the need to love one another. They express a desire to win the unsaved for Christ. They emphasize the joy of the Lord a lot! Fellowship and prayer are important to them. But there is a serious imbalance.

Neither am I claiming that my own church, or any church for that matter, comes out very well when compared to the early church. Every group struggles to come up to biblical standards, and falls short. But what troubles me about those caught up in the Toronto Blessing is their failure to *admit* these discrepancies. Many pastors and churches, I know, acknowledge shortcomings and endeavour to redress deficiencies. The enthusiasm, emotion and worldwide attention generated by the events in Toronto, however, has led them to believe they are in the vanguard of an authentic move of the Holy Spirit. What others see as excesses and aberrations they claim are the very evidences of renewal. They seem to feel they are an outpost constructed by God himself to mark the new frontier towards which other churches should be pressing.

What do we make of the decision by the Association of Vineyard Churches (AVC) to separate themselves from the Toronto Airport Christian Fellowship? Does this indicate a determination on the part of the AVC to distance themselves from the exotic phenomena associated with the Toronto Blesssing? Yes, I believe it does. And I do trust that there will be a move on the part of the whole AVC back towards a more biblical position. John Wimber has expressed concern for discipleship. However, I have my doubts.

Many of those who have been the most supportive of events in Toronto are Vineyard leaders from both the US and Canada. Excitement about the Toronto Blessing permeates the whole Vineyard movement. This should come as no surprise to John Wimber. The Toronto Blessing grew out of the soil of Vineyardism. Without Vineyard emphases, and John Wimber himself, there could have been no 'blessing'. Everything practised in the Toronto church, from the format of the 'renewal' meetings to the phenomena themselves, has been a part of the Vineyard experience for well over a decade. Since Toronto leaders operate on the basis of a whole set of Vineyard presuppositions, any differences are a matter of degree and not of kind.

As Steve Long, administrator at the Toronto church, assured me in an interview in February 1996, both John Arnott and John Wimber have apologized to each other for failures in communication. 'We remain Vineyard in everything but name. The breach has already healed over. This is not a separation so much as a release. Wimber has released us to move in the new direction God is leading us.' And John Wimber has left the door open for a review of the decision to disassociate from the Toronto Fellowship.

My reasons for rejecting the Toronto Blessing are the same reasons I have for rejecting Vineyardism. Some individual adherents and churches in the AVC demonstrate beliefs and practices consistent with more traditional evangelicals. But the movement as a whole should be rejected for the following reasons.

1. Their attitude towards the Scriptures

Among the five distinguishing marks of a true revival, Jonathan Edwards lists an increased love for the Scriptures: 'The Spirit that operates in such a manner as to cause in men a greater regard for the Holy Scriptures, and establishes them more in their truth and divinity is certainly the Spirit of God... The devil would never attempt to beget in persons a regard to that divine word which God has given to be the great and standing rule for the direction of his church in all religious matter, and all concerns of their souls, in all ages.'[4] Instead of leading people to warm themselves by a fire kindled through the contemplation and proclamation of God in his Word, the Vineyard has kindled a strange fire!

Anti-intellectualism

Instead of emphasizing the transformation and development of the mental capacities through a passionate approach to the Scriptures, followers are exhorted to empty their minds, to become open to the irrational and to stop worrying about reason and logic (cf. ch. 11).

Experience judges Scripture

Instead of Scripture being the supreme court in all matters of faith
and practice, feelings, impressions, physical manifestations and all
manner of experiences drive the movement (cf. ch. 13).

Doctrine is devalued

Instead of participants glorying in the great doctrines of the faith,
they are encouraged to cast aside their theological moorings (cf. ch.
12).

Preaching becomes a poor cousin

Instead of preaching being the powerful tool the Spirit uses, as he
has throughout history, to kindle and encourage revival, it is sadly
neglected. Testimonies, singing, healings, words of prophecy and
all the physical phenomena overshadow God speaking through
powerful preaching (cf. ch. 12).

Discipleship is bound to suffer

Jesus prayed that the Father would sanctify his disciples 'by the
truth; your word is truth' (John 17:17). Lack of emphasis on the
content and application of the Bible is bound to produce anaemic
disciples in the years ahead.

Cheryl Thomson writes about her experience at a Toronto-area
Vineyard fellowship even before the onset of the Toronto Blessing:
'But teaching at our Vineyard fellowship did not emphasize the
Bible and the basic tenets of Scripture the way even I, with my
"arrested spiritual development", hoped they would. After our
marriage I saw my husband increasing his familiarity with Vineyard
choruses, and spending quality time in music rehearsals, while the
Word of God lay untouched.'[5]

The perception that believers should expect the healing of deep
inner problems instantaneously is projected. John Arnott describes
what has been happening as an exciting and unexpected party in
which 'People are laughing and rolling and crying and getting so
empowered that emotional hurts from childhood were just lifted

off...'⁶ Doubtless, this can and does happen. But ordinarily, God uses the means of grace over a period of time to renew people through the transforming of their minds (Rom. 12:2).

An expectation that God commonly solves problems instantaneously short-circuits the role that suffering and tribulation play in character development. 'We also rejoice in our sufferings, because we know that suffering produces perseverance; perseverance, character; and character, hope. And hope does not disappoint us, because God has poured out his love into our hearts by the Holy Spirit, whom he has given us' (Rom. 5:3-5).

The modern emphasis on inner healing, much stressed by Wimber, is a biblical wasteland that deserves much more thorough reflection than I can give in this book. The expectation of sudden inner healing usually fails to give hurting disciples the time and biblical teaching they need. It tends to devalue the self-examination, conviction and confession that are so necessary to lead a person to repentance. And without repentance, forgiveness cannot be enjoyed. Failure to adequately lay the groundwork of faith in the atoning sacrifice of Christ that generates the peace of heart we find through revelling in our justification will produce short-lived feelings of release. Even if the deep hurts experienced should be due to false guilt or misery produced by others, the teaching of the Word is crucial for long-term healing to occur.

2. The place of Christ

As noted earlier, Jonathan Edwards also highlights the central importance of glorifying Jesus Christ the Lord. Supporters of the Toronto Blessing would be the first to claim that they do this. They sing of Jesus. Those 'slain in the Spirit' profess to have been drawn nearer to Christ. But Edwards asserted that it was not enough to talk about Christ. It must not be 'any mystical, fantastical Christ: such as the light within.'⁷

The emphasis of the Toronto Blessing — unconsciously perhaps, but very definitely — turns the attention of people away from Jesus Christ as he is present in the Word of God to a mystical impression of Christ. I make this assertion for the following reasons (cf. ch 14).

Physical phenomena

In spite of the fact that there is no scriptural evidence to support the belief that the Holy Spirit produces falling down and lying prone for extended periods, shaking, pogoing, hysterical laughing, animal sounds, staggering around like a drunk, whirling one's head in a blur of motion, or nausea, the movement encourages the occurrence of such things. Every meeting leads inexorably towards 'ministry time', when prayer is made for the Spirit to manifest himself by reproducing physical phenomena such as these. This illustrates, not a passion for Christ, but a passion for a personal experience that one can claim to be from Christ. This search for spectacular feelings and experiences is merely a subtle form of the spiritual consumerism of the 1990s (cf. ch. 8).

Miraculous signs and wonders

Testimonies about healings, visions, dreams, etc. fill up much of the space in meetings and literature, directing people's attention away from Christ. (cf. chs 16, 17).

Prophecy

Prophecy is given much more attention than Christ (cf. chs 18, 19).

The Holy Spirit

Every Christian draws strength and comfort from the indwelling presence of the Comforter. The God-ordained role of the Holy Spirit in this era is to turn the attention of all of us to Jesus Christ the Lord. Vineyard preaching and practice instead turn the searchlight on what they suppose to be the Holy Spirit. Actually they present this blessed Person as if he were a commodity to be passed around, a liquid to refresh us, a force to generate personal ecstasy. In a typical meeting we hear a lot about 'soaking in the Spirit', 'the fire of the Spirit', 'the river of the Spirit', etc. Scant attention is given to the place of the atoning sacrifice of Christ as the basis for our redemption, regeneration, justification, adoption, sanctification and glorification.

Christ commissioned us to go into all the world and preach the gospel. That gospel centres on great redemptive events — the death, resurrection, ascension and session of Christ. Great Christ-centred preaching characterized the early church as it did the great historic revivals. This emphasis is missing from the Toronto Blessing.

3. Harmony with other Christians

Another of Jonathan Edwards' five distinguishing marks of a work of the Spirit is 'a spirit of love to God and man'. This is manifest in 'high and exalting thoughts of the Divine Being,' and in a sincere love for other Christians.[8] In the early church this brotherly love was exhibited by their joining with other believers, their commitment to fellowship and the harmony that existed in the group.

The élitism manifest in the movement leads those outside it to feel they are deprived unless they have also shared in the Vineyard experiences and subscribe to the Vineyard vision of power evangelism. The appeal to come to Toronto — or wherever the 'blessing' is being shared — is yet another incarnation of the old two-tier spiritual caste-system. In other groups this caste-system reared its head as 'seeking the second blessing', or 'the baptism of the Holy Spirit with speaking in tongues'. Now it is: 'Have you received the Toronto Blessing?'

The excitement and media attention surrounding this approach may be very effective in building the Toronto church and a 're-newal' network, but it is very destructive to the church at large. People are being drawn away from their own churches to join a Vineyard-style church. Or they are going back to their churches to pass on the 'blessing'. As result, confusion and division are being introduced on a massive scale.

The movement professes a desire to bless the whole church. Ron Allen, pastor of the Fort Wayne Vineyard said, 'This move of God is bigger than the Vineyard. This is God's way of bringing His Church together to reach a city.'[9] Vineyard leaders cannot understand why other Christians don't jump on the bandwagon. Well, in this book, I have given dozens of reasons why. Instead of bringing the church together, the Toronto Blessing, and Vineyardism, is tearing it apart. On 5 December 1995 the Vineyard denomination was itself riven by casting its Toronto church adrift.

In my own Baptist denomination, not far from where I live, one church has almost collapsed, another has been split, at least one has been taken over by Vineyard sympathizers and several others are being seriously influenced. In each of these churches godly, mature Christian leaders who have given their lives to build up churches in a tough society have been sidelined or deeply hurt. Some have had to leave.

Stories of division and confusion could be multiplied around the world. Instead of the 'Toronto Blessing' being an unmixed blessing, it has proved to be a baneful distraction. This is happening, not because believers who do not support it are Pharisees, nor because they are stubborn or inflexible, but because the Vineyard has spawned a movement that is a serious departure from 'the faith once and for all delivered to the saints'. Many mature believers see in its divisiveness proof that it is not a movement energized by the Holy Spirit.

4. The Holy Spirit has little to do with the Toronto Blessing

The Holy Spirit cannot be the source of a movement that fails to spotlight Jesus Christ and his cross, that produces unbiblical physical manifestations, that judges reality by impressions instead of the Scriptures, that does not emphasize preaching, that fails to produce serious conviction of sin, that devalues the great doctrines that the Spirit himself caused to be written down, that downplays reason and the mind, that treats him as a commodity to be passed around and that encourages disorder and repetitive singing. Instead we have a movement driven by expectation and suggestibility in the context of emotionally charged meetings. It is a movement that has all the characteristics of mass hypnotism. In large measure the movement is driven by the incredible energy of people who want to believe so badly that what is happening is of the Holy Spirit that they believe their own publicity!

Why this love affair with exotic experiences? J. I. Packer, in his book *A Quest For Godliness,* discusses the need we have today for the Puritan balance of warm godliness and sober scholarship. The Puritans combined a 'flaming zeal for God' with a passion for practical Christian living. Those who flock to Toronto, instead of displaying this passion for Christ in his Word and in his world strike me as being examples of the 'restless experientialists' Packer mentions. He says that their outlook is one of 'casual haphazardness and fretful impatience, of grasping after novelties, entertainments, and "highs", and of valuing strong feelings above deep thoughts.

They have little taste for solid study, humble self-examination, disciplined meditation, and unspectacular hard work in their callings and their prayers. They conceive the Christian life as one of exciting extraordinary experiences rather than of resolute rational righteousness.'[10]

This experiential restlessness, manifest in an impatience with the classic disciplines of the Christian life, speaks of an evangelical movement seriously frayed at the edges. Instead of helping to knit up the tangled edges of evangelicalism, the Vineyard is bent on speeding up the unravelling process.

I do not believe that power evangelism, as proposed by Wimber, or phenomena, as seen at Toronto, will evangelize our world. No, I firmly assert that a far greater impact is made on sinners by Christ-like character. In different contexts this is called the fruit of the Spirit, salt, light, holiness or godliness. Why seek the exotic when we have fourteen indispensable signs of the Spirit's activity as recorded at Pentecost? These are the 'salt and light signs' of the Spirit that will always characterize a genuine work of God. When sinners undergo an internal revolution, that transformation spills over into all human relationships. Then we have real revival!

This era is no darker than many others. What we need is light — the light of lives transformed by the Spirit through the production of these ongoing evidences of his mighty work. Perhaps the Vineyard and the Toronto Blessing will be the burr under the saddle of evangelicalism that will provoke us to renewed passion for the things of God. Too many evangelicals are complacent, contented and lethargic. The salt is not very salty. The light is dim. But we must not let the Prince of Darkness persuade us that the pursuit of manifestations will cause the flame of witness to flare. All that will do is kindle strange fire.

William Carey has often been called 'the father of modern missions'. His passion for the lost and for the Saviour blazed a path thousands have followed. As the nineteenth century dawned his friend John Ryland made a point that we need to reiterate today: 'The ordinary influences of the Holy Spirit are of far more importance to individuals who partake of them, than his extraordinary gifts; that is, it is better to be a saint than a prophet; better to be holy, than to be inspired; better to be directed into the love of God, than into the knowledge of futurity. Herein the blessed Spirit communicates himself in his own proper nature, as the Spirit of holiness.'[11]

Would I encourage my friends to go to Toronto to seek the 'blessing'? Would I want my family or the church at large to drink at the Vineyard fountain? Is their vision of the evangelical landscape the vision I have for my grandchildren? Decidedly not! Instead, may the light of genuine revival illumine our benighted age, and may a passion for biblical holiness burn within.

Appendix I
Summary of events of the Great Awakening

1734-37, 1740-42	Awakening in America, under Jonathan Edwards, the Tennents and others.
Mid-1730s-1740s	Awakening in Britain
27 June 1736	George Whitefield preaches his first sermon.
1737	Thousands of souls are awakened in Bristol, London, etc.
1738	Whitefield goes to Georgia. The Wesleys return to Britain and are converted.
1739	Rejection in the established churches moves Whitefield to follow the example of the Welshmen Howel Harris and Daniel Rowland into the open air. The response is phenomenal.
	John Wesley preaches against the reformed faith, opening a breach in the movement. Manifestations are encouraged in Bristol.
Early 1740s	In America James Davenport and Andrew Croswell encourage phenomena as proof of conversion. Davenport later repents and writes retractions.
	Charles Chaucy uses the phenomena to attack the revival in America. His objections to Edwards' Calvinism and the excesses in the revival probably contributed to his later founding of the Unitarians.
1736-48	Edwards writes a series of works defending and defining the revivals:

A Narrative of Surprising Conversions (1736), in which he describes the remarkable events that took place in Northampton in the initial years of the revival. This influences others on both sides of the Atlantic.

Distinguishing Marks of a Work of the Spirit of God (1741), in which he uses 1 John 4 to list nine things that *do not* prove a work of God one way or the other and five sure signs of a work of God.

Some Thoughts concerning the Present Revival of Religion in New-England (1743), in which he defends the revival against its critics, including a section on his wife's experiences.

A Treatise concerning Religious Affections (1746), in which he tackles problems created by friends within the movement such as Davenport and Croswell. He seeks to define genuine Christian experience in the light of the phenomena. He further elaborates the lists of signs that cannot be relied upon and signs that definitely distinguish Spirit-produced emotions from wildfire enthusiasm.

An Humble Attempt to Promote Explicit Agreement and visible Union of God's People in Extraordinary Prayer for the Revival of Religion and the Advancement of Christ's Kingdom on Earth, pursuant to Scripture-Promises and Prophecies concerning the Last Time (1748), in which he used Zechariah 8:20-22 to call believers to join together in prayer for revival

Appendix II
Jonathan Edwards' list of 'no-signs' — signs that neither prove nor disprove the presence of a work of God

Assessing a spiritual movement can prove difficult and delusive. We may take some indicators as infallible marks of a work of God when in reality they may prove nothing at all. Jonathan Edwards knew this very well. In his *The Distinguishing Marks of a Work of The True Spirit*, published in 1741, Edwards listed a number of negative signs, 'no-signs' as he called them, that neither prove nor disprove a work of God.

John Stackhouse summarizes these principles:

Genuine renewal movements in the past had demonstrated some or all of these signs, he asserted, but so had clearly spurious ones. It was therefore a mistake for either critics or proponents of the revival to focus attention upon these ambiguous qualities ...

(1) that the work is carried on in an unusual way;

(2) that it produces strong effects on the bodies of participants;

(3) that it prompts a great deal of attention (Edwards called it 'noise'!);

(4) that it stirs people's imaginations;

(5) that it is promoted too much by the influence of example and testimony;

(6) that it results in imprudent conduct;

(7) that errors in judgement and even 'delusions of Satan' are intermingled with it;

(8) that some of its professed converts later fall into scandal; and

(9) that its preachers insist too much on the terrors of God's wrath.[1]

In his *The Religious Affections*, published in 1756, Edwards extended his list of 'no-signs' to twelve, most of which I have listed below:

1. It is no sign one way or the other, that religious affections are very great, or raised very high;

2. that great effects are produced on the bodies of participants;

3. that people are fervent, fluent and abundant in talking about spiritual things;

4. that good feelings arise unbidden — they may come from false spirits who often give false comforts and joys;

5. that they come from texts of Scripture suddenly brought to mind, since the devil loves to pervert Scripture;

6. that they produce love, since some may have religious love but not saving grace. Christian love may be counterfeited; ...

9. that they spend much time in external duties of worship and religion;

10. that they praise and glorify God with their mouths;

11. that they show great confidence that what they have experienced is divine;

12. that the truly godly are deeply affected and pleased by their profession.

Notes

Strange fire from Toronto
1. Tom Wolfe, *The Me Decade and the Third Great Awakening,* Bantam, 1977, p.164.
2. Cheryl Thomson, 'Not Just — A Memoir of "The Vineyard":1986-1994', private paper, p.5.
3. John Armstrong, 'The Me Generation and Modern Revival Movements,' *Reformation & Revival Update,* Nov./Dec. 1995.
4. Wolfe, *The Me Decade,* p.163.
5. An open letter for general distribution from John Arnott, Toronto Airport Vineyard, 12 December 1995.
6. *Ibid.*
7. *Ibid.*
8. *Ibid.*

Chapter 1 — Experiencing the 'Toronto Blessing'
1. Doug Koop, '"Fire" still ablaze at Toronto church,' *Christian Week,* 31 October 1995, p.4.
2. Statistics in the May/June 1995 issue of *Spread the Fire* list a cumulative attendance of 400,000: first-time attendance of 133,000; 15,000 pastors and church leaders; 7,000 commitments and recommitments. Doug Koop's article, cited in note 1, raises the figure to 600,000. Subsequent contacts put the figure as 700,000 and climbing.
3. Steve Long, 'The Airport Vineyard: an insider's story,' *Christian Week,* May 1995, p.10.
4. *Ibid.*
5. Lynda Hurst, 'Laughing all the way to heaven,' *Toronto Star,* 3 December 1994, p.A24.
6. *Ibid.*
7. Tom Harpur, 'What the "mighty wind from Toronto" feels like,' *Toronto Star,* 20 November 1994, p.E12.
8. Nick Needham, 'Have we gone mad?,' *Banner of Truth* magazine reprinted with permission in *Jaiza,* May 1995, p.4.
9. *Ibid.*

10. Doug Koop, '"Toronto Blessing" garnering worldwide attention', *Christian Week,* 23 August 1994, p.4.
11. Long, 'The Airport Vineyard: an insider's story,' p.10.
12. Hurst, 'Laughing all the way to heaven,' p.A1.
13. Gail Reid, 'Blessing hits talk show,' *Christian Week,* 11 July 1995, p.18.

Chapter 2 — Surfing the Third Wave
1. Clark H. Pinnock, 'Can't tell God how and where to work,' *The Canadian Baptist,* March 1995, p.9.
2. C. Peter Wagner, *The Third Wave of the Holy Spirit,* Servant, 1988.
3. Victor Budgen, *The Charismatics and the Word of God,* Evangelical Press, 1989, p.181.
4. *Ibid.,* p.183.
5. *Ibid.,* pp.186,187.
6. *Ibid.,* p.188.
7. John Stackhouse, Jr, 'Background to blessing,' *Faith Today,* March/April 1995, p.24.
8. See *Power Evangelism* and *Power Healing* by John Wimber and Kevin Springer, Harper & Row, 1986 & 1987.
9. Material in this section is taken from James A. Beverley's research found in his book, *Holy Laughter & The Toronto Blessing,* Zondervan, 1995, pp 38-41,133.
10. *Ibid.,* p.46.
11. Guy Chevreau, *Catch The Fire,* HarperCollins Publishers, 1995, p.21.
12. *Ibid.*
13. *Ibid.*
14. Beverley, *Holy Laughter and the Toronto Blessing,* p.54.
15. Chevreau, *Catch The Fire,* p.24.
16. See Beverley, *Holy Laughter and the Toronto Blessing,* p.89 and John Arnott in a message delivered at the Toronto Airport Vineyard on 18 November 1994 entitled 'Dynamics of Receiving Spiritual Experiences' quoted on page 14 of *Excerpts from Vineyard Church Transcripts,* prepared by Bob Hunter for Christian Research International (hereafter called *CRI transcripts*).
17. James A. Beverley, 'Toronto Blessing update: notes from a friendly critic,' *Christian Week,* 31 October 1995, p.11.
18. *Ibid.*

Chapter 3 — Confusing signals
1. Long, 'The Airport Vineyard: an insider's story'.
2. *Ibid.*
3. Hurst, 'Laughing all the way to heaven', p.A24.
4. Long, 'The Airport Vineyard: an insider's story'.
5. Hurst, 'Laughing all the way to heaven', p.A24.
6. Guy Chevreau, '"Grade A" fruit', *Faith Today,* March/April 1995, p.26.
7. Chevreau, *Catch The Fire,* p.145.
8. *Ibid.,* pp.146-9.
9. *Ibid.,* p.166.
10. *Ibid.,* pp.176-82.
11. Long, 'The Airport Vineyard: an insider's story,' p.10.

12. Quoted by Gail Reid, 'Blessing hits talk show', p.19.
13. Wimber, *John Wimber Responds To Phenomena.*
14. Board Report in Memorandum of 14 October 1994 from the Association of Vineyard Churches.
15. John Wimber, *Vineyard Reflections* (John Wimber's leadership letter), 'Refreshing, Renewal, and Revival,' Memorandum of 14 October 1994, p. 2.
16. *Ibid.,* p. 3.
17. *Ibid.,* p. 6.
18. Letter from Gary Best to John and Carol Arnott, 15 December 1995, re perspective of AVC Canada on reasons for disengagement, posted on Internet.
19. John Wimber, 'Notice of Withdrawal of Endorsement from the Toronto Airport Vineyard,' 13 December 1995.
20. Letter from Gary Best to John Arnott, 15 December 1995.
21. Arnott, open letter,12 December 1995.
22. *Ibid.*
23. E-mail from Richard Riss to John Arnott, 4 December 1995.
24. Arnott, open letter, 12 December 1995.
25. John Wimber, AVC Notice to Vineyard Pastors, 13 December 1995.
26. Ibid.
27. Long, 'The Airport Vineyard: an insider's story'.

Chapter 4 — A potpourri of evangelical responses

1. Comments at a conference in Hertfordshire reported in the *Evangelical Times,* July 1995, p.3.
2. Editorial, *Faith Today,* May 1994, p.46.
3. Reid, 'After the Laughter,' *Faith Today,* March/April 1995, p.20.
4. Pinnock, 'Can't tell God how and where to work,' p.10.
5. Gail Reid, 'After the Laughter,' p.19.
6. David Reed, 'The Toronto Mixed Blessing,' Praxis Workshop put on by World Vision, 25 April 1995.
7. Justin Dennison, 'Grapes of Wrath or Blessing?' *Evangelical Baptist,* February 1995, pp. 20-21.
8. Daniel Lundy, 'Signs and Wonders Today,' *The Gospel Witness,* 18 May 1995, pp.4-5.
9. Larry Matthews, editorial, 'The best and the worst,' *The Canadian Baptist,* March 1995, p.7.
10. Beverley, *Holy Laughter and the Toronto Blessing,* p.29.
11. Reid, 'After the Laughter,' p.22.
12. Needham, 'Have we gone mad?', p.5.
13. *Ibid.*
14. *Ibid.*
15. *Ibid.*
16. Letter from Ken Fast in *Faith Today,* May/June 1995, p.10.
17. Quoted by Reid in *After the Laughter,* p.23.
18. *Ibid.,* p.23.
19. *Ibid.,* p.21.
20. Jonathan Edwards, *A Treatise Concerning Religious Affections,* Yale University Press, 1959, p.95.

21. John F. MacArthur, *Reckless Faith,* Crossway Books, 1994, p.174.
22. *Ibid.,* p.175.
23. Ken Birch, 'No Laughing Matter,' *The Pentecostal Testimony* (official organ of The Pentecostal Assemblies of Canada), February 1994, p.27.
24. *Ibid.*
25. Dr Joseph R. Chambers, '"Strange Fire" in the Lord's Vineyard,' *Liberation,* Spring 1995, p.8.
26. Long, 'The Airport Vineyard: an insider's story,' p.10.
27. John Wimber, Internal report to "All Vineyard Pastors," Memorandum of 14 October 1994.
28. Long, 'The Airport Vineyard: an insider's story'.
29. Cheryl and Steve Thomson, letter to the editor of *Faith Today,* May/June 1995, p.8.
30. Rev. Gordon Williams, *Vineyard Experience — Written for the Body of Christ,* an eleven-page description of his experiences and concerns, p.1.
31. *Ibid.*
32. Interview on *W5,* undated TV programme aired over CBC, Toronto.
33. *Ibid.*
34. See B. B. Warfield, *Counterfeit Miracles,* Banner of Truth Trust, reprint 1976.
35. Harpur, 'What the "mighty wind from Toronto" feels like,' *Toronto Star,* 20 November 1994, p.E12.
36. Letter in *Evangelical Times,* July 1995.

Chapter 5 — Shots across the bow

1. Beverley, *Holy Laughter and the Toronto Blessing,* p.146.
2. James Ryle, *It's Enough To Make You Cry,* quoted in *Excerpts from Vineyard Church Transcripts — Canada & U.S.A. — with Commentary,* prepared by Bob Hunter for Christian Research International, Shelburne, Ontario, 1995, p.1.
3. Comments by John Arnott recorded on a CBC radio programme, *Sunday Morning,* undated.
4. Chevreau, *Catch The Fire,* p.122.
5. William DeArteaga, audiotape of Toronto Airport Vineyard 9:15 a.m. meeting on 13 October 94.
6. DeArteaga, *Quenching The Spirit,* pp.32,55.
7. Ian Murray, *Jonathan Edwards,* Banner of Truth Trust, reprint 1992, pp.216-17.
8. *Ibid.,* p.217.
9. MacArthur, *Reckless Faith,* p.40.
10. *Ibid.,* p.39.
11. Larry Matthews, 'The best and the worst,' *The Canadian Baptist,* March 1995, p.7.
12. Association of Vineyard Churches, *Board Report,* Sept/Oct. 1994, p.2.

Chapter 6 —The Vineyard pro and con

1. John Wimber's Leadership Letter, p.6.
2. Vineyard Christian Fellowship, Toronto Airport, 6 March 1994, *Our Statement of Faith.*

We believe there is one God who lives for ever in three persons; Father, Son, and Holy Spirit.

That the Bible is God's Word to the world, speaking to us with authority and without error.

We believe in the divinity of Jesus Christ the Son, in His virgin birth, His sinless life, His miracles, His death for us on the cross, in His shed blood, His ascension to the Father, and in His personal physical return to rule the earth in power and love.

We believe that all mankind is lost in sin and selfishness and needs to turn from it and trust personally in the Saviour, Jesus Christ, being born anew by the Holy Spirit's power into God's family.

We believe the Holy Spirit lives in us as believers and brings love, joy, peace, patience, kindness, goodness, faithfulness, humility, and self-control into our lives. He works in and through us with His charismatic gifts.

We believe in the resurrection of every person; to eternal life for the believer and eternal judgement for the lost.

We believe in unity for all believers in our Lord Jesus Christ and seek community together: to become more like Him in every way, who is the head of His body, the Church. We are called to love Him and one another and are enabled to do this only as His life flows in and through us.

3. Grant Hochman, 'What is a cult?', *Christian Week,* 11 July 1995, p.7.

4. Hunter, *Excerpts from Vineyard Church transcripts,* p.90, emphasis his.

5. Comments from an interview on an undated broadcast on CBC radio.

6. Reed, 'The Toronto Mixed Blessing'.

7. Lundy, 'Signs and Wonders Today,' pp.4,5.

8. Daniel Lundy, Lecture given at Ajax Baptist Church, Ontario, 1 April 1995.

9. John Piper, *Desiring God,* Multnomah Press, 1986.

10. Beverley, *Holy Laughter and the Toronto Blessing,* p.152.

11. John Wimber, 'Introducing prophetic ministry,' *Equipping the Saints,* Fall 1989, p.6

12. *Ibid.*

13. Beverley, *Holy Laughter and the Toronto Blessing,* p.133.

14. Don Lewis, *Assessing The Wimber Phenomenon,* Regent College, June 1985.

15. Comments made by speaker at Airport Vineyard, 8 September 1994.

16. Williams, *Vineyard Experience,* p.10.

17. Thomson, 'Not Just— A Memoir of "The Vineyard"', p.19.

18. Rick Joyner, 'A Vision of the Twelve Cities,' *The Morningstar Journal,* Charlotte, North Carolina: vol. 2, No. 3.

19. Thomson, 'Not Just — A Memoir of "The Vineyard"', pp.18,19.

20. Toronto Airport Vineyard, 11 October 1995.

21. Chevreau, *Catch the fire,* p.61.

22. Gordon Fee, *The First Epistle to the Corinthians,* Eerdmans, 1987, p.697.

23. A brochure advertising 'Gifts of the Spirit Classes', from 3 October 1994 to 15 May 1995.

24. Beverley, *Holy Laughter and the Toronto Blessing,* pp.154-5.

Chapter 7 — Supreme court or round-table discussion?
1. *The Westminster Confession of Faith,* Article I, Section 10.
2. Toronto Airport Christian Fellowship, *Statement of Faith.*

Chapter 8 — Phenomena — biblical or bizarre?
1. David Lewis, *Healing, Fantasy or Fact?,* Hodder & Stoughton, 1989, pp. 175, 286.
2. Bill Jackson, *What in the World is Happening to us?* Vineyard Campaign, Urbana, Illinois, May 1994, p.3.
3 *Ibid.*
4. Chevreau, *Catch the Fire,* p.13.
5. *Ibid.,* p.52.
6. Needham, 'Have we gone mad?', p.4.
7. Jackson, *What in the World is Happening to us?* p.3.
8. *Ibid.,* pp.6,9.
9. Speaker at Toronto Airport Vineyard, 8 September 1994.
10. Jackson, *What In The World Is HappeningTo Us?* p.3.
11. Needham, 'Have we gone mad?', p.4.
12. Jackson, *What in the World is Happening to us?* p.3.
13. *Ibid.*
14. John Arnott, Pastor's Meeting, 19 October 1994, *CRI transcripts,* p.80.
15. Byran Mode, Toronto Airport Vineyard, 14 July 1995.
16. Needham, 'Have we gone mad?', p.4.
17. As told by Wes Campbell, Toronto Airport Vineyard, 14 October 1994, *CRI transcripts,* p.22.
18. Randy Clark, Let the Fire Fall Conference, Anaheim Vineyard, July 1994, *CRI transcripts,* p.23.
19. August 1994 issue of *Charisma Magazine,* p.24, *CRI transcript,* p.24.
20. Jackson, *What in the World is Happening to us?* p.7.
21. *Ibid.*
22. Birch, 'No Laughing Matter,' p.27.
23. Warren Smith, 'Holy Laughter or Strong Delusion?' *SCP Newsletter,* Fall 1994, pp.5,8.
24. Chevreau, *Catch the Fire,* pp.14,16.
25. *Ibid.,* pp.16-17.
26. The term 'easy-believism' is used to highlight the problem posed by people who profess faith in Christ but do not display the fruit of saving faith. They may have gone forward in response to an invitation but never have been truly saved. Their faith is general but not transforming in that they are not moved to perseverance as obedient disciples of Christ.
27. Jackson, *What in the World is Happening to us?* p.7.
28. *Vineyard newsletter,* March 1994, vol. 01.
29. Reported in *Spread the Fire,* May/June 1995, p.25.
30. Randy Clark, Let The Fire Fall Conference, Anaheim Vineyard, July 1994, *CRI transcripts,* p.26.
31. Jackson, *What in the World is Happening to us?* p.6.
32. *Ibid.,* p.6.
33. *Ibid.,* p.7.

34. Needham, 'Have we gone mad?', p.4.
35. Cited by Beverley, *Holy Laughter and the Toronto Blessing*, p.12, from Robert Hough, 'God Is Alive and Well and Saving Souls on Dixon Road,' *Toronto Life Magazine*, February 1995, p.31.
36. Beverley, *Holy Laughter and the Toronto Blessing*, p.69.
37. Clark, *CRI transcripts*, p.26.
38. *Memorandum of Association of Vineyard Churches*, 14 October 1994.
39. Steve Long, 'What About Animal Noises?,' *Spread The Fire*, October 1995, pp.17,30.
40. Wes Campbell, *Spiritual and Physical Manifestations*, undated.
41. Needham, 'Have we gone mad?', p.5.
42. Beverley, *Holy Laughter and the Toronto Blessing*, ch. 7. See also p.207.
43. Chevreau, *Catch the Fire*, pp.40-41, italics his.
44. *Ibid.*, p.41, italics his.
45. *Memoirs of David Brainerd*, quoted in Chevreau, *Catch the Fire*, pp.43-4.
46. Beverley, *Holy Laughter and the Toronto Blessing*, pp.123-4.
47. Steve Witt, 'Ox in the Nursery,' *Spread the Fire*, October 1995, p.13.
48. *Spiritual Counterfeits Project Newsletter*, 19:2, p.14.
49. *Ibid.*
50. *Ibid.*
51. *Ibid.*
52. *Ibid.*
53. *Ibid.*
54. Chevreau, *Catch the Fire*, p.127.

Chapter 9 — A needle in a historical haystack

1. Jackson, *What in the World is Happening to us?* p.3.
2. B. B. Warfield, *Counterfeit Miracles*, Edinburgh: The Banner of Truth Trust, first published 1918, reprinted 1976, pp.21,23,25-6.
3. Cited from John Wimber, *Spiritual Gifts Seminar* notes, p.12, by Bill Jackson, *Cessationism*, Vineyard Christian Fellowship, 1995.
4. Jonathan Edwards, *Charity and its Fruits*, Banner of Truth, 1969, cited in McHale, p.78.
5. Warfield, *Counterfeit Miracles*, p.11.
6. *Ibid.*, pp.11-12.
7. *Ibid.*, p.13.
8. *Ibid.*, p.10.
9. Footnote of Roy J. Deferrari in his translation of *Eusebius Pamphili: Ecclesiastical History, Books 1-5*, Fathers of the Church, Inc., 1953, p.311.
10. *Ibid.*, pp.315-16.
11. Gary W. McHale with Michael A. G. Haykin, *The 'Toronto Blessing': A Renewal From God?*, vol. 1, *Historical Perspectives*, Canadian Christian Publications, 1995, p.21.
12. *Ibid.*, p.22.
13. *Ibid.*, p.27.
14. Eusebius, *Ecclesiastical History*, 4.15.
15. McHale & Haykin, *The 'Toronto Blessing'*, p.37.
16. Wimber, *Power Evangelism*, p.155.

17. Cited by McHale & Haykin, *The 'Toronto Blessing'*, p.54.
18. Warfield, *Counterfeit Miracles*, p.36.
19. *Ibid.*, p.10.
20. *Ibid.*, p.12.
21. *Ibid.*, p.29.
22. Bill Jackson, *Cessationism*, cited in McHale & Haykin, *The 'Toronto Blessing'*, p.305.
23. V. Raymond Edman, *The Light in Dark Ages*, Van Kampen Press, 1949, p.302.
24. *Ibid.*, pp.301-2.
25. *Ibid.*, p.301.
26. John Woodbridge, *Great Leaders of the Christian Church*, Moody Press, 1988, p.176, cited in McHale & Haykin, *The 'Toronto Blessing'*, p.61.
27. Cited in McHale & Haykin, *The 'Toronto Blessing'*, p.61, from Simony-Tournely, *The Catholic Encyclopedia* Encyclopedia Press, Inc., 1913, p.516.
28. Jackson, *Cessationism*.
29. Roland Bainton, *The Reformation of the Sixteenth Century*, Beacon Press, 1952, p.117.
30. John Calvin, *Institutes*, Book IV, Chapter III.
31. James Atkinson, *The Great Light, Luther and Reformation*, Eerdmans by arrangement with Paternoster Press, 1968, p.172, italics mine.
32 Martin Luther, *Defense and Explanation of All the Articles of Dr Martin Luther Which Were Unjustly Condemned by the Roman Bull*, cited by David Otis Fuller in *Valiant for the Truth*, McGraw Hill, 1961, p.121.
33. Peter Lewis, *The Genius of Puritanism*, Carey Publications, 2nd ed., 1979, pp.11,14.
34. *Ibid.*, p.12.
35. *Ibid.*, p.12.
36. Edman, *The Light in Dark Ages*, p.358.
37. Ruth A. Tucker, *From Jerusalem to Irian Jaya*, Academie Books (Zondervan), 1983, p.71.
38. *Ibid.*, pp.72-4.
39. Bill Jackson, *What in the World is Happening to us?*, p.6.
40. Christopher Rule, 'George Fox and Early Quakerism,' *Reformation Today*, No. 95, p.15.
41. Keith Crim, General Editor, *The Perennial Dictionary of World Religions*, Harper and Row, 1981, pp.310-12 .

Chapter 10 — The Great Evangelical Revivals

1. Michael A. G. Haykin, *Revivals and Signs and Wonders*, Canadian Christian Publications, 1994. Much of the material in this paragraph is gleaned from this work, pp.6-7. This work has also been a source of guidance to many of the quotations in this chapter.
2. Arnold Dallimore, *George Whitefield. The Life and Times of the Great Evangelist of the Eighteenth-Century Revival*, Cornerstone Books, 1980, vol. I, p.104.
3. *Ibid.*, vol. I, p.109.
4. George Whitefield's *Journals*, Banner of Truth, 1960, pp.84-5.
5. Dallimore, *George Whitefield*, vol. I, pp.115-16.

6. *Ibid.,* vol. I, p.119.

7. John Gillies, *Memoirs of the Life of the Reverend George Whitefield, M.A.,* E. & C. Dilly, 1772, p.28 (cited by Dallimore, *George Whitefield.,* vol. I, pp.263-4).

8. Cited by Dallimore, *George Whitefield,*vol. I, p.130.

9. Dallimore, *George Whitefield,* vol. 2, p.128.

10. R. Tudor Jones, *Evangelical Revival in Wales: A Study in Spirituality,* in James P. Mackey, ed., *An Introduction to Celtic Christianity,* T & T. Clark, 1989, p.238 (Cited by Haykin, *Revivals and Signs and Wonders,* p.27).

11. George Whitefield, *Indwelling in the Spirit,* in *Sermons on Important Subjects,* Thomas Tegg, 1833, p.433.

12. *The Methodist Magazine,* 1849, p.165 (Cited in Dallimore, *George Whitefield,* vol. 1, p.328).

13. 'Enthusiasm,' in *A Dictionary of the English Language,* London: 1755.

14. 'Walking with God' in *Select Sermons of George Whitefield,* Banner of Truth Trust, 1958, p.104.

15. Haykin, *Revivals and Signs and Wonders,* p.18.

16. Quoted from George Whitefield, *Sermons on Important Subjects,* Thomas Tegg, 1833, p.432.

17. *Ibid.*

18. Haykin, *Revivals and Signs and Wonders,* p.26.

19. John Wesley, *The Nature of Enthusiasm,* 21, Wesley's Standard Sermons, ed. Edward H. Sugden, 4th ed.; The Epworth Press, 1956, II, 95-96 (Cited by Haykin, *Revivals and Signs and Wonders,* p.25).

20. See Dallimore, *George Whitefield,* ch. 18.

21. *The Journal of John Wesley,* London, Wesleyan Methodist Bookroom, vol. 2, p.185 (Cited by Dallimore, *George Whitefield,* vol. I, p.316).

22. Dallimore, *George Whitefield,* vol. I, p.317.

23. *Ibid.,* vol. I, p.325, italics mine.

24. *Ibid.*

25. *Ibid.*

26. *The Journal of Charles Wesley,* Wesleyan Methodist Bookroom, 2 vols, entry for 5 August 1740.

27. *Ibid.,* 4 June 1743.

28. Quoted in Dallimore, *George Whitefield,* vol. 1, pp. 328-9.

29. *The Journal of John Wesley,* vol. 2, p.298 (Cited in Dallimore, *George Whitefield,* p.329).

30. Dallimore, *George Whitefield,* p.330.

31. A letter mentioned in *John Wesley's Journal,* vol. 2, pp.299-300.

32. Charles Wesley's *Journal,* 12 June 1740, quoted in Dallimore, *George Whitefield,* vol. 1, p.330.

33. Dallimore, *George Whitefield,* vol. I, pp.330-31.

34. Haykin, *Revivals and Signs and Wonders,* footnote, p.23.

35. Cited in Dallimore, *George Whitefield,*vol. 1, p.417.

36. Dallimore, *George Whitefield,*vol. I, pp.421-2.

37. Jonathan Edwards, *A Narrative of Surprising Conversions,* 1736, reprinted Banner of Truth Trust, 1965, p.30, italics his.

38. Edwards, *Narrative of Surprising Conversions,* p.30, quoted in Dallimore, *George Whitefield,* vol. 1, pp. 422-3.

39. Edwards, *Narrative of Surprising Conversions,* pp.37-8, quoted in Dallimore, *George Whitefield,* vol. 1, p. 424.

40. Dallimore, *George Whitefield,* vol. 1, p. 425.

41. *Ibid.,* p.427.

42. Chevreau, *Catch the Fire,* footnote on p.77.

43. Eleanor Mumford in a tape of her experiences in Toronto cited by John Legg.

44. Murray, *Jonathan Edwards,* p.193.

45. Dallimore, *George Whitefield,* pp.428-9.

46. Haykin, *Revivals and Signs and Wonders,* p.32.

47. Cited by McHale & Haykin, *The Toronto Blessing,* p.83.

48. McHale & Haykin, *The Toronto Blessing,*p.84.

49. Haykin, *Revivals and Signs and Wonders,* p.33.

50. Murray, *Jonathan Edwards,* p.225.

51. *Ibid.,* p.217.

52. Edwards, *The Religious Affections,* p.59.

53. Beverley, *Holy Laughter and the Toronto Blessing,* pp.78,80.

54. Iain H. Murray's review in *The Banner of Truth,* March 1995, pp.28-9, emphasis his.

55. Haykin, *Revivals and Signs and Wonders,* pp.40-41.

56. *Ibid.,* pp.41-2.

57 Letter to Mary Carey, 14 December 1789 (Baptist Missionary Society Archives, Angus Library, Regent's Park College, Oxford), cited by Haykin, *Revivals and Signs and Wonders,* pp.42-3.

58. See review of Iain Murray's book, *Revivals and Revivalism, The Making and Marring of American Evangelicalism,* Banner of Truth Trust, in *Reformation Today,* September/October1994, p.30.

59. Jackson, *What In The World Is Happening To Us?,* p.4.

60. *Ibid.,* p.5.

61. Murray, *Revivals and Revivalism,* p.374.

62. Brian M. Abshire, *The Real Seduction of Biblical Christianity — 18th Century Revivalism and the Destruction of American Christian Culture,* Chalcedon Report, September 1994, p.22.

63. Dallimore, *George Whitefield,* vol. I, p.137.

64. Charles G. Finney, *Revivals of Religion,* Chicago: Moody Press, 1962.

65. Murray, *Revival and Revivalism,* p.249.

66. Abshire, *The Real Seduction of Biblical Christianity,* p.23.

67. George Whitefield, 'Walking with God' in *Select Sermons of George Whitefield,* London: The Banner of Truth Trust, 1958, p.104.

68. Jonathan Edwards, *Distinguishing Marks of a Work of the Spirit of God,* 1741.

69. Haykin, *Revivals and Signs and Wonders,* p.35.

70. Murray, *Jonathan Edwards,* p.216.

71 Cited by Murray *Jonathan Edwards,* on pp.235-6 from Edwards' *Some Thoughts concerning the Present Revival.*

72. D. Martyn Lloyd-Jones, *Revival,* Wheaton: Crossway, 1987, pp.146-7.

Chapter 11 — Divine disorder or cultivated chaos?

1. John Wimber, 'Refreshing, Renewal, and Revival', in *Vineyard Reflections: John Wimber's Leadership Letter,* July/August, 1994, p.1.

2. Quoted in Chevreau, *Catch The Fire,* p.154.

3. Beverley, *Holy Laughter and the Toronto Blessing,* p.34.

4. Chevreau, *Catch The Fire,* p.24.

5. John Arnott at Holy Trinity, Brompton, England, 14 February 1995, *CRI transcripts,* pp.36-7.

6. John Arnott, Toronto Airport Vineyard, *Dynamics of Receiving Spiritual Experiences,* 8 November 1994, *CRI transcripts,* p.14, italics mine.

7. Jack Deere, Toronto Airport Vineyard, 20 November 1994, *CRI transcripts,* p.42.

8. Wes Campbell, Toronto Airport Vineyard, Oct. 14, 1994, *CRI transcripts,* p.84.

9. Ibid., pp.86,88.

10. Lloyd-Jones, *Revival,* pp.60-61.

11. A letter received by Jewel van der Merwe, Discernment Ministries, Lapeer, Michigan, and read out at the Discernment Ministries Conference at Missisauga, Ontario on 2 March 1996.

12. Rodney Howard-Browne, *The Reality of the Person of the Holy Spirit,* pp.31-2, cited in *CRI transcripts,* p.24.

13. Quoted in Beverley, *Holy Laughter and the Toronto Blessing,* p.100.

14. Lloyd-Jones, *Revival,* p.74.

Chapter 12 — Theology — modern whipping boy

1. Toronto Airport Vineyard, 8 September 1994.

2. Beverley, *Holy Laughter and the Toronto Blessing,* p.75.

3. John Wimber, Healing Seminar Series, audiotapes, 3 vol. unedited, 1981.

4. Lewis, *Assessing The Wimber Phenomenon,* Regent College, June 1985.

5. *Ibid.*

6. *Ibid.*

7. G. Thomas Morton, 'Pilgrimage of the Post-Charismatics,' *Eternity,* Feb. 1980, pp.21-5.

8. William DeArteaga, Toronto Airport Vineyard, 13 October 1994, *CRI transcripts,* p.76.

9. Chevreau, *Catch the Fire,* p.70.

10. *Ibid.,* p.68.

11. DeArteaga, *Quenching the Spirit,* p.32.

12. *Ibid.,* p.55.

13. *Ibid.,* p.83.

14. Vine, *An Expository Dictionary of New Testament Words,* Old Time Gospel Hour edition, n.d., p.307.

15. J. I. Packer, *Hot Tub Religion,* Tyndale Publishers Inc., 1987.

16. Mary Audrey Raycroft, 'Ministering Life,' *Spread the Fire,* August 1995, p.21.

17. *Ibid.*

18. Memorandum of 14 October 1994, p.2 of Board Report.

19. John MacArthur, *Songtime USA* radio interview, cited in *CRI transcripts,* p.77.

20. John Wimber, *Healing Seminar Series,* audiotapes, 3 vol. unedited, 1981.

21. William DeArteaga, Toronto Aiport Vineyard, 13 October 1994, *CRI transcripts,* pp.32-3.

22. *CRI transcripts,* p.48.

23. Lewis, *Assessing the Wimber Phemonenon.*

24. *Ibid.*

25. *The Gospel Witness,* 18 May 1995, pp.9-13.

26. Lundy, lecture at Ajax, 1 April 1995.

27. Beverley, *Holy Laughter and the Toronto Blessing,* pp.26-30.

28. Todd Hunter, *Revival In Focus,* Mission Vieto Vineyard, 23 October 1994, from *CRI transcripts,* p.20.

29. *The Perennial Dictionary of World Religions.*

30. Beverley, *Holy Laughter and the Toronto Blessing,* p.123.

31. *Ibid.,* p.127.

32. William W. Menzies, *Anointed to Serve, The Story of the Assemblies of God,* Gospel Publishing House, 1971, p.32, cited in *CRI transcripts,* p.5.

33. *CRI transcripts,* p.10.

34. *Ibid.,* pp.7-8.

35. Summarized in Beverley, *Holy Laughter and the Toronto Blessing,* p.61 from Hank Hanegraaff, *Christianity in Crisis,* Harvest House, 1993, pp.59-276.

36. Randy Frame, *Word Faith under Fire,* comments of speaker Hank Hanegraaff at a conference in Philadelphia in September 1994, *Christianity Today,* 24 October 1994, p.85.

37. Beverley, *Holy Laughter and the Toronto Blessing,* p.61.

38. DeArteaga, *Quenching the Spirit,* p.228.

39. *Ibid.,* p.55.

40. Alan Morrison, a letter to the UK Evangelical Alliance declining their invitation to attend a consultation on the Toronto Blessing, 'EA Toronto consultation "a confusion"', *Evangelical Times,* July 1995, p.10.

41. *Ibid.*

42. Letter from Rev. Don McCallum, pastor of Kortright Presbyterian Church, Guelph, Ontario, 6 June 1995 to Jeremy Sinnott.

43. Question on 20 January 1995, Toronto Airport Vineyard, to Randy Clark in response to this message 'Run With The Fire', 1 Year Anniversary Message, *CRI transcripts,* p.28.

44. Ibid., p.27.

45. Beverley, *Holy Laughter and the Toronto Blessing,* p.153.

46. Charles H. Spurgeon, *Autobiography, Volume 1: The Early Years* Banner of Truth, 1962 edition.

Chapter 13 — Putting the experiential cart before the scriptural horse
1. Dallimore, *George Whitefield,* vol. 1, p.110.

2. Morton, 'Pilgrimage of the Post-Charismatics,' p.23.

3. John MacArthur, from an undated sermon series entitled 'Charismatic Chaos'.

4. John Wimber, 'Refreshing, Renewal, Revival,' *Vineyard Reflections,* John Wimber's Leadership Letter, July/August 1994, p.6.

5. *Ibid.*

6. Beverley, *Holy Laughter and the Toronto Blessing,* p.84.

7. Wimber and Springer, *Power Evangelism,* p.89.

8. *Ibid.,* p.88.

9. John Wimber, 'Healing: An Introduction,' cassette tape 5, *CRI transcripts,* p.77.

10. Wes Campbell, 'Spiritual and Physical Manifestations of the Holy Spirit,' Toronto Airport Vineyard, 15 October 1994, *CRI transcripts,* p.76.

11. Chevreau, *Catch the Fire,* p.154, italics his.

12. *Ibid.,* p.156.

13. *Ibid.,* p.62, italics his.

14. *Ibid.,* p.63

15. *Ibid.,* pp.64-5.

16. *Ibid.,* p.71, italics his.

17. News report by Krysia P. Lear, 'Groundbreaking Conference Explores Evangelicalism,' *Faith Today,* July/August 1995, p.49.

18. *Ibid.,* p.50.

19. *Ibid.*

20. Abshire, *The Real Seduction of Biblical Christianity,* p.23.

21. See John Ankerberg & John Weldon, *Protestants & Catholics, Do They Now Agree?,* Harvest House, 1995.

22. From Inez Smith Davis, *The Story of the Church,* Herald Publishing House, 1943, pp.230-32, cited by Nader Mikhaiel in *The Toronto Blessing — Slaying in the Spirit — The Telling Wonder,* self-published, Earlwood, Australia, 2nd edition, 1995, pp.1-2.

23. A prayer of Rubi'a al-'Adwiyya, a Muslim mystic cited in John A. Subhan, *Sifism, Its Saints and Shrines,* Lucknow Publishing House, India, 1960, p.16.

24. Jalalu'd-Din Rumi, Muslim mystic of the thirteenth century, *Ibid.,* p.39.

25. *Ibid,* p.40.

26. H. A. Maxwell Whyte, *Dominion Over Demons,* Banner Publishing, 1973, p.85.

27. A professor of theology and apologetics at Reformed Episcopal Seminary in Philadelphia.

28. Morton, *Pilgrimage of the Post-Charismatics,* p.21.

29. *Ibid.*

30. *Ibid.*

31. *Ibid.,* p.22

Chapter 14 — Is Christ front and centre?

1. Jonathan Edwards, *The Distinguishing Marks of a Work of the Spirit of God,* originally published in 1741 contained in *Select Works of Jonathan Edwards,* Banner of Truth Trust, 1965, vol. I, pp.109-10.

2. *Ibid.,* p.110.

3. Quoted by Reid, 'After the laughter,' p.20.

4. Larry Randolph, 'Pursuing Jesus Before His Gifts,' Prophetic School — Part 3, Toronto Airport Vineyard, 19 November 1994, *CRI transcripts,* p.72.

5. Chevreau, '"Grade A" Fruit,' p.26.

6. Eleanor Mumford, 29 May 1994, *CRI transcripts,* p.29.

7. Chevreau, *Catch the Fire,* pp.160,163.

8. *Ibid.,* p.53.

9. Ron Allen, 'From Refreshing To Power Evangelism,' Toronto Airport Vineyard, 13 October 1994, *CRI transcripts,* p.16.

10. *CRI transcripts,* p.17.

11. John Armstrong, 'In Search of Spiritual Power,' article in *Power Religion,* ed. Michael Scott Horton, Chicago: Moody Press, p.81.

12. Grudem, *Power & Truth,* p.34, footnote.

13. Wimber & Springer, *Power Evangelism,* p.57.
14. Jack Deere, Toronto Airport Vineyard, 20 November 1994, *CRI transcripts,* p.79.
15. John Arnott, Toronto Airport Vineyard, Pastor's Meeting, 19 October 1994, *CRI transcripts,* p.89.
16. Summarized by MacArthur, *Reckless Faith,* p.62 from *What Happens When Christians Use Bad Language,* Barna Research Group, Ltd, 21 February 1994.
17. Chevreau, *Catch the Fire,* see pp.160,163.
18. Lundy, lecture at Ajax, 1 April 1995.
19. Grudem, *Power & Truth,* pp.13-14.
20. *CRI transcripts,* p.37.
21. J. I. Packer, *Keep in Step with the Spirit,* Old Tappan, New Jersey: Revell, 1984, pp.65-6.
22. Edwards, *Distinguishing Marks of a Work of the Spirit of God,* pp. 109-10.

Chapter 15 — Is this really a movement of the Holy Spirit?
1. Editorial comments from John Arnott in *Spread the Fire,* March/April 1995 issue, p.2 and May/June issue, p.2
2. Jackson, *What in the World is Happening to Us?,* p.1.
3. Chevreau, *Catch the Fire,* p.vii.
4. Daina Doucet, 'David Mainse: A Channel For God, A TV Ministry Experiences the Blessing,' *Spread the Fire,* May/June 1995, p.5.
5. *Ibid.,* p.7
6. Gary Pritchard, 'British Church: Laughing in the Rain,' *Spread the Fire,* August 1995, p.10.
7. Gail Reid, 'Doing "Cobble Time"', *Spread the Fire,* August 1995, p.13.
8. *Ibid.*
9. *Ibid.*
10. Hurst, 'Laughing all the way to heaven', p.A24.
11. Beverley, *Holy Laughter and the Toronto Blessing,* pp.95-6.
12. *Ibid.,* pp.13-14.
13. Carol Wimber, 'A Hunger for God,' in Kevin Springer, ed., *Power Encounters,* San Francisco: Harper & Row, 1988, p.12.
14. Mikhaiel, *Slaying in the Spirit.* I acknowledge Mikhaiel's help in discovering most of the sources in this section on hypnosis.
15 Francis MacNutt, *Overcome by the Spirit,* Chosen Books.
16. Mikhaiel quotes from at least the following books on hypnotism:

    Theodore X. Barber, *Hypnotism, Imagination and Human Potentialities,*
       Pergamon Press Inc., 1974.
    Wolfgang Luthe, *Autogenic Therapy,* Vol. V, Grune & Stratton, 1970.
    Richard S. Sandor, *Brenham's New Studies in Hypnotism,* International
       University Press, 1980.
    Ernest R. Hilgard, *The Experience of Hypnosis,* Harbinger Book, Harcourt,
       Brace & World, Incl., 1968.
    Encyclopedia Britannica, 1971.
    Timothy Hall and Guy Grant, *SuperPsych,* Methuen of Australia, 1976.
    Anatol Milechnin, *Hypnosis,* John Right & Sons Ltd, 1967.

Peter W. Sheehan and Campbell W. Perry, *Methodologies of Hypnosis,* Lawrence Erlbaum Associates, 1976.

Peter L. N. Naish, *What is Hypnosis?,* Open University Press, 1986.

17. Taken from Lewis, *Healing, Fantasy or Fact?,* p.286.

18. *Ibid.,* p.175.

19. Dr Patrick Dixon, *Signs of Revival,* Kingsway, 1994, p.75.

20. See Mikhaiel, *Slaying in the Spirit,* ch. 2, pp.19-42.

21. *Ibid.,* ch. 1.

22. *Ibid.,* p.26 quoting Francis MacNutt, *Overcome by the Spirit,* Chosen Books, 1984.

23. *Ibid.,* p.27 quoting Charles and Frances Hunter, *Since Jesus Passed By,* Time-Light Books, 1973, p.17.

24. Anatol Milechnin, *Hypnosis,* John Right & Sons Ltd., 1967, p.179.

25. Mikhaiel, *Slaying in the Spirit,* pp.27-8.

26. *Ibid.,* p.27.

27. See Beverley, *Holy Laughter and the Toronto Blessing,* ch. 7, especially pp. 119-20.

28. MacNutt, *Overcome by the Spirit,* p.137.

29. Mikhaiel, *Slaying in the Spirit,* p.44.

30. Cited by Tony Payne, 'No Laughing Matter,' article in *The Briefing,* Issue 146/7, p.7.

31. Patrick Dixon, *Signs of Revival,* Kingsway, 1944, pp.259-60, cited by Mikhaiel.

32. Dixon, *Signs of revival,* p.269.

33. See Ray Yungen, *For Many Shall Come in my Name,* Solid Rock Books, 1991, or other studies of the New Age Movement.

34. John Wimber, Internal Report to "All Vineyard Pastors," 14 October 1994.

35. John Arnott, Toronto Airport Vineyard, 'Dynamics of Receiving Spiritual Experiences', 18 November 1994, *CRI transcripts,* p.14.

36. Jackson, *What in the World is Hapening to us?* p.9.

37. See Dallimore, *George Whitefield,* vol. 1, pp.326-30.

38 Williams, *Vineyard Experience,* pp.4,7,10.

39. Cheryl & Steve Thomson, letter to editor published in 'Crosstalk', *Faith Today,* March/April 1995.

40. Thomson, 'Not Just — A Memoir of "The Vineyard"', p.21.

41. Chevreau, *Catch the Fire,* p.127.

42. Mikhaiel, *Slaying in the Spirit,* p.75.

43. Tim Stafford, 'Testing the Wine from John Wimber's Vineyard,' *Christianity Today,* 8 August 1986, p.19, emphasis mine.

44. John Arnott, Pastor's Meeting, Toronto Airport Vineyard, 19 October 1994, *CRI transcript,* p.34.

45. Todd Hunter, *Revival In Focus,* Mission Vieto Vineyard, 23 October 1994, *CRI transcript,* p.29, italics mine.

46. Albert James Dager, *Holy Laughter, Rodney Howard-Browne and the Toronto Blessing,* Media Spotlight, 1995, p.13.

47. Chevreau, *Catch The Fire,* p.153.

48. Thomson, 'Not Just — A Memoir of "The Vineyard"', p.6.

49. Long, 'The Airport Vineyard: an insider's story'.

50. Beverley, *Holy Laughter and the Toronto Blessing,* p.17.
51. Reid, 'After the Laughter,' p.23.
52. Dick Sutphen, Transcript, *The Battle for Your Mind: Persuasion and Brainwashing Techniques Being Used On The Public Today,* undated, pp.1-10, cited by Dager, *Holy Laughter, Rodney Howard-Browne and the Toronto Blessing,* pp.12-13.
53. *Ibid.*
54. *Ibid.,* comments in brackets are mine.
55. *Ibid.,* p.13.
56. Williams, *Vineyard Experience,* p.10.
57. Mikhaiel, *Slaying in the Spirit,* p.39.
58. Dager, *Holy Laughter, Rodney Howard-Browne and the Toronto Blessing,* p.13.
59. Milechnin, *Hypnosis,* p.74, cited by Mikhaiel, *Slaying in the Spirit.*
60. MacNutt, *Overcome by the Spirit,* p.159.
61. Beverley, *Holy Laughter and the Toronto Blessing,* p.158.
62. Meeting on 14 July 1995.
63. Beverley, 'Toronto Blessing update,' *Christian Week,* 31 October 1995, p.11.
64. Tim Thornborough, 'Making your mind up,' *The Briefing,* No. 146/7, St Matthias Press, n.d., pp.16-17.

Chapter 16 — Power in the Vineyard

1. The term probably originated with Alan Tippet.
2. Michael Scott Horton, ed., *Power Religion,* Moody Press, 1992.
3. Wayne Grudem, *Power and Truth, A Response To 'Power Religion,'* Vineyard Position Paper No. 4, Association of Vineyard Churches.
4. Rich Nathan, *A Response to 'Charismatic Chaos' the book written by John F. MacArthur, Jr, Vineyard Position Paper No. 5,* Association of Vineyard Churches, April 1993.
5. Wimber and Springer, *Power Evangelism* (revisd edition,1992), p.78.
6. *Ibid.*
7. See Wimber and Springer, *Power Evangelism,* 1986 ed., pp.11,31.
8. *Ibid.,* pp.91-106.
9. Wimber and Springer, *Power Evangelism,* 1992 ed., p.78.
10. Armstrong, *Signs and Wonders in Biblical Perspective.*
11. Wimber and Springer, *Power Evangelism,* 1992 ed., p.78.
12. *Ibid.,* p.79.
13. Grudem, *Power and Truth,* p.24.
14. Armstrong, *Signs and Wonders in Biblical Perspective.*
15. Stanley K. Fowler, 'Signs and Wonders Today: Some Theological Reflections,' reprint from *Baptist Review of Theology,* vol. 3, No. 2, Fall 1993, p.2 , summary from *Power Evangelism,* 1986, p.46.
16. Armstrong, *Signs and Wonders in Biblical Perspective.*
17. Marc Dupont, 'Prophetic School — Part 3,' Pastor's Meeting, Toronto Airport Vineyard, 16 November 1994, *CRI transcripts,* p.79.
18. Wimber and Springer, *Power Religion,* 1986, pp.66-90.
19. Westminster Confession, V:1,7.
20. Fowler, 'Signs and Wonders Today', p.6.

21. See chapters 8 and 15 and Beverley, *Holy Laughter and the Toronto Blessing,* pp.119-20.
22. John E. MacArthur, *The Charismatics,* Grand Rapids: Zondervan, 1978, pp.143-9.
23. Nathan, *A Response to 'Charismatic Chaos',* p.12.
24. Wimber and Springer, *Power Healing,* pp.169-70.
25. Brochure from Toronto Airport Fellowship advertising the Healing School for 22-25 November 1995.
26. John Armstrong, 'In Search of Spiritual Power,' article in *Power Religion,* p.76.
27. Morton, *Pilgrimage of the Post-Charismatics,* p.22.

Chapter 17 — Why I reject the Vineyard power trip
1. Fowler, 'Signs and Wonders Today,' p.3, italics his.
2. Grudem, *Power & Truth,* p.20.
3. *Power Religion,* pp.126,133.
4. Grudem, *Power & Truth,* p.39.
5. Fowler, 'Signs and Wonders Today,' p.5.
6. I searched for every reference in the epistles to healing, miracles, signs and wonders, tongues and their interpretation, prophecy, prophets and the casting out of evil spirits. I did not include lying wonders or references to false prophets, since that would prove the opposite. Dating is consistent with *The Lion Handbook of the Bible,* Lion Publishing, 1973, pp.574-8.
7. The comparison is a rough comparison only and does not take into account the number of chapters in which signs and wonders are mentioned or omitted. If individual chapters were charted, the difference would be even more profound.
8. I included any mention of signs and wonders, with the exception of lying signs and wonders. Miracles, healing, raising the dead, tongues, casting out of evil spirits and predictions were all tabulated.
9. Warfield, *Counterfeit Miracles,* pp.10,29.

Chapter 18 — Navigating the prophetic wave
1. Beverley, 'Toronto Blessing update', p.11.
2. Witt, *Ox in the Nursery,* Spread The Fire, Oct. 1995, p.13.
3. Marc Dupont, 'Prayer of the Prophetic,' Part 2, Toronto Airport Vineyard, Catch The Fire Conference, 14 October 1994, *CRI transcripts,* p.66.
4. An analysis by Bob Hunter, Christian Research Institute, Shelburne, Ontario, *CRI Excerpts,* p.37. Christ was mentioned 143 times while prophets or prophecy were mentioned 372 times in thirty transcripts — 2.6 times more often.
5. David Pytches, *Some Said It Thundered: A Personal Encounter with the Kansas City Prophets,* 2nd ed., Nashville: Oliver-Nelson, 1991, p.18.
6. *Ibid.*
7. Beverley, *Holy Laughter & The Toronto Blessing,* p.132.
8. *Ibid.,* p.125.
9. *Ibid.,* pp.126-7.
10. *Ibid.,* p.133.
11. *Ibid.*
12. Wayne Grudem, *The Vineyard's Response to The Standard,* Vineyard Position Paper No. 3, June 1992, p.17 (A response to the critique of John Armstrong carried

in articles in *The Standard*, a publication of the Baptist General Conference between October 1990 and July 1991).

13. *Ibid.,* p.17.

14. Tucker, *From Jerusalem to Irian Jaya,* p.173.

15. From an article by John Armstrong in *The Standard,* July 1991, p.21.

16. Grudem, *Vineyard's Response to The Standard,* p.18.

17. Jack Deere, from printed notes for Workshop 2, entitled, *A Demonic Doctrine Illustrated,* distributed at a Vineyard Conference in Australia in 1990, quoted by Mark Thompson, 'Spirititual Warfare, II,' *The Briefing,* St Matthias Press, April 1990, p.11 or p.18, depending on the version. Wayne Grudem affirms the veracity of this quote by repeating it in *Power & Truth,* p.55

18. Grudem, *Power & Truth,* p.55.

19. *Spread The Fire,* October 1995, p.10. See also p.21.

20. *Ibid.,* p.21.

21. *Ibid.,* p.2.

22. *Ibid.,* p.2.

23. Raycroft, *Ibid.,* p.35.

24. Interview of Paul Cain and Jack Deere, *Ibid.,* p.10.

25. Kevin Springer, 'Paul Cain — A New Breed of Man', *Equipping,* Fall 1989, p.11.

26. Beverley, 'Toronto Blessing update,' p.11.

27. *Spread The Fire,* March/April 1995, p.23.

28. Raycroft, *Spread the Fire,* October 1995, p.21.

29. *Ibid.,* p.35.

30. Mike Bickle, *Ibid.,* p.9.

31. *Ibid.,* pp.8-9.

32. Needham, *Have We Gone Mad?,* p.3.

33. Raycroft, *Spread the Fire,* October 1995, p.35.

34. Marc Dupont, *The True Ministry of a True Prophet,* Spread the Fire, Oct. 1995, p.7.

35. Dupont, 'Prayer of The Prophetic,' Part 2, *CRI transcripts,* p.66.

36. Raycroft, *Spread The Fire,* October 1995, p.21.

37. Wesley Campbell, *Close Encounters of the Divine Kind, Ibid.,* pp.6,32. Some of these examples are from 1987.

38. Witt, 'Ox in the Nursery,' p.13.

39. *Ibid.,* p.14, I have recently had independent confirmation of a rise in these claims about nausea and prophecy.

40. Beverley, 'Toronto Blessing update,' p.11.

41. Editorial, 'Meet The Challenge Canada,' *Spread the Fire,* May/June 1995, p.29. James Watt paraphrases this from his memory of *The Light & the Glory,* by Peter Marshall. The editor writes that James Watt, a Canadian in Washington, has a ministry of calling Canadian Christians to intercede for Canada.

42. *Ibid.,* p.29.

43. *Ibid.,* p.31.

44. Doug Koop, *Holy laughter lifting spirits,* Christian Week, 15 March 1994, p.2.

45. Hurst, 'Laughing all the way to heaven,' p.A24.

46. Roger Mitchell, 'Book on Prophetic: "Safe Reading"', *Spread the Fire,* October 1995, p.29.

47. Bickle, *Growing in the Prophetic,* cited by Mitchell, *Spread the Fire,* October 1995 p.32.

48. James Ryle, *Hippo in the Garden,* Creation House, 1993, pp.259, 261, italics his.

49. John Arnott, 'Moving Into Increasing Anointing,' *Spread the Fire,* May/June 1995, p.2.

50. John Wimber, from a taped message preached in his church in January 1989, from *Foundation* magazine, Nov./Dec. 1989 (Cited by McHale & Haykin, *The Toronto Blessing,* vol. I, p.90).

51. Jack Deere, *Surprised by the Power of the Spirit,* Grand Rapids: Zondervan Publishing House, 1993, pp.173-4.

52. James Beverley writes, 'Bob Jones was disciplined for major sin (involving prophetic abuses related to sexual misconduct) in the fall of 1991.' *Holy Laughter & The Toronto Blessing,* p.131.

53. *Ibid.,* p.85.

54. Jonathan Edwards, *Some Thoughts Concerning the Present Revival of Religion in New England,* from *The Works of Jonathan Edwards,* 2 vols., Banner of Truth Trust, 1976, I, p.404.

Chapter 19 — Vineyard prophecy in biblical perspective

1. Portions of this section have been adapted from my book *Church — No Spectator Sport,* ch. 10.

2. O. Palmer Robertson, *The Final Word,* Banner of Truth Trust, 1993, pp.52-3, italics mine.

3. *Ibid.,* p.73.

4. *Foundation,* Nov./Dec. 1989, cited by McHale & Haykin, *The Toronto Blessing,* vol. I, p.90.

5. *Spread The Fire,* October 1995, p.10.

6. Springer, 'Paul Cain — A New Breed of Man,' p.11.

7. Raycroft, *Spread The Fire,* October 1995, p.35.

8. Beverley, *Holy Laughter and the Toronto Blessing,* p.128.

9. Albert James Dager, *Latter-Day Prophets,* Media Spotlight, 1990 edition revised and expanded in 1995, p.3.

10. Beverley, *Holy Laughter and the Toronto Blessing,* p.57.

11. E. H. Andrews, *The Promise of the Spirit,* Evangelical Press, 1982, p.215.

12. Robertson, *The Final Word,* p.6.

13. *Ibid.,* p.15.

14. B. B. Warfield, 'The Biblical Idea of Revelation,' in *Revelation and Inspiration,* Grand Rapids: 1981 reprint. p.23.

15. Robertson, *The Final Word,* p.16, italics his.

16. George Smeaton, *The Doctrine of the Holy Spirit,* Banner of Truth Trust, reprinted 1980, p.152.

17. Robertson, *The Final Word,* pp.69-70.

18. *Ibid.,* p.60.

19. Cited by Anthony Coppin, Article in *Reformation Today,* No. 97, May/June 1987, p.22.

20. Mike Bickle, 'Prophet Margins,' *Spread the Fire,* October 1995, p.10.

21. Robertson, *The Final Word,* pp.16-17.

22. Bickle, *Prophet Margins*, p.10.

23. John Piper, *Compassion, Power and the Kingdom of God*, part II, p.4.

24. Wayne Grudem, *The Gift of Prophecy in the New Testament and Today*, Kingsway Publications, 1988, p.96f.

25. Robertson, *The Final Word*, p.113.

26. *Ibid.*, p.111 (The quotation is from John Calvin, *Commentary upon the Acts of the Apostles*, Baker Book House, 1984, vol. II, p.268).

27. Rick Joyner, 'The Prophetic Ministry,' *The Morning Star Prophetic Newsletter*, no date, vol. 3, No. 2, p. 4, from *CRI transcripts*, p.7.

28. Jack Deere, Toronto Airport Vineyard, 20 November 1994, *CRI transcripts*, p.65.

29. *Ibid.*

30. Piper, *Compassion, Power and the Kingdom of God* part I, p.4.

31. *Ibid.*, part II, p.4.

32. Beverley, *Holy Laughter and the Toronto Blessing*, p.132.

33. James A. Beverley, 'John Wimber, the Vineyard, and the Prophets: listening for a word from God,' *The Canadian Baptist*, March/April 1992, p.36.

34. Marc Dupont, 'What In The World Is God Doing In '95?', *Spread the Fire*, March/April 1995, p.23

35. Bickle, *Prophet Margins*, p.9, italics mine.

36. *Ibid.*

37 Wright, *Church — No Spectator Sport*, chs 9 and 10 contain a fuller treatment of this subject.

38. Packer, *Keep in Step with the Spirit*, p.217.

39. Quoted by Flynn, *Nineteen Gifts of the Spirit*, p.52.

40. Needham, 'Have we gone mad?', p.4.

41. Mike Bickle, 'Principles For Nurturing The Prophetic Ministry, Introduction to the Prophetic,' January 1989, *CRI transcripts*, p.61.

42. Wes Campbell, 'Pastoring the Prophetic,' Catch The Fire Conference, Toronto Airport Vineyard, 13 October 1994, *CRI transcripts*, p.64.

43. James Ryle, 'Sons of Thunder,' Boulder Valley Vineyard tape ministry, preached 1 July 1990.

44. Grudem, *Vineyard's Response to The Standard*, p.17.

45. Grudem, *The Gift of Prophecy*, p.262.

46. *Ibid.*, p.131.

47. Ryle, *Hippo in the Garden*, p.31.

48. MacArthur, *Reckless Faith*, p.185.

49. John Blattner, 'Pitfalls of Prophecy and How to Avoid Them,' *Equipping The Saints*, Fall 1989, pp.19-20.

50. *Ibid.*, p.14.

51 *Ibid.*, p.19.

52. Garry Friesen, *Decision Making & the Will of God*, Multnomah Press, 1980, p.130.

53. *Ibid.*, pp.130-31.

54. *Ibid.*, p.131.

55 Jonathan Edwards, *Thoughts on the Revival, Works* IV.II, p.404.

56. Haddon Robinson, *Decision Making by the Book*, Victor Books, 1991, p.18.

57. Robertson, *The Final Word*, p.9.

58. Term coined by Piper, *Compassion, Power And The Kingdom of God*, part II, p.2.

59. Grudem, *Vineyard's Response to The Standard*, p.17.

Chapter 20 — The Indispensable Signs of Pentecost

1. Robertson, *The Final Word*, p.12.

2. John MacArthur, *Body Dynamics*, p.20.

3. Eugene H. Peterson, *The Message — the New Testament in Contemporary English*, Navpress, 1993, p.421.

4. Edwards, *Distinguishing Marks of a Work of the True Spirit, Works*, vol. I, pp.113-14.

5. Thomson, 'Not Just — A Memoir of "The Vineyard"', p.8.

6. John Arnott, Pastor's Meeting, Toronto Airport Vineyard, 19 October 1994, *CRI transcripts*, p.80.

7 Edwards, *Distinguishing Marks of a Work of the True Spirit*, p.110.

8. *Ibid.*, pp.115-17

9. Chevreau, *Catch the Fire*, p.152.

10. J. I. Packer, *A Quest For Godliness*, Wheaton, Illinois:, Crossway Books, 1990, p.30.

11. From a sermon entitled, 'The Love of the Spirit,' *Pastoral Memorials: Selected from the Manuscripts of the Late Revd John Ryland, D.D.*, B. J. Holdsworth, 1828, vol. II, p.42.

Appendix II

1. John G. Stackhouse, Jr, 'What light does history shed on the Toronto Blessing?', *Faith Today*, March/April 1995, p.24.

Bibliography

Material from the Association of Vineyard Churches

Mike Bickle, 'Administrating Prophecy in the Church,' *Equipping The Saints,* Fall, 1989, p.24 (This same article is modified slightly and reprinted in *Spread The Fire,* October 1995).

John Blattner, 'Pitfalls of Prophecy and How to Avoid Them,' *Equipping The Saints,* Fall 1989, p.14.

Wes Campbell, *Spiritual and Physical Manifestations,* an undated pamphlet.

Randy Clark, Let the Fire Fall Conference, Anaheim Vineyard, July 1994, *CRI transcripts,* pp.23,26.

William DeArteaga, *Quenching the Spirit,* Lake Mary, Florida: Creation House, 1992.

Jack Deere, printed notes for a workshop entitled 'A Demonic Doctrine Illustrated,' distributed at a Vineyard conference in Australia in 1990, quoted by Mark Thompson, 'Spiritual Warfare, II,' *The Briefing,* Sydney, Australia: St Matthias Press, April 1990, p.11 or p.18, depending on the version. (Wayne Grudem affirms the veracity of this quote by repeating it in *Power & Truth, A Reponse To Power Religion,* Vineyard Position Paper No. 4, p. 55.)

Jack Deere and Paul Cain, interview, *Spread the Fire,* October 1995, p.10.

Jack Deere, *Surprised by the Power of the Spirit,* Grand Rapids: Zondervan Publishing House, 1993, pp.173-4.

Wayne Grudem, *The Vineyard's Response to The Standard,* Vineyard Position Paper No. 3, June 1992 (a response to the critique of John Armstrong carried in articles in *The Standard,* a publication of the Baptist General Conference between October 1990 and July 1991).

Wayne Grudem, *Power & Truth, A Response To 'Power Religion,'* Vineyard Position Paper No. 4, Anaheim, California: The Association of Vineyard Churches, undated.

Wayne Grudem, *The Gift of Prophecy in the New Testament and Today,* Wheaton, Ill.: Crossway Books, 1988 (also published in Britain by Kingsway Publications).

Todd Hunter, *Revival In Focus,* Mission Vieto Vineyard, 23 October 1994, from *CRI transcripts,* pp.20,29.

Bill Jackson, *What In The World Is Happening To Us?* Vineyard Campaign, Urbana, Illinois: May 1994.

Bill Jackson, *Cessationism,* Urbana, Illinois: The Vineyard Christian Fellowship, 1995.

Rick Joyner, 'A Vision of the Twelve Cities,' *The Morningstar Journal,* Charlotte, North Carolina, vol. 2, No. 3.

Rick Joyner, 'The Prophetic Ministry', *The Morning Star Prophetic Newsletter,* vol. 3, no. 2, p.4 from *CRI transcripts,* p.7.

Rich Nathan, *A Response to 'Charismatic Chaos' the book written by John F. MacArthur, Jr,* Vineyard Position Paper No. 5, Anaheim, California: The Association of Vineyard Churches, April 1993.

Memorandum from the Association of Vineyard Churches, 14 October 1994, including 'John Wimber Responds To Phenomena', Board Report, 'Summary Report on the Current Renewal and the Phenomena Surrounding it', A memorandum from Todd Hunter, National Coordinator, to all Vineyard Pastors.

John Piper, *Compassion, Power And The Kingdom of God — The authority and nature of the gift of prophecy,* paper summarizing two sermons given at Bethlehem Baptist Church, 25 March 1990, part 2.

James Ryle, *Hippo in the Garden,* Lake Mary, Fla.: Creation House, 1993.

James Ryle, 'Sons of Thunder', Longmont, Colo., Boulder Valley Vineyard tape ministry, sermon preached 1 July 1990.

James Ryle, 'It's Enough to Make You Cry,' message quoted in *CRI transcripts,* p.1.

Kevin Springer, 'Paul Cain — A New Breed of Man,' *Equipping,* Fall 1989, p.11.

Kevin Springer, ed., *Power Encounters,* San Francisco: Harper & Row, 1988.

C. Peter Wagner, *The Third Wave of the Holy Spirit,* Ann Arbor, Mich.: Servant, 1988.

John Wimber and Kevin Springer, *Power Evangelism,* San Francisco: Harper & Row, 1986.

John Wimber and Kevin Springer, *Power Evangelism: Revised and Expanded with Study Questions,* San Francisco: Harper, 1992, p. 78.

John Wimber and Kevin Springer, *Power Healing,* San Francisco: Harper & Row, 1987.

John Wimber, 'Spiritual Gifts Seminar,' notes, p.12, quoted by Bill Jackson, *Cessationism,* Urbana, Illinois: The Vineyard Christian Fellowship, 1995.

John Wimber, 'Healing: An Introduction,' cassette tape 5, *CRI transcripts,* p.77.

John Wimber, from a taped message preached in his church in January 1989, *Foundation* magazine, Nov./Dec. 1989.

John Wimber, 'Introducing prophetic ministry,' *Equipping the Saints,* Fall 1989, p.4.

John Wimber, 'Healing Seminar Series,' audiotapes, 3 vols, unedited, 1981.

John Wimber, *Vineyard Reflections,* John Wimber's Leadership Letter, 'Refreshing, Renewal, and Revival', July/August 1994.

Carol Wimber, 'A Hunger for God,' in Kevin Springer, ed., *Power Encounters,* San Francisco: Harper & Row, 1988, p.12.

Evaluations of the Vineyard Movement

John Armstrong, 'In Search of Spiritual Power,' article in *Power Religion,* ed. Michael Scott Horton, Chicago: Moody Press, p.81.

John Armstrong, *Signs and Wonders in Biblical Perspective,* Seminar at Toronto Baptist Seminary, 6 May 1995.

Stanley K. Fowler, 'Signs and Wonders Today: Some Theological Reflections,' reprint from *Baptist Review of Theology,* vol. 3, No. 2, Fall 1993.

Bob Hunter, *Excerpts From Vineyard Church Transcripts — Canada & U.S.A. — with commentary,* Shelburne, Ontario: Christian Research International, 1995 (referred to as *CRI transcripts*).

Dr Don Lewis, *Assessing The Wimber Phenomenon,* Regent College, June 1985.

John MacArthur, *Songtime USA* Radio Interview, cited in *CRI transcripts,* p.77.

Tim Stafford, 'Testing the Wine from John Wimber's Vineyard,' *Christianity Today,* 8 August 1986, p.19.

Cheryl Thomson, *Not Just — A Memoir of 'The Vineyard': 1986-1994,* Toronto: Strangers and Pilgrims Christian Evangelism Fellowship, 1994.

General material cited about the Toronto Blessing

James A. Beverley, 'John Wimber, the Vineyard, and the Prophets: listening for a word from God,' *The Canadian Baptist,* March/April 1992, p.36.

James A. Beverley, *Holy Laughter and The Toronto Blessing,* Grand Rapids: Zondervan, 1995.

James A. Beverley, 'Toronto Blessing update: notes from a friendly critic', *Christian Week,* 31 October 1995, p.11.

Ken Birch, 'No Laughing Matter,' *The Pentecostal Testimony* (official organ of the Pentecostal Assemblies of Canada), February 1994, p.27.

Dr Joseph R. Chambers, '"Strange Fire" in the Lord's Vineyard', *Liberation,* Spring 1995, p.8.

Charisma magazine, August 1994, Rodney-Howard Browne on laughter, p.24, CRI transcripts.

Guy Chevreau, *Catch The Fire,* London: HarperCollins, 1994.

Guy Chevreau, '"Grade A" fruit,' *Faith Today,* March/April 1995, p.26.

Albert James Dager, 'Holy Laughter, Rodney Howard-Browne and the Toronto Blessing', *Media Spotlight,* Redmond, Washington: 1995.

Justin Dennison, 'Grapes of Wrath or Blessing?,' *Evangelical Baptist,* February 1995, pp. 20-21.

Daina Doucet, 'David Mainse: A Channel For God, A TV Ministry Experiences the Blessing,' *Spread the Fire,* May/June 1995, p.5.

Ken Fast, letter in *Faith Today,* May/June 1995, p 10.

The Gospel Witness, special issue, *Signs and Wonders Today — A Biblical Response,* 18 May 1995.

Tom Harpur, 'What the "mighty wind from Toronto" feels like', *Toronto Star,* 20 November 1994, p.E12.

Robert Hough, 'God Is Alive and Well and Saving Souls on Dixon Road,' *Toronto Life* magazine, February 1995, p.31.

Rodney Howard-Browne, *The Reality of the Person of the Holy Spirit,* pp.31-32, cited in *CRI transcripts.*

Lynda Hurst, 'Laughing all the way to heaven,' *Toronto Star,* 3 December 1994, p.A24.

Doug Koop, 'Holy laughter lifting spirits', *Christian Week,* 15 March 1994, p.2.

Doug Koop, '"Toronto Blessing" garnering worldwide attention', *Christian Week,* 23 August 23 1994, p.4.

Doug Koop, '"Fire" still ablaze at Toronto church', *Christian Week,* 31 October 1995, p.4.

Daniel Lundy, 'Signs and Wonders Today,' *The Gospel Witness,* 18 May 1995, pp.4-5.

Daniel Lundy, Lecture given at Ajax Baptist Church, Ontario, 1 April 1995.

Evangelical Times, News report of a conference in Hertfordshire, July 1995, p.3.

Larry Matthews, editorial, 'The best and the worst,' *The Canadian Baptist,* March 1995.

Rev. Don McCallum, pastor of Kortright Presbyterian Church, Guelph, Ontario, letter dated 6 June 1995 to Jeremy Sinnott.

Gary W. McHale with Michael A. G. Haykin, *The 'Toronto Blessing' A Renewal From God?*, vol. 1, *Historical Perspectives*, vol. 3, *Jonathan Edwards: The Man, his Experience and his Theology*, Richmond Hill, Ontario: Canadian Christian Publications, 1995.

Nader Mikhaiel, *The Toronto Blessing — Slaying in the Spirit — The Telling Wonder*, Earlwood, Australia: self-published, 2nd edition, 1995.

Alan Morrison, a letter to the UK Evangelical Alliance declining their invitation to attend a consultation on the Toronto Blessing, 'EA Toronto consultation "a confusion"', *Evangelical Times*, July 1995, p.10.

Nick Needham, 'Have We Gone Mad?', article from the *Banner of Truth* magazine reprinted in *Jaiza*, May 1995, p .4

Tony Payne, 'No Laughing Matter,' *The Briefing*, Issue 146/7, p.7.

Clark H. Pinnock, 'Can't Tell God How and Where to Work', *The Canadian Baptist*, March 1995, p.10.

Gary Pritchard, 'British Church: Laughing in the Rain', *Spread the Fire*, August 1995, p.10.

Dr David Reed, *The Toronto Mixed Blessing*, Praxis Workshop put on by World Vision, 25 April 1995.

Gail Reid, 'After the laughter,' *Faith Today*, March/April 1995, p.20.

Gail Reid, 'Blessing hits talk show,' *Christian Week*, 11 July 1995, p.18.

Gail Reid, 'Doing "Cobble Time",' *Spread the Fire*, August 1995, p.13.

Warren Smith, 'Holy Laughter or Strong Delusion?', *SCP Newsletter*, Fall 1994, pp.5,8.

Spiritual Counterfeits Project Newsletter, 19:2, p.14.

Cheryl & Steve Thomson, letter to editor published in 'Crosstalk', *Faith Today*, March/April 1995.

Cheryl and Steve Thomson, letter to the editor of *Faith Today*, May/June 1995, p.8.

Tim Thornborough, 'Making your mind up', *The Briefing*, No. 146/7, London: St Matthias Press, undated, pp.16-17.

Rev. Gordon Williams, *Vineyard Experience — Written for the Body of Christ*, an eleven-page description of his experiences and concerns.

W5, undated TV programme aired over CBC, Toronto.

Material from the Toronto Airport Vineyard

Mike Bickle, 'Prophet Margins', *Spread the Fire*, Ocober 1995, p.10.

Brochure advertising 'Gifts of the Spirit Classes', from 3 October 1994 to 15 May 1995.

Brochure advertising the Toronto Airport Vineyard Healing School, 22-25 November 1995.

Wesley Campbell, 'Close Encounters of the Divine Kind', *Spread the Fire,*
October 1995, pp.6,32.

Randy Clark, Response to question on his message 'Run With the Fire',
One Year Anniversary Message, 20 January 1995, Toronto Airport
Vineyard, *CRI transcripts,* p. 28.

Marc Dupont, 'What in the World is God Doing in '95?', *Spread the Fire,*
March/April 1995, p.23.

Marc Dupont, 'The True Ministry of a True Prophet', *Spread the Fire,*
October 1995, p.7.

Steve Long, 'The Airport Vineyard: an insider's story', *Christian Week,* 9
May 1995, p.10.

Steve Long, 'What About Animal Noises?', *Spread the Fire,* October
1995, pp.17,30.

Spread the Fire, magazine published by the Toronto Airport Vineyard,
issues May/June, March/April, August, October, December 1995.

Mary Audrey Raycroft, 'Ministering Life', *Spread the Fire,* August 1995,
p. 21.

Vineyard newsletter, March 1994, vol. 01.

Vineyard Christian Fellowship, Toronto Airport, 6 March 1994, *Our
Statement of Faith.*

Steve Witt, 'Ox in the Nursery', *Spread the Fire,* Ocober. 1995, p.13.

Messages

Ron Allen, 'From Refreshing to Power Evangelism', Toronto Airport
Vineyard, 13 October 1994, *CRI transcripts,* p 16.

John Arnott, Pastor's Meeting, Toronto Airport Vineyard, 19 October
1994, *CRI transcripts,* pp. 80,89, also pp. 34, 80, research.

John Arnott, 'Dynamics of Receiving Spiritual Experiences', Toronto
Airport Vineyard, 8 November 1994, *CRI transcripts,* p.14.

John Arnott at Holy Trinity, Brompton, London, 14 February 1995, *CRI
transcripts,* pp.36,37.

John Arnott, personal notes, Toronto Airport Vineyard, 4 October 1995,
17 January 1996.

Mike Bickle, 'Principles for Nurturing the Prophetic Ministry, Introduction to the Prophetic', January 1989, *CRI transcripts,* p.61.

Wes Campbell, 'Pastoring the Prophetic', Catch the Fire Conference,
Toronto Airport Vineyard, 13 October 1994, *CRI transcripts,* p.64.

Wes Campbell, Toronto Airport Vineyard, 14 October 1994, *CRI transcripts,* pp. 22,84.

Wes Campbell, 'Spiritual and Physical Manifestations of the Holy Spirit',
Toronto Airport Vineyard, 15 October 1994, *CRI transcripts,* p.76.

William DeArteaga, audiotape of 9:15 a.m meeting on 13 October 1994,
also *CRI transcripts,* pp.32,33,76.

Jack Deere, Toronto Airport Vineyard, 20 November 1994, *CRI transcripts,* pp. 42,65,79.

Marc Dupont, 'Prayer of the Prophetic', Part 2, Toronto Airport Vineyard, Catch the Fire Conference,14 October 1994, *CRI transcripts,* p.66.

Marc Dupont, Prophetic School — Part 3, Pastor's Meeting, Toronto Airport Vineyard, 16 November 1994, *CRI transcripts,* p.79.

Byran Mode, Toronto Airport Vineyard, 14 July 1995.

Eleanor Mumford, 29 May 1994, *CRI transcripts,* p.29.

Larry Randolph, 'Pursuing Jesus Before his Gifts', Prophetic School — Part 3, Toronto Airport Vineyard, 19 November 1994, *CRI transcripts,* p.72.

Historical books and articles

Brian M. Abshire, *The Real Seduction of Biblical Christianity — 18th Century Revivalism and the Destruction of American Christian Culture,* Chalcedon Report, September 1994.

James Atkinson, *The Great Light, Luther and Reformation,* Grand Rapids: Eerdmans by arrangement with Paternoster Press, Exeter, 1968.

Roland Bainton, *The Reformation of the Sixteenth Century,* Boston: Beacon Press, 1952.

Victor Budgen, *The Charismatics and the Word of God,* Evangelical Press, 1989.

Letter to Mary Carey, 14 December 1789, Baptist Missionary Society Archives, Angus Library, Regent's Park College, Oxford.

Arnold Dallimore, *George Whitefield. The Life and Times of the Great Evangelist of the Eighteenth-Century Revival,* Westchester, Illinois: Cornerstone Books, 1980, vols I, II (published in Britain by the Banner of Truth Trust).

Inez Smith Davis, *The Story of the Church,* Independence, Missouri: Herald Publishing House, 1943.

Roy J. Deferrari, footnote in his translation of *Eusebius Pamphili: Ecclesiastical History, Books 1-5,* New York: Fathers of the Church, Inc., 1953, p.311.

V. Raymond Edman, *The Light in Dark Ages,* Wheaton: Van Kampen Press, 1949.

Jonathan Edwards, *Charity and its Fruits,* Edinburgh: Banner of Truth Trust, 1969.

Jonathan Edwards, *The Distinguishing Marks of a Work of the Spirit of God,* originally published in 1741, contained in *Select Works of Jonathan Edwards,* vol. 1, London: Banner of Truth Trust, 1965.

Jonathan Edwards, *A Narrative of Surprising Conversions,* 1736, reprinted London: Banner of Truth, 1965.

Jonathan Edwards, *Some Thoughts Concerning the Present Revival of Religion in New England*, from *The Works of Jonathan Edwards*, 2 vols, Edinburgh: Banner of Truth Trust, 1976, I.

Jonathan Edwards, *A Treatise Concerning Religious Affections*, New Haven, Conn.: Yale University Press, 1959.

Jonathan Edwards, *The Works of Jonathan Edwards, Thoughts on the Revival*, IV II, London: Ball Arnold & Co., 1834.

Eusebius, *Ecclesiastical History*, 4.15.

Charles G. Finney, *Revivals of Religion*, Chicago: Moody Press, 1962.

Randy Frame, *Word Faith under Fire*, comments of speaker Hank Hanegraaff at a conference in Philadelphia in September of 1994, *Christianity Today*, 24 October 1994.

David Otis Fuller, 'Defense and Explanation of All the Articles of Dr Martin Luther Which Were Unjustly Condemned by the Roman Bull,' article in *Valiant for the Truth*, New York, McGraw Hill, 1961.

John Gillies, *Memoirs of the Life of the Reverend George Whitefield, M.A.*, London: E. & C. Dilly, 1772.

Michael A. G. Haykin, *Revivals and Signs and Wonders*, Richmond Hill, Ontario: Canadian Christian Publications, 1994.

R. Tudor Jones, 'Evangelical Revival in Wales: A Study in Spirituality', in James P. Mackey, ed., *An Introduction to Celtic Christianity*, Edinburgh: T & T. Clark, 1989.

Peter Lewis, *The Genius of Puritanism*, Haywards Heath, Sussex, Carey Publications, 2nd ed., 1979.

D. Martyn Lloyd-Jones, *Revival*, Wheaton: Crossway, 1987.

William W. Menzies, *Anointed to Serve, The Story of the Assemblies of God*, Springfield, Missouri: Gospel Publishing House, 1971.

The Methodist Magazine, 1849, p. 165, Cited in Dallimore, *George Whitefield*, vol. 1, p. 3.

Iain Murray, *Jonathan Edwards*, Edinburgh: Banner of Truth Trust, reprint 1992.

Iain Murray, *Revival and Revivalism: The Making and Marring of Ameican Evangelicalism 1750-1858*, Edinburgh: Banner of Truth Trust, 1994.

Review of Iain Murray, 'Revival and Revivalism: The Making and Marring of American Evangelicalism' in *Reformation Today*, Sept/ Oct. 1994, p.30.

Christopher Rule, 'George Fox and Early Quakerism', *Reformation Today*, No. 95, p.15.

John Ryland, D. D., 'The Love of the Spirit', *Pastoral Memorials: Selected from the Manuscripts of the Late Rev. John Ryland, D. D.*, London: B. J. Holdsworth, 1828, vol. II, p.42.

Charles H. Spurgeon, *Autobiography, Volume 1: The Early Years*, Edinburgh: Banner of Truth, 1962 edition.

Simony-Tourneley, *The Catholic Encyclopedia*, New York: The Encyclopedia Press, Inc., 1913.

Ruth A. Tucker, *From Jerusalem to Irian Jaya*, Grand Rapids: Academie Books (Zondervan), 1983.

John Wesley, 'The Nature of Enthusiasm', 21, *Wesley's Standard Sermons*, ed. Edward H. Sugden, 4th ed.; London, The Epworth Press, 1956, vol. II, pp.95-6.

The Journal of Charles Wesley, London: Wesleyan Methodist Bookroom, n.d. 2 vols.

George Whitefield's *Journals*, London: Banner of Truth, 1960.

George Whitefield, 'Indwelling in the Spirit', in *Sermons on Important Subjects*, London: Thomas Tegg, 1833.

George Whitefield, *Select Sermons of George Whitefield*, London: The Banner of Truth Trust, 1958.

Tom Wolfe, *The Me Decade and the Third Great Awakening*, New York: Mauve Gloves & Madmen, Clutter and Vine, Bantam, 1977.

John Woodbridge, *Great Leaders of the Christian Church*, Chicago: Moody Press, 1988.

General books and articles

E. H. Andrews, *The Promise of the Spirit*, Evangelical Press, 1982.

John Ankerberg & John Weldon, *Protestants and Catholics, Do They Now Agree?*, Eugene, Oregon, Harvest House, 1995.

John Armstrong, 'The Me Generation and Modern Revival Movements', *Reformation & Revival Update*, Nov./Dec. 1995.

What Happens When Christians Use Bad Language, Barna Research Group, Ltd., 21 February 1994.

John Calvin, *Commentary upon the Acts of the Apostles*, Grand Rapids: Baker Book House, 1984, vol. II.

John Calvin, *Institutes*, Book IV.

Anthony Coppin, article in *Reformation Today*, No. 97, May/June 1987, p.22.

Keith Crim, ed., *The Perennial Dictionary of World Religions*, San Francisco, Harper and Row Publishers, 1981.

Albert James Dager, *Latter-Day Prophets*, Media Spotlight, 1990 edition revised and expanded in 1995.

Patrick Dixon, *Signs of Revival*, Eastbourne: Kingsway, 1994.

Gordon Fee, *The First Epistle to the Corinthians*, Grand Rapids: Eerdmans, 1987.

Leslie B. Flynn, *Nineteen Gifts of the Spirit*, Wheaton, Illinois: Victor, 1981.

Garry Friesen, *Decision Making & the Will of God,* Portland, Oregon: Multnomah Press, 1980.

Hank Hanegraaff, *Christianity in Crisis,* Eugene, Oregon: Harvest House, 1993.

Grant Hochman, 'What is a cult?', *Christian Week,* 11 July 1995.

Michael Scott Horton, ed., *Power Religion,* Chicago: Moody Press, 1992.

Charles and Frances Hunter, *Since Jesus Passed By,* Van Nuys, California: Time-Light Books, 1973.

Krysia P. Lear, 'Groundbreaking Conference Explores Evangelicalism', *Faith Today,* July/August 1995, p.49.

David Lewis, *Healing, Fantasy or Fact,* London: Hodder & Stoughton, 1989.

The Lion Handbook of the Bible, Herts, England: Lion Publishing, 1973.

John F. MacArthur, *The Charismatics,* Grand Rapids: Zondervan, 1978.

John F. MacArthur, *Reckless Faith,* Wheaton: Crossway Books, 1994.

John F. MacArthur, undated sermon series entitled *Charismatic Chaos.*

Francis MacNutt, *Overcome by the Spirit,* New Jersey: Chosen Books, 1984.

G. Thomas Morton, 'Pilgrimage of the Post-Charismatics', *Eternity,* February 1980, pp. 21-5.

J. I. Packer, *Keep in Step With the Spirit,* Old Tappan, New Jersey: Revell, 1984.

J. I. Packer, *Hot Tub Religion,* Wheaton: Tyndale Publishers., 1987.

J. I. Packer, *A Quest for Godliness,* Wheaton, Illinois: Crossway Books, 1990.

Eugene H. Peterson, *The Message — the New Testament in Contemporary English,* Colorado Springs: Navpress, 1993.

John Piper, *Desiring God,* Portland: Multnomah Press, Portland, Oregon: Multnomah Press, 1986.

David Pytches, *Some Said It Thundered: A Personal Encounter with the Kansas City Prophets,* 2nd ed., Nashville: Oliver-Nelson, 1991.

O. Palmer Robertson, *The Final Word,* Edinburgh: The Banner of Truth Trust, 1993.

Haddon Robinson, *Decision Making by the Book,* Wheaton, Ill.: Victor Books, 1991.

George Smeaton, *The Doctrine of the Holy Spirit,* Edinburgh: The Banner of Truth Trust, Reprint, 1980.

John Stackhouse, Jr, 'Background to Blessing', *Faith Today,* March/April 1995, p.24.

John A. Subhan, *Sufism, Its Saints and Shrines,* Lucknow, India: The Lucknow Publishing House, 1960.

Vine, *An Expository Dictionary of New Testament Words,* Lynchburg, Virginia: The Old Time Gospel Hour edition, undated.

B. B. Warfield, *Counterfeit Miracles,* Edinburgh: The Banner of Truth Trust, first published 1918, reprinted 1976

B. B. Warfield, 'The Biblical Idea of Revelation', in *Revelation and Inspiration,* Grand Rapids: 1981 reprint.

Westminster Confession of Faith.

H.A. Maxwell Whyte, *Dominion Over Demons,* Springdale, PA: Banner Publishing, 1973.

Eric E. Wright, *Church — No Spectator Sport,* Evangelical Press, 1994.

Books on hypnotism

Theodore X. Barber, *Hypnotism, Imagination and Human Potentialities,* New York: Pergamon Press Inc., 1974.

Wolfgang Luthe, *Autogenic Therapy,* vol. V, New York: Grune & Stratton, 1970.

Richard S. Sandor, *Brenham's New Studies in Hypnotism,* New York: International University Press, 1980.

Ernest R. Hilgard, *The Experience of Hypnosis,* New York: Harbinger Book, Harcourt, Brace & World, Incl., 1968.

Timothy Hall and Guy Grant, *SuperPsych,* Sydney: Methuen of Australia, 1976.

Nader Mikhaiel, *The Toronto Blessing — Slaying in the Spirit — The telling Wonder,* Earlwood, Australia: self-published, 2nd ed., 1995.

Anatol Milechnin, *Hypnosis,* Bristol: John Right & Sons Ltd, 1967.

Peter W. Sheehan and Campbell W. Perry, *Methodologies of Hypnosis,* New York: Lawrence Erlbaum Associates, 1976.

Peter L. N. Naish, *What is Hypnosis,* Philadelphia: Open University Press, 1986.

Dick Sutphen, Transcript, *The Battle for Your Mind: Persuasion and Brainwashing Techniques Being Used On The Public Today,* undated.

Index